THE NIKONIAN CHRONICLE

From the Year 1241 to the Year 1381

(Volume Three)

WITHDRAWN

Edited, Introduced and Annotated

by

Serge A. Zenkovsky

Translated

by

Serge A. and Betty Jean Zenkovsky

THE KINGSTON PRESS, INC.

Princeton, New Jersey 08542

ISBN   0-940670-02-X

Printed in the United States of America
Published by
The Kingston Press, Inc.
P.O. Box 1456
Princeton, NJ 08542

The preparation of this volume and costs associated with its publication were supported by the Translations and Publications Programs of the National Endowment for the Humanities, an independent federal agency.

CONTENTS

PREFACE TO VOLUME III OF
THE NIKONIAN CHRONICLE

In the present, third, volume of the English critical edition of *The Nikonian Chronicle* the translators follow the same methods which were used in Volumes One and Two. For technical reasons the division into volumes in this English edition does not correspond to the divisions in the original Russian edition as it was published in Volumes XI-XIII in *Polnoe sobranie russkikh letopisei (Complete Collection of Russian Chronicles)*, St. Petersburg, 1892-1904 (further abbreviated, *PSRL*). In this volume the text of the entries for the years 1241-1345 follows that published in Volume X of *PSRL*, while the entries for the years 1345-1381 are translated from the Russian text which appeared in Volume XI of *PSRL*.

As we pointed out in the Foreword to Volume One, the original Russian text of this so-called *"Nikonian Chronicle"* was compiled in the 1520's in the offices of the Metropolitan of All Russia, most probably under the guidance and editorship of Metropolitan Daniel, himself. Still, the main work of compilation was certainly done by professional chroniclers who had before them a wide variety of material, a considerable part of which is no longer extant. As a result of the compilation of this chronicle on the basis of various sources, one quite often finds in *The Nikonian Chronicle* a repetition of descriptions of the same events or documents because the original compilers probably tried to preserve all available materials but were uncertain which sources were more reliable.

Furthermore, the chroniclers of the 1520's were unaware of the considerable differences in the Russian calendar and the calculations of years which were common from the eleventh to early fifteenth centuries. As we wrote in the Foreword to Volume One, the writers of earlier chronicles, which were used by the compilers of the *Nikonian*, had three different dates for starting the year. The original Russian and widely Slavic custom was to begin the year with the commencement of spring on March 1. Sometimes they also used the Byzantine calendar system, which began the year with September 1 before this March 1. In the twelfth and thirteenth centuries in certain regions, however, there appeared a third system, usually called the "Ultra March Calendar," according to which the Russians started the year also on March 1, but before, not after, the Byzantine New Year which began on September 1.

There are also a number of puzzles in determining the years of events because in the early period of Russian history in the Christian Near East there were likewise various systems employed for determining the year. Since the eleventh century the standard Byzantine system of chronology was based on the presumption that Christ was born in the 5508th year after the creation of the world; but there were also other systems for calculating the Christian Era. They based their chronology on the presumption that Christ was born 5505 years after the creation of the world (as in Byzantium, also, but before the tenth century). Still others (*i.e.*, Antiochia in Syria), considered Christ was born 5500 years after the creation of the world, and even 5493, etc. Unaware of all these complex chronological calculations for the calendar existing in the tenth to the twelfth centuries, and probably in order to avoid mistakes, the compilers of *Nik.* sometimes repeated the same event under various years, indicating basically the year which they found in the source material available to them. For these reasons, we find in *Nik.*, as well as in practically all medieval Russian chronicles, considerable confusion in chronology up to the end of the fourteenth century. The same events are to be found in different chronicles under differing, though close, years.

We do not wish to go into further details of these complexities of the calendar and eras, but refer the reader to a more elaborate discussion of this problem, in Section V of the *Introduction* to Volume One of *The Nikonian Chronicle* in this English edition.

We must likewise keep it in mind that the events were described mostly on the basis of the earliest original recordings. In many instances, however, these were not available to the writers of *The Nikonian Chronicle*, or had become illegible due to wear and tear over the centuries. Therefore the compilers of *Nik.* sometimes, although rarely—and it is so-indicated by the present Editor—misspelled the names of localities or persons mentioned in earlier chronicles which, in their time, had become forgotten. As far as possible, this Editor has restored the original spelling of such names when they could be found in chronicles which preceded *Nik.* In some instances the chronicle writers had at their disposal only later versions of the descriptions of events or characterizations of heroes and saints which, themselves, had become embellished by yet previous scribes or chroniclers. The most striking case of this is the description of the Battle of Kulikovo, for which the compilers of *Nik.* used some later extensive versions in which they could find more details, but likewise more embellishment and inventiveness by the scribes or writers of these later sources.

Despite this complex problem of dating the calendar and finding the original discussion of events under later embellishments and addenda, *The Nikonian Chronicle* still remains of unique importance because, as we have already mentioned in the preceding Volumes One and Two, it has preserved a considerable amount of material which was later lost and is now completely unavailable to historians and researchers of our time. We find in it many details from the provincial chronicles of Rostov, Riazan', Tver', Nizhnii Novgorod and others which perished during the turbulent centuries of Russian history when Russian cities—built largely of wood—fell victim so often to conflagration, sacking and destruction by enemies.

This English critical edition of *The Nikonian Chronicle* could be achieved only with the assistance of several organizations and a considerable number of friends and colleagues in the academic world. The generous help of the National Endowment for the Humanities, whose financial support made possible the labor of several years' preparation of the present English edition, is particularly gratefully remembered by the Editor and his co-translator. We must especially thank Dr. Susan Mango of that Endowment, who, over the years of our contact with NEH, gave us most generously of her time and advice.

The American Council of Learned Societies financially assisted the translators' travel to Russia in 1979, where they were able to visit local libraries and archives, and to consult colleagues specialized in medieval Russian history, literature and, especially, chronicle-writing. In Leningrad, Dr. Dmitri S. Likhachev, member of the Academy of Sciences of the U.S.S.R. and head of the Sector of Old Russian Literature, greatly helped the Editor in permitting him to work in the library and offices of this Sector, and by providing most valuable advice and elucidation of a number of problems of Russian chronicle-writing and of Russian history. Dr. Likhachev's *Russkie letopisi* (Moscow-Leningrad, 1947), as well as many other of his works, were of particular assistance to the translators and Editor of this English critical edition of *Nik*. His colleagues in the Sector of Old Russian Literature, especially L. A. Dmitriev; the latter's wife, R. P. Dmitrieva, whose *Bibliografiia russkogo letopisaniia* (Moscow-Leningrad, 1962) is of particular importance for all scholars dealing with Russian chronicles; O. V. Tvorogov; O. A. Belobrova and G. M. Prohorov of the same Sector greatly assisted this Editor with their counsel, advice and bibliographical references. We also gratefully remember Professors N. S. Demkova and R. G. Skrynnikov of the University of Leningrad.

In the Depository Library of Handwritten Books and Manuscripts of the Pushkin House of the Adacemy of Sciences in Leningrad we received a number of valuable suggestions from V. P. Budaragin, head of the Drevnekhranilishche.

In Moscow, several scholars, specialists in Old Russian history, members of the Institute of History of the Academy of Sciences, likewise assisted the present Editor with their advice and suggestions. I remember with particular gratitude the late A. A. Zimin, probably the most outstanding specialist in Russian history of the fifteenth to sixteenth centuries, who—although gravely afflicted by illness—nonetheless most graciously granted several hours of sessions in which the problems of Old Russian history and Russian historical writing, especially in the sixteenth century, were discussed. Dr. Boris Kloss, author of *Nikonovskii svod i russkoe letopisanie XVI-XVII v.* (Moscow, 1980), greatly assisted this Editor during the discussions of the sources and writers of *Nik*. His above-mentioned book is the most detailed and useful discussion of *The Nikonian Chronicle* and of late Russian chronicle writing.

The Editor must likewise thank for their advice and encouragement several American colleagues, among whom he would especially like to mention Professor Valerie Tumins of the University of California at Davis, Professor Ralph Fisher of the University of Illinois, and Professor Mark Szeftel of the University of Washington, Seattle. Many other American colleagues and librarians were of great help, providing us with their advice and asistance in finding the materials of importance for a critical discussion of the problems of Russian chronicles and, especially, of the *Nikonian*. They are all remembered with deep gratitude.

Finally, I would like to thank Professor Josef Rysan of Vanderbilt University, and Dean Robert Chauvin and President Pope Duncan of Stetson University for their help and encouragement.

The most invaluable assistance in translating and preparing these volumes for publication was given by my wife, co-translator and research associate, Betty Jean Bubbers Zenkovsky. Without her, I would hardly ever have undertaken such monumental work and certainly would have been unable to bring it to an end. Her aid and patience are most gratefully appreciated.

Finally, our thanks are due to the editors of The Kingston Press—Professor George Pahomov, Dr. Nikolas Lupinin and Professor Max Kortepeter. Their efforts and cooperation were extremely beneficial in bringing about the final publication of such a complex work as this chronicle.

It is obvious that I, as the Editor, am solely responsible for all possible errors in translation, dates and commentaries to be found in this critical English edition of *The Nikonian Chronicle*.

Serge A. Zenkovsky
Daytona Beach, Florida
August, 1984

INTRODUCTION TO VOLUME III
OF THE NIKONIAN CHRONICLE

1. *Political Significance of the Era, 1241-1381*

A convenient title for this third volume of the English critical edition of *The Nikonian Chronicle*, which embraces the years 1241-1381, would be "Russia under the Tatar-Mongols."[1] In 1237-1241 the heirs of Genghis Khan completed subjugation of all the Russian lands and established their firm control over them. About one and a half centuries later, in 1380, Russian armies under Prince Dmitrii of Moscow—later known as Dmitrii "Donskoi"—inflicted the first crushing defeat upon the joint Tatar forces of the Golden Horde, led by Khan Mamai.[2]

Conquest and domination of Russia by the Tatars lasted altogether over two centuries because the battle of Kulikovo, despite all its importance, did not put an end to some control over Russia by these Asian nomads. This Tatar domination left profound and ineradicable traces on Russia's past and present, and on the West's attitude toward and relations with Russia.

1. Here, we call these Asian conquerors "Tatar-Mongols" because both names were originally the names only of some Mongol clans. Later, in Russia, they became known as "Tatars," although the bulk of their armies was neither Mongol nor Tatar, but, primarily, Turkic-speaking nomads of Central Asia and southern Russia—largely, the Polovetss, who called themselves "Kipchak" and were known in the West as "Kumans." The name, "Mongol," is now used only to identify the really "Mongol-speaking" population of Asia. Vladimirtsov, B. la., *Chenghiz Khan*, Berlin/Moscow, 1922; and his *Obshchestvennyi stroi Mongolov*, Leningrad, 1934. See, also, R. Grousset, *Les Conquérants du Monde*, Paris, 1944.

2. In *Nik.*, whose compilers used for the fourteenth century the Byzantine calendar which started the new year on September 1, the battle of the Don—or Kulikovo—which occurred on September 8, appears under the year, 1381, and not 1380, as it should according to the modern calendar.

The most disastrous results of the Tatar Yoke were Russia's isolation from the West, mass decimation and abduction of the population, and the destruction of cultural and economic centers. Weakened by the Asian invaders, Russia was unable to withstand the pressure of her Western neighbors, and some decades after the Tatar conquest most of Russia's western and southern lands were taken by Poles and Lithuanians. Almost immediately after the Tatar conquest Russia's rapacious Western neighbors, seeing her plight, started to attack her western borders. The first were the Swedes under Earl Birger, who, in July, 1240, invaded the Novgorodian land in the region of the Neva river.[3] They were defeated by Prince Alexander "Nevsky." Two years later, he had to fight and defeat the German "Crusaders" of the Livonian Order, who entered northwestern Russia near Pskov.

While the Swedes and the Livonian Knights were stopped, Lithuania and—from the early fourteenth century—the Poles, as well, systematically encroached upon the west Russian principalities. By the end of the fourteenth century all Russian territories roughly west of the line, Pskov—upper Don river, were in the hands of Poles or Lithuanians. Even other, more eastern Russian lands came under considerable political influence from the Polish-Lithuanian Commonwealth. Novgorod—whose territories embraced the entire Russian north from Narva to the Urals —and such close-lying principalities near Moscow as Tver' and Riazan' in the fifteenth century vacillated in their political allegiance between Lithuania and Moscow.

In 1385 the marriage of Grand Prince Jagaillo of Lithuania and the Polish Queen Jadwiga, and then the resulting political union of both countries, created on Russia's western border a powerful confederation which at times was joined by Bohemia and Hungary. Indeed, in the later fourteenth and fifteenth centuries the Jagellonian empire was the most powerful entity in all Europe. The heirs of Jagaillo commanded not only all central and

3. This occurred in 1241, according to the Old Russian "March" calendar used in *Nik.* in this instance. They were defeated by Prince Alexander—later known as Alexander "Nevsky." Two years later, he had to fight and defeat the German "Crusaders" of the Livonian Order, who entered northwestern Russia near Pskov.

east central Europe from the Baltic to the Black Sea but nearly swallowed the remaining Russian lands.

Thus, the small remaining eastern Russia, itself divided into a multitude of petty rival principalities, became solidly insulated from the West. Swedes, the Livonian Order and the Polish-Lithuanian Commonwealth so jealously guarded the routes from Russia to the West that Russia became almost completely inaccessible to and forgotten by Western Europe. At that time only Novgorod had some commerce with the West, and still this trade was very onesided because while Western merchants—primarily, Germans—would come to Novgorod, they would not permit Russian tradesmen to sell their merchandise on the Western markets.

In view of this situation it is small wonder that in the thirteenth to fifteenth centuries and later, Western Europe forgot Russia's existence and no longer considered her part of the European Christian community. Before the Mongol invasion there had been very active economic, dynastic and even cultural contacts between Russia and the West. Russia's princes and princesses had married rulers and scions of rulers of Germany, Sweden, Norway, France, Hungary and other Western countries (as well as of Byzantium). Even one Anglo-Saxon king, Edmund the Ironside (d. 1016), and later the wife and daughter of Harold, the last Anglo-Saxon king, killed in 1066 at Hastings, had found refuge in Russia, where Harold's daughter, Gita, married the prince of Kiev, Vladimir Monomakh. (The mother of this same Vladimir was a Byzantine princess.) Although the Russians had embraced Byzantine Orthodox Christianity and not Roman Catholicism, and despite the strife between Constantinople and Rome, neither Russians nor West Europeans had paid much attention to this confessional difference.

Russia's conquest by the Mongol Tatars, however, drastically curtailed these relations with Western Europe and greatly altered West Europeans' attitude toward Russians. In the Western mind, deliberately or not, Russia ceased to belong to the traditional European Christian world and came to be viewed as a part of the Asian empire, and even as Asia. It was forgotten that for centuries the Russians had formed a protective shield guarding the West from the Asian nomads—Pechenegs, Kumans and, now, Tatar-Mongols. Although the Russians were defeated and incorporated over a longer period of time into the realm of Genghis Khan's heirs, they nonetheless caused their Tatar overlords enough trouble and worry as to prevent the latter from making further westward incursions. After Batu's successful raids into Poland, Bohemia, Hungary and the Balkans in the 1240's, the Tatars were too preoccupied with keeping their Russian subjects under control so as to venture into another offensive against the West. Despite conquest and the centuries-long Asian yoke, however, Russia did not undergo any significant impact of the culture, and none of the religion, of their Tatar rulers. They became neither Asian nor nomadic, and the Russians' religion, culture and way of life remained much the same as it had been before Batu's invasion.

In Batu's armies, in his administration and, especially, in the economy of the Golden Horde there was already a considerable number of Moslems, and the impact of Islam on the Horde grew stronger with every year. Indeed, Batu's son, Khan Berke (1258-1266), was a devout Moslem; and later on, Khan Uzbek (1313-1341) made Islam the official confession of the Golden Horde. Still, neither religiously nor culturally was Russia affected by the Islamic ways of her overlords or the latters' officials and merchants. There were practically no conversions of Russians into Islam, with the exception of a few isolated cases of some Russians who resided in the Khans' capital, Sarai. The only tangible impact of the Mongol Yoke on medieval Russia may be found in the organization of the army, in the adoption of new weapons, and in some financial, commercial and monetary terminology. But while a large number of Greek words became deeply implanted in the Russian language, there remain now just some dozens of Tatar words in the Russian lexicon.

Mediterranean Europe, the Balkans, Sicily and southern Spain, which were similarly conquered by Moslem Arabs, bear till now the traces of Moslem influence, for the populations of these regions were largely Islamicized—in Sicily, till the twelfth century; in Spain, till the sixteenth; and in the Balkans, until now. Examples of Moslem art are scattered throughout all the countries of the Balkans, southern Italy and southern Spain, but we do not find any of these in original Russian lands. The famous Oriental cupolas of Vasilii Blazhennyi in Moscow, crowned by the Cross and erected after Ivan's conquest of Kazan', symbolize not the impact of Islam or Asia on Russia but, rather, the victory of

Russians over Asia and Moslems. With the exception of some dynastic marriages in the Middle Ages, there was little inter-marriage between the Asian conquerors and the Russians, and there is practically no Asian blood in the veins of Russians. To the contrary, there is considerable Russian blood in the veins of Ta-tars because, when abducting Russian slaves—especially, women—the Tatars accepted these slaves into their own families.

Nonetheless, Western Europe, Russia's neighbors and, es-pecially, Rome, tried to justify Western aggression against Rus-sia by religious and cultural considerations. We have already mentioned the attacks by Swedes and German crusaders, who claimed that their inroads into Russian territory were made with the purpose of converting the "schismatics." In 1253, being un-der strong pressure from Poland, Daniel of Galicia was forced to accept his crown from the Roman Catholic Pope, thus recog-nizing at least for several years the supreme authority of Rome (which he renounced in 1260). Occupation of Galicia and Volynia by the Poles in the fourteenth century led to Catholic pressure on the Orthodox population there, and in 1340 Pope Benedict XII gave his blessing to King Casimir of Poland to start a crusade against the "schismatic people of Russia." Three years later, in 1343, Pope Clement VI gave King Casimir financial support to fight "Tatars, Russians and Lithuanians."[4] Purposeful political and religious confusion of Russians with Tatars—*i.e.*, of Eastern Christians ("schismatics") with infidels—prompted Pope Urban V to give a plenary indulgence to participants in a crusade against pagan "Lithuanians, Tatars and other infidels and schismatics." This identification of Orthodox Christian Russians with pagan or Moslem Tatars became very convenient and can easily be found in a number of historical writings and pamphlets. Even at the present time in contemporary studies of current Russia, and of her atheistic and communist rulers there can be heard the echo of old claims that Russians are not a part of Europe but, rather, an Asian nation. It is interesting to recall that Russians captured by Tatars and sold as slaves to Italy and southern France were called "white Tatars" there. Centuries later, Napoleon remarked,

---

4. Meyendorff, 65-66, who quotes A. Theiner, *Vetera monumentae historia Poloniae*, Rome, 1860.

"Scratch a Russian and you will find a Tatar," and a similar theme could be heard in the cheap slogans of British politicians who organized the Crimean campaign of 1853-1855. Subsequently, similar inferences are to be found in many of the writings of Karl Marx. Historians like to forget that for half a millenium Russia formed a Christian rampart against the Asian invaders and that Russians were the first among the Europeans to defeat the Moslem Tatars, thereby stopping the advance of the Asian and Islamic conquerors.

2. *Populational Losses and Destruction of Cultural-Economic Centers*

As mentioned above, conquest of Russia by the Tatar-Mongols resulted in deep and often tragic relations between Russia and Western Europe, and in the attitude of Russia's immediate Western neighbors toward her state and people. Even more immediately damaging was the very process of conquest, which brought irreparable human, cultural and economic losses. During the conquest nearly all major cities—with the exception of Novgorod, Pskov and Smolensk, which the Tatars could not attain in the course of their invasion—were destroyed and the inhabitants were decimated or abducted (the women and children, particularly) into captivity and slavery. These abductions furnished the Tatars not only with additional slave manpower and concubines but also with a prized market commodity since the Tatars would sell large numbers of captives to buyers from Central Asia and the Near East or to Genoese slave merchants in the Crimea.

Constant raids into Russia by the Khans' commanders or by semi-independent Tatar lords perpetuated the practice established by the Polovetss of periodic renewal of slave supplies for these markets. The most important of these raids recorded in the chronicles occurred in 1252, 1254, 1258, 1273, 1281, 1282, 1283, etc., and lasted with the same frequency until nearly the mid-fourteenth century. During many of these raids—as, for instance, in 1293—large cities and towns were completely destroyed and burned, endless numbers of people were killed or captured. According to medieval Italian documents, an average price for a "white Tatar slave" (as the Russians were called) was about "136-139 lira apiece," although an apparently exceptionally beautiful seventeen-year-old "white Tatar" girl was sold to southern France

—Rousillon, in the Oriental Pyrenees—for 2,093 liras. In general, female slaves were twice as expensive as male.[5] In the fourteenth centuries slaves from Eastern Europe were among the most valuable merchandise in the Mediterranean region. As late as 1572, during their raid on Moscow, the Crimean Tatars captured and killed about one million people, of which one-quarter was sold for ridiculously low prices because of an oversupply on the slave market. They went to the Near East, to North Africa and to the Mediterranean countries of Europe.

Besides these constant massacres and abductions into slavery, Russia suffered from frequent conscriptions of men into the Mongol armies. In 1245 almost immediately after the conquest, for the purpose of conscription and the levying of taxes, the Tatars ordered a census of the population, divided Russia into census districts called *tumen* or *tma* (that is, ten thousand), and then into smaller districts of a thousand and of a hundred. The late Professor George Vernadsky estimated that Russia's total population in 1276 was between 8,600,000 and 10,000,000.[6] The present writer, however, feels that such a number is greatly exaggerated because Vernadsky considered that each household consisted of twenty persons. The number of persons per household should be considerably lower, since many members of the households were either slain or taken captive during the invasion and subsequent raids. Russian soldiers had to participate, as part of the Mongol army, in a number of campaigns which took them to the Near East, Central Asia and even to China. Obviously, very few of them returned home. Some perished during the campaigns, some died from disease. Besides soldiers, the Tatars would take a great many skilled craftsmen back to the Golden Horde and to the city of Karakorum, capital of the Mongol Empire. Thus, the population of Russia was reduced in four ways: killed during raids, abducted as slaves, drafted as soldiers, or conscripted as craftsmen. This systematically weakened the human resources of the country throughout the entire period of Tatar domination in Russia and even in the later centuries as long as the Tatar raids lasted. In fact, the last major raids against

5. M. D. Poluboiarinov, *Russkie liudi v Zolotoi orde*, Moscow, 1978.

6. Vernadsky, III, p. 219.

Central Russia occurred in the late sixteenth century, while a lesser raid against Volynia and Podolia took place in the late eighteenth.

In taking cities, the Tatar-Mongols would usually destroy and burn them both during the fighting with the local populations and after their seizure, so as to punish the defenders and teach a lesson to their next prey. Since the cities were economic centers of regions, their destruction and the massacre of their inhabitants, craftsmen and merchants, together with subsequent abductions, inflicted heavy blows on the country's economy. In the years 1237-1241 practically all the cities of eastern, central and southern Russia were razed and some—*i.e.*, Riazan'—never recovered.[7] According to reports of eyewitnesses, mostly incidental Western travellers, there remained in Kiev just some dozen households while the other important southern city, Pereiaslavl' Russkii, became a completely Tatar place.

The economy of eastern and southern Russia suffered, moreover, from a rerouting of trade from such Russian cities as Kiev, Chernigov, Pereiaslavl', Vladimir and others to Sarai, capital of the Golden Horde, where now the products of Russia would come as bounty or taxes. The latter, paid mostly in goods, were so heavy and so diversified that there remained very little to be sold within Russia, itself, especially in the thirteenth century when taxes were collected either by Tatar officials—the so-called *baskaks*, or by their tax farmers, who were mostly Moslem merchants from Central Asia or the Near East.

Destruction of most Russian cities—with the above-mentioned exception of Novgorod and a couple of other places in the northwestern part of the country—likewise meant the wholesale destruction of the cultural centers. The spread of culture, which has always been the almost exclusive domain of the churches and of monasteries located in the cities and in especially richer regional centers, was consequently totally disrupted. Because of the destruction of these cultural centers, literacy, as well as literary and artistic production, steadily decreased throughout at least the first century following the invasion. Only toward the

7. Present Riazan' is not the old Riazan' but the former Pereiaslavl' Riazanskii, which was renamed "Riazan' " only in the eighteenth century.

mid-fourteenth century, when a new monastic and cultural revival commenced, can we observe some literary and artistic progress.

3. *Chronicle Writing in the Years 1241-1381*

In the meantime, the chronicle becomes very dry and the annual entries are often reduced to the mere enumeration of deaths of princes, plagues, Tatar inroads and extremely short reports of political events. A casual perusal of the *Laurentian Chronicle* for the years, 1241-1419 shows that these approximately two centuries take up only some sixteen pages because the chroniclers had so little to say or to learn of.[8] Even in the much later *Muscovite Late XV Century Chronicle* the period, 1241-1381, takes only seventy-four pages.[9]

The Nikonian Chronicle in this respect is very different from the earlier local chronicles written during the time of the Tatar Yoke. Besides its basic text, which is taken largely from the so-called *Chronographic Redaction of the Fifth Novgorodian Chronicle*,[10] it includes a large amount of other materials. The latter were taken from the chronicles of various principalities, primarily from Tver', Novgorod, Riazan', Rostov, *a.o.* To these was added some material of not purely historical nature. They were the lives of saints, stories about the battles and other literary works written not as historical reportage but rather as literature for edification. They are more lyrical glorifications of the saints and princes and of their saintly or heroic deeds, rather than materials for the political, cultural or institutional historiography of Russia. These works, introduced into the chronicles at a later time, often contain, nonetheless, more interesting details about the life and psyche of the Russian people than do the materials which record strictly historical events. Such inclusion of diverse materials concerning the years, 1241-1381, lends *The Nikonian Chronicle* the form of a historical-literary anthology, although formally it is

8. See the *Laurentian Chronicle* in the so-called *Academic Suzdalian* version, *PSRL,* Vol. I.

9. See *PSRL,* Vol. XXV.

10. See Introduction to *The Nikonian Chronicle*, Vol. I. This *Chronographic Redaction* remained unpublished. This editor could not gain access to this most important source for *The Nikonian Chronicle.*

still divided into annual entries which provide extremely valuable and interesting sources for understanding Russia's past at that time.

LIST OF TITLES OF ENTRIES
IN VOLUME THREE OF *THE NIKONIAN CHRONICLE*
1241 A.D.-1381 A.D.
[The titles in brackets were added by the Editor.
The other titles are as they appear in *Nik.*]

BIBLIOGRAPHY AND BIBLIOGRAPHICAL ABBREVIATIONS
(Only the most essential works are mentioned here)

Baumgarten	Baumgarten, N. de, *Généalogie des branches reignantes en Russie*, in *Or. Chr.*, 1934.
Berezhkov	Berezhkov, N. G., *Khronologiia russkogo letopisaniia*, AN Moscow, 1963.
Bréhier	Bréhier, L, *La vie et la mort de Byzance*, Albin Michel, Paris, 1969.
Dal'	Dal', V. I., *Tolkovyi slovar' zhivogo russkogo iazyka*, M. 1861-67.
Dmitriev	Dmitriev, L., *Zhiteinye povesti russkogo severa*, AN, L. 1973.
Dmitrieva	Dmitrieva, R., *Bibliografiia russkogo letopisaniia*, AN M-L, 1962.
Galician Chr.	*Galitskaia letopis'*, part of *Hyp.*, *PSRL*, Vol. 2.
Golubinskii	Golubinskii, F., *Istoriia russkoi tserkvi*, Vols. 1 and 2, in four parts, M. 1900-1917.
Hyp.	*Ipatievskaia letopis'*, *PSRL*, Vol. 2.
Ioasaf. Chr.	*Ioasafovskaia letopis'*, Moscow, 1950.
IRL	*Istoriia russkoi literatury*, AN, M-L, 1943-1948, Vols. I-II.
IRL X-XVII VV.	*Istoriia russkoi literatury X-XVII v.v.*, Ed., Dmitriev, L. and Likhachev, D. M., 1980.
Kartashev	Kartashev, A. V., *Ocherki po istorii russkoi tserkvi*, Paris, 1959, Vols. I and II.
Kliuchevskii	Kliuchevskii, V., *Kurs russkoi istorii*, M. 1937, Vols. I, II.
Kloss	Kloss, B., *Nikonovskii svod i russkoe letopisanie XVI-XVII vv.*, Nauka, Moscow 1980.
Khronograph	*Khronograf 1512*, *PSRL*, Vol. 22.
Kuz'min	Kuz'min, L.G., *Nachal'nye etapy drevnerusskogo letopisaniia*, Izdat. Moskovskogo Universiteta, 1977.
Laur.	*Lavrentievskaia letopis'*, *PSRL*, Vol. 1.
Likhachev, *Letopisi*	Likhachev, D.S., *Russkoe letopisanie*, AN, M-L 1957.
Likhachev, *Nasledie*	Likhachev, D.S., *Velikoe nasledie*, Sovremennik, Moscow 1975.

Lit. Cal.	*Liturgical Calendar and Rubrics*, St. Vladimir's Seminary Press, New York, 1979.
Makarii	Bulgakov, Makarii, *Istoriia russkoi tserkvi*, Vols. 1-17, SPb, 1866-1883.
Mayendorff	Mayendorff, John, *Byzantium and the Rise of Russia*, Cambridge University Press, 1981.
Meshcherskii	Meshcherskii, N.A., *Istoriia voiny iudeiskoi I. Flaviia*, M. 1958.
Migne	Migne, J.P., *Patrologiae cursus completus*, Series Graeca, Paris, 1860 H., Vol. 102, 105.
Musc. Late 15th C.	*Moskovskii letopisnyi svod kontsa piatnadtsatogo veka*, *PSRL*, Vol. 25.
Musc. Late 15th C., Abbr.	*Sokrashchennye moskovskie letopisnye svody kontsa 15-go veka*, *PSRL*, Vol. 27.
Nasonov	Nasonov, A.N., *Istoriia russkogo letopisaniia*, M. 1969.
Nasonov	Nasonov, A.N., *Mongoly i Rus'*, M. 1940.
Nik.	*Patriarshaia ili Nikonovskaia letopis'*, *PSRL*, Vols. 9-13.
Novg. Kom. and *Novg.Syn.*	*Novgorodskaia pervaia letopis' starshego i mladshego izvodov*, Moscow-Leningrad, 1950.
Novg. Chr.	*Novgorodskaia letopis'* in *PSRL*, Vol. 3-4.
Or. Chr.	*Orientalia Christiana* (serial), Rome.
Pashuto	Pashuto, V.T., *Vneshniaia politika drevnei Rusi*, Nauka, M. 1968.
Poluboiarinov	Poluboiarinov, M.D., *Russkie liudi v Zolotoi Orde*, M. 1978.
Prokhorov	Prokhorov, G. M., *Povest' o Mitiae*, Publ. A.N. SSSR, L.1978.
Rashid	Rashid ad Din, *Sbornik letopisei*, A.K. Arends, trans., M-L 1946.
PSRL	*Polnoe sobranie russkikh letopisei (Complete Collection of Russian Chronicles)*, 1841--, AN Moscow, Vols. 1-34.
RIB	*Russkaia istoricheskaia biblioteka*, SPB 1872-1927 (39 vols.).

Roty	Roty, Martine, *Dictionnaire Russe-Francais des Termes en Usage en Église Russe*, Paris, IES, 1980.
Rogozh. Let.	*Rogozhskaia letopis'*, publ. in *PSRL*, Vol. 15.
SIE	*Sovietskaia istoricheskaia entsiklopediia*, Vols. 1-16, M. 1961-1976.
Simeon. Chr.	*Simeonovskaia letopis'*, *PSRL*, Vol. 18.
Sof.	*Sofievskaia letopis'*, *PSRL*, vols. 5-6.
Soloviev	Soloviev, S.M., *Istoriia Rossii s drevneishikh vremen. I-X* (in 30 vols.) M., 1959-1966.
Suzd. Acad.	*Suzdal'skaia letopis'*, see *Laur.*, *PSRL*, vol. 1.
TODRL	*Trudy otdela drevnerusskoi literatury*, AN SSSR, Vols. 1-34, Leningrad, 1932.
Tvorogov	Tvorogov, O.B., *Drevnerusskie khronografy*, AN, L. 1975.
Tver'. let.	*Tver'skaia letopis'*, in *PSRL*, Vol. 15.
Tver'. Sbornik	*Tver'skoi sbornik*, in *PSRL*, Vol. 15.
Ustiuzh. Chr.	*Ustiuzhskii letopisnyi svod*, AN Moscow, 1950.
Vasiliev	Vasiliev, A.A., *History of the Byzantine Empire*, Univ. of Wisc. Press, 1958, Vols. 1-2.
Vernadsky	Vernadsky, G., *History of Russia*, Vol. 3, Yale U.P., 1953.
Volynian Chr.	*Volynskaia letopis'*, part of *Hyp.*, *PSRL*, Vol. 2.
Vladimir. Let.	*Vladimirskii letopisets*, *PSRL*, Vol. 30.
Zenkovsky	Zenkovsky, S., *Medieval Russia's Epics, Chronicles and Tales*, 2nd rev. ed., E.P. Dutton & Co., New York, 1969.
Zimin	Zimin, A.A., Introduction to the *Ioasafovskaia letopis'*, above.

LIST OF ABBREVIATIONS
(Libraries and Manuscripts)
(For the locations of *mss.*, see Introduction to Volume I)

AN	Adademiia Nauk (Academy of Sciences, USSR)
BAN	Biblioteka Akademii Nauk (Library of the Academy of Sciences), USSR, Leningrad.
Chron. red. 5 Novg.	*Chronographic redaction of the Fifth Novgorodian Chronicle*, in *ms.* only, in GIM.
GIM	Gosudarstvennyi istoricheskii muzei (State Historical Museum), Moscow.
GBIL	Gosudarstvennaia biblioteka imeni Lenina (Lenin State Library), Moscow.
Obol.	*Obolenskii ms. redaction of The Nikonian Chronicle.* See Ch. I of Intro. to Vol. I.
Patr.	*Patriarshii ms. redaction of The Nikonian Chronicle,* See Ch. I of Intro. to Vol. I.
Radziwill Chr.	*Radzivillovskaia letopis'*
SIE	*Sovietskaia istoricheskaia entsiklopediia* Vol. I-XVI, Moscow 1961-1976.

GLOSSARY OF RUSSIAN AND BYZANTINE TERMINOLOGY

ARCHIMANDRITE — Abbot, head of a large, prominent monastery.

BASKAK — Mongol Tatar official, mostly a tax collector in Russia.

BOGATYR' — An outstanding, unusually strong and brave warrior.

BOIARIN, BOIAR — A noble of high rank. Since the thirteenth century the boiars formed an exclusive group out of which were chosen the prince's councillors and high officials.

CHETVERT', or CHET' — (1) A measure of grain, varying from 134 to 288 American pounds; (2) An Old Russian land unit of about 1.35 acres.

DEN'GA — Basic monetary unit since the fourteenth century (from Mongol *Tamga*—seal). A ruble contained usually 100 Novgorodian or 200 Moscow *den'gas*.

DRUZHINA — A prince's retinue or bodyguard; permament nuclues of a prince's armed force.

GOST' — Wholesale merchant; later, in the fifteenth-seventeenth centuries, the top and very small group of the business class.

GRIVNA — A unit of weight of about 410 grams.

IARLYK — A charter of the khan of the Golden Horde granting a principality to the Russian princes.

INDICTION — Byzantine unit of chronology: a fifteen-year period. The year begins September 1.

KAZAK (COSSACKS) — Originally, Turkic nomads, not connected with a tribe; frontiersmen; later, free Russian settlers along the rivers of the prairie.

KHRONOGRAF — From Greek, Chronograph—a type of Byzantine historical writing organized into the reigns of the emperors; and, in Russia, of the princes and tsars.

KUNA — The marten fur. It was a monetary unit in ancient Russia.

xxxi

LETOPIS'	Historical writings of Old Russia, organized under yearly entries.
LOGOTHET	In Russian, *logofet*: high Byzantine office, in charge of financial affairs, primarily.
METROPOLIA	A large bishopric. In Russia the entire territory and administration of the Church.
METROPOLITAN	Metropolitan bishop, head of the Russian Church.
NAMESTNIK	Local administrator and judge, appointed by the grand prince.
NOGATA	A monetary unit of *kuna* (see above) system, usually equal to 2½ *rezana*, or $1/20$ *grivna kun*.
NOMOCANON	Byzantine codex of ecclesiastic law and, partially, civil law. After Russia's Christianization it also became the Russian codex of canon law.
OKOL'NICHII	A high official, just under *boiar*; often member of the Boiar Duma.
POPRISHCHE	A measure of distance, usually equivalent to one *versta*.
POSADNIK	An elected high official or commissioner. In Novgorod, the elected chief administrator. In Kievan Russia, an official appointed by the prince.
PUD	A measure of weight, equivalent to forty pounds (since the eighteenth century).
RUBLE	Basic unit of Russian monetary system since the fourteenth century. Equivalent to 100 Novgorodian or 200 Muscovite kunas. (Since the sixteenth century, 200 and 100 kopeks.)
SAZHEN'	A linear unit equivalent to three arshins, or seven feet.
SCHEMA	The second and highest monastic tonsure. Very strict rules.
SLUGA	A servitor in medieval Russia; in the army, equal to a squire.
STOL'NIK	A court official who aided the prince at table. Later, a high official just beneath a *boiar*.

THEOTOKOS

"One who gave birth to God." The Orthodox term for the Virgin Mary. (In Russian, *"Bogoroditsa."*)

TYSIATSKII

Literally, the commander of a troop of one thousand men. In all the major cities, tysiatskiis commanded city soldiers and militias.

ULUS

A tatar term for a state or part of a state under Tatar domination.

VECHE

A town meeting. After the thirtenth century, it disappeared except in Novgorod and Pskov, where the *veche* became a kind of citizens' council, meeting on the main city square.

VERSTA

A unit of distance of about $^2/_3$ of a mile, or 1,063 klm.

VOEVODA

A high official, appointed by the prince. He may be an army or detachment commander, or chief military, administrative or judicial officer, or the governor of a territory.

USHKUINIK

From *ushkui*, a river boat: Novgorodian adventurers or freebooters who raided along the rivers of northern Russia and the Volga.

GENEALOGICAL TABLES

1. The House of Moscow
2. The House of Tver'
3. The House of Lithuania
4. The House of Genghis Khan and of the Golden Horde

The dates in these tables, as well as in the text of *The Nikonian Chronicle*, may be different from those in other chronicles or in the works of modern historians. This is to be explained by the fact that chroniclers in various regions of Russia used different dates for beginning the New Year (*i.e.*, March 1, September 1, or March 1 of the following year), and even different eras for chronology. See the *Preface* to this volume and the *Introduction* to Volume One of *The Nikonian Chronicle*.

GENEALOGY OF THE PRINCES OF THE HOUSE OF MOSCOW

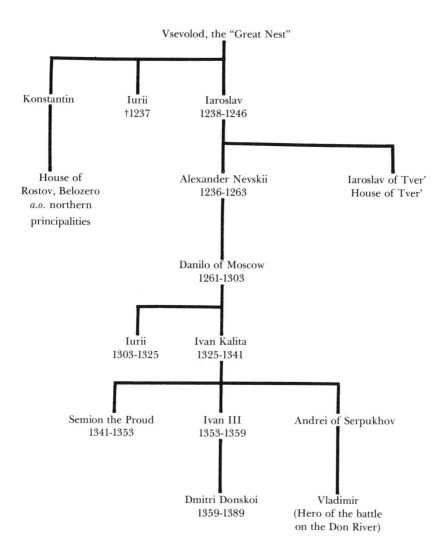

Vsevolod, the "Great Nest"

Konstantin

Iurii
†1237

Iaroslav
1238-1246

House of
Rostov, Belozero
a.o. northern
principalities

Alexander Nevskii
1236-1263

Iaroslav of Tver'
House of Tver'

Danilo of Moscow
1261-1303

Iurii
1303-1325

Ivan Kalita
1325-1341

Semion the Proud
1341-1353

Ivan III
1353-1359

Andrei of Serpukhov

Dmitri Donskoi
1359-1389

Vladimir
(Hero of the battle
on the Don River)

THE HOUSE OF TVER'

Vsevolod, the "Great Nest"

Iaroslav
1238-1246

Alexander Nevskii, 1236-1263   Iaroslav of Tver'
(Novgorod & Vladimir   1247-1271
See House of Moscow)

Mikhail
1285-1319

Dmitrii   Alexander   Vasilii of Kashin
1319-1325   1325-1339

Vsevolod

Mikhail II   House of Kashin
1368-1399

From the House of Tver' branched out the Houses of Kashin, Mikulin, Kholm, Dorogobuzh, *a.o.*

THE HOUSE OF LITHUANIA—POLAND

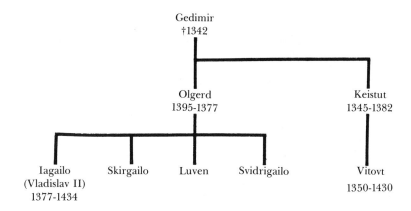

Jagellonian Dynasty in Lithuania, Poland, at times, also, in Hungary and Bohemia

THE HOUSE OF GENGHIS KHAN AND OF THE GOLDEN HORDE
[Dzhuchi' Ulus]

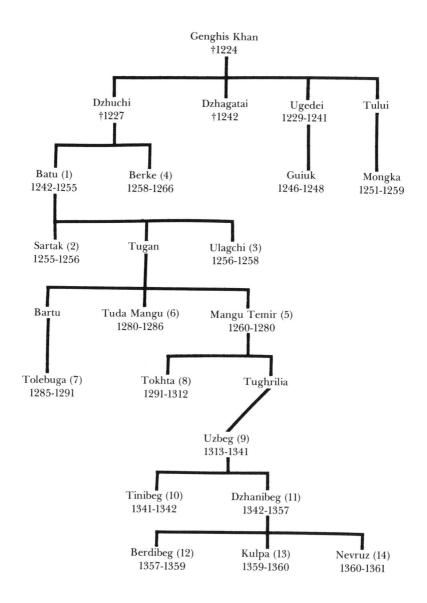

THE NIKONIAN CHRONICLE

(1241-1381)

This pious, noble and praiseworthy Grand Prince Aleksandr Iaroslavich was eighth in the line of autocrat Tsar Grand Prince Vladimir Sviatoslavich, who was equal to the Apostles because he enlightened the Russian land through Holy Baptism. He was also eleventh in the line of Riurik, and he was loved by God, God-favored and praiseworthy. For his many and glorious virtues he was deserving of both the people's and God's praise, and thus it was from his youth and his earliest years. He was taught all manner of blessed deeds by his wise-in-God, pious father, the ruling prince, Iaroslav Vsevolodich, and by his holy mother, God-loving Princess Feodosia, who, after being tonsured a nun, received the monastic name of Euphrosinia. He was introduced by them to all manner of good instruction.

Fear of God settled in his heart and he observed God's Commandments and behaved according to them, very much respecting the clergy and monks.

Throughout his whole youth he strictly observed the wisdom of humility;

he abstained and stayed awake [praying at night] and he observed purity of soul and of body,

he followed the rules of humility and rejected vainglory,

---

1. The present version of *The Life of Aleksandr Nevskii* is divided among several annual entries and interspersed with reports on some other events. Its original version was apparently written by someone contemporary to the Prince, most probably by Metropolitan Cyril, between 1263 and 1283. The story contains some eyewitness reports of the events and some elements of heroic epics. Later it was reworked in the *vita* style and considerably adorned. See D. S. Likhachev's articles in *TODRL*, Vol. V (1947). An earlier version of this *vita* has already been rendered in English. See Zenkovsky, pp. 224-236.

he controlled the desires of his flesh because he was aware that gluttony may destroy chastity,

and could prevent him from remaining awake, and would harm his virtues.

On his lips were constantly divine words which were sweeter than honey.

He would read the Scripture carefully

and he was filled with the desire to follow its words and practice them in deed.

His parents could see that he succeeded in these virtues,

that he was strict and always strove to please God,

that in his habits he did please God, that he burned with divine and heavenly desires,

that he was a good and honorable person among men,

that he cared for nothing other than the best fruit of man's spiritual perfection;

that he steadily hid his own virtue for the sake of humble wisdom.

Although he was honored by God with the honor of the earthly kingdom, had a spouse and children, he still achieved greater wisdom than any other man. He was mature in his behavior, his beauty of life was equal to Joseph the Beautiful. His power was like that of Solomon and his voice could be heard by all as a trumpet. His bravery was as that of the Roman Emperor Vespasian, the son of Nero,[2] who conquered all Judea. Indeed, the latter mustered his troops and ordered the storming of Antipas' city.[3] When the citizens made a sortie and defeated the Roman troops, he, alone by himself, threw the citizens to the city's gates and laughed at his troops, telling them, "Why did you leave me alone?" And such was this Grand Prince Aleksandr Iaroslavich, who defeated everyone and was never defeated. He was very merciful, in the same way as was his God-preserved father, Iaroslav; but in every respect he followed in his steps, giving as ransom for captives much gold and silver. And he would send it to Khan Batu, to the Horde, to ransom the captive Russian people who were taken prisoner by the godless Tatars. Thus did he ran-

2. Vespasian (A. D. 69-79) was *not* the son of Nero (A. D. 54-68).

3. Antipas (4 B. C. - A. D. 39) was Tetrarch of Galilea and Pereae, and died before Vespasian conquered Judea (A. D. 69).

som them and deliver them from evil labor and many misfortunes   **1241**
and unhappiness.

He, himself, was always protected by God and was never injured by any of his enemies. The Lord bestowed His mercy abundantly upon him and he was feared and dreaded by his enemies, and people everywhere trembled at his name. Wisdom and wit were given him as they had been given to Solomon. Above all, he loved justice, and he instructed his boiars to preserve it, to adhere to it, telling them parables from Divine Scripture: that they should learn God's Wisdom, should abstain from drunkenness, and be humble before God; that they should never forget how to judge righteously and not be influenced by the mighty, not to accept bribes, not to injure anyone; but to protect the offended from the hand of the offender; that they should not accept more than they ought; and that they should be satisfied with their fees. And he repeated this continually unto them, sometimes threatening them with his own power, sometimes reminding them of eternal salvation, when they would have to render an accounting at the terrifying Judgment of Christ's Law.

The boiars and his other men, seeing the wisdom given him by God, could not contend with him but promised unanimously to behave as he commanded them. And so he ruled the dominion given him by God courageously and bravely according to the Divine Commandments, and his renown spread through distant countries so that many people tried to see him.

When the people learned that godless Khan Batu, with God's permission, had caused much evil in the great Russian land, this blessed Aleksandr went to Novgorod, with his father, Iaroslav, remaining there to rule; and divine power did not allow the pagans even to approach the limits of the land of great Novgorod. They [Aleksandr and Iaroslav] stayed there and combatted inimical, hostile Lithuanians and Germans, while the murderous Tatars, by God's help, did no manner of battle against them.

THE BATTLE OF THE NEVA

Once, in order to see him powerful people from the Western land calling themselves the servants of God[4] came to Grand Prince

---

4. Servants of God: in this case these are probably Western Catholic monks and missionaries.

1241   Aleksandr Iaroslavich, grandson of Vsevolod, great grandson of
Iurii Dolgorukii, gr. gr. grandson of Vladimir Monomakh, gr. gr.
gr. grandson of Vsevolod, gr. gr. gr. gr. grandson of Iaroslav,
gr. gr. gr. gr. gr. grandson of Great Vladimir. They did so just as
the Queen of Sheba went to Solomon to see him and to hear his
wisdom. Likewise these came to see Aleksandr because his renown had spread everywhere. Returning, they told their people,
"Brethren! We have travelled to many countries and have seen
many people, but nowhere have we seen such a man, such a king
among kings and prince among princes." These words of praise
concerning the bravery and wisdom of blessed Aleksandr were
heard by the king[5] of some part of Rome[6] living in a northern
country; and he became overfilled with envy and hatred, growing
proud in his mind. He decided to take advantage of the moment,
for he was aware of Batu's conquest of Russia. This king of this
land hoped to swallow up the remaining part of Russia, and in his
pride he said, "I will go and I will capture Great Novgorod and
other cities, and I will turn the Slavic people into my slaves, and I
will defeat Grand Prince Aleksandr, himself, or I will take him
prisoner." And he assembled many people—masters, bishops,
Swedes, Murmans, Suomi, Em',[7] filled his ships with many regiments and marched with heavy forces. Breathing a militant spirit,
he crossed the sea and went over the river Neva, trembling with
rage and wishing to seize Ladoga and Great Novgorod, the entire
region of Novgorod up to Valaam.[8] The Most Gracious and Most
Merciful Manloving God, however, wanted to protect and defend
His dominion from the evil cunning of foreigners, and so this
madman labored in vain because his intentions were contrary to
the Will of God.

Soon after their arrival came the tidings that the Swedes were
marching toward Ladoga, and they [the Swedes] sent their envoys to Aleksandr Iaroslavich, saying, "Resist if you can; but I
have already arrived here and I will capture you, and you and

5. "King" here means *"yurl"* (earl, count) Birger Magnusson, royal
brother and the actual ruler in place of the weak king, Eric Laespe
(1223-1250).

6. Here is meant Roman Catholic Northern Europe.

7. Murmans, Suomi, Em': Finno-Ugric tribes of present Finland.

8. Ladoga: an old Russian city on Lake Ladoga; Valaam—a Russian
monastic center on Lake Ladoga.

your sons will be my slaves." When Aleksandr heard these words **1241**
his heart burned and he went to the chruch of Holy Sophia.
There, kneeling before the altar, he prayed tearfully, saying,
"Lord God, Who ordered that another's borders not be crossed:
be the Judge, also, of this one and forbid him to invade countries
that are not his." Then he arose and went to Archbishop Spiridon,
bowing, and received his blessing; then he left the church and encouraged his hosts, saying, "God is in truth, not in power." And
he mounted his horse and marched against the enemy troops,
even being unable to send tidings to his father because the enemy
soldiers were approaching. In addition, not many Novgorodians
were able to assemble as they had to march rapidly against the
enemy. He came against them on Sunday, the fifteenth day of the
month of July, when the Council of Six Hundred Thirty Fathers
of Chalcedon, and the Holy Martyrs Cyril and Julita, and holy
Grand Prince Vladimir, who Christianized all the Russian land
and who was called "Basil" after Holy Baptism, are remembered.

ABOUT PELGUSIUS OF IZHORA

Aleksandr's voevoda was an elder, a notable, from the Izhora
land, by the name, Pelgusius—Philip, in Holy Baptism—who was
charged with guarding the seashore. He greatly respected the
Holy Martyrs Boris and Gleb, and although he lived among his
own [Finnic] tribe, which was pagan, he still observed Lent and
abstinence on Wednesdays and Fridays; therefore God let him
see an awesome vision about which we will speak shortly. This
Pelgusius glimpsed the enemy host and he went to meet Prince
Aleksandr Iaroslavich to tell him of the great forces of the Varangians. When he was on the shore of the sea, guarding the two
routes, he held vigil all night. As the sun began to rise he heard an
awesome noise coming from the sea, and he saw a ship approaching. In its midst stood the Holy Martyrs Boris and Gleb in red
vestments, with their hands on their shoulders. The oarsmen of
the ship, however, were covered as though by fog. And Boris said
to Gleb, "Brother Gleb! Order them to row faster. Let us help
our kinsman, Grand Prince Aleksandr Iaroslavich." When Pelgusius saw this vision and heard these voices coming from the
Holy Martyrs Boris and Gleb, he was seized by great fear and
trembling and he remained thus until the ship moved out of his
sight. Thereupon he hurried to Grand Prince Aleksandr Iarosla-

1241   vich, upon whom he gazed with joyful eyes, and he confessed to him alone what he had seen and heard. The latter told him, "Speak of this to no one until God acts as He desires."

[SIX HEROES OF THE BATTLE ON THE NEVA]

And so he marched quickly against them and toward the sixth hour of the day there was a great battle against the Romans.[9] They slew a great many Romans, and he even left a seal on the king's face with his sharp sword. Then in the host of Grand Prince Aleksandr Iaroslavich there appeared six brave men battling courageously beside him. The first one was by name Gavrila Oleksich. This one rode onto the boat and, seeing that the king's son was fleeing from his hands, from the ship, he rode after him on boards to the very ship from which they were descending. He rode to the ship before him and then turned, and was thrown from the boards, together with his horse, into the sea. Thanks to God's will, he escaped from them unharmed. Then he rode further and battled staunchly with the commander in the midst of his troops, and thus did he kill their commander, Spiridon. Their bishop was also killed there.

The second Novgorodian was named Zbyslav Iakunovich. This one rode his horse continuously against the enemy, doing battle only with an axe. He had no fear in his heart and several fell at his hand. All wondered at his power and bravery.

The third was Iakov from the land of Polotsk, who was one of the Prince's hunters. He attacked the [Swedish] troops with a sword, behaving valiantly; and he was praised by the Prince.

The fourth Novgorodian was named Misha. He charged on foot with his troops and he destroyed three of the Romans' ships.

The fifth was among the young ones, named Savva. He rode against the great tent of the king which had a golden top, and he cut the [supporting] pole, whereupon the tent fell. When Grand Prince Aleksandr Iaroslavich's regiments saw the tent fall they rejoiced.

The sixth among his squires was Ratmir. He also fought on foot, and he was surrounded by many Romans. Wounded many times, he fell and thus passed away.[10]

9. "Romans" here means the Roman Catholic Swedes.

10. All six of these names are found in *Novg. Kom.*

All this I heard from my lord, Prince Aleksandr Iaroslavich, **1241** and from others who were witnesses of this battle. It was a miracle similar to the one which occurred in olden times during the reign of King Hezekiah, when Jerusalem was attacked by Sennacherib, the king of Assyria, who wanted to capture the Holy City: suddenly an angel of the Lord appeared and slew 185,000 Assyrian warriors, and early the next morning their bodies were found there, all dead. The same happened after Aleksandr Iaroslavich's victory: after he defeated the king [Earl Birger] on the other shore of the Izhora, which Aleksandr's regiments did not reach, numerous enemy were found slain by the Lord's angels. And so they [the Russians] found the bodies of many dead who were killed there. The remaining enemy fled and there were three ships full of the bodies of great commanders. They sank the ships with them on the Neva Sea[11] but for the others they dug graves and cast an endless number into them. Also, many were wounded and they escaped in the night.

Among the Novgorodians who fell were Konstantin Lugatinich, Giuriata Pineshchinich, Namest, Drochilo Nezdilov, son of a tanner,[12] and, altogether, twenty men fell, including the people of Ladoga, or perhaps fewer. God alone knows.

Grand Prince Aleksandr Iaroslavich returned with great victory, glorifying and thanking God and saying, "Most Gracious Lord, I thank Thee and glorify Thy Holy Name; I called upon Thee in the days of my sadness and Thou didst not abandon me, Thy servant, and Thou deliveredst me from my enemies. They were proud and they fell; and we rose up and won. Thou warmly lovest everyone who sincerely repents and Thou drawest near everyone who seeks Thee in awe and love. Thou dost not despise those who look to Thee alone, but Thou helpest them; and all those who, with all their souls, address themselves to Thy Majesty Thou dost not disdain, but aidest; and Thou assistest those who address Thee with all their souls, and Thou helpest when they petition Thee, Thou glorifiest those who glorify Thee. Thou art the only Giver of blessings and Thine is the glory, the

11. Apparently, the Neva river or the Gulf of Finland.

12. Corrected according to *Novg. Syn.*; in *Nik.*, the spelling differs somewhat.

13. This prayer is not found in earlier chronicles. It belongs to the *vita* tradition.

1241   Father, Son and Holy Ghost, now and ever and unto the ages and ages. Amen."[13]

The same year Batu's Tatars defeated the Hungarians, captured the king's son, Menush, and brought him and a great multitude of high commanders to Batu.

The same year Batu's Tatars killed Prince Mstislav of Ryl'sk.

[ALEXANDER LEAVES NOVGOROD]

The same year [6748/1240 in *Novg. III.*] the Novgorodians disagreed with Aleksandr Iaroslavich [Nevskii] and there was subversion in Novgorod. Together with his mother, his princess and the entire court, Aleksandr went to his father, Grand Prince Iaroslav Vsevolodich of Vladimir. Remaining for a short time with his father, he then departed to be prince in Pereiaslavl', which is located on Lake Kleshchino.

The same year [6748 in *Novg. III.*] the Germans,[14] with the people of Medved', Veliad' and Iur'ev, and together with Prince Iaroslav Vladimirich, captured Izborsk. When these tidings that the Germans had taken Izborsk arrived in Pskov, the entire city marched against them, and there was a fierce battle. There was great carnage among them. The Germans killed voevoda Gavrila Goreslavich, and defeated the people of Pskov, slaying many in pursuit, others they captured. And they chased them to the city, setting fire in the suburbs; and there was much evil. They burned the churches, the holy icons and the church property, and devastated many towns around Pskov. They besieged the city for one week but were unable to take it. They captured many children of good men and took them into captivity, then retreated. And so it continued, without peace; but the Germans had the advantage over the people of Pskov because the latter were betrayed by Tverdila Ivanovich with some other men, and he began to rule in Pskov in agreement with the Germans, campaigning against the Novgorodian towns. And the other people of Pskov fled to Novgorod with their wives and children because of the German violence.[15]

The same year [6748/1240 in *Novg. III.*] after the victory and departure of Grand Prince Aleksandr Nevskii, even the same

14. German knights of the Livonian Order.

15. The text follows quite closely *Novg. Syn.*

winter, Germans and Chud' from the western lands came against **1241** Vod'.[16] They campaigned everywhere and levied a tribute from them. In the land of Kopor'e they built a fortress in the domain of Grand Prince Aleksandr, but that was not the entire evil. They took Tesovo and marched up to thirty versts from Novgorod, killing merchants everywhere as far as Luga and Sabol', then returned to their own land with a great many captives, having imposed tribute on the various towns.

Then the people of Novgorod sent a petition to Grand Prince Iaroslav Vsevolodich asking him to send his son to be prince there; and he gave them his son, Prince Andrei, although they still requested Grand Prince Aleksandr; but he did not give him to them. Then the men of Novgorod returned to Novgorod and reported there all of Iaroslav's speeches—that he would not give them Grand Prince Aleksandr to rule them.

The same year [6748/1240 in *Novg. III.*] the Novgorodians, according to their custom, convened the veche and sent Archbishop Spiridon with the boiars and leading men again to Grand Prince Iaroslav Vsevolodich, petitioning him and asking him to send them Grand Prince Aleksandr Iaroslavich. With the above-mentioned boiars and leading men of Novgorod, Archbishop Spiridon came to Grand Prince Iaroslav Vsevolodich in Vladimir, speaking in the name of Novgorod, and he petitioned him, asking that Grand Prince Aleksandr Iaroslavich become prince of Novgorod. Then they acknowledged that the men of Novgorod were wrong in every way: "It was not right," they said, "to initiate this subversion and to have a disagreement with your son, Grand Prince Aleksandr. Give up your dislike for Great Novgorod and give us your son, Prince Aleksandr, to be our prince." And so he gave them his son, Aleksandr, to be their prince.

The same year [6748 in *Novg. III.*] Lithuanians and Germans fought in the Novgorodian land and caused much evil, then returned home.

The same year Batu's Tatars took the land of the Bulgars which is on the rivers Volga and Kama.

In the year 6750/1242. [6749 in *Novg. III.*] Grand Prince Aleksandr Iaroslavich came to Novgorod, and with him were

16. Chud': Estonians, in this case. Vod': Finnic tribes in the Novgorodian land; Germans: in this case, Livonian knights.

1242   Archbishop Spiridon and the boiars. The Novgorodians met
him with crosses at the city gates, he ascended to the Grand Principality with great honor, and there was vast rejoicing in Novgorod. When he came to Novgorod he hanged many traitors.
Soon thereafter he marched with the levies of Novgorod, Ladoga,
Karela and Izhora[17] against the German town of Kopor'e, and he
destroyed that city to its foundations, slew Germans and brought
some to Novgorod; others he permitted to go to the German land
because he was merciful above all measure. He hanged the traitors among the Vod' and Chud', then returned to Pereiaslavl',
which is on Lake Kleshchino.

In the year 6751/1243. [6749/1241 in *Sof. V.*] The Germans gathered in their land[18] and defeated the troops of Pskov,
then put their administrators in Pskov. Hearing of this, Prince
Aleksandr Iaroslavich became very sad about the shedding of
Christian blood, and without losing time, seized by fervent divine
faith, he marched to Novgorod with his brother, Andrei, and
with all his troops. Coming to Novgorod, he bowed to the cathedral of Holy Sophia with prayer and tears.

THE BATTLE ON THE ICE

In the year 6751/1243. Grand Prince Aleksandr marched
against the Germans with his brother, Andrei, with the Novgorodians, and with the levies of the Niz land, with great forces.
He did thus so that they should not boast and say, "We will dishonor the Slavic race, take the city of Pskov and assign our administrators to the city." He [Aleksandr] occupied all the roads to
Pskov and then unexpectedly, entered Pskov and captured the
Germans, the Chud' and the German administrators, sent them
in chains to Novgorod, and liberated the city of Pskov from captivity.

Then he marched into the German land, campaigned there,
burned, slew many and captured others; but the Germans were
proud and they assembled another host, saying, "Let us go to defeat Prince Aleksandr and capture him," and they marched with
their hosts. When Aleksandr's vanguard saw them, they were
seized with great fear, gazing upon their many troops, and they
reported this to Prince Aleksandr Iaroslavich. He became very

17. Karela and Izhora: Finnic tribes north of Novgorod.
18. In Livonia.

sad, went to the church of the Holy Trinity [in Pskov] and prayed   **1243**
there, weeping and shedding tears; and then he marched toward
the German land. At that time it was winter. When he was in
their land he sent all his troops on forays. On one of these forays
the Germans killed voevoda Damash and Kerbert, the posadnik's
brothers—strong and very brave men. With them, more people
were slain, some were taken captive, and some hurried to Grand
Prince Aleksandr Iaroslavich; he then began to prepare his
troops. When the Grand Master[19] learned of this, he advanced
against Aleksandr with all his bishops and with all his forces which
were in their land, and he received help from the queen. They all
gathered on the lake called "Chudskoe."[20] When Grand Prince
Aleksandr Iaroslavich saw them he retreated beyond the lake.
The Germans and the Chud' marched against him. The Grand
Prince aligned his regiments on Lake Chud' and on the land near
Voronii Kamen' [Crows' Rock]. He strengthened his spirit with
the sign of the Cross and marched onto [icy] Lake Chudskoe.
There was a great multitude [of troops] in both hosts. His
father, Grand Prince Iaroslav Vsevolodich, sent to his aid his
younger brother, Andrei, with many of his warriors, and therefore Grand Prince Aleksandr had a multitude of brave men, and
they were as strong as in ancient times were the men of King
David. And so the warriors of Grand Prince Aleksandr became
filled with martial spirit and their hearts became like those of
lions, and they were light as eagles. They said, "Our honorable
and dear Prince! Now is the time to sacrifice our lives for you."
Grand Prince Aleksandr raised his hand toward heaven and said,
"God! Be Judge between me and them, and help us, God, just
as Thou didst help Moses against Amalek, and my forefather,
Prince Iaroslav, against accursed Sviatopolk."

It was Saturday and the sun was rising when the two hosts
clashed. The Germans and the Chud', being in a formation
shaped like a pig, thrust through the [Russian] regiments, and
there was an evil and great battle for the Germans and the Chud'.
There were tremors from the breaking lances and there was noise
of swords clashing. They moved over the frozen lake but the ice
could not be seen because it was all covered with blood. I heard
from a witness who told me that he saw the Divine Host overhead,

19. "Grand Master"— "Grossmeister": the head of the Livonian
Order.

20. Chudskoe lake, near Pskov.

1243   which came to help Grand Prince Aleksandr; and he was victorious, thanks to the strength of God, to Holy Sophia and to the Holy Martyrs Boris and Gleb, who shed their blood for the sake of their people. The [heavenly Russian] warriors heaved their shoulders and slashed with swords, moving as if on air; and the others had no refuge whither to flee, and they were pursued for seven versts on the ice, up to the Subolich shore. Five hundred Germans were killed there, and an endless number of Chud'. Fifty important Germans were captured—powerful commanders—and they were brought to Novgorod. Some others drowned in the water, and some, gravely wounded, escaped. This battle occurred on the fifth of April, to the glory of the Holy Theotokos, when the Holy Martyr Claudianus is remembered. And so God glorified Grand Prince Aleksandr before all hosts in the same way as He glorified Joshua, the son of Nun, at Jericho. The German had said, "We will take Grand Prince Aleksandr captive," but God turned them over unto his hand; and there was never an enemy who could resist him in battle.

Grand Prince Aleksandr returned with great glory. His host took many captives and they were carried next to the horses, even those who are called "knights." Thus Grand Prince Aleksandr approached the city of Pskov, where he was met before the city by the abbots and priests in vestments and with crosses, and by a great many people chanting, "Glory to God and to Grand Prince Aleksandr Iaroslavich!" Lord, Our Helper! Thou didst help gentle David defeat the aliens, and Thou didst help our pious prince with his army of the Cross to liberate the city of Pskov from aliens, from strangers, by the hand of Grand Prince Aleksandr Iaroslavich.

And the name of Grand Prince Aleksandr Iaroslavich began to spread through all lands, from the Varangian Sea to the Pontic Sea,[21] to the Caspian Sea, to the land of the Tiveretses,[22] to Mt. Ararat, and to the other side of the Varangian Sea, and to the Arabian mountains and even up to Great Rome. And his name spread before ten thousand and ten thousand, and before thou-

21. Varangian Sea: the Baltic sea. Pontic Sea: the Black Sea.

22. In *Nik.*: "*Do moria Khupozhskogo.*" The name is unclear; perhaps it is a misspelling of "Khvalisskoe," Caspian. Tiveretses *(Tivertsy):* a Russian tribe which, according to *The Primary Chronicile,* occupied in the ninth to eleventh centuries the land between the Black (Pontic) Sea and the Danube and Dniestr rivers.

sands and thousands. And so he came to Novgorod with great **1243**
victory.

The same year on the eighteenth of the month of May, the
day of Holy Martyr Alexander, there was a sign in Pskov in
the monastery of St. John the Theologian before the icon of
the Holy Saviour, over the grave of the wife of Prince Iaroslav
Vladimirich. [The princess] had been killed by her stepson at
the town of Medvezhaia Golova [Bear's Head]. For twelve days
myrrh issued forth from the icon, filling four wax cups as into a
glass vessel. Taking counsel, the people of Pskov sent two wax
cups with myrrh as a blessing to Novgorod, to the Archbishop and
to the people of Novgorod, leaving another two in Pskov. Oh,
verily, a most marvelous Miracle! The myrrh flowed from the dry
wood as if from a spring. Glory to Thee, Our God, because Thou
givest us, Thine undeserving servants, such a blessing. We rely
upon Thee, Lord Almighty, because Thou, Who lovest mankind,
carest for us and bestowest Thy mercy upon us wretches!

CONCERNING THE VENERABLE BARLAAM, WONDERWORKER OF KHUTYN'

The same year the venerable and highly virtuous great wonderworker Barlaam, Abbot of Khutyn', whose lay name was
Aleksei Mikhailovich, passed away.[23] He lived a very holy life
and pleased God in perfection; he passed to Him with joy, into
eternal bliss; he was glorified by God, by eternal memory and
his innumerable miracles, which are related in the solemn reading on his memorial day.

The same year [6750/1242 in *Vozn.*] the Germans sent
[envoys] to Novgorod, bowing and saying, "Whatever we have
taken by lance and sword—Pskov, Luga and Latygola[24]—all this
we relinquish, and those people whom we captured we will exchange: you release ours and we will send you yours. And we
will also release all the captives from Pskov." And so they made
peace and both let all the captives go.

The same year [6750/1242 in *Sof. V.*] the Lithuanians began
to ravage the Novgorodian land. Aleksandr marched against
them and defeated their seven hosts with a single one; and he
slew many of them and captured others. Those captives he at-

23. In *Novg.* Barlaam's lay name is Viacheslav Prokshinich.

24. As originally, in *Novg.* and *Syn.* In *Nik.*, it reads, erroneously,
"Pskov, Vetluga, Latygoda."

1243 tached to the tails of the horses, abusing them, and thus they were taken [to Novgorod] with his warriors, and since that time his name has been renowned.

The same year [6750/1242 in *Novg. III.*] Grand Prince Iaroslav Vsevolodich went to Khan Batu, to the Golden Horde, and he sent his son, Konstantin, to the Great Khan. Batu honored Iaroslav and let him go, giving him seniority over all the Russian land, and he returned with great honor to his land.

In the year 6752/1244. [In 6750/1252 in *Sof. V.*] Prince Vladimir Konstantinovich of Uglich, grandson of Vsevolod, Great Grandson of Iurii Dolgorukii, gr. gr. grandson of Vladimir Monomakh, gr. gr. gr. grandson of Vsevolod, gr. gr. gr. gr. grandson of Iaroslav, gr. gr. gr. gr. gr. grandson of Great Vladimir, and his nephews, Prince Boris Vasil'kovich of Rostov and Prince Vasilii Vsevolodich, went to the Golden Horde to Khan Batu to ask for *iarlyk*.[25] He heard them, pondered, gave them their domains and let them return with honor.

The same year Feodosiia, wife of Grand Prince Iaroslav Vsevolodich, died in Novgorod and she was buried in the St. George monastery. As a nun, she was tonsured under the name, Euphrosinia, because at that time they used to give the monastic name not according to the first letter [of her lay name] but the name was bestowed according to the name of the saint on whose day the person was tonsured.

[PRINCE KONSTANTIN JOURNEYS TO BATU AND THE GREAT KHAN]

In the year 6753/1245. Prince Konstantin Iaroslavich, grandson of Vsevolod, great grandson of Iurii Dolgorukii, gr. gr. grandson of Vladimir Monomakh, came to the city of Vladimir to his father, Iaroslav Vsevolodich, with honor, from Batu's Golden Horde, as well as from visiting [Guyuk] the son of the Great Khan in Karakorum [in Mongolia].[26]

---

25. *Iarlyk:* in Mongol, a charter to rule or of privileges.

26. Batu—himself the son of Genghis Khan's senior son, Dzuchi —became virtually an independent head of the Golden Horde, which reached from Central Asia to the Carpathian mountains, and for some decades into the Balkan peninsula. His suzerains, also heirs of Genghis Khan (d. 1226), the Great Khans, or emperors, of the Mongol Empire, resided first in a tent capital, later in the city of Karakorum, on the river Orkhon, which flows into Lake Baikal; Emperor Kubilai transferred it

[PRINCE ALEKSANDR DEFEATS THE LITHUANIANS]

The same year [6754/1246 in *Novg. IV*] the Lithuanians campaigned at Torzhok and in the Bezhetskii district. Prince Iaroslav Vladimirich, together with the people of Novyi Torzhok, pursued them, and there was a battle which the Lithuanians won. They slew many people, captured horses and returned to their land. The voevoda of Tver', however, pursued them, together with Iavid and Erbet,[27] with the people of Tver' and Dmitrov, as well as with Prince Iaroslav Vladimirich, who was with the men of Novyi Torzhok. A great battle ensued at Toropets and they fought all day. The Lithuanians won and the [Russian] princes fled to Toropets; but that same night Prince Aleksandr Iaroslavich with the Novgorodians came to their aid, and there was very great joy: they embraced and kissed each other. On the morrow they mustered their troops and clashed with the Lithuanians. There was a great battle and an evil massacre, and they defeated the Lithuanians. They took from them all the captives, and from thence the Novgorodians returned home; but Prince Aleksandr with his personal guard nonetheless pursued them [the Lithuanians], and defeated them at Zhizhich, from whence only a few escaped. Then he took his son from the city of Vitebsk and marched to Novgorod, on his way encountering another host whom he did not fear to oppose: there ensued a great battle, and thanks to divine aid and the help of the Most Pure Theotokos, he defeated the enemy and came home with joy.

The same year [6754/1246 in *Vozn.*] Grand Prince Iaroslav

in 1260-1270 to Peking, permitting him to control his Chinese dominions more easily. The capital of the Golden Horde was Sarai, on the lower Volga. From 1242 to 1246 there was an interregnum in the Mongol empire. Actual power was in the hands of Ugedei's dowager, Khatun (Royal Dame) Turakina, who endeavored to secure the throne for her son, Guyuk, who probably became a Nestorian Christian and, after his election by the Kurultai, reigned from 1246 to 1276. Karakorum, capital of Genghis Khan's empire, was founded by Genghis Khan in 1220 but was abandoned as a city in the sixteenth and seventeenth centries. *Kurultai* was a council of Mongol ruling lords and Genghis Khan's descendants, usually summoned only to elect a new Great Khan or decide about important new campaigns.

27. As in *Novg.*; in *Nik.*, "Iavedei and Kerbet," apparently Tatar commanders.

1245 Vsevolodich, grandson of Iurii Dolgorukii, great grandson of Vladimir Monomakh, and his kin: his nephew, Prince Vladimir Konstantinich; his other nephew, Vasil'ko of Rostov; the latter's sons, Boris and Gleb; his other nephew, Vsevolod; the latter's son, Vasilii Vsevolodich, the grandson of Konstantin, great grandson of Vsevolod, gr. gr. grandson of Iurii Dolgorukii, gr. gr. gr. grandson of Vladimir Monomakh, [all] went to the Golden Horde to Khan Batu.

In the year 6754/1246. Prince Sviatoslav Vsevolodich and Prince Ivan Vsevolodich, grandsons of Iurii Dolgorukii, great grandson of Vladimir Monomakh, with their nephews returned from the Tatars to their domains; but Khan Batu dispatched Grand Prince Iaroslav Vsevolodich to the sons of the Great Khan [to Mongolia].

CONCERNING THE HOLY MARTYRS,
GRAND PRINCE MIKHAIL VSEVOLODICH OF CHERNIGOV
AND HIS BOIAR, FEDOR, WHO SUFFERED TOGETHER[28]

When Khan Batu, waging war, came for the first time through the forest and conquered the Riazan' land, and the cities of Kolomna, Moscow and Vladimir, and the entire Orthodox domain, except Novgorod, he returned thereafter to his prairie. From thence the Tatars marched to conquer the Kievan land, and they took Pereiaslavl' Russkii, Chernigov and Kiev, where at that time Prince Mikhail, son of Vsevolod Chermnyi, grandson of Sviatoslav, great grandson of Oleg, gr. gr. grandson of Sviatoslav, gr. gr. gr. grandson of Vsevolod, gr. gr. gr. gr. grandson of Iaroslav, gr. gr. gr. gr. gr. grandson of Great Valdimir, was grand prince. Batu dispatched his commander, Mongka Khan, to see the city of Kiev. He went, fulfilled Khan Batu's command and sent a certain message to Grand Prince Mikhail Vsevolodich in Kiev; but the latter not only did not accept the envoy, he also offended him. When Mongka Khan[29] cunningly dispatched other envoys with flattery, Mikhail killed his envoys and then, himself, fled to Hungary with all his family. The Tatars pursued but did not catch

28. For another, probably earlier, version of Prince Mikhail's martyrdom and a discussion of it, see Serebriansky, N., *Drevne-russkie kniazheskie zhitiia*, Moscow, 1915.

29. Mongka, son of Genghis Khan's junior son, Tului; from 1251 to 1259, the Great Khan.

him. Then Batu, himself, came to the city of Kiev with all his   **1246**
forces and not only occupied the city of Kiev but also submitted
and subjugated all the cities and the entire Orthodox land there.
Then he went to Hungary, conquering everything up to the Danube river and Moldavia, and he remained there for three years.
When Prince Mikhail Vsevolodich learned that Batu had left
for Hungary, he returned thereupon to Kiev and saw his whole
land destroyed, as well as the city of Kiev, and he wept greatly and
shed tears. Then he went to Chernigov to be grand prince there.

Batu waged war against the Hungarians, defeating them,
and returned to his prairie [on the lower Volga]. And he placed
his governors and administrators everywhere, in all the Russian
cities; and then he commanded all the Russian princes remaining
in Russia to come to him and to bow before him. Before [their
arrival] he commanded his wizards[30] to build two bonfires and to
force all the Russian princes and boiars to pass between these
fires and to bow to a bush, to their idols and to the fire. And of the
gifts which were brought to the Khan, some were cast into the
fire; and then they [the princes] were conducted to the Khan, and
many [of the princes] obeyed his command for the sake of glory
in this rapidly perishing world. Seeing the princes going to the
Horde and performing such rites, Grand Prince Mikhail Vsevolodich became greatly discomfited by this. Summoning his grandson, Prince Boris Vasil'kovich of Rostov[31] and his boiar, Fedor, he
told them, weeping many tears, "Do you see this woe and misfortune among our generation—that we, Christians and ob-
servors of Christ's Commandments, believing in Him, nonetheless
deny Him by performing the Khan's commands? Let us en-
deavor, my beloved, to be martyred for Christ, and then we will
reign with Him in the ages. Let us trample Satan under foot, as
well as the commands of his servant, the impure Khan." And
these words were sweet to his boiar, Fedor. So he began to prepare himself for the journey. Together with his boiar, Fedor, he

30. At that time most of the Mongols, including Batu, himself, were
Shamanist pagans. Their wizards, or priests, were called "Shaman"; but
there were among them, even among the descendants of Genghis
Khan, some Christians, predominantly Nestorians, as well as Buddhists
and Moslems.

31. Boris Vasil'kovich was the son of Mikhail's daughter, Maria of
Rostov.

spoke his thoughts to his spiritual shepherd, John. His spiritual father, John, strengthened him so that he would not weaken; and he—Prince Mikhail—with his boiar, Fedor, told him of their intentions. Then he, the priest John, gave them Holy Communion to be with them during their journey, as well as his blessing, and let them depart saying, "May Lord God strengthen you with the Power of the Holy and Lifegiving Ghost, and adorn you with the crown of martyrdom."

Grand Prince Mikhail Vsevolodich of Chernigov, together with his grandson Boris Vasil'kovich of Rostov, and with his boiar, Fedor, went to the Horde, to Khan Batu. And upon their arrival, Khan Batu was told of them. Then Khan Batu summoned his wizards and told them, "Deal according to your custom with the Russian Grand Prince Mikhail, and then conduct him to me." The wizards told Mikhail, "The Khan summons you; come hither." When they came to the place where bonfires had been prepared on both sides, many Russian princes with their boiars passed between the fires and bowed to the sun, to the fire and to their idols, doing thus for the sake of the glory of this world. Then the Khan's wizards told Mikhail and his boiar, Fedor, "You, too, must pass between the bonfires and bow to the sun and to the fire." But Mikhail said, "It does not befit us Christians to pass between the fires or to bow to the sun and to the fire, and the Khan should not give such orders. We worship and venerate Our Lord God, Jesus Christ, Who created all and Who is glorified in the Trinity. But we do not worship your loathesome gods, who are idols, and we do not render them any honor. You, Khan, are mortal and a perishing man. We are ready to render you honor and bow before you, because you bear power and have received from God your kingdom and the glory of this rapidly perishing world; but we will not reject Christ-God, nor will we bow before your material gods, and you will never force us to do so. All things were created by God to serve man."

When Khan Batu heard about such bravery and the determination of Grand Prince Mikhail and his boiar, Fedor, he was moved and said, "This is a great man;" and he sent him his master of the table [stolnik], by the name of Eldega, ordering him to talk with him calmly and quietly. The latter came and told him, "Prince Mikhail! I am sent hither by Khan Batu to tell you the following: listen to me and bow to the sun and to the moon, and

if you do, you will receive great honor from me and I will bestow
my favor upon you, and I will make you glorious and honorable
throughout all the Russian land; but if you do not obey me, you
will die an evil death." Mikhail answered, "The Khan says to bow
to the sun and to the moon and to the fire; but all these things are
given to serve man, and I will not obey the Khan." And Eldega,
the Khan's master of the table, said, "The sun is in the sky and no
one can touch it and the moon is in the sky and no one can touch it
or know about it; and fire destroys all, and no one can withstand
it." Then Mikhail responded, "God is everywhere. He has no
beginning and He is Unseen and there is only One, His Son, Who,
before all the ages, was begotten by His Father without any mother, then, at the end of the ages, was born [into our world] from
His Mother without His Father, but by the intention of His Father
and with the action of His Holy and Lifegiving Ghost. He created
the heavens, the land, all that is seen and the unseen: the sun, the
moon, the stars, the land, sea and rivers, and everything which is
upon the land. And He also created the first man, Adam, from
whom we all descend. And He gave him all creatures to serve
him: the sun, moon and stars; and man is commanded by God not
to worship any person or any thing either in the sky or on the low
land, but only the One God; and we worship His saints because
they are the true servants of God and they pray for us, and they
are our intercession before God. And thus it is. Your Khan has
promised me a reign and glory in this rapidly passing world; but
this whole world is impermanent and quickly passes; everything
changes rapidly in this temporal age. Even your Khan does not
know anything about himself: today he is the ruler, tomorrow he
may be a pauper. Today he is healthy, tomorrow he may be ill;
today he shines with bodily beauty, tomorrow he may stink with
pus and worms; today he is alive, tomorrow he may be dead."

The Khan's master of the table was astonished at the speech
of Mikhail and told him, "Prince, Mikhail! I have never heard
such words from any other man. You are vastly wise and you
should be merciful toward yourself." But Mikhail answered,
"Lord God created me and I believe in Him and I go to Him, and
He will let me into the Eternal Kingdom." The master of the
table, Eldega, said, "You have soon to die." And Mikhail responded, "Death for Christ is life to me." And Eldega said, "Give
instructions concerning your possessions because very soon the

1246   Khan's word will bring you death." Mikhail answered, "I gave away my possessions for the sake of Christ-God. I came naked from my mother's womb and naked shall I go again as I came." [*Eccl.* 5:15, paraph.] Then his grandson, Prince Boris Vasil'ko-vich of Rostov, came to him with many tears, weeping, and so did many other Russian princes and boiars weep and shed tears; and they urged him, "Do as the Khan wishes. You should not perish, and we do not want to perish because of you. God knows that what we do now, we are forced to do. When we return to our land, we and all the land will take your sin upon us, and throughout the land we will accept a spiritual punishment for you. Thus you would do much good for the Russian land, and for all of us."

Boiar Fedor was greatly worried at these speeches because he feared that he—Mikhail—would become too weak to confess Lord God before the khans and princes; and he told him, weeping and shedding tears, "My lord; Prince Mikhail! Do not forget the instruction of your spiritual father, John, who told you from the Gospel that the Lord says, 'Whosoever confesseth Me before people, I will confess him before My Father in Heaven. And whosoever rejecteth Me before people, him will I reject before My Father in Heaven.'" Mikhail heard these words with joy and sweetness because boiar Fedor was greatly wise; and he suggested to his lord to obtain the greatest possession.

Then his grandson, Prince Boris Vasil'kovich of Rostov, insisted uninterruptedly with tears and weeping that he follow the Khan's will; but he—Mikhail—embraced him and kissed him and said, "My child, Boris! Christians are supposed to confess God with faith and by deeds because even so faith, if it have not works, it is dead, in itself, according to the Apostle. [*James* 2:17] And in another place the Lord speaks with the mouth of the Apostles: 'These people honoreth Me with their lips but their hearts are far from Me; and in vain do they worship Me.'" [*Mark* 7:6-7] Then his grandson, Boris, told him, "On this earth you are my only mentor and comforter." Mikhail said, "What is on earth is nothing because here all passes and perishes rapidly, and here all is a dream or like smoke, while the heavenly blessings are real and eternal." Then Mikhail summoned his priest, received from him Holy and Divine Communion, and rejoiced in the spirit, saying, "My Lord God Almighty! I thank Thee because Thou permittest me, an unworthy and sinful man, to receive Divine Communion.

Help me also to receive a martyr's crown for Thy Sake, and remit **1246** me my sins. Blessed be Thou unto the ages and ages. Amen." Then he said to the Khan's master of the table, Eldega, "Go and tell Khan Batu what Mikhail says: I will not bow to your gods; I will not venerate them; and I will not follow your lawless order."

This was announced to the Khan, and with fierceness he sent [his men] to torture him badly, and then put him to death; they approached and began to torture him but he said, "I am Christian and I will not venerate any creatures, but only the Creator, and I will not follow the lawless order of the Khan." And after his many tortures, someone who had once been Christian but had then rejected the Christian faith approached him and with a knife cut off the honorable head of the holy great martyr, Mikhail, and threw it afar off from the body; but the head still spoke, "I am Christian," and everyone marvelled at this miracle.

Thereafter they cajoled and entreated boiar Fedor, and offered him his prince's principality, but he said, "Why do you offer me glory in this short-lived and vain world? It was I, myself, who advised my prince to do thus." Then he reproached them and offended their gods. They tortured him at length and cut off his head, saying, "These mad ones did not want to venerate the sun and the moon, and therefor they are unworthy even to be gazed upon!" Those accursed ones did not comprehend that the sun and moon are creatures of God given man to serve man. These holy martyrs, Grand Prince Mikhail and boiar Fedor, passed away on the twentieth day of the month of September of the year 6754/1246. Their bodies were cast to the dogs to be devoured, but for many days they remained untouched. Then there appeared above their bodies a fiery pillar. This pillar shone for many fair dawns with many candles, and there were to be heard angelic voices, chanting. The faithful who happened by there saw this with joy and, tearfully, they buried their holy bodies to the glory of Lord God, Who performs most glorious miracles on behalf of His saints. And His is the glory for the ages unto the ages. Amen.

The same year Khan Batu let Prince Boris Vasil'kovich of Rostov go to his son, Khan Sartak.[32] This Sartak honored him

32. Khan Sartak was the son of co-ruler of Khan Batu. After the latter's death *circa* 1255, he ruled for one or two years, 1255-1256.

1246 and allowed him to depart with honor to Russia, to his own domain.

The same year [6755/1247, *Novg. IV*; 6756/1248, *Laur.*] Grand Prince Iaroslav Vsevolodich was in the Great Horde [in Mongolia] with the sons of the Great Khan. There he was calumniated by Fedor Iarunovich to Khan Batu, and he endured many difficulties with the Tatars for the sake of the Russian land. They released him quite awearied. He journeyed a short while from the sons of the Great Khan, and on the thirtieth day of the month of September he died a hard death among aliens.[33] Of those it is said in the Scriptures, "Nothing is more deserving before God than that a man lay down his life for another." [*John* 15:13 paraph.] This Grand Prince sacrificed his life for others and for the Russian land, and God granted him the heritage of the just. He was merciful to everyone and would always give unhesitatingly whatever was asked.

In the year 6755/1247. Prince Aleksandr [6754/1246 in *Sof. V*] received in Novgorod tidings of the death of his father, Grand Prince Iaroslav Vsevolodich, and he journeyed from Novgorod to Vladimir. Together with his uncle, Sviatoslav Vsevolodich, grandson of Iurii Dolgorukii, and with his brothers, he lamented his father.

The same year [6755/1247 in *Laur.*] after the death of his brother, Iaroslav Vsevolodich, Prince Sviatoslav Vsevolodich ascended to the throne of the Grand Principality of Vladimir, and he assigned his nephews, Prince Aleksandr Iaroslavich, Prince Andrei, Konstantin, Afanasii, Daniil, Mikhail, Iaroslav and Vasilii to the cities as had been willed by his brother, Grand Prince Iaroslav Vsevolodich; and he did not alter the latter's will.

The same year Prince Andrei Iaroslavich, son of Vsevolod, grandson of Iurii Dolgorukii, great grandson of Vladimir Monomakh, went to the Horde to Khan Bastu, and he was received with honor by him.

33. According to the Catholic missionary, monk John Piano Carpini, who was at that time in Karakorum, Grand Prince Iaroslav was poisoned by Khatun Turakina, Guyuk's mother. Karamzin doubts Carpini's veracity but Vernadsky finds it plausible because, in his opinion, Carpini's information, gathered among the Russians residing in Karakorum, is usually accurate. Vernadsky, III, 143; see also *SIE*, vol. 16, p. 983; and Nasonov, A.N.: *Mongoly i Rus'*, M., 1940.

ALEKSANDR'S JOURNEY TO THE HORDE AND TO KHAN BATU, WHO WAS ASTONISHED BY HIM AND WHO RENDERED HIM GREAT HONOR.

The same year Khan Batu of evil fame heard of the honorable bravery and invincible courage of God-protected Grand Prince Aleksandr, and about his many and most glorious victories over his enemies; and he sent him his envoys, who said, "Prince Aleksandr! The most glorious prince of the Russian dominions! I know how reasonable you are because God has submitted many nations to me, and they all obey my authority. You are the only one who has not submitted to my power. Now, harken! If you intend to keep your land undamaged, then hurry to me at once and you will view the honor and glory of my realm, and you will win benefices for yourself and for your land." Grand Prince Aleksandr, wise in God, pondered concerning his holy father, Iaroslav, who had journeyed to the Horde without caring for this passing realm, and who had sacrificed his life there for the sake of his faith and for the sake of his people [*John* 15:13 paraph.], thereby winning for himself the Heavenly Kingdom; therefore, he, blessed Aleksandr, following the example of his pious father's deeds, also decided to go to the Horde for the purpose of protecting the Christians. He arrived at the glorious city of Vladimir with vast forces and his arrival was awesome. Word of his awesome arrival spread down to the mouth of the Volga, and the women of the Moabites[34] frightened their children with his name, saying, "Hush! Grand Prince Aleksandr is coming!" In Vladimir he remained but a short time, receiving the blessing of Bishop Cyril, and without delay he continued his journey. Coming to Khan Batu, God's blessing shown upon him everywhere. When Khan Batu saw him he marveled and told his magnates, "It is true, what you have told me—that there is none equal to this prince," and he greatly honored him and gave him gifts. Thus does God astound those whom He selects, and He puts it into the mind of the impure that they should be ashamed of themselves and that they should respect those people. Then, together with his brother, Andrei Iaroslavich, he sent him to the sons of the Great Khan.[35]

34. "Moabites": in this case this biblical name is applied to the Tatars.
35. "Great Khan": that is, to their capital, Karakorum.

1247   The same year Khan Batu of ill renown, with a multitude of warriors, waged war against western Hungary and the northern land, which he had not reached before, and he destroyed many cities, occupying them; no one could resist him. He imprisoned many princes and commanders, whom he dispatched to his son, Sartak. Remaining there the entire year, he waged war, captured and rendered unto the sword and fire all those who did not want to submit to him.

The same year Berdy Bek, an important nobleman of Batu's, was killed in Hungary.

In the year 6756/1248. There was a portent on the moon. It became as though covered with blood, and then disappeared.

[BATU'S WAR AGAINST VARAZHDIN]

The same year Khan Batu waged war up to the city of Varazhdin, in Hungary,[36] destroying many cities and capturing all, and none could resist him. Then he came to Varazhdin, which is located in the middle of the Hungarian land. There were very few of the usual trees. All the trees were grapevines, and there was an abundance of all fruit and all manner of wines. This fortress was surrounded from all sides by water, and was extremely well fortified, and no one feared to remain within it. In the middle of the fortress was a very high tower.[37] At that time the ruler of the Hungarian land and of the Czechs and Germans, and of Pomerania, and of the land up to the Great Sea[38] was Vladislav.[39] Once there was Orthodoxy in the land of Hungary because they

36. Varazhdin: probably now Petrovarazhdin, near Novi Sad, in northern Serbia.

37. In *Nik.*, *stolp; stolp,* or, in Greek, *style,* is a kind of pillar or column with a platform on top, on which the ascetic stylites would live for years, remaining thus in the open air, praying and sometimes preaching. The word, *stolp,* however, may likewise denote a tower, particularly in this text, because this Vladislav was a ruler and not an ascetic stylite.

38. "Great Sea" may denote the Baltic or the North Sea.

39. At the time of Batu's invasion, the Hungarian king was Bela IV (1235-1270). The only Vladislav who was simultaneously king of Bohemia and of Hungary was Vladislav II Jagellonian (1476-1516) of Bohemia, from 1471; he was also king of Hungary from 1490. However, during the invasion by Batu of the southern Danubian (Pannonian) plain, there was in Serbia King Stephan Vladislav (1234-1243), who was the

received Holy Baptism from the Greeks.[40] Since the Hungarians **1248** did not translate the Scriptures into their language, the Romans [Catholics] succeeded in winning them to their heresy. And from that time up to the present they have been in unity with Rome.

This aforementioned King Vladislav also obeyed the Roman church, until St. Sava, Archbishop of Serbia, came to him and convinced him to join the Greek religion, the true Christian faith; but he did so secretly, not openly, because he feared that the Hungarians would revolt on account of that. St. Sava remained there for five months, instructing him concerning the Orthodox Greek faith; and then he returned home, leaving only one priest with Vladislav. And he remained there as if he were one of the king's servants.

Khan Batu, arriving in the Hungarian land, destroyed all its cities and captured the people because King Vlaslav, whom St. Sava had named "Vladislav," did not manage to gather all his people because of the vast distances.

In the meantime, King Vladislav remained many days on the above-mentioned tower, very much aggrieved, taking no bread or water and imploring Christ-God, with tears, to change His wrath to mercy and deliver him from his enemies. From the tower on which he stayed, he glimpsed his sister, fleeing to him from the fortress; but the Tatars caught and imprisoned her and took her to Batu.

Seeing all this, King Vladislav wailed still more and shed tears, praying to Christ God that He with His help and mercy deliver him from his enemies. While he was praying the tears flowed from his eyes as river streams, falling upon the marble, which they penetrated. To this day can be seen the traces of these tears on the marble of that tower. From this the lords and all those who were with him realized that help and mercy were forthcoming

brother of St. Sava. and during whose reign the Mongol invasion of Hungary occurred (the Mongols defeating the Hungarians at Mati on April 11, 1241). This entire apocryphal story of King Vladislav is of Balkan origin. The Mongols crossed Bosnia, northern Serbia and Croatia in the winter of 1240-1241, going as far south as Cattaro. K. Jireček, *Istorija Srba*, I, 226, Beograd, 1922.

40. The Pannonian Slavs were Christianized in the mid-ninth century by Cyril and Methodius shortly before the Hungarians occupied the Pannonian plain.

1248   from God. Soon thereafter a person approached, very fair and awesome, and all those with the king were seized by fear and trembling. This person approached the king and said, "Because of your tears, Lord God gives you victory over Khan Batu. March at once against him." The people gazed upon the face of the speaker but could see him no more.

And so the king descended from the tower and saw a saddled horse standing quietly by, not held by anyone, with a battle axe on it. From this he perceived that there would be aid from God. King Vladislav at once mounted this horse, took up the battle axe in his hand, sallied from the fortress with his host, all those who were with him, and unexpectedly and stealthily charged the camp of Khan Batu. At that time Batu had but a small troop because all his Tatars were dispersed in raids, and those Tatars who were with him were the same hour defeated by the wrath of God and were as dead, and they fled in great shame. Seeing his misfortune, Khan Batu knew not what to do, and he also fled, pursued by the wrath of God; and with him was the king's sister. Accompanied by his warriors, King Vladislav chased him, killing many Tatars; he reached Khan Batu, with whom he fought, but the king's sister began to aid Batu. Vladislav approached, cried out loudly, wept tearfully and prayed for Lord God's help; and with God's help he killed Khan Batu, as well as his sister with him.[41] With his lords and all his warriors, he occupied Batu's camp and the Tatars, unaware of what had occurred, were taken prisoner upon their return to this camp by the Hungarians, who put them to death and took vast wealth from them. Those, however, who wanted to embrace the Christian faith were left alive. And so Lord God with His invisible power put to death the impure Khan and his endless

---

41. Batu was not killed in Hungary, but died in 1255 in his capital, Sarai, on the Volga. Batu retreated from Central Europe and did not proceed with the conquest of the West because two of his main commanders, both also grandsons of Genghis Khan and both future Great Khans, or Emperors, of the Mongols, gave up campaigning and returned to Mongolia. They were Guyuk (Emperor, 1246-1248) and Mongka (Emperor, 1251-1255). Batu also followed them in order to influence the election of the Great Khan, or Emperor, in view of the death of Emperor Ugedei (1229-1241), the third son and successor to Genghis Khan. At that time the Mongol Emperor (Great Khan) was elected by the Kurultai, or the *diet* of Mongol lords, and Genghis Khan's descendants.

power, and so the Scripture was fulfilled which says, "Vengeance **1248** is Mine, says the Lord." [*Rom.* 12:19 paraph.] A bronze statue of King Vladislav on his horse, holding his battle axe with which, thanks to the invincible power of God, he killed Khan Batu and also his sister, was cast and placed on a tower in the middle of the fortress so that everyone, unto the last generation, might view it and remember this event; and it remains there to the present day.
[This is the end of the story about Batu.]

The same year Prince Boris Vasil'kovich of Rostov, grandson of Konstantin, great grandson of Vsevolod, gr. gr. grandson of Iurii Dolgorukii, gr. gr. gr. grandson of Vladimir Monomakh, married the daughter of Prince Iaroslav of Murom.

The same year Prince Mikhail, also called "Khorobrit," son of Iaroslav, grandson of Vsevolod, great grandson of Iurii Dolgorukii, gr. gr. grandson of Vladimir Monomakh, cast out from the Grand Principality of Vladimir his uncle, Grand Prince Sviatoslav Vsevolodich, grandson of Iurii Dolgorukii, great grandson of Vladimir Monomakh; and he, himself, ascended to the Grand Principality of Vladimir.

The same year [6757/1249 in *Novg. IV.*] Grand Prince Mikhailo Iaroslavich Khorobrit of Vladimir did battle against Lithuania, and the Lithuanians killed him, Grand Prince Mikhail Iaroslavich of Vladimir, grandson of Vsevolod, great grandson of Iurii Dolgorukii, gr. gr. grandson of Vladimir Monomakh. Blessed Cyril, Bishop of Rostov, sent for his body and buried it in the church of the Most Pure Theotokos in Vladimir. His brothers, the princes of Suzdal', marched against the Lithuanians and defeated them at Zubchev.

In the year 6757/1249. Prince Gleb Vasil'kovich, grandson of Konstantin, great grandson of Vsevolod, gr. gr. grandson of Iurii Dolgorukii, traveled to the Horde to Sartak, the son of Khan Batu.[42] Khan Sartak honored him greatly and let him return to his domain. The same year Prince Aleksandr Iaroslavich [Nevskii] and his brother, Prince Andrei, returned [from Mongolia] from the sons of the Great Khan. The latter assigned to

42. Sartak became co-ruler with Batu during the last years of Batu's life.

1249 Aleksandr Kiev and all the Russian land,[43] while his brother, Prince Andrei, was given the Grand Principality of Vladimir.[44]

The same year, on the twenty-seventh day of the month of December, Prince Vladimir Konstantinovich, grandson of Vsevolod, great grandson of Iurii Dolgorukii, gr. gr. grandson of Vladimir Monomakh, gr. gr. gr. grandson of Vsevolod, gr. gr. gr. gr. grandson of Iaroslav, gr. gr. gr. gr. gr. grandson of Great Vladimir, passed away in Vladimir. His body was taken to his patrimony of Uglich Pol'e, where it was buried in the church of St. Saviour. His sons were Andrei and Roman.

The same year Prince Vasilii Vsevolodich passed away. He was the grandson of Konstantin, great grandson of Vsevolod, gr. gr. grandson of Iurii Dolgorukii, gr. gr. gr. grandson of Vladimir Monomakh, gr. gr. gr. gr. grandson of Vsevolod, gr. gr. gr. gr. grandson of Iaroslv, gr. gr. gr. gr. gr. grandson of Great Vladimir; and his body was taken from Vladimir to his patrimony of Iaroslavl', where it was buried in the church of the Most Pure Theotokos on the eighth day of the month of February. His sons [*Sic!*] were Vasilii.

In the year 6758/1250. Prince Boris Vasil'kovich of Rostov traveled to the Golden Horde, to Khan Sartak, son of Batu. Khan Sartak greatly honored him and allowed him to return to his patrimony.

[METROPOLITAN CYRIL MOVES TO SUZDALIA]

The same year His Holiness Cyril, Metropolitan of Kiev and all Russia, traveled from Kiev to Chernigov. He came to Riazan', then went to the Suzdalian land, where he was met with great honor by the princes and boiars.[45]

---

43. That is, most probably, the region of Kiev, Pereiaslavl' and Chernigov only.

44. The chronicler speaks of the "sons" of the Great Khan because in 1248-1257 there was an interregnum in Karakorum, during which the grandchildren of Genghis Khan struggled for the imperial succession.

45. The arrival of Cyril, Metropolitan of Kiev and all Russia, in Vladimir was of paramount political and ecclesiastic importance. Later Cyril settled in Vladimir, *de facto* thus transferring the See of the Metropolitan of all Russia from Kiev to the Suzdalian land, while his successors

The same year Grand Prince Sviatoslav, son of Vsevolod, **1250** grandson of Iurii Dolgorukii, great grandson of Valdimir Monomakh, together with his son, Dmitrii, travelled to Khan Sartak, Batu's son, in the Golden Horde; he and his son were received with honor by the Khan.

The same year Prince Andrei Iaroslavich, grandson of Vsevolod, great grandson of Iurii Dolgorukii, gr. gr. grandson of Vladimir Monomakh, married in Vladimir the daughter of Danilo Romanovich; the wedding was performed in the church of the Holy Theotokos of the city of Vladimir by His Holiness, Metropolitan Cyril of Kiev and all Russia, and by Cyril, Bishop of Rostov. There was great solemnity, much happiness and great rejoicing.

In the year 6759/1251. [6758/1250 in *Novg. III.*] His Holiness Cyril, Metropoitan of Kiev and all Russia, together with Cyril, Bishop of Rostov, travelled from Vladimir to Novgorod, where he was met with Great honor by Grand Prince Aleksandr Iaroslavich and the latter's leading men. He was greeted by a procession with crosses, by the entire Sacred Council, archimandrites and abbots and a multitude of people, and the Novgorodians beseeched him to consecrate them Dalmatus as their bishop.

The same year Grand Prince Aleksandr Iaroslavich [Nevskii] became gravely ill, but Lord God and His Most Pure Mother were merciful to him, thanks to the prayers of His saintly intercessors, His Holiness Cyril, Metropolitan of Kiev and all Russia, Archbishop Dalmatus of Novgorod and Bishop Cyril of Rostov and the entire Sacred Council, as well as by his late parents and forefathers.

The same year there was much rain and many floods which inundated everything—grain and hay. The great bridge of Novgorod was washed away into the Volkhov River, and in the fall the freezes killed all the grain.

The same year Prince Gleb Vasil'kovich, grandson of Konstantin, great grandson of Vsevolod, gr. gr. grandson of Iurii Dolgorukii, went to his partrimony of Belozero, and this year was peaceful.

---

moved from Vladimir to Moscow, thereby making it the ecclesiastic center of the land. After the Mongol invasion, Kiev and its region became almost entirely devastated and depopulated.

In the year 6760/1252. The same year Grand Prince Aleksandr [Nevskii] again went to the Golden Horde to the new khan, Sartak, leaving the glorious city of Valdimir and all the Suzdalian land in the care of his brother, Prince Andrei [Iaroslavich] of Suzdal'. The latter was endowed with honor and bravery but he paid little heed to the administration of his dominion: he excelled in the hunt of beasts and attended the counsel of young minds. Therefore because of them there was much disturbance and perfidy among the people, and difficulties in his domain. And this happened because God permitted it.

The same year Khan Sartak sent his commander, Nevrui, as well as Khan Katiak and Khan Ali-beg the Brave with other Tatars, to wage war against this Prince Andrei Iaroslavich of Suzdal', the son of Vsevolod, grandson of Iurii Dolgorukii. On the eve of St. Boris' Day the godless Tatars forded the Kliazma near Vladimir and stealthily marched toward the city of Pereiaslavl' [Zalesskii]. In the morning of St. Boris' Day Grand Prince Andrei Iaroslavich of Suzdal' [hearing of their raid] became worried about his situation and said, "Lord! How long are we going to fight among ourselves and bring the Tatars against each other? I would rather flee to foreign lands than be in the friendship and service of the Tatars." He summoned his warriors and then, with his regiments, Grand Prince Andrei met them [the Tatars]. The two hosts clashed and a great battle ensued. By the wrath of God for our ever-increasing sins we were defeated by the pagans and Grand Prince Andrei escaped only with difficulty. He went to Great Novgorod but the Novgorodians did not want to receive him; then he went to Pskov, where he remained awhile, awaiting his princess. When his princess arrived, he departed with her for the German city of Kolyvan'.[46] He left his princess there while he, himself, journeyed beyond the sea to the Swedish land. The master of Sweden received him with honor and then he sent to Kolyvan' for his princess, with whom he then sojourned for a certain time in the Swedish land. [Before he left Russia] the Tatars pursued him and nearly caught him at the city of Pereiaslavl' [Zalesskii], which is on Lake Kleshchino. But God and the Most Pure Theotokos protected him. The Tatars

46. Kolyvan', now Revel or Talinn.

searched for him, scattering hither and thither, but he escaped **1252** from them after having been grand prince for three years. The Khan's son, Nevrui, with his Tatars, took Pereiaslavl' [Zalesskii] on Lake Kleshchino, capturing Prince Iaroslav's widow and children, and killed her, but they took Iaroslav's children into captivity. They also killed their [the Russians'] voevoda, Zhidislav, and took all their people into captivity, stealing all their possessions, and then they returned to the Golden Horde.

The same year [6761/1253 in *Novg. IV*] Grand Prince Aleksandr Iaroslavich [Nevskii], grandson of Vsevolod, great grandson of Iurii Dolgorukii, came from the Horde with much honor. His Holiness Cyril, Metropolitan of Kiev and all Russia, met him with a procession and crosses, with the Sacred Council and with a multitude of people. Because he had received the Khan's charter to rule, His Holiness, Metropolitan Cyril, took him to the throne of the grand prince of Vladimir, the throne of his father, Iaroslav Vsevolodich, and they built there a church in memory of [the victims of] the invasion of Nevrui.

The same year [6759/1251 in *Sof. V*] the Tatars released from the Golden Horde Prince Oleg Ingvarich of Riazan', grandson of Igor', great grandson of Gleb, and permitted him to go to his patrimony.

The same year on the third day of the month of February Grand Prince Sviatoslav Vsevolodich passed away. He was the grandson of Iurii Dolgorukii, great grandson of Vladimir Monomakh, gr. gr. grandson of Vsevolod, gr. gr. gr. grandson of Iaroslav, gr. gr. gr. gr. grandson of Great Vladimir.

In the year 6761/1253. The church of the Holy Martyrs Boris and Gleb was consecrated in Rostov by Cyril, Bishop of Rostov, in the presence of the pious princes, Boris of Rostov and Gleb of Belozero, both sons of Vasil'ko, grandchildren of Vsevolod, gr. gr. grandchildren of Iurii Dolgorukii.

The same year a son, Dmitrii, was born to Prince Boris Vasil'kovich of Rostov.

The same year the Novgorodians under Prince Vasilii Aleksandrovich [the son of Nevskii], grandson of Iaroslav, defeated the Lithuanians at Toropets. At the same time the people of Pskov defeated the Germans at Pskov.

In the year 6762/1254. [6761/1253 in *Vozn.*] Grand Prince Iaroslav Iaroslavich of Tver' gave up his domain of Tver' and

1254 went to Pskov. The people of Pskov received him with great honor.

The same year [6763/1255 in *Laur.*] a son, Konstantin, was born to Prince Boris Vasil'kovich of Rostov.

In the year 6763/1255. [6762/1254 in *Vozn.*] After the Sunday of Easter week, Prince Konstantin of Uglich passed away and his body was taken to Vladimir. He was the son of Iaroslav, grandson of Vsevolod, great grandson of Iurii Dolgorukii, gr. gr. grandson of Vladimir Monomakh, gr. gr. gr. grandson of Vsevolod, gr. gr. gr. gr. grandson of Iaroslav, gr. gr. gr. gr. gr. grandson of Great Vladimir. His body was met by his brother, Prince Aleksandr Iaroslavich [Nevskii], as well as by their spiritual father, Metropolitan Cyril, the entire Sacred Council and all his boiars with a multitude of people; and it was buried in the church of the Most Pure Theotokos in Vladimir.

The same year the Novgorodians invited Grand Prince Iaroslav Iaroslavich of Tver' to come from Pskov to Novgorod, and so he became prince of Novgorod and they expelled from Novgorod Prince Vasilii Aleksandrovich, grandson of Iaroslav, great grandson of Vsevolod, gr. gr. grandson of Iurii Dolgorukii; he rapidly dispatched tidings to his father, Aleksandr Iaroslavich [Nevskii] of Vladimir, and went to Torzhok to await his father there. Grand Prince Aleksandr Iaroslavich, together with his cousin, Dmitrii Sviatoslavich, grandson of Vsevolod—these princes Aleksandr and Dmitrii were sons of two brothers— marched with many warriors toward Torzhok, where he was met by his son, Vasilii. From thence he marched to Novgorod, where he was met by Reteshka the Novgorodian with greetings: "Prince Iaroslav Iaroslavich has fled from Novgorod." Then, according to their old tradition, the Novgorodians summoned the *veche*: "Brethren! Let us be firm for the Most Pure Theotokos, for Novgorodian justice and for our patrimony, and whether in death or in life, we will not spare ourselves." Then the Novgorodians sent their archbishop, Dalmatus, with their senior men to Grand Prince Aleksandr Iaroslavich, asking him to give up his wrath. He told them, "Turn over to me my enemy, posadnik Ananii. If you do not extradite him to me, I will do battle against you." And the Novgorodians deliberated at length concerning this. Then Grand Prince Aleksandr Iaroslavich sent to them, saying, "If you do not want to extradite my enemy, posadnik Ananii, then take away from him the office of posadnik and I will give up my **1255** wrath." The Novgorodians assembled and said, "This was the machination of Prince [Iaroslav] and of our own trespassers of the oath. God and Holy Sophia should judge them because they instigated us to quarrel with the prince [Aleksandr]." They deprived Ananii of the office of posadnik, which they gave to Mikhail Stepankovich; and then they concluded peace with Grand Prince Aleksandr Iaroslavich, according to all their Novgorodian liberties, confirming it with him by a pledge on the Cross. Then Prince Aleksandr Iaroslavich marched into Novgorod, where he was met by Archbishop Dalmatus and [a procession] with crosses of the entire Sacred Council; and so Grand Prince Aleksandr Iaroslavich brought his son, Vasilii, to be prince in Novgorod, [6764/1256 in *Vozn.* and *Novg. III.*] while he, himself, marched away from them, from Novgorod, with great honor; and there was peace and great tranquility.

In the year 6764/1256. The princes went to Gorodets and to Novgorod; but Prince Boris Vasil'kovich of Rostov went to the Horde with many gifts. Prince Aleksandr Iaroslavich [Nevskii] also sent the Tatars his envoys with many gifts. Prince Boris Vasil'kovich of Rostov went to Khan Ulagchi [of the Golden Horde], presented him gifts and was greatly honored; and he returned to his patrimony with great honor.

The same year Grand Prince Aleksandr Iaroslavich marched with the levies of Suzdal' against the Em',[47] defeated them and returned home with many captives.

The same year Prince Aleksandr Iaroslavich marched with the levies of Suzdal' to Novgorod and from thence, together with the Novgorodians, he marched against the Swedish land and against the Chud'. They went through impassable places where they could not distinguish day from night and where there was permanent darkness. Thus they marched, campaigning throughout all the Pomor'e.[48] And they returned home with many captives and with vast booty.

In the year 6765/1257. Grand Prince Aleksandr Iaroslavich Nevskii] of Vladimir, Grand Prince Boris Vasil'kovich of Rostov and Grand Prince Andrei Iaroslavich of Suzdal' went with many

47. Em': a Finnic tribe north of Novgorod.
48. Pomor'e: the shore of the Finnish Gulf.

1257 presents to the Golden Horde, where [Khan] Ulagchi honored them; and they returned with great honor to their patrimony.

The same year Prince Gleb Vasil'kovich married [a Tatar princess] in the Horde and he returned to his patrimony from the Khan, from the land of the Khan [the Golden Horde] with great honor.

The same winter [6765/1257 in *Laur.*] the census takers came from the Golden Horde and took a census in the lands of Suzdal', Riazan' and Murom; and they assigned there their own officers of tens, hundreds, thousands and ten thousands. Completing their work, they returned to the Golden Horde. They did not include in their census only the archimandrites, abbots, priests, deacons, members of the clergy and others working for the church: that is, all those who attend Lord God and the Most Pure Theotokos, and who are connected with the Lord's House and who serve in the divine churches.

In the year 6766/1258. [6764/1256 in *Sof V.*] Grand Prince Oleg of Riazan' passed away during Holy Week, on Wednesday, after being tonsured a monk and shorn to the *schema*. He was buried in the church of the Holy Saviour on the eighth day of the month of March, on the day of the Holy Martyr Phetinia of Samaria. After him, his son, Roman, became Grand Prince of Riazan'.

The same year Grand Prince Aleksandr Iaroslavich [Nevskii] of Vladimir, Grand Prince Andrei Iaroslavich of Suzdal', Prince Boris Vasil'kovich of Rostov and Grand Prince Iaroslav Iaroslavich of Tver' went to the [Golden] Horde and honored Khan Ulagchi and all the lords and commanders of the Golden Horde; and they departed for Russia with great honor, each returning to his own patrimony the same fall.

That winter Prince Boris Vasil'kovich of Rostov and his brother, Prince Gleb Vasil'kovich, with his princess [who was a Tatar] returned from the Horde to Rostov, bowed to the Most Holy Theotokos and crossed themselves before Her Icons, and they received a blessing from their spiritual father, Bishop Cyril, as well as from their mother, Grand Princess Maria.

*[THE TATAR CENSUS]

The same year [6765/1257 in *Vozn.*] the census takers came from the Tatar land to Vladimir and then these census takers of

the Golden Horde, together with Grand Prince Aleksandr Iaroslavich of Vladimir, with Andrei Iaroslavich of Suzdal' and with
Prince Boris Vasil'kovich of Rostov went to take a census of the
Novgorodian land. When the people of Novgorod heard about
this they became very upset. When the Tatar census taker came
with Grand Prince Aleksandr Iaroslavich to Novgorod, as well as
with the other Russian princes, Prince Vasilii Aleksandrovich of
Novgorod fled from his father, from Novogorod, to Pskov. The
Tatars began to levy tribute, and the Novgorodians did not accept this. They gave many gifts, however, to the Khan and to his
envoys, and let them go in peace; but they killed their posadnik,
Mikhalko, as well as the other posadnik Mikhalko, whom they also
killed, while posadnik Ananii passed away. Then the office of
posadnik was given to Mikhalko Fedorovich, and the office of
tysiatskii to Zhidiata Domozhirovich.[49] Prince Aleksandr Iaroslavich drove his son, Vasilii, from Pskov and sent him to Niz.[50]
And he executed the latter's druzhina: some had their noses and
ears cut off, some had their eyes taken out and hands cut off.
They were those who advised Prince Vasilii to do thus [to resist
the Tatars] as he did. In this way the evil people perished in an
evil manner, and the Tatar census takers went with peace, being
satisfied.

The same year the Lithuanians waged war against Torzhok
and the Novgordians gathered their troops and marched against
them. A great battle ensued, which the Lithuanians won, and
much evil befell the people of Novyi Torzhok.

The same year the Tatars raided the entire Lithuanian land
and then, with many captives and wealth, they went back to their
encampments.

In the year 6767/1259. Mikhalko, the man of Pinsk, came to
Novgorod, declaring the following: "If you are not taken in the
census of the Khan of the Golden Horde, then the Tatar host will
march in to Nizovskaia land and much grief will come to all." The
Novgorodians took fright and agreed to be counted. They sent
their envoys to the Golden Horde, to the Khan, with many gifts,

49. "Zhirokha" in *Novg.*

50. *Niz,* or *Nizovskaia zemlia;* "the lowland": the land south of the
Novgorodian region—primarily the Volga-Oka region.

1259 petitioning him to turn aside his wrath and asking him to take a census of all their land, as he wanted.

The same year [6766/1258 in *Laur.*] the Tatar census takers came to Vladimir from the Horde. Taking with them Grand Prince Aleksandr Iaroslavich of Vladimir, Prince Andrei Iaroslavich of Suzdal' and Prince Boris Vasil'kovich of Rostov, they went to Novgorod and took a census of the land of Novgorod and Pskov, but did not take a census of the archimandrites, abbots, priests, deacons, monks, or all members of the clergy, and attendants of the churches, all those who pray to Lord God and to the Most Pure Theotokos and who reside in the Lord's House, and who celebrate in the divine churches. The Tatars took their census and returned to the Golden Horde, and there was great peace and tranquility in Novgorod. The Novgorodians, however, asked Prince Aleksandr Iaroslavich to remain there, and they honored him. He set his son, Dmitrii, as prince of Novgorod, while he, himself, went to the city of Vladimir. Arriving in Rostov, he bowed to the ground before the Icon of the Most Pure Theotokos, crossed himself before Her Icon and received a blessing from his spiritual father, Bishop Cyril, saying, "My father, Lord! Thanks to your prayer, I arrived in Novgorod in good health; and now I have returned hither from Novgorod, likewise in good health." Blessed Bishop Cyril, the Grand Princess, Prince Boris and Prince Gleb honored him with great love. He sojourned with them for a certain time in great concord, worshipped Lord God and the Most Pure Theotokos, made devotions before Her holy Icon and received a blessing from his spiritual father, Bishop Cyril, and from the Grand Princess; and from thence he went to Vladimir, to his patrimony.

In the year 6768/1260. There was peace.

In the year 6769/1261. A son, Daniil, was born to Grand Prince Aleksandr Iaroslavich [Nevskii].

The same year Bishop Cyril of Rostov, because of his advanced age and great exhaustion, gave up his bishopric and Ignatius, archimandrite of the monastery of the Epiphany, was invested in his place with the approval and blessing of Cyril, Metropolitan of Kiev and all Russia.

The same year Prince Andrei [of Uglich], son of Vladimir,[51]   **1261**
grandson of Konstantin, great grandson of Vsevolod, gr. gr.
grandson of Iurii Dolgorukii, gr. gr. gr. grandson of Vladimir
Monomakh, gr. gr. gr. gr. grandson of Vsevolod, gr. gr. gr. gr.
gr. grandson of Iaroslav Vladimirich, died in his patrimony of
Uglich-Pol'e, and he was buried in the chuch of St. Saviour in
Uglich.

The same year His Holiness Cyril, Methopolitan of Kiev and
all Russia, elevated Mitrophanes to bishop of Sarai.[52]

In the year 6770/1262. On the twenty-first day of the month of
May Blessed Bishop Cyril of Rostov passed away and was buried
in the church of the Most Pure Theotokos in Rostov.

The same year on the nineteenth day of the month of September, Metropolitan Cyril of Kiev and all Russia, in the presence
of pious Prince Boris Vasil'kovich of Rostov and his brother, Gleb
Vasil'kovich of Belozero, consecrated Ignatius bishop of Rostov.

The same year all the cities in Russia held counsel about the
Tatars because Khan Batu placed his administrators in all the
Russian cities, as did his son, Sartak, after killing [*Sic!*] Batu; and
after Sartak, so did the other [khans]. The Russian princes, having agreed among themselves, drove the Tatars from their cities
because there was always violence from them. The rich ones would
farm out from the Tatars the collection of taxes, and then would
greedily increase their own benefit; therefore many people were
forced to accept serfdom in order to pay the interest. And so the
Russian princes drove the Tatars away, and some were killed,

---

51. In *Nik.* it is stated erroneously that Prince Andrei of Uglich was
the grandson of Vasil'ko Konstantinovich, but in actuality he was the
grandson of Grand Prince Konstantin Vsevolodich of Vladimir. See
N. de Baumgarten, *Généalogies des branches régnantes des Rurikiches du
XIII au XVI siècles*, Vol. XXXVI (No. 99) of *Orientalia Christiana*, Roma,
1934, p. 60, Table XI.

52. Sarai, on the lower Volga, was the capital of the Golden Horde.
There was always a large number of Orthodox Russians there; consequently, Metropolitan Cyril established there a special diocese. The
bishop of Sarai was also a sort of liaison with the Horde for the Russian
Church and the Russian princes.

1262 others became Christian in the Name of the Father, Son and Holy Ghost. At that time in Iaroslavl' they killed Zossima the Apostate, who had given up the Christian faith, and his monastic vows, and had become a very wicked Moslem. He was the favorite agent of the Khan's envoy, Titak, and he caused much harm to the Christians; therefore the Orthodox Christians killed him and threw his body to the dogs to be eaten.

The same year [6772/1264 in *Novg. IV.*] Grand Prince Iaroslav Iaroslavich, grandson of Vsevolod; Prince Dmitrii Aleksandrovich, grandson of Iaroslav Iaroslavich; the former's son-in-law, Konstantin; Tovtivil of Polotsk; and the Novgorodian host all marched with great forces against the German city of Iuriev.[53] And although the city had three lines of fortified walls around it, they took it in one single assault, killing the Germans. Among our men, a good and brave man was shot in the city: this was Petr Miasnikovich. And they also killed Iakov, a courageous nail-maker, and Il'ia Dektiarev, and the smith, Izmail. They were very courageous and very daring men.

In the year 6771/1263. A son, Mikhail, was born to Prince Gleb Vasil'kovich of Belozero.

[THE PASSING OF GRAND PRINCE ALEKSANDR NEVSKII]

The same year [6700/1262 in *Sof. V.*] Grand Prince Aleksandr Iaroslavich [Nevskii], grandson of Vsevolod, great grandson of Iurii Dolgorukii, gr. gr. grandson of Vladimir Monomakh, gr. gr. gr. grandson of Vsevolod, gr. gr. gr.gr. grandson of Iaroslav, gr. gr. gr. gr.gr. grandson of Great Vladimir, went for the fourth time to Khan Berke of the Golden Horde;[54] and he spent the winter there. He became very ill and was permitted to return to Russia; but on the fourteenth day of the month of November before reaching the city of Gorodets [his condition worsened] and he was tonsured monk and shorn to the *schema*. He passed away that same night. On the twenty-third day of the same month of November they brought his body to Vladimir and placed it in the church of the Most Pure Theotokos. When His Holiness

53. Iur'ev, now Tartu or Dorpat.

54. Berke was a brother of Batu's. He was a stern ruler who embraced Islam and made it for the first time the religion of the Golden Horde (1258-1266).

Cyril, Metropolitan of Kiev and all Russia, wanted to put into his **1263** hand a charter absolving his sins and Monk Sebastian tried to open his hand, he—Prince Aleksandr—himself, raised his hand as if alive, and everyone marvelled at this. When His Holiness, Metropolitan Cyril of Kiev and all Russia, placed the charter in his hand he closed his hand as if he were alive. He was buried in the city of Vladimir, in the monastery of the Nativity of the Most Pure Theotokos, after having ruled [in Vladimir for ten years. His [surviving] sons were Vasilii, Dmitrii, Andreii and Daniil of Moscow.

In the year 6772/1264. After [Grand Prince Aleksandr], his brother, Grand Prince Iaroslav Iaroslavich of Tver', ascended to the Grand Principality of Vladimir and he became grand prince of Vladimir and Novgorod.

The same year [6771/1263 in *Vozn.*] the Novgorodians drove out from Novgorod Prince Dmitrii Aleksandrovich.

The same year [6771/1263 in *Vozn.*] Grand Prince Iaroslav Iaroslavich went to Novgorod and the Novgorodians accepted him with joy and great honor. At that time [6771/1263 in *Vozn.*] in Novgorod he married, taking to wife the daughter of Iurii Mikhailovich.

The same year [6771/1263 in *Vozn.*] Grand Prince Andrei Iaroslavich of Suzdal', grandson of Vsevolod, great grandson of Iurii Dolgorukii, gr. gr. grandson of Vladimir Monomakh, gr. gr. gr. grandson of Vsevolod, gr. gr. gr. gr. grandson of Iaroslav, gr. gr. gr. gr. gr. grandson of Great Vladimir, passed away. His sons were Iurii and Mikhail.

[LITHUANIAN AFFAIRS]

The same year [6771/1263 in *Hyp.*] there was a rebellion in Lithuania. They rebelled against their prince. Grand Prince Mindaugas was killed by his own relatives, who, unbeknownst to all, had conspired. Then they began to quarrel about his wealth, and they killed Tovtivil, Prince of Polotsk; they also put in irons the boiars of Polotsk, and they asked the people of Polotsk to turn over to them Tovtivil's son because they also wanted to kill him; but he fled to Novgorod with his men. Thereafter the Lithuanians assigned their own prince to Polotsk and they released the people of Polotsk whom they had [earlier] arrested, together with their prince.

1264   This Grand Prince Mindaugas [of Lithuania] had a son [6670/1262 in *Hyp.*] by the name, Voishelk, who previously had given up everything—father, mother, his right to be prince, and everything he possessed, and had gone to Mt. Sinai. There, he was baptised and learned how to read, and he was a very deserving and highly virtuous monk. He stayed there for ten years, then went back to his own land. Grand Prince Mindaugas, being pagan, attempted lovingly to persuade him to give up his life as a monk, but he did not listen and built a monastery among the Christians, and lived there, working for God and endeavoring in many labors.

In the year 6773/1265. [6771/1263 in *Hyp.*] When Voishelk learned of the assassination of his father, Grand Prince Mindaugas, he became greatly afflicted and said, "My Lord God! Thou seest this injustice. Thy Name will be glorified so that the lawless ones should not boast of their dishonor. Give me strength and power to march against them, for the Sake of Thy Name, so that Thy Name will be glorified everywhere." And so he put aside the vestments of a monk, promising to don them again three years hence, although he did not in the least break the [other] rules and regulations for a monk. He assembled a large host—the friends and supporters of his father, Grand Prince Mindaugas—and he marched against the pagan Lithuaninas and Chud',[55] capturing everyone who lived there. He remained there a whole year, baptised many of them, and built churches and monasteries; but some others escaped to Pskov with their wives and children, where they accepted divine baptism. He arranged everything for good, then assigned his chief commander, Andrei Daniilovich, to be grand prince there. Then he returned to his monastery and again put on the vestments of monk, and endeavored in his difficult and highly virtuous labors. At a great age, after many labors, he passed away to God.

In the year 6774/1266. The grand prince of Kostroma, Vasilii Iaroslavich the junior, grandson of Vsevolod, great grandson of Iurii Dolgorukii, was married in Kostroma by Ignatius, Bishop of Rostov, in the Church of St. Theodore.

---

55. Chud': Estonians. In the thirteenth century only Russians, who formed the greatest part of the population of Lithuania, were Christians. Ethnic Lithuanians remained pagan till the end of the fourteenth century.

The same year Berke, Khan of the Golden Horde, passed **1266** away and the violence of the Tatars over Russia lessened.

The same year [6773/1265 in *Hyp.*] there appeared a star in the west from which there extended a long ray, like a tail, in the direction of the south. This star remained for thirteen nights, then became invisible.[56]

The same year [6773/1265 in *Novg. IV.*] the Lithuanian prince, Dovmont, came to Pskov with his entire clan. There he was baptised and was given the name, Timotheus; and the people of Pskov asked him to be their prince. He selected the best and bravest people of Pskov and then took his druzhina—altogether, three hundred of them—and marched and captured the entire Lithuanian land, his own patrimony. He captured the wife of Prince Gerden and two of her children, young princes, and marched back to Pskov. He crossed the river Dvina, marched for five versts and camped on the river Dvina, having left two scouts— Davyd and Luka—with a single troop. And he let the other two hundred men go to Pskov with the captives. In the meantime, Prince Gerden returned to his land and, seeing it devasted, chased after Dovmont with seven hundred warriors, to catch him: with him were Gogort, Lumbei, Liugailo and other Lithuanian princes. They came to the river Dvina and, crossing it, camped on the shore. Then the scouts came to Dovmont, telling him of this large host. He told his druzhina, "We have before us either death or life; so let us be brave men for the sake of the Holy Trinity, for the holy churches and for the Christian faith."[57] There remained with them, however, only ninety of his troops; but he prayed to Lord God, to the Most Pure Theotokos, and to Holy Martyr, Leontius, who was remembered that day, and marched against them [against the Lithuanians], and defeated them. They killed there Grand Prince Gogort and other princes, and slew many Lithuanians, trampling others into the river. Some of them were driven by the river Dvina to the Gandov Island; but they were also killed, there. Gerden, himself, barely escaped with a few troops, [while among Dovmont's troops] only

56. This was most probably a comet.

57. The church of the Holy Trinity was the main church of Pskov, and therefore the Holy Trinity was considered by the people of Pskov to be their heavenly protector.

1266   one man of Pskov was killed. Prince Dovmont came to Pskov with many captives and much booty.

The same year [6773/1265 in *Vozn.*] Grand Prince Iaroslav Iaroslavich marched from Vladimir to Novgorod with a great many troops. He wanted to wage war against Pskov, against Prince Dovmont; but the Novgorodians were unwilling to do this, so he returned home, leaving in Novgorod his nephew, Prince Dmitrii Aleksandrovich, grandson of Iaroslav, great grandson of Vsevolod, gr. gr. grandson of Iurii Dolgorukii.

In the year 6775/1267. There was a great disturbance in Novgorod. The same year the Narva section of Novgorod burned. The same year the Novgorodians, under the command of Elevferii[58] and Prince Dovmont of Pskov, and with the levies of Pskov, campaigned in Lithuania and killed Prince Gerden.

In the year 6776/1268. A son, Vasilii, was born to Prince Boris Vasil'kovich.

The same year [6774/1266 in *Novg. IV.*] the Novgorodians with Prince Iurii Andreevich, grandson of Iaroslav, great grandson of Vsevolod, gr. gr. grandson of Iurii Dolgorukii, campaigned in the land beyond the river Narva, and they sent to the city of Iaroslavl', to Prince Dmitrii Aleksandrovich, asking him to come to their aid. They also sent to the city of Vladimir, to Grand Prince Iaroslav Iaroslavich, asking him to come to Novgorod and gather a host against the Germans; but he sent to them, to Novgorod, in his place, his sons, Sviatoslav and Mikhail, and other princes; and those began to build wall-batteringrams in the bishop's court. Then the Germans sent their envoys, people of Velyad, of Riga, of Iuriev and from other cities, saying, cunningly, "Why do you want to shed blood in vain? Let us have peace and concord, and then your merchants will come to us and our merchants will go to you, and we will have neither fighting nor offense. But if you want to fight, there are for this purpose the people of Kolyvan' and Rakovor."[59] And so their bishops and their knights of God gave an oath on the Cross, and so they made peace.[60]

58. "Eleferii Sbyslavich," in *Novg.*; "Elerferii" in *Nik.*

59. That is, "You may fight them: the people of Kolyvan', (now Tallin, or Revel') and Rakovor (Wesenberg). We will neither join them nor aid them."

60. By "their knights of God" are meant the knights of the Livonian Order, who in principle were considered knights-monks.

[THE RUSSIAN CAMPAIGN AGAINST THE GERMANS AT RAKOVOR] **1268**

The same year [6775/1267 in *Sof. V.*] all the aforementioned princes assembled in Novgorod: they were Prince Dmitrii Aleksandrovich; Prince Sviatoslav Iaroslavich, grandson of Iaroslav; his brother, Mikhail; Iurii Andreevich, grandson of Aleksandr; Konstantin, son-in-law of Aleksandr; Prince Dovmont of Pskov, with the levies of Pskov; Iaropolk, and a multitude of warriors; and on the twenty-third day of the month of February, with many other princes, they marched in strong forces toward the German city of Rakovor. Entering this land, they took three routes and campaigned there at length. Marching forward, they encountered a great inaccessible cave in which many Chud' were hiding; and so it was impossible to do battle with them. Thus, they remained at this cave for three days; a master sapper cleverly directed water against them, and they all were forced to flee from the cave. They were all slain and their wealth was taken. Then [the Russians] marched to Rakovor. Approaching the river Kigora[61] they were met by the Germans in great strength—there were as many of them as the sand. This happened because all the German land [Livonia] gathered there. Then the princes began to align their regiments: the Novgorodian forces faced the great German "iron swine;"[62] Prince Dovmont with the levies of Pskov formed the center; Prince Dmitrii Aleksandrovich and Prince Sviatoslav Iaroslavich, grandson of Iaroslav, were both above them on the right wing; while Prince Mikhail Iaroslavich was on the left hand, with many princes. The Russian force was very large, so that it was impossible to count them. The two hosts clashed in battle. [First] they began to test each other, little by little; then they became angry and started the big battle. It was an evil massacre and blood flowed like water so that the horses could not gallop. Bodies lay all around like ricks of hay or shocks of rye. Many Novgorodians were killed by this armored "iron swine" formation, and many boiars and squires of the Russian princes fell. Many people of Pskov and Ladoga were killed there. This happened on the eighteenth day of the month of February, on Saturday of Shrovetide; and many Orthodox people wept. Then the princes shouted loudly, praying and shedding tears to Lord

61. Should be Kiula; *Novg.*
62. "Iron swine": a wedge-like formation of armored cavalry knights.

1268 God and the Most Pure Theotokos to come to their aid because they were sorely aweoried and everyone was afraid and trembled. Then, unexpectedly, Lord God and His Most Pure Mother aided the Russian princes, and the Germans fled, not pursued by anyone but only by divine wrath. The Russian princes followed after, slaying them, as far as three marches and seven versts before Rakovor. Then they returned and remained near the bones [of those killed in battle] for three days; then they marched to Novgorod, and Prince Dmitrii Aleksandrovich went from Novgorod to Pereiaslavl', and the other princes went to their own places.

The same year Prince Dovmont of Pskov campaigned through inaccessible approaches against the people of Verui, and he captured many and went as far as the sea; he campaigned along the seashore [the Gulf of Finland] and returned to Pskov with many captives.

The same year Prince Gleb Vasil'kovich of Belozero returned from the Golden Horde, gravely ill. He remained ill for a long time, then, thanks to the mercy of God and the Most Pure Theotokos, he recovered.

In the year 6777/1269. Prince Dmitrii Sviatoslavich, grandson of Vsevolod, great grandson of Iurii Dolgorukii, gr. gr. grandson of Vladimir Monomakh, gr. gr. gr. grandson of Vsevolod, gr. gr. gr. gr. grandson of Iaroslav, gr. gr. gr. gr. gr. grandson of Great Vladimir, passed away. Before his death, he was tonsured and received the *schema* from Bishop Ignatius of Rostov. At that time there were with him his mother and Prince Gleb Vasil'kovich. Suddenly, he recovered his speech and began talking. Gazing upon the bishop with joyful eyes, he said, "Lord father, Bishop Ignatius! You have fulfilled your duty to God, preparing me for the long route into the eternal ages, and you have crowned me, a warrior, to appear before Our King, Christ, the Lord." Thereupon he quietly and peacefully gave up the ghost, and was buried in the church of St. Michael in the Iuriev monastery.

The same year, during All Saints' week, the Germans marched against Pskov, burned the suburb and remained near the city for ten days. Causing much evil, they then retreated, campaigning in the surrounding towns. Prince Iurii Andreevich, grandson of Iaroslav, heard of this and with the Novgorodians marched toward Pskov. When the Germans learned this they re- **1269** crossed the river and stopped fighting.

The same year there was a disturbance in Novgorod and they [the Novgorodians] started fighting among themselves. Some wanted to send for Grand Prince Iaroslav Iaroslavich of Vladimir to request him to aid them in obtaining a conclusive peace with the Germans; others, however, did not want to send anyone to Grand Prince Iaroslav Iaroslavich of Vladimir.

The same year Grand Prince Iaroslav Iaroslavich, grandson of Vsevolod, went to Novgorod, being angered at the posadniks, and this was the reason for the disturbance among them. Therefore Grand Prince Iaroslav Iaroslavich grew wroth and returned to Vladimir. Then they [the Novgorodians] sent him a humble petition because there was no peace with the Germans. He listened to their petition and returned from Brodnichi, and so he came to them in Novgorod and they acted according to his will.

The same year Grand Prince Iaroslav Iaroslavich, grandson of Vsevolod, sent to Vladimir to assemble troops for the campaign against the Germans. A strong force was gathered; with them came the Great Baskak, Amragan,[63] his son-in-law, Aidar, and many Tatars. Hearing this, the Germans took fright and trembled, and sent their envoys with a humble petition and many gifts. In their petition they [the Germans] promised [Iaroslav] to do everything he wanted, and gave the Great Baskak[64] and all the Tatar nobles many gifts, as well as to other Tatars. They were frightened at the very name of Tatar; and so they acceded to the will of Grand Prince Iaroslav Iaroslavich, relinquished the entire region of Narova and returned all the captives.

The same year Mitrophanes, Bishop of Sarai, gave up his bishopric of Sarai and sent his resignation, written by his own hand, to the Metropolitan of Kiev and all Russia.

The same year His Holiness Cyril, Metropolitan of Kiev and all Russia, appointed Theognost bishop of Pereiaslavl' Russkii and Sarai.

---

63. Amragan in *Novg.*; Armagan, *Musc.*; Iargaman in *Nik.*

64. Great Baskak: the chief Tatar administrator in the subjugated Suzdalian lands.

1270   *In the year 6778/1270.* The Novgorodians became tumultuous and summoned the veche. They wanted to cast out from
Novgorod Grand Prince Iaroslav Iaroslavich, and killed his
friends and advisors and sacked their estates and possessions.
They sent a missile to Gorodishche[65] to Grand Prince Iaroslav
Iaroslavich in which they enumerated all his faults: "Oh, Prince!
Why do you practice injustice? And why do you keep so many
hawks and falcons? You took from us all the waters of the Volkhov, and even other waters which you gave to your snarers of
ducks. And you keep too many hounds; and you took away from
us the hare-hunt and gave it to your own hunters; and then you
appropriated the estate of Aleksei Mortkin.[66] And you took much
silver from Nikifor Matveevich, Roman Boldyrev and Varfolomei
Alekseevich.[67] And why do you drive from us the foreigners living
here? And you have many other faults, Prince. Now, Prince,we
can no longer abide your violence! Prince! Depart peacefully
from us and we will look for another prince!" On the morrow
Grand Prince Iaroslav Iaroslavich sent them his son, Sviatoslav,
and his tysiatskii, Andrei Vratislavich, who bowed to the veche and
said, "Forgive me this and then I will not act any longer thus. I
pledge to you on the Cross that all will be done according to your
liberties." The Novgorodians, however, responded, "Prince, we
do not want you. Depart from us in peace. If you do not, we will
cast you out. We do not want you." Then Grand Prince Iaroslav
Iaroslavich, grandson of Vsevolod, departed from them, from
Novgorod, and went to Vladimir, where he began to gather a
host, intending to campaign against Novgorod. He sent Ratibor
to the Tatar Khan of the Golden Horde, asking him to fight Novgorod. He told them, "The Novgorodians do not obey me or
pay their tribute to you. They have cast out your tax collectors
and killed some of them. They have cast me out with dishonor and
they speak offensively of you." And so the Khan sent his host
against them. The Novgorodians sent to Pereiaslavl' for Prince
Dmitrii Aleksandrovich, grandson of Iaroslav, great grandson of

---

65. Gorodishche: suburban residence of the Novgorodian princes.

66. Mortkinich, in *Novg.*

67. In *Novg.*: "from Nikifor Manushkinich, Roman Boldyzerich
and Varfolomei."

Vsevolod; but he refused to go, saying, "I do not want to take the **1270**
throne from my uncle, Iaroslav Iaroslavich." The Novgorodians
were very saddened because Grand Prince Iaroslav Iaroslavich
gathered a strong force. Hearing of this, Prince Vasilii Iaroslavich
of Kostroma, grandson of Vsevolod, great grandson of Iurii
Dolgorukii, gr. gr. grandson of Vladimir Monomakh, sent his
envoys to Novgorod, saying, "I render honor to the Most Pure
Theotokos and to the men of Novgorod. I have heard that my
brother, Grand Prince Iaroslav Iaroslavich, is marching with a
host against Novgorod, and that our nephew, Prince Dmitirii
Aleksandrovich of Pereiaslavl', Prince Gleb Rostislavich of
Smolensk (grandson of Mstislav), and the Tatar Khan have also
sent their hosts against you. I am sorry for you, my patrimony."
Then they sent envoys to him, petitioning humbly; and so he went
to the Golden Horde, to the Khan, and the Tatar host was withdrawn because he succeeded in convincing the Khan, telling all
as it had happened. He said, "The Novgorodians are right and
my brother, Grand Prince Iaroslav Iaroslavich, is wrong." The
Khan greatly honored him and he was happy that he did not have
to dispatch his hosts.

Grand Prince Iaroslav Iaroslavich with his children and with
Prince Gleb Rostislavich of Smolensk,[68] grandson of Mstislav and
great grandson of Davyd, however, marched, warring, to Novgorod. The Novgorodians built fortifications in the vicinity of
their city on both its banks [of the river Volkhov], and strongly
fortified the city, itself. And so they mustered men from the whole
land, as well as men of Pskov; also, they brought Germans to
help them, and they moved to Gorodishche in strong force.
There they camped, armed and in armour, which shone as water.
Grand Prince Iaroslav Iaroslavich, as well as the other princes,
hearing of this, marched toward them; and coming to Rusa, they
camped there. Then he sent an envoy to the Novgorodians, saying, "Why do you dislike me? What are my faults? I repent of
everything [of any wrong I have done] and I will never act in the
same way in the future. All my princes will vouch for me." The
Novgorodians, though, answered him, "Prince! You intended to
start a war against our [Holy Patron], Holy Sophia.[69] Now, Prince,

68. In *Nik.*, "of Pereiaslavl'."
69. Holy Sophia was the cathedral of Novgorod.

1270 you know that we are ready to die for Holy Sophia and for each other. It is [a question of] our honor and glory. We have no prince now but we have the Lord God, Holy Sophia and justice on our side. We do not want you." And so the Novgorodians remained firm. Grand Prince Iaroslav Iaroslavich, grandson of Vsevolod, however, sent to his spiritual father, Cyril, Metropolitan of Kiev and all Russia, asking him how to resolve this situation honorably and imploring him to vouch for him to the Novgorodians. And he said, "I will never betray my word. Please try it for me, my father, and bring us to peace. Although they speak badly of me, I will never behave in like manner in future against them. It is your duty to bring about peace, especially among us, your real [spiritual] children."

His Holiness Cyril, Metropolitan of Kiev and all Russia, sent an epistle to Novgorod in which he wrote, "Lord God granted power to the Apostles, permitting them to bind and to unbind; and we [bishops] are their successors. And so we, the Apostolic heirs, bearers of the Image of Christ and of His Power here, in this case I, the present shepherd of all Russia—I instruct and command you according to God: Fear God, respect the prince. Do not fight in vain and do not shed blood. Any fault or any sin can be repented and forgiven. If Grand Prince Iaroslav Iaroslavich is in any way at fault with regard to you, he is absolved and forgiven for all these, and he does not intend to behave in such wise again. I vouch for him and you must accept him with due honor. If, however, in your wrath you have pledged an oath on the Cross to each other not to accept Grand Prince Iaroslav Iaroslavich, grandson of Vsevolod [as your lord], I release you from this oath, forgive you and give you my blessing. Do not fight! Do not shed blood! Be at peace and in accord! If you do not obey me, I will place a spiritual punishment upon you."[70] Thereupon the Novgorodians sent to Grand Prince Iaroslav Iaroslavich, offering peace; and so they made peace, confirming it with an oath on the Cross that all would be in accordance with their ancient Novgorodian liberties, as it had been in their land from its very beginning. And so they accepted Prince Iaroslav Iaroslavich in Novgorod and rendered him great honor.

70. "Spiritual punishment": in this case, probably, excommunication.

The same year Grand Prince Iaroslav Iaroslavich went from   **1270**
Novgorod to Vladimir.

[PASSION MARTYR ROMAN, PRINCE OF RIAZAN']

The same year Grand Prince Roman Ol'govich of Rostov, grandson of Ingvar, great grandson of Igor', gr. gr. grandson of Gleb, was calumniated in the Golden Horde before the Khan. It was said that he spoke irreverently of the Great Khan and that he offended the latter's faith; and so he, the Khan, sent the Tatars against him. They wanted to force him to join their faith, but he answered them, "It is not fit for an Orthodox Christian to give up his Orthodox faith and to accept the pagan Moslem faith." They began to beat him, but he said, "I am Christian and the Christian faith is, verily, a holy one, while your Tatar faith is a pagan one." They did not want to hear such words from him and so they cut out his tongue and put a kerchief in his mouth; then they cut off all his members and threw them away: they cut off his fingers and toes, his hands and his lips, and his ears and other members, and so there remained just his trunk. They skinned him down from the head, and, finally, put the head on a lance. This new martyr is equal in his passions to St. James of Persia.

Oh, beloved princes of Russia! Do not be seduced by the vain, shortlived and tempting glory of this world because there are deep pitfalls therein. Such glory is but a passing one and disappears as a shadow, departs as smoke. It is like unto a dream. No one can bring anything into this world and none can take anything with him, leaving this world. You came naked, from the womb of your mother, and you will leave this world naked. [*Eccl.* 5:15 paraph.] Do not be evil toward each other and do not desire whatsoever belongs to others; do not injure your junior kin because their angels[71] see the face of Your Father, Who is in Heaven. Care for true justice, humility, patience, purity, love and mercifulness, and then you will be fulfilled with the joy of the saints. Thus did this Prince Roman win the Heavenly Kingdom through his passions, and the Crown from the Lord's hand, as did

---

71. According to Orthodox teaching, each person has a guardian angel.

1270 [earlier] his kin, Grand Prince Mikhail Vsevolodich of Chernigov, because they suffered for the sake of Christ and the Orthodox Christian faith.[72] He [Prince Roman] was killed on the nineteenth day of the month of July.

In the year 6779/1271. Grand Prince Vasilii Aleksandrovich, grandson of Iaroslav, great grandson of Vsevolod, gr. gr. grandson of Iurii Dolgorukii, gr. gr. gr. grandson of Vladimir Monomakh, gr. gr. gr. gr. grandson of Vsevolod, gr. gr. gr. gr. gr. grandson of Iaroslav, gr. gr. gr. gr. gr. grandson of Great Vladimir, passed away.

The same year [6778/1271 in *Vozn.*] the following princes went to the Khan, to the Golden Horde: Iaroslav Iaroslavich [of Vladimir], grandson of Vsevolod; his brother, Vasilii Iaroslavich of Kostroma; and his nephew, Dmitrii Aleksandrovich of Pereiaslavl' [Zaleskii].

The same year during the fifth week of Great Lent there was a portent on the sun. The sun disappeared before dinner, and then again became full.[73]

The same year the dowager princess of Prince Vasil'ko passed away. At that time, there were with her her son, Boris, with his princess and his children, but [her other son] Prince Gleb was then in the Horde with the Khan. She passed away to God, quietly and humbly. Bishop Ignatius and all the Sacred Council buried her with fitting funeral chants in the church of St. Saviour in her own monastery.

The same year Grand Prince Iaroslav Iaroslavich, grandson of Vsevolod, great grandson of Iruii Dolgorukii, gr. gr. grandson of Vladimir Monomakh, gr. gr. gr. grandson of Vsevolod, gr. gr. gr. gr. grandson of Iaroslav, gr. gr. gr. gr. gr. grandson of Great Vladimir, passed away on his journey from the Horde. He ruled the Grand Principality of Vladimir after his brother, Aleksandr Iaroslavich, for eight years. His body was taken to Tver'. Bishop Simon of Tver' buried him with the fitting funeral chants in the church of the Holy Wonder Workers Kos'ma and Damian in Tver'. After him to the throne of Vladimir there ascended his brother, Vasilii junior, of Kostroma, the son of Iaroslav, grandson

72. Grand Prince Mikhail of Chernigov was killed by the Tatars for refusing to worship their gods. See entry under 6754/1246.

73. There was a partial eclipse of the sun on March 23, 1270.

of Vsevolod, great grandson of Iuruii Dolgorukii, gr. gr.grandson   **1271**
of Vladimir Monomakh, gr. gr. gr. grandson of Vsevolod, gr. gr.
gr. gr. grandson of Iaroslav, gr. gr. gr. gr. gr. grandson of Great
Vladimir, and so he became grand prince of Vladimir and Novgorod.

The same year a son, Mikhail, was born to Grand Prince Iaroslav Iaroslavich, after the latter's death.

The same year Manuel Paleologue became the first emperor
of Byzantium, after the rule of the Latins. He drove out the Latins from Constantinople and ruled over Byzantium for twenty-
four years.[74]

ABOUT DOVMONT

The Grand Master of Riga[75] wondered about the bravery and
courage of Prince Dovmont of Pskov, and he marched toward
Pskov with great forces, in ships, boats, by horseback, and with
wall-batteringrams. When Prince Dovmont of Pskov heard
about this, he went to the church of the Holy Trinity, removed
his sword and laid it before the holy altar, and began to pray tearfully. After long prayers and many tears Abbot Isidor, with all the
members of the clergy, took his sword and girdled him with it.
After blessing him, he let him go. Dovmont did not wait for the
Novgorodian troops and, with only the levy of Pskov, he marched
forward, relying upon the help of the Holy Trinity, the Most Pure
Theotokos and the Holy Siants; and thanks to his bravery and
courage, he defeated the German troops. He wounded the Grand
Master [of the Livonian Order], himself, in the face, and captured others, while the remaining ones fled. This happened on
the eighth day of the month of June.

The same year [6780/1272 in *Novg. IV.*] the Germans undertook evil action in the land of Pskov, but Prince Dovmont of Pskov
marched against them, campaigned in their land of the Chud',
and returned with many captives.

74. It was not Manuel, but Michael VIII Paleologue, Emperor of
Nicea, who, in 1261, not 1271, drove the Latin "Crusaders" from Constantinople, and thus restored the Byzantine Empire. He died in 1282.

75. That is, Grand Master of the German Livonian Order.

1272   *In the year 6780/1272.* [6781/1273 in *Novg. IV.*] The Novgorodians sent to Pereiaslavl' [Zaleskii] to Prince Dmitrii Aleksandrovich, grandson of Iaroslav, great grandson of Vsevolod, asking him to become prince of Novgorod. When Grand Prince
[of Vladimir-Novgorod] Vasilii Iaroslavich, grandson of Vsevolod, learned of this, he sent against him his voevoda Simeon,
while he, himself, marched to Pereiaslavl' and from thence to
Torzhok. Arriving there, he burned Torzhok and assigned his
namestnik to it, then returned.

The same year his voevoda Simeon occupied several Novgorodian regions and returned to Vladimir, to Grand Prince
Vasilii Iaroslavich, grandson of Vsevolod, with many captives.

In the year 6781/1273. Grand Prince Vasilii Iaroslavich,
grandson of Vsevolod, great grandson of Iurii Dolgorukii, together with Iargaman, Great Baskak of Vladimir, and with Khan
Aidar and with many Tatars of the Khan's, fought in the Novgorodian land and returned to Vladimir with many captives.

The same year Grand Prince of Tver', Sviatoslav Iaroslavich,
grandson of Iaroslav, great grandson of Vsevolod, gr. gr. grandson of Iurii Dolgorukii, marched with the Khan's Tatars and campaigned in the Novgorodian lands of Volokh, Bezhichi and
Vologda; and he returned to Tver' with many captives.

The same year grain was very expensive in Novgorod and
the Novgorodian merchants in Vladimir, Tver' and Kostroma
were arrested and robbed.

The same year Prince Dmitrii Aleksandrovich, grandson of
Iaroslav, marched to Tver' with the hosts of all the Novgorodian
lands. They—the Novgorodians—sent to Vladimir, to Grand
Prince Vasilii Iaroslavich, grandson of Vsevolod [the Great Nest]
their envoys, Simeon Mikhailovich, Lazar' Moiseevich and Stepan
Dushilovich, saying, "Do not desire Novgorod, and whatsoever
of the Novgorodian possessions you have taken, please return
them. And the Novgorodian merchants whom you robbed, arrested and imprisoned should all be returned with their wares,
without any discussion; and you should live with us in peace and
amity."

Grand Prince Vasilii Iaroslavich, grandson of Vsevolod
[the Great Nest] let the envoys go with honor; but he did not
agree to make peace. Then Prince Dmitrii Aleksandrovich,
grandson of Iaroslav, great grandson of Vsevolod [the Great

Nest], marched with a Novgorodian host to Torzhok; but at that **1273** time the voevodas of Grand Prince Vasilii Iaroslavich were already in Torzhok, and the Novgorodians became distressed, and there was great fear and trembling among them; and they said, "Woe to us from all sides! Here is the Grand Prince of Vladimir, and there is the Grand Prince of Tver'; and there is the Great Baskak of the Khan with the Tatars; and all the Niz land is against us!" They asked Grand Prince Vasilii Iaroslavich, grandson of Vsevolod, to be their prince, and they wanted to be rid of Prince Dmitrii Aleksandrovich. Seeing this, he took fright, gave up Novgorod and went to Pereiaslavl' [Zalesskii]. Then the Novgorodians sent a petition to Grand Prince Vasilii Iaroslavich, asking him to come to Novgorod. The same year [6782/1274 in *Novg. III.*] Grand Prince Vasilii Iaroslavich, grandson of Vsevolod, great grandson of Iurii Dolkgorukii, went to Novgorod. The Novgorodians went to meet him and bowed, and accepted him [as their prince] with honor.

In the year 6782/1274. Metropolitan Cyril came from Kiev to Vladimir, bringing with him Serapion, archimandrite of the Cave monastery, to be bishop of Vladimir and Suzdal'.[76]

The same year [6781/1273 in *Novg. VII.*] the Novgorodians saw that their bishop, Dalmatus, had become completely exhausted and was ready to give up the life of this vain age. They came to him sadly and, bowing deeply to him, asked, "Lord, father, shepherd and our teacher, Archbishop Dalmatus! Please give your blessing to another shepherd and teacher in your stead, so that he will be with us in your place." He answered, "It is not meet that I should do so—rather, it should be done by God and the Most Pure Theotokos. If you want my humble advice, you have [a good candidate in either] Abbot Davyd or John, in St. George's monastery; and you have my spiritual father [confessor], Clement. You may select whomsoever you wish." They preferred his spiritual father, Clement, who was noted by God,[77]

76. Bishop Serapion was an eloquent preacher and skilful writer whose sermons have been preserved. Two of them are included in S. Zenkovsky: *Medieval Russia's Epics, Chronicles and Tales*, E. P. Dutton & Co., N.Y., 1974.

77. According to the Novgorodian tradition, they probably cast lots, and the lot fell to Clement.

1274 and Archbishop Dalmatus gave him his blessing with his own hand. The same year Dalmatus, Archbishop of Novgorod, passed away. The same year the Novgorodians sent Clement with their leading man to Kiev, to Cyril, Metropolitan of Kiev and all Russia, to be consecrated bishop of Novgorod.

The same year [6781/1273 in *Novg. IV.*] the Grand Princess Feodora, wife of Grand Prince Gleb, passed away and Ignatius, Bishop of Rostov, together with the Sacred Council, chanted the funeral hymns over her body, and she was buried in the church of the Most Pure Theotokos in the city of Rostov.

The same year Pavel Semenovich, posadnik of Novgorod, passed away.

In the year 6783/1275. Vasilii Iaroslavich, grandson of Vsevolod, journeyed to the Golden Horde.

The same year there were portents on the sun. The whole sun was surrounded with circles, and in the middle of the circles were crosses; these circles were blue, green, yellow, crimson and red, and there were spines along these circles; and this occurred on the third day of the month of May.[78]

The same year Serapion, Bishop of Vladimir, Suzdal' and Nizhnii Novgorod, passed away and was buried in Vladimir, in the cathedral of the Most Pure Theotokos with golden cupolas. He was very learned, and strong in Divine Scripture.

The same year [6782/1274 in *Hyp.*] the Tatars and the Russian princes campaigned against Lithuania. They waged war there, and returned with many captives.

The same year in Russia[79] and in Novgorod there was a second census ordered by the khan of the Horde; and they counted everyone but the priests, monks and members of the clergy.

The same year a bear with three legs was killed.

The same year [6782/1274 in *Novg. III.*] the office of posadnik of Novgorod was given to Mikhail Mikhailovich.

The same year there were portents in the skies. The same year there was awesome thunder in the city of Vladimir, and lightning struck the deacon in the holy cathedral church of the

78. It was probably a so-called atmospheric halo.

79. In this case, "Russia" means the region of present east central, southern and a portion of western Russia, which paid tribute to the Golden Horde.

Most Pure Theotokos; this happened during the Eucharist when **1275** he came out to read the litany, and all the people fell down from great fear and were as if dead.

In the year 6784/1276. His Holiness Cyril, Metropolitan of Kiev and all Russia, appointed Theodor, then abbot of the monastery of St. Constantine and St. Helen, to be bishop of Vladimir, Suzdal' and Nizhnii Novgorod.

The same year Grand Prince Vasilii Iaroslavich, grandson of Vsevolod, great grandson of Iurii Dolgorukii, returned from the Golden Horde of the Tatars to Vladimir.

The same year all the city of Tver' burned. There remained only one church.

The same year in Kiev, Clement was consecrated Archbishop of Novgorod by Cyril, Metropolitan of Kiev and all Russia. He went from Kiev to his diocese in Novgorod.

The same winter in the month of November there was a portent on the moon, which completely disappeared, then reappeared.

The same winter Grand Prince of Vladimir, Vasilii the Junior, son of Iaroslav, grandson of Vsevolod, great grandson of Iurii Dolgorukii, gr. gr. grandson of Vladimir Monomakh, gr. gr. gr. grandson of Vsevolod, gr. gr. gr. gr. grandson of Iaroslav, and gr. gr. gr. gr. gr. grandson of Great Valdimir, passed away in Kostroma; and on this occasion the princes assembled together: there were Boris Vasil'kovich of Rostov; Gleb Vasil'kovich of Belozero; Prince Mikhail Ivanovich, grandson of Vsevolod; Prince Dmitrii Aleksandrovich of Pereiaslavl', grandson of Iaroslav, great grandson of Vsevolod; and Prince Fedor Rostislavich of Iaroslavl', grandson of Mstislav, great grandson of Davyd, gr. gr. grandson of Monomakh, gr. gr. gr. grandson of Iaroslav, gr. gr. gr. grandson of Great Vladimir. And with them were a multitude of boiars and people. Ignatius, Bishop of Rostov, together with the Sacred Council, chanted the funeral hymns over his body, and he was buried in the church of St. Theodore in Kostroma. He was very virtuous, loved God with all his heart, loved the people and was merciful toward all without guile; and he was very attentive toward the holy churches: he greatly respected the bishops as his superiors and shepherds, loved greatly and respected the whole clergy and the monks, and was meek, forgiving those who had sinned against him. He lived forty years

1276 from his birth and became Grand Prince of Vladimir and Novgorod for five years, after his brother, Grand Prince Iaroslav Iaroslavich. His sons were . . . [*Sic!*] After him, his nephew, Prince Dmitrii Aleksandrovich, grandson of Vsevolod, great grandson of Iurii Dolgorukii, assumed the grand principality of Vladimir.

The same year the Novgorodians sent a petition from Novgorod to Vladimir, to Grand Prince Dmitrii Aleksandrovich, grandson of Iaroslav Vsevolodich, calling him to Novgorod.

The same year Prince Boris Vasil'kovich of Rostov, grandson of Konstantin, married his senior son, Prince Dmitrii.

In the year 6785/1277. Grand Prince Dmitrii Aleksandrovich, grandson of Iaroslav, great grandson of Vsevolod, gr. gr. grandson of Iurii Dolgorukii, came to Novgorod, and he was received with honor by the Novgorodians.

The same year the princes went to the Horde: they were Grand Prince Boris Vasil'kovich of Rostov, grandson of Konstantin, great grandson of Vsevolod, gr. gr. grandson of Iurii Dolgorukii, with his princess and his children; his brother, Prince Gleb Vasil'kovich, of Belozero with his son, Mikhail; Prince Fedor Rostislavich of Iaroslavl', grandson of Mstislav, great grandson of Davyd, gr. gr. grandson of Rostislav, gr. gr. gr. grandson of Mistislav, Gr. gr. gr. gr. grandson of Valdimir Monomakh, gr. gr. gr. gr. gr. grandson of Iaroslav, gr. gr. gr. gr. gr. gr. grandson of Great Vladimir.

PRINCE FEDOR OF IAROSLAVL'

It should be kept in mind, however, that Prince Fedor Rostislavich of Iaroslavl' was by birth not from the Iaroslavl' [branch of princes] but from the Smolensk [branch].

And hearken, now! Grand Prince of Kiev Vladimir Vsevolodich Monomakh had a senior son named Mstislav, and the principality of Smolensk was given to him; later, after his father's death, he became grand prince of Kiev, where he died. Usually, however, he continued to be called "Prince of Smolensk." His son, Rostislav, also became grand prince of Smolensk, as did Rostislav's son, Davyd, who likewise became grand prince of Smolensk. Davyd's son was Mstislav, and Mstislav's son was Rostislav; and this Prince Rostislav [of Smolensk] had [three] sons: Fedor, about whom we speak, and his brothers—Gleb and **1277** Mikhail. The two latter offended him—Fedor—by giving him only the city of Mozhaisk, while his brother, Gleb, became grand prince of Smolensk. Prince Fedor Rostislavich, about whom we now speak, was prince of Mozhaisk, and was unmarried. [About the same time] the grand prince of Iaroslavl' was Vsevolod Konstantinich, grandson of Iurii Dolgorukii, great grandson of Vladimir Monomakh. This Vsevolod Konstantinich of Iaroslavl' had a son, Vasilii, and this Vasilii Vsevolodich of Iaroslavl' had a daughter. When Prince Vasilii Vsevolodich of Iaroslavl' passed away in Iaroslavl', there remained after his death in Iaroslavl' his dowager princess and his daughter. Then Prince Fedor Rostislavich communicated from Mozhaisk with Prince Boris Vasil'kovich of Rostov, with his brother, Prince Gleb Vasil'kovich of Belozero, and with the dowager princess of Vasilii Vsevolodich of Iaroslavl', telling them that he wanted to marry the latter's daughter. And so he married her, and subsequently became grand prince of Iaroslavl', receiving the principality of Iaroslavl'. He started ruling there together with his mother-in-law, and he was greatly virtuous.[80]

At that time there was a tradition[81] of going to the Horde, to the Khan, and receiving a yarlyk[82] from the Khan in his name— [in this case] for the principality of Iaroslavl'. Consequently, he [Fedor] had to travel with others to the Khan of the Horde. Together with him was Prince Andrei Aleksandrovich, grandson of Iaroslav, great grandson of Vsevolod; and with them many other [princes] journeyed to the Horde, each on account of his own principality. And so they joined together for the journey. When they came to the Khan of the Golden Horde they were recieved with honor.

The same year Grand Prince Boris Vasil'kovich of Rostov, son of Konstantin, grandson of Vsevolod, great grandson of

80. This long resumé of Prince Fodor's background and marriage is specific to *Nik.* and probably was meant to point out the fact that the princes of Iaroslavl' and their descendants—*i.e.*, the Princes Kurbskii and others—did not belong to the original Suzdalian line of Riurikovich princes running from Iurii Dolgorukii, Vsevolod the Great Nest, etc.

81. Actually, the rule.

82. "Iarlyk": a charter permitting a prince to rule.

1277 Iurii Dolgorukii, became ill in the Horde and asked to be tonsured a monk; however, his Princess Maria prevented him from so doing because she hoped that he would live. And so he confessed to his spiritual father, repented and lived piously for a number of days.

In the year 6786/1278. [6785/1277 in *Laur.*] Grand Prince Boris Vasil'kovich of Rostov, grandson of Konstantin, great grandson of Vsevolod, great gr. grandson of Iurii Dolgorukii, gr. gr. gr. grandson of Vladimir Monomakh, gr. gr. gr. gr. grandson of Vsevolod, gr. gr. gr. gr. gr. grandson of Iaroslav, gr. gr. gr. gr. gr. gr. grandson of Great Vladimir, passed away in the Golden Horde on the sixth day of the month of September, when the Holy Martyr Euthymia is remembered. His Princess Maria with his son, Dmitrii, brought his body from the Golden Horde to Rostov. Ignatius, Bishop of Rostov, together with the Sacred Council, chanted the funeral hymns over his body, and he was buried in Rostov in the left side of the cathedral church of the Most Pure Theotokos on the thirteenth day of the month of November, when Our Holy Father John Chrysostom is remembered. His sons were Dmitrii and Konstantin. After the passing of Grand Prince Boris Vasil'kovich, his brother, Gleb Vasil'kovich of Belozero became grand prince of Rostov. At that time there still remained with the khan of the Golden Horde Grand Prince Gleb Vasil'kovich of Rostov, grandson of Konstantin, great grandson of Vsevolod, great gr. grandson of Iurii Dolgorukii; his nephew, Prince Konstantin Borisovich, grandson of Vasil'ko, great grandson of Konstantin, gr. gr. grandson of Vsevolod; Prince Fedor Rostislavich of Iaroslavl', grandson of Mstislav, great grandson of Davyd; Prince Andrei Aleksandrovich, grandson of Iaroslav, great grandson of Vsevolod; and, with them, many other princes, boiars and servants. At that time Khan Mangu Temir[83] decided to do battle, and he ordered all the aforementioned princes to make ready. Soon thereafter Khan Mangu Temir, himself, and the Russian princes, set out campaigning, and Lord God helped the Russian princes, for they took the Ossets' glorious city of Dadakov, in winter on the eighth day of the month of February when the Holy Martyr Theodore Stratilat and the Holy Prophet, the

83. Of the Golden Horde, 1266-1279.

seer of the heart, Zachariah, are remembered.[84] They took many **1278** captives and a great amount of wealth, while some of their enemies were slain and their city was burned. Khan Mangu Temir greatly honored the Russian princes, praised them and gave them all presents, then let them go to Russia to their own domains with great honor and many gifts.

The same year Grand Prince Gleb Rostislavich of Smolensk, grandson of Mstislav, great grandson of Davyd, gr. gr. grandson of Rostislav, gr. gr. gr. grandson of Mstislav, gr. gr. gr. gr. grandson of Vladimir Monomakh, gr. gr. gr. gr. gr. grandson of Vsevolod,[85] gr. gr. gr. gr. gr. gr. grandson of Iaroslav, gr. gr. gr. gr. gr. gr. gr. grandson of Great Vladimir, passed away.

The same winter [6785/1277 in *Vozn.*] Grand Prince Dmitrii Aleksandrovich, grandson of Iaroslav, great grandson of Vsevolod, together with the levies of Suzdal' and Novgorod, waged war against the Karels. He conquered all their land and returned with a great many captives.

The same winter [6785/1277 in *Vozn.*] in the month of February there was a portent on the sun. The sun became encircled by circles. In the middle of them was a cross, and outside the circles there were four suns.[86] Above the sun was a large arch with the horns turned toward the north.

The same year Prince Gleb Vasil'kovich of Rostov came back from the Horde from Khan Mangu Temir, together with whom he fought in the war [in the Caucasus]; and with him was his son, Mikhail, and his nephew, Konstantin Borisovich, grandson of Vasil'ko. They brought many captives with them and much wealth, and they were greatly honored by the khan. On the thirteenth day of the month of June when the reverend Father Onuphrius of the desert is remembered, he returned to the city of Rostov. It was the week of All Saints and he thanked Lord God and the Most Pure Theotokos and all the saints. He entered the

84. Ossets: Also, the Iassy or Alans, in the central Caucasus. Vernadsky (III, 124) presumes that Dadakov was later Dzauji-gäu, subsequently Vladikavkaz (now Ordzhonikidze), the Ossets' stronghold on the river Terek.

85. This last name is missing in *Nik*.

86. This was probably another instance of the so-called atmospheric halo.

1278   holy church and prayed to Lord God and to the Most Pure Theotokos, making the Sign of the Cross before Her holy icon; and
he received a blessing from his spiritual father, Ignatius, Bishop of
Rostov, and there was great joy in Rostov.

The same year Grand Prince Gleb Vasil'kovich of Rostov
married his son, Mikhail, to the daughter of Grand Prince Fedor
Rostislavich of Iaroslavl'. The wedding took place in the church
of the Most Pure Theotokos in Iaroslavl' and was performed by
Ignatius, Bishop of Rostov. There were present Prince Gleb
Vasil'kovich of Rostov, himself; his nephew, Konstantin Boriso-
vich, grandson of Vasil'ko, great grandson of Konstantin; Prince
Davyd Konstantinovich of Galich[87] and Dmitrov, grandson of
Iaroslav, great grandson of Vsevolod, gr. gr. grandson of Iurii
Dolgorukii; and Davyd Davidovich; as well as a number of boiars.
And a great many people came thither, and there was great joy
in Iaroslavl'. This happened on the fifteenth day of the month of
July when the Holy Martyr Cyril and his mother, Julita, are remembered. Grand Prince Gleb Vasil'kovich, grandson of Konstantin, great grandson of Vsevolod, offered a great banquet in
the city of Iaroslavl' and honored the father of his daughter-in-
law, [Prince] Fedor Rostislavich Chernyi, his princess and his
children, as well as his son-in-law, Davyd Konstantinovich,
[Prince] of Galich and Dmitrov, as well as his boiars and his
squires.

The same year pious Prince Andrei and his wife, Ustinia,
passed away.

The same year Grand Prince Gleb Vasil'kovich of Rostov
sent his son, Mikhail, to the Tatars [of the Golden Horde] to aid
them in their war, and with him there went the father of his
daughter-in-law, Prince Fedor Rostislavich Chernyi of Iaroslavl'.

[THE PASSING OF PRINCE GLEB VASIL'KOVICH]

The same year Grand Prince Gleb Vasil'kovich of Rostov
passed away. He was the grandson of Konstantin, great grandson
of Vsevolod [Great Nest], gr. gr. grandson of Iurii Dolgorukii, gr.

87. This city of Galich is in the Suzdalian land.

gr. gr. grandson of Vladimir Monomakh, gr. gr. gr. gr. grandson **1278**
of Vsevolod, gr. gr. gr. gr.gr. grandson of Iaroslav, gr. gr. gr. gr.
gr. gr. grandson of Great Vladimir; and he lived from the time
of his birth for forty-one years. After the Tatar conquest [of
Russia] [this Prince Gleb] from his youth served the Tatars, and
thus he succeeded in protecting many Christians from the Tatar
offenses: he would console the sorrowful, and he never spared
drink or food but provided them to the needy; he gave alms to
the unfortunate, to paupers, to pilgrims, orphans and widows,
remembering the words of God, "Inasmuch as ye did unto
one of these brethren, even these last, ye did give unto Me."
[*Math*. 25:40.] And He said, "Blessed are the merciful for they
shall obtain mercy." [*Math*. 5:7.] And [King] David said, "Blessed is he who considereth the poor, and blessed is he who cares for
the paupers and the poor, for in the day of evil Lord God will deliver him.. The Lord will preserve him and keep him alive and he
shall be blessed upon the earth, and deliver not thou him unto the
will of his enemies." [*PS*. 41:1-3] And his son, Solomon, also said,
"One cleanses himself of sins through alms and faith," and "One
who gives to the poor, lendeth unto God." [*Prov*. 16:17, reph.]
And the saint prophet Daniel said, "Break thy sins by righteous-
ness and thine iniquities by showing mercy to the poor." [*Dan*. 4:2]
And great [John] Chrysostom said, "Just as water extinguishes
fire, so do alms purify sins." [This Prince Gleb Vasil'kovich] gave
countless alms to those who asked; he built many churches, which
he beautified with icons and books; he greatly respected the clergy
and monks, and he was full of love and mercy toward all; he was
humble and hated pride, remaining aloof from it as from the serpent. When, by God's will, he departed this vain and rapidly passing life, he passed to the Lord meekly and quietly, thus joining
his father, grandfather and ancestors; after his passing he left
those who knew him in sadness and tears. Bishop Ignatius of
Rostov, together with the Sacred Council, chanted the customary
funeral hymns and buried him in the church of the Most Pure
Theotokos in Rostov.

His sons were [*Sic!*] Mikhail, who succeeded him in his domain of Belozero. In the city of Rostov after Gleb Vasil'kovich's
passing there ascended to the throne his nephews: Prince Dmitrii
Borisovich, grandson of Vasil'ko, and the latter's brother, Konstantin Borisovich.

1278   The same year in Uglich Pol'e there passed away the Grand Princess Avdot'ia [Eudoxia], dowager of Vladimir Konstantino-vich.

The same year Grand Prince Dmitrii Aleksandrovich of Vladimir occupied [the town of] Tetiakov [Dadakov in the Caucasus].

The same year very many people died from various diseases.

The same year the Tatars came to Riazan', caused much evil and returned home.

In the year 6787/1279. On the twenty-first day of February there was a portent on the moon, which completely disappeared; it reappeared before dawn, but not in full light.[88]

The same year there was a portent on the sun.

The same year Grand Prince Iurii Andreevich of Suzdal', grandson of Iaroslav, great grandson of Vsevolod [Great Nest], gr. gr. grandson of Iurii Dolgorukii, gr. gr. gr. grandson of Vladimir Monomakh, gr. gr. gr. gr. grandson of Vsevolod, gr. gr. gr. gr. gr. grandson of Iaroslav, gr. gr. gr. gr. gr. gr. grandson of Great Vladimir, passed away. After him his brother, Mikhail Andreevich, ascended to the throne of Suzdal'.

The same year Grand Prince Mikhail Rostislavich of Smolensk passed away, the grandson of Mstislav, great grandson of Davyd, gr. gr. grandson of Rostislav, gr. gr. gr. grandson of Mstislav, gr. gr. gr. gr. grandson of Vladimir Monomakh, gr. gr. gr. gr. gr. grandson of Vsevolod, gr. gr. gr. gr. gr. gr. grandson of Iaroslav, gr. gr. gr. gr. gr. gr. gr. grandson of Great Vladimir. After him Prince Fedor Rostislavich Chernyi of Iaroslavl' ascended to the throne of his patrimony, the grand principality of Smolensk.

The same year Grand Princess of Iaroslavl', by the name of Marina, the dowager of Vsevolod Konstantinovich, who was grandson of Vsevolod and great grandson of Iurii Dolgorukii, passed away and was buried in Iaroslavl'.

The same year Prince Dmitrii Borisovich, grandson of Vasil'ko, great grandson of Konstantin, gr. gr. grandson of Vsevolod [Great Nest] took away some districts from Prince Mikhail Glebovich of Belozero, grandson of Vasil'ko, great grandson of

88. Probably an eclipse of the moon.

Konstantin, gr. gr. grandson of Vsevolod; and he did so sinfully **1279** and unjustly, in such manner offending and violating the rights of his kin. Oh! The evil greed of humankind and accursed pride! And would Lord God tolerate it and remain silent, and would He not avenge His offended servants who appeal to Him, weeping and shedding tears?

The same year Theognost, Bishop of Sarai, came for the third time from the Greek land, from Constantinople. He was sent by His Holiness Cyril, Metropolitan of Kiev and all Russia, and by Khan Mangu Temir of the Golden Horde, to Emperor Michael Paleologue of Byzantium, with a charter from His Holiness Metropolitan Cyril and from Khan Mangu Temir, and with gifts from them both.

The same year the Tatars campaigned in Lithuania and the Russian princes marched with them. They returned home with many captives and booty.

The same year at night there was a portent on the moon, which entirely disappeared. It was not visible until dawn, and did not reappear even when there was light.[89]

In the year 6788/1280. Grand Prince Davyd Konstantinovich of Galich and Dmitrov, grandson of Iaroslav, great grandson of Vsevolod, gr. gr. grandson of Iurii Dolgorukii, gr. gr. gr. grandson of Vladimir Monomakh, passed away.

The same year Ignatius, Bishop of Rostov, covered the roof of the Most Pure Theotokos in Rostov with lead, and laid red marble on the floor.

The same year His Holiness Cyril, Metropolitan of Kiev and all Russia, as was his habit, left Kiev and visited all the cities of Russia, teaching, punishing and instructing. He went to the Suzdalian land and heard from some people that Ignatius, Bishop of Rostov, had dealt unjustly with the body of his late prince, Gleb Vasil'kovich, of Rostov. He accused him cruelly and nine weeks after the latter's death he removed his body, at midnight, from the cathedral church, abusing it dishonorably. He ordered that he be buried in the land of the monastery of the princess, dedicated to the Holy Saviour. For this action Cyril, Metropolitan of

89. Probably another eclipse of the moon.

1280   Kiev and all Russia, interdicted Ignatius from celebrating the sacred services; and this punishment lasted until Prince Dmitrii Borisovich of Rostov, grandson of Vasil'ko, interceded on his behalf with the Metropolitan. Then the Metropolitan pardoned him, saying, "Do not be so proud! And do not believe that you are without sin. You should rather absolve and forgive people, than interdict or excommunicate them so often. We obtain absolution of the sins of our brethren, and God's mercy is hidden in the mercy of our neighbors. Weep, my child, and repent unto death for this improper and shameless impertinence. You condemned him before he was convicted by Divine Judgment, yet, while he was alive, you respected him, accepted gifts from him, would eat and drink with him, passed time and rejoiced with him. At that time you could have corrected his offenses, but you did not correct him; now you want to punish him cruelly, by interdicting and excommunicating him. If you want to help him, do so by giving alms to the poor, praying and celebrating sacred and divine liturgies for the salvation of his soul." And so, having greatly punished and instructed Bishop Ignatius, His Holiness Metropolitan Cyril absolved him and gave him his blessing to officiate [as bishop], and to celebrate all sacred and divine services. He consoled him so that the latter would not feel too greatly hurt.

The same year there were awesome thunderstorms, powerful winds, strong whirlwinds, great tempests, much lightning which killed many people; and many burned from it. The whirlwinds were so strong that they tore out whole houses with their foundations, with people and with entire households, and carried them off. In such manner the Lord demonstrated His warning, reminding and bringing us to repentance. He does not want the death of a sinner, but wants him to become converted and live.

The same year Clement, Archbishop of Novgorod, came to Cyril, Metropolitan of Kiev and all Russia, and received a blessing from him. He also came to see Grand Prince Dmitrii Aleksandrovich [of Vladimir], grandson of Iaroslav, concerning peace and concord between him and the Novgorodians.

The same year, the seventh day of the month of December, when our Holy Father Ambrosius, Bishop of Milano, is remembered, His Holiness Cyril, Metropolitan of Kiev and all Russia, passed away in Pereiaslavl' in the Suzdalian land. Present were

Grand Prince Dmitrii Aleksandrovich of Vladimir; Clement, Archbishop of Novgorod; Ignatius, Bishop of Rostov; and Fedor, Bishop of Vladimir and Suzdal'. They chanted over his body, placed it in the casket and took him to Vladimir, from whence they bore it to Kiev and again chanted; and all the Russian bishops, with the entire Sacred Council, celebrated the funeral service and buried him in the cathedral church of Kiev.

The same year Grand Prince Dmitrii Aleksandrovich of Vladimir, with his kin, marched to Novgorod to wage war. The Novgorodians sent him their archbishop, Clement, with a petition, entreaties and gifts. He listened to the archbishop, accepted the gifts and returned with his kin to Vladimir.

The same year there were portents in the sky: there was a fiery cloud in the western land from which sparks fell onto the earth. It remained for awhile and disappeared.[90]

In the year 6789/1281. There were dissension and great enmity between the two grand princes of Rostov, Dmitrii Borisovich and his brother, Konstantin Borisovich. When Bishop Ignatius of Rostov tried to reconcile them and to bring about concord between them, only greater hostility ensued. Prince Konstantin journeyed from Rostov to Vladimir, to Grand Prince Dmitrii Aleksandrovich, grandson of Iaroslav. Then Grand Prince Dmitrii Borisovich of Rostov began to gather an army and to fortify the city, fearing his kin and seized by great sadness; and the entire city of Rostov was upset. Bishop Ignatius journeyed from Rostov to Vladimir and beseeched Grand Prince Dmitrii Aleksandrovich [not to fight]; then Grand Prince Dmitrii Aleksandrovich, with Ignatius, Bishop of Rostov, and his boiars, went to Rostov, and the bishop arranged peace and concord among them. There was great festivity and all rejoiced. Then Grand Prince Dmitrii Aleksandrovich returned to the city of Vladimir.

[THE STRUGGLE FOR THE GRAND PRINCIPALITY OF VLADIMIR]

The same winter Prince Andrei Aleksandrovich, grandson of Iaroslav, great grandson of Vsevolod [Great Nest], junior broth-

90. Probably the phenomenon of "falling stars."

1281 er of Grand Prince Dmitrii Aleksandrovich of Vladimir, went to the Golden Horde seeking to replace his brother as Grand Prince [of Vladimir]; his consorts and aides were Semion Tonil'evich and many others. He gave to the Khan[91] and to the great lords [of the Golden Horde] many presents, supplied them all with wealth, and cajoled them, thus obtaining the Grand Principality of Vladimir in the place of his senior brother, Grand Prince Dmitrii Aleksandrovich. He received tidings from Russia, however, that Grand Prince Dmitrii Aleksandrovich was assembling a large army and was fortifying the city, unwilling to accept the Khan's decision to deprive him of the Grand Principality, as had been decided by the Khan; and he even announced this to the Khan. The latter, though, ordered his commanders, Kav Gadeh and Al Chedai, to march [to the aid of Andrei Aleksandrovich] with the Tatar forces. Prince Andrei Aleksandrovich came to Murom with the Tatars from the Khan of the Golden Horde, as well as with his advisor and consort, Semion Tonilevich, and with many other aides; and he sent for Prince Mikhail Ivanovich of Starodub, the grandson of Vsevolod [Great Nest], great grandson of Iurii Dolgorukii; and for all the other Russian princes. When they arrived and held counsel, their entire army marched to Pereiaslavl' against Grand Prince Dmitrii Aleksandrovich.

Grand Prince Dmitrii Aleksandrovich received these tidings, and fled with his wife and children, with his boiars and all his court, to Novgorod, and occupied the city of Kopor'e. The Novgorodians, though, marched cunningly toward Lake Il'mero, pretending that they would let him go from thence because he intended to escape beyond the sea. There was much altercation among them. The Novgorodians then told Grand Prince Dmitrii Aleksandrovich, "Prince! We do not want you! Better that you depart from us of your own will. If you do not leave from hence, you will be captured by the Tatars, who will take you to the Khan of the Golden Horde; and we will not help you." He gave up Kopor'e and fled beyond the sea. The Novgorodians did not take him prisoner and allowed him to go, but they forcibly captured two of his daughters and his boiars, with their wives and children, saying, "These we will hold as hostages until all your boiars and

91. Apparently, to Khan Tuda Mangu.

squires leave Kopor'e; and then we will release them." And so   **1281**
they separated on the first day of the month of January.

The Tatars scattered about the entire land, seeking Grand Prince Dmitrii Aleksandrovich, and ravaged everything around Murom, Vladimir, Iur'ev, Suzdal', Pereiaslavl', Rostov, Tver', and up to Torzhok and even farther, close to Novgorod. They tried to catch up with Grand Prince Dmitrii Aleksandrovich but were unable to do so, and returned home. In the meantime Grand Prince Andrei Aleksandrovich, grandson of Iaroslav, great grandson of Vsevolod, gr. gr. grandson of Iurii Dolgorukii, entered the city of Vladimir and ascended to the throne of the Grand Principality. He offered a great banquet and gave many gifts to the lords of the Horde, Kav Gadeh, Al Chedai and other Tatars; and he let them return to the Golden Horde, to the Khan. Thus, with many captives, they went to the Horde.

The same year Prince Dmitrii Aleksandrovich came from beyond the sea to Pereiaslavl'. At that time in Kopor'e there were still his boiars and squires, and his treasury and all his property. His son-in-law, Prince Dovmont of Pskov, came from Pskov and took over in Kopor'e all the treasury of his father-in-law, as well as his boiars and his squires, and led them from Kopor'e and sent to his father-in-law, Grand Prince Dmitrii Aleksandrovich. He went further and took the city of Ladoga because there were many men there of Grand Prince Dmitrii Aleksandrovich. He also took them from thence, also sending them to his father-in-law, Grand Prince Dmitrii Aleksandrovich.

In the meantime the Novgorodians marched toward Kopor'e, destroyed the fortifications, and sent envoys to Vladimir, to Prince Andrei Aleksandrovich, asking him to come to Novgorod. He went to them in Novgorod, became prince there, and the Novgorodians rendered him great honor. Grand Prince Dmitrii Aleksandrovich went to the city of Pereiaslavl', where he began to assemble an army, and he fortified the city. Numerous men began to gather there from everywhere. The same year a messenger came from Novgorod to Prince Andrei Aleksandrovich saying, "Your senior brother, Grand Prince Dmitrii Aleksandrovich, has settled in the city of Pereiaslavl'. He is gathering a huge army and many men are coming to him from all parts." And so he gathered the Novgorodian levy and made an agreement with them concerning everything.

1282   *In the year 6790/1282.* Prince Andrei Aleksandrovich marched from Novgorod to Vladimir, taking with him many Novgorodians, posadnik Semion Mikhailovich and another posadnik, Iakov Dmitrievich, with all military arms. He feared his senior brother, Grand Prince Dmitrii Aleksandrovich, who was in Pereiaslavl' with strong forces, summoning an army from all parts. Prince Andrei Aleksandrovich arrived in Vladimir, honored the Novgorodians and let them return, commanding them to guard Torzhok and Novgorod. Posadnik Semion Mikhailovich and Iakov Dmitrievich guarded Torzhok, not allowing the namestniks of Grand Prince Dmitrii Aleksandrovich to enter Torzhok. Prince Andrei Aleksandrovich marched from Vladimir to Gorodets and from thence he went to the Golden Horde, to the Khan.

The same year Prince Andrei Aleksandrovich journeyed to the Golden Horde to the Khan [Tuda-Mangu] with his advisor and consort, Semion Tonil'evich and with many other consorts. He was received by the Khan with honor. Prince Andrei, with his consorts, told the Khan and all present his own truth concerning his senior brother, making his brother responsible for all the fault. "He does not want to obey you, Khan; nor does he want to pay you his tribute." And so, for the second time he aroused the Khan's wrath against his senior brother.

The same year there was a portent in the sky.

The same year Grand Prince of Tver', Sviatoslav Iaroslavich, grandson of Iaroslav, great grandson of Vsevolod, gr. gr. grandson of Iurii Dolgorukii, together with the levies of Tver', as well as Grand Prince of Moscow Danilo Aleksandrovich, grandson of Iaroslav, great grandson of Vsevolod, gr. gr. grandson of Iurii Dolgorukii, with the levies of Moscow, and also with the posadniks of Novgorod and the levy of Novgorod, marched toward Pereiaslavl' to fight against Grand Prince Dmitrii Aleksandrovich. When the latter learned this he looked toward Heaven, sighed, shed tears and said, "Lord! See this injustice: I have offended none of them, nor do I intend to do them any injustice. Why do they rise up against me? Why do they chase me unceasingly, seeking to take my soul from me? And they want to destroy my druzhina, and even to annihilate all memory of me. My Lord God! Help me and save me." And so he wept greatly, mounted his horse and marched against them with his warriors toward the city of Dmitrov. Not reaching Dmitrov, he camped thereby for five days, and so they negotiated, whereupon, having made peace, **1282** they went back.

The same year Prince Andrei Aleksandrovich was sent a large army from the Khan, under Tura-Temir and Alyn, with many Tatars from the Golden Horde; and with them he marched against his senior brother, and Grand Prince Dmitrii Aleksandrovich, grandson of Iaroslav; and they caused the Christians much harm. But Grand Prince Dmitrii Aleksandrovich with his druzhina, princes, children and entire court fled to the horde of Khan Nagai, to whom he told everything in order, relating it with tears, and gave him and his nobles many gifts. Khan Nagai listened to him and kept him in honor.[92]

The same year the Tatars campaigned against Lithuania and then returned to the Horde with a large number of captives.

In the year 6791/1283. A Greek named Maxim was consecrated Metropolitan of Kiev and all Russia by the Patriarch of Constantinople.

The same year the Saracens besieged Constantinople with a strong army, ravaged many regions and returned with a great number of captives.

The same year His Holiness Maxim, Metropolitan of Kiev and all Russia, who was Greek by birth, came from Byzantium, from Constantinople.

The same year the Lithuanians fought against the Germans and they returned with many captives.[93]

The same year Grand Prince Dmitrii Aleksandrovich came from the Horde, from the Khan [Nagai] and made peace with his brother, Prince Andrei Aleksandrovich of Gorodets.[94]

---

92. Nagai or Nogai (1230?-1300), great great grandson of Genghis Khan (Dzhuchi line). An army commander in the Golden Horde. After the death of Batu's son and heir, Berke (1255-1266), Nagai became virtually an independent ruler of the territory between the Danube and Don rivers and manipulated the khans of the Golden Horde. With his help Tokhta (1291-1312) overthrew Khan Tele Buga and himself became Khan. In 1300, however, Tokhta fought and killed Nagai. Nasonov, A. N., *Mongoly i Rus'*, Moscow-Leningrad, 1940.

93. By "Germans" is meant the German Orders of Teutonian and Livonian Knights.

94. Apparently, Grand Prince Dmitrii skillfully used the rivalry between Nagai and Tele Buga, and received the *iarlyk* (a patent for ruling) from the former.

1283   The same year His Holiness Maxim, Metropolitan of Kiev and all Russia, visited the Khan of the Golden Horde and the same year he returned to Russia from the Horde.

The same year Grand Prince Dmitrii Aleksandrovich of Vladimir, grandson of Iaroslav, sent two of his boiars, Antonii and Feofan, to Kostroma stealthily to seize Semion Tonil'evich in order to investigate him in detail concerning everything, and then to kill him. They went, carried out his order, arrested Semion Tonil'evich in Kostroma, then interrogated him in all details. Semion told them, "You interrogate me in vain because I served my lord, Prince Andrei Aleksandrovich, faithfully and honestly; and if between the brothers there was any discord, offense or disagreement, they, themselves, are aware of that; I only know that I had to serve my lord with all my heart!" Antonii and Feofan told him, "You incited the Khan of the Golden Horde and you brought Tatars to fight our lord, Grand Prince Dmitrii Aleksandrovich!" But Semion Tonil'evich replied, "I know nothing of this. If you want, verily, to learn of it, ask my lord, Prince Andrei Aleksandrovich." Antonii and Feofan told him, "Since you did not want to tell our lord anything about what your lord plotted, is plotting and intends to plot, we must kill you." But Semion said, "Your advice is vain because your lord agreed with my lord on peace and concord, and they confirmed their agreement with a pledge on the cross. How can it be peace and concord on the side of your lord, and your side, if you want to kill his boiar? Verily, your deed is a vain one." And so, on the order of Grand Prince Dmitrii Aleksandrovich, Semion Tonil'evich was killed in Kostroma.

The same year Prince Andrei Aleksandrovich of Gorodets began to dissent from his brother, Grand Prince Dmitrii Aleksandrovich of Vladimir, because little by little he learned from the people that his boiar, Semion Tonil'evich, had been killed on the latter's order. Prince Andrei Aleksandrovich of Gorodets was greatly saddened by his death and so there arose new quarrels and dissension and still worse enmity between them.

The same year there was an awesome portent in the sky.

The same year there were great thunderstorms, lightning and winds with fearful tornadoes.

In the year 6792/1284. All the bishops of Russia were summoned to Kiev to Maxim, Metropolitan of Kiev and all Russia.

The same year there was a portent in the sky and the sun disappeared.

ABOUT EVENTS IN THE PRINCIPALITY OF KURSK   **1284**

The same year there occurred great misfortune in the Grand Principality of Kursk. There was the custom among the khans of the Horde that the khans and their nobles levy tribute from the entire Russian land. Sometimes some Russian princes would farm out the tax collection and then the princes, themselves, would collect the taxes and take them to the Horde; but sometimes the Tatar merchants from the Horde, for their own benefit, would farm out the levy of taxes in the Russian principalities, and in this way would gain great benefits. There was at that time a Tatar noble named Ahmet, who was very evilly cunning, greedy and sly. He was the son of Temir and he was Baskak[95] for the principality of Kursk. There were several Tatar Baskaks in the other cities of the Russian land, and they were very powerful. This Baskak Ahmet would farm out from the Tatars the collection of all districts in the principality of Kursk, and through the collection in these districts he caused many hardships for the princes and common people of the principality of Kursk. But this was not all, for, besides that, he built two large settlements in the principality of Oleg, Prince of Ryl'sk and Vorgola, and Prince Sviatoslav of Lipetsk. He brought many people from all parts to these settlements, and they could have from him whatever they wanted. In this way the population of these settlements grew rapidly, and there were markets there and all manner of craftsmen, so that these two settlements were like big cities. People from them would go around and cause great violence and offense in the principality of Kursk, and they ravaged everything around Vorgola, Ryl'sk and Lipetsk. Prince Oleg of Ryl'sk and Prince Sviatoslav of Lipetsk were kin and were sometimes amicable, other times would quarrel and fight. Sometimes they would rob the settlement of this Ahmet, Baskak of the Kursk principality. There were complaints about them from Ahmet and, finally, they were reconciled with Ahmet; but the Khan of the Horde did not know it. When the population of this settlement grew very large and there was more and more violence from them in the lands of Oleg and Sviatoslav, then Oleg and Sviatoslav began to discuss it, and they held many councils about this. After receiving the advice and support of his kin, Prince Sviatopolk of Lipetsk, Prince Oleg of Ryl'sk and Vorgola

95. "Baskak": Tatar tax collector. About Nagai, see Fn. 92.

1284   went to the Golden Horde, to his Khan Tele Buga, with a complaint [about Ahmet and Khan Nagai].

Khan Tele Buga [Nagai's rival] gave Prince Oleg his bailiffs to destroy the settlements [of Ahmet] and return the people from thence to Prince Oleg's land. When Prince Oleg of Ryl'sk and Vorgola was still with the Khan in the golden Horde, his kin Prince Sviatoslav of Lipetsk, marched with troops against these settlements of Ahmet's, robbed them and then went to the Horde to his kin, Oleg, to Khan Tele Buga, with a complaint about Baskak Ahmet. The Khan gave them his bailiffs and sent them back to their patrimonies in Russia. When Prince Oleg and his kin, Sviatoslav, came with the Tatars they ordered their people to rob both these settlements; and some of the people there were killed, some were captured, and others were put in irons; and their own people were brought back to their patrimonies.

At that time Baskak Ahmet was in Khan Nagai's other horde. Learning that his settlements in Russia had been ravaged by Oleg, Prince of Ryl'sk and Vorgola, and by his kin, Prince Sviatoslav of Lipetsk, he became greatly upset and went to Khan Nagai to calumniate Prince Oleg. He said, "Prince Oleg and his kin, Sviatoslav of Lipetsk, are princes in name only; as a matter of fact, however, they are mere robbers and they, my Khan, are your enemies. They are preparing war. If you, my Khan, do not trust me and want, verily, to know what is really occurring, then send your falconer to the principality of Oleg, where there are many hunting places with swans, so that they catch some swans for you and also obtain information about Prince Oleg, and catch him. These falconers should invite Prince Oleg to you. If Oleg accedes to your will, than I am a liar and Oleg is right."

Khan [Nagai] sent his falconers to carry this out and thereafter they summoned Prince Oleg to him; but Oleg did not go to Khan Nagai of the Horde because he was afraid: although he had not robbed these settlements, his people and his kin, Prince Sviatoslav of Lipetsk—without seeking Oleg's advice—had robbed them; they had gone at night to these settlements and had ravaged them. Therefore Oleg was afraid and pondered what to do because people called them robbers; and between Oleg and his kin, Sviatoslav, there was great discord. The Khan's falconers heard of all this, caught the swans and returned to the Horde to Khan Nagai, summoning Oleg to Nagai; but Oleg would not come.

They told all this to Khan Nagai, adding, "Your Baskak Ahmet   **1284**
was right: Princes Oleg and Sviatoslav are robbers and do not obey
you. We caught swans in the swan-hunting places but Oleg did not
heed your summons and offended us, and does not want to come
to you. You should realize that Oleg is prepared to fight you."

Khan Nagai became very angry and summoned Ahmet,
Baskak of Kursk, telling him, "Prince Oleg is guilty before you
and he wants to fight me; therefore I am sending my troops against
him and you should accompany them." He summoned his noble,
Temir, with his Tatars, and told him, "Go with these Tatars against
Prince Oleg, devastate his principality, and turn over his boiars
to Baskak Ahmet that he may do what he wants with them; then
bring Prince Oleg, himself, to me." The Tatars came campaign-
ing to the city of Vorgola on the thirteenth day of the month of
January after Epiphany. It was a very severe winter and very cold.
When Prince Oleg heard of this he escaped to the Golden Horde
[of Khan Tele Buga] with his wife and children, while his relative,
Prince Sviatoslav of Lipetsk, fled into the forests of Voronezh. The
Tatars chased Prince Oleg but could not catch him. Other Tatars
chased Prince Sviatoslav but likewise could not catch him, while
Oleg's boiars fled after him.

When the Tatars who pursued Oleg returned they captured
Oleg's boiars, thirteen senior boiars. They occupied all of Oleg's
and Sviatoslav's principalities, remaining there twenty days and
devastating the entire principalities; and thus the settlements
[of Ahmet's] became crowded with people, with all manner of
cattle and with all the wealth of Vorgola, Ryl'sk and Lipetsk. There
they camped and ordered that Oleg's boiars be brought to them:
these boiars were put in German irons by pairs. At that time there
happened to be in that land important merchants from Germany
and Constantinople, and they, also, were brought and put into
the German irons. When they [the Tatars] learned that they were
merchants they ordered that they be released from the irons and
that all their merchandise be restored to them and that they not be
harmed in any way. And they told them, "You are merchants and
do business here. You travel through all lands and you may tell
everywhere that whosoever undertakes a quarrel with his baskak
will suffer the same fate as those princes." They turned over Oleg's
senior boiars to Baskak Ahmet, saying, "Such were the words of
the Khan: you may do with them whatever you want." And they

1284   returned to the Horde to their Khan Nagai, with many captives and wealth, devastating the entire land. Baskak Ahmet killed and hanged on trees the boiars who were turned over to him, and went with them [the Tatars] to the Horde. In his two settlements he left his two brothers and Tatars with them; there were also many Russians serving him. He ordered them [his brothers] to guard the settlements, but he did not dare to remain in Russia because he had not caught any of the princes. He established a tribute, and so taxes and revenues were levied. All this occurred because of our sins, because of the princes' injustice, because they lived in injustice and dissension. And I have still to write concerning it; but let us leave off here because it is too long, and the end of the story will be finished in the next year.

In the year 6793/1285. There was a portent in the sky.

The same year [6792/1284 in *Laur.*] Baskak Ahmet came to the Horde to Khan Nagai, leaving his two brothers in his two settlements in order to guard those settlements. One of these brothers marched from one settlement to the other and thirty-five Russian people serving with them marched along with them. Prince Sviatoslav of Lipetsk received tidings of this and he decided with his boiars and with his druzhina, without seeking Oleg's counsel, to seize them on their way. When they marched unguarded he attacked them with his druzhina and killed twenty and five Russian people and two Tatars; but both of Baskak Ahmet's brothers escaped to the settlement, and so the people of the settlement were gathered and they fought with Prince Sviatoslav. Many were killed on both sides. Prince Sviatoslav did this without Oleg's knowledge and he intended to do something worthy; but, as a matter of fact, he caused great damage to himself and to Oleg. And not only did he do this, but he did not want to repent it because humility destroys all the devil's intrigues and plots. And so great enmity arose.

The same year [6792/1284 in *Laur.*] after Easter, during St. Thomas' Sunday, the two brothers of Ahmet, Baskak of Kursk, as well as people from the settlement, escaped to Kursk. On the morrow, Monday, the other people of the settlement also fled, and many rumors and great hatred developed. Prince Sviatoslav of Lipetsk, however, did not become humble because he did not care for all this. He was not afraid because he believed that no one could defeat him. Baskak Ahmet sent him an envoy from the Horde in order to be reconciled with him, but he killed that envoy.

The same year [6792/1284 in *Laur.*] Prince Oleg of Ryl'sk   **1285**
and Vorgola came from the Golden Horde, from Khan Tele Buga.
He commanded that a memorial service be celebrated for his
slain boiars, as well as for all those who had been killed. Then he
sent envoys to his kin, Prince Sviatoslav of Lipetsk, asking, "Why
brother, did you cause all this? You turned your and my justice
into injustice; you won for me and for yourself the reputation of
robbers. Till now, you have committed much brigandage and last
winter you destroyed the Baskak's settlements; even now, during
their journey, you have defeated his brothers and robbed his
settlements. You, yourself, brother, know what the Tatars' customs are; but we are Christians, and for us injustice and robbery
are not right. All these deeds are repulsive and hateful, and everyone will receive revenge from God for such deeds, in this age and
in the future. Repent, my brother, and live according to Christian
law. Go to the Horde and try to console and win Khan Nagai and
his nobles."

But Prince Sviatoslav of Lipetsk answered, "Why do you worry?
Why do you concern yourself with my affairs? I am responsible
for myself, and I will do whatever I wish. Although I robbed the
Baskak's settlements, I was right because I did not hurt a human
being, but a beast. And, especially, I took revenge against our
enemies, the infidel pagan Tatars. Why should God and the
people reproach me for this, that I have killed pagan bloodletters?"

Prince Oleg of Ryl'sk and Vorgola said, "I have an agreement
with you that we should act in unanimity and that we should hold
counsel with each other—I with you and you with me. And you
forgot this, your pledge on the cross, and considered it as nought.
Now the Tatars have come to us, waging war, and I had to escape
to the Golden Horde, to the Khan, but you did not go [for the
second time] to the Golden Horde with me; you remained in
the Russian land; you stayed with all these boiars in the Voronezh
forest in order to rob. Thus you did, and you robbed greatly,
causing much harm and misfortune to me and to yourself; and
so you destroyed my principality and yours, to the end. If you
had accompanied me to the Golden Horde, perhaps with divine
aid we could have won support from the Khan of the Golden
Horde; but you turned to brigandage, you committed all manner
of unbelievable injustice, and even now you remain in your principality considering that you have committed no sin. You believe
that you can do everything, but you can do nothing. Now you

1285   go neither to your Khan Tele Buga nor to Khan Nagai in order to justify yourself, and so one misfortune is added to another, one trouble to another. I wonder how God will judge me and you?"

After a certain time Prince Oleg went to Khan [Tele Buga] in the Golden Horde. He returned with Tatars from the Golden Horde and, following the Khan's order, he killed his kin, Prince Sviatoslav of Lipetsk. Prince Aleksandr ascended to the principality of Lipetsk after his brother, Sviatoslav. He wept greatly and shed tears over his brother, Prince Sviatoslav, who was killed by Oleg, Prince of Ryl'sk and Vorgola. He could not suffer this and he went to the Horde, to the Khan, with many gifts, and he received an army from him. When he came with Tatars he killed Prince Oleg of Ryl'sk and Vorgola, and his two sons, Davyd and Semion. This story is lengthy but important, and numerous details have been omitted because of its length; but it may be that even this short story may result in weeping and tears by some person who has a good mind.

The same year [6792/1284 in *Novg. III.*] Prince Andrei Aleksandrovich of Gorodets, grandson of Iaroslav, great grandson of Vsevolod, gr. gr. grandson of Iurii Dolgorukii, made an agreement with the Novgorodians, and he pledged on the cross that they would never give up Novgorod; and the Novgorodians also pledged to him they would never look for another prince; and this agreement was made in Torzhok. The same year [6792/1284 in *Novg. III.*], however, Grand Prince Dmitrii Aleksandrovich, grandson of Iaroslav, assembled large forces and campaigned against his junior brother, Prince Andrei Aleksandrovich of Gorodets. The latter took fright and the Novgorodians also gave him up. And so he [Prince Dmitrii] marched with Tatars toward Novgorod and did much harm in their land. The Novgorodians petitioned him, and Grand Prince Dmitrii Aleksandrovich became their prince.

The same year His Holiness Maxim, Metropolitan of Kiev and all Russia, according to his custom travelled the entire Russian land instructing, punishing and administering. So he came to Novgorod, where he was met by Grand Prince Dmitrii Aleksandrovich with great honor. Then he went to Pskov, where he was also rendered great honor.

The same year Prince Andrei Aleksandrovich of Gorodets brought the khan's son from the Golden Horde against his senior

brother, Grand Prince Dmitrii Aleksandrovich. While the Tatars   **1285**
were raiding here and there, Grand Prince Dmitrii Aleksandrovich
gathered large troops, marched against them, and the khan's son
escaped to the Horde while Grand Prince Dmitrii Aleksandrovich
captured the boiars of his brother, Andrei.

In the year 6794/1286. Grand Prince Roman of Briansk campaigned against Smolensk. He burned the suburb, attacked the
city, devastated the district and the towns, and went back.

The same year [6793/1285 in *Laur.*] with the blessing of
Simon, Bishop of Tver', Grand Prince Mikhail Iaroslavich of
Tver', grandson of Iaroslav, great grandson of Vsevolod, gr. gr.
grandson of Iurii Dolgorukii, with his mother, Grand Princess
Oksinia, rebuilt the cathedral church which was previously dedicated to Cosma and Damian; and they dedicated it to the transfiguration of the Holy Saviour, and they built it of stone.

The same year [6793/1285 in *Laur.*] the Lithuanians fought
against Aleshki and other estates of the Bishop of Tver'; but the
people of Tver' assembled with the people of Moscow, Volokh,
Novyi Torg, Dmitrov, Zubtsev and Rzhev and they defeated them
and chased them away. They recaptured the [the Russian] captives
[taken by the Lithuanians] and captured their Prince Dovmont.

The same year Prince Ivan Dmitrievich of Pereiaslavl' [Zal-
eskii], grandson of Aleksandr, gr. grandson of Iaroslav, gr. gr.
grandson of Vsevolod, gr. gr. gr. grandson of Iurii Dolgorukii,
married the daughter of Prince Dmitrii Borisovich of Rostov,
grandson of Vasil'ko.

In the year 6795/1287. [6794/1286 in *Laur.*] The princes of
Rostov, Dmitrii Borisovich, grandson of Vasil'ko, and his brother,
Konstantin Borisovich, divided their patrimony. The senior
brother, Prince Dmitrii Borisovich, remained in Rostov; his junior
brother, Prince Konstantin Borisovich, settled in Uglich Pol'e,
while their cousin, Prince Mikhail Glebovich, grandson of Vasil'ko,
settled in Belozero. The same year [6794/1296 in *Laur.*] a son,
Aleksandr, was born to Prince Dmitrii Borisovich of Rostov. The
same year [6794/1296 in *Laur.*] a son, Mikhail, was born to Grand
Prince Konstantin Borisovich of Uglich [Pol'e].

The same year [6794/1286 in *Laur.*] Theodore, Bishop of
Vladimir, Suzdal' and Nizhnii Novgorod passed away.

The same year Grand Prince Dmitrii Aleksandrovich, grandson of Iaroslav, waged war against Tver'; but the Grand Prince of

1287   Tver', Mikhail Iaroslavich, grandson of Iaroslav, gr. grandson of Vsevolod, marched to meet him with his troops and so they both came to Kashin; and negotiating there, they were reconciled.

The same year Simon, Bishop of Tver', consecrated the wooden church of St. Saviour in Tver'. It was inside a stone one which was larger but not completed, and he celebrated church services there while the masters continued to work on the stone church of St. Saviour.

The same year the foundation of the church of Holy Martyrs Boris and Gleb was laid in Rostov with the blessing of Ignatius, Bishop of Rostov.

In the year 6796/1288. His Holiness Maxim, Metropolitan of Kiev and all Russia, consecrated in the cathedral of Holy Sophia in Kiev a certain Iakob to be bishop of Vladimir, Suzdal' and Nizhnii Novgorod.

The same year wonderworker Ignatius, Bishop of Rostov, passed away.

The same year on the fourteenth day of the month of June the church of St. Michael in Rostov burned, having been struck by lightning.

The same year Blessed Simon, Bishop of Tver', passed away. He was very virtuous, a good preacher and mighty in the books of Divine Scripture. He feared no prince but ruled, verily, accord- to the words of Christ; he did not quarrel with anyone; he interdicted all those who caused injustice; he was honest, greatly wise and he greatly respected the clergy, monks, the poor, the orphaned and widows. He interceded for the offended, spared the injured and was dreaded by all those who committed injustice. Everyone feared him and trembled. On the third day of the month of February, when Holy Simon, the Receiver of the Saviour, and Anne, the Prophetess, are remembered, his sacred and blessed body was buried on the right side of the church of St. Saviour.

The same year lord Elortai of the Golden Horde, son of Temir, waged war against Riazan'. He devastated Riazan', Murom, and the land of the Mordva. He caused much harm and returned home.

The same year Grand Prince Dmitrii Aleksandrovich, grandson of Iaroslav, gr. grandson of Vsevolod, gr. gr. grandson of Iurii Dolgorukii, started to fight with Grand Prince Mikhail Iaroslavich of Tver', grandson of Iaroslav, gr. grandson of Vsevolod, gr. gr. grandson of Iurii Dolgorukii; Prince Mikhail of Tver' began to gather troops, while Grand Prince Dmitrii of Vladimir **1288** also began to assemble his army, and with him were his brothers and his kin: Prince Andrei Aleksandrovich of Gorodets and Grand Prince Daniel Aleksandrovich of Moscow. And together with them was Prince Dmitrii Borisovich of Rostov, grandson of Vasil'ko, gr. grandson of Konstantin. They marched [6797/1289 in *Novg. IV*] toward Kashin, camping near Kashin for nine days, devastating everything and burning Kosniatin. From thence they intended to march toward Tver' but Grand Prince Mikhail marched against them with his army, and so they negotiated, were reconciled and went home.

In the year 6797/1289. [6798/1290 in *Vozn.*] His Holiness Maxim, Metropolitan of Kiev and all Russia, in the cathedral church of Holy Sophia in Kiev, consecrated Tarasius, abbot of the monastery of St. John the Theologian, to be bishop of Rostov.

The same year Grand Prince Mikhail Iaroslavich of Tver', grandson of Iaroslav, together with his mother, Grand Princess Oksin'ia, sent abbot Andrew of the monastery of the Most Pure Theotokos, to Kiev, to Maxim, Metropolitan of Kiev and all Russia; and there [6798/1290 in *Novg. IV.*] he was consecrated Bishop of Tver'. This one was a Lithuanian by birth, the son of Prince Erden' of Lithuania.[96]

The same year Prince Dmitrii Borisovich of Rostov, grandson of Vasil'ko, gr. grandson of Konstantin, gr. gr. grandson of Vsevolod, gr. gr. gr. grandson of Iurii Dolgorukii, and his brother, Prince Konstantin Borisovich of Uglich, went to the Golden Horde to the khan, with their wives; and the khan entertained them with honor.

The same year the Tatars campaigned against Lithuania and returned to the Horde with many captives.

The same year the khan of the Golden Horde released with honor Prince Dmitrii Borisovich of Rostov and his brother, Prince Konstantin Borisovich of Uglich.

In the year 6798/1290. The cathedral diocesan church of the Holy Saviour was consecrated by Andrew, Bishop of Tver'. This bishop was Lithuanian by birth, son of the Lithuanian Prince Erden'.[97]

96. "Gerden'," in earlier entries.
97. "Gerden'," in earlier entries.

1290   The same year a son, Ivan, was born to Grand Prince Dmitrii Aleksandrovich of Vladimir.

The same year Prince Dmitrii Borisovich of Rostov marched toward Tver' with the Novgorodians, who were under the Novgorodian voevoda, posadnik Andrei; but the people of Tver' and of Novgorod made peace, and Prince Dmitrii Borisovich of Rostov, with his levies of Rostov, marched to Kashin. And then they became reconciled and went home.

The same year posadnik Samoila Rodionovich was killed in Novgorod. The Novgorodians assembled in armour, stormed the Prussians' street and robbed and burned their houses.

The same year there was tumult among the Tatars, but it was quiet in Russia.

In the year 6799/1291. The daughter of Grand Prince Iaroslav Iaroslavich of Tver', who was a virgin, was shorn to holy, angelic, monastic orders in a nunnery.

The same year there was a portent on the moon. First, it was red as blood, and then it darkened.

The same year [6798/1290 in *Laur.*] there was tumult in the Horde between Khan Tokhta, who fought Tele Buga, and Sool-gui; and Tokhta overcame them.

The same year Khan Nagai killed Khans Tele Buga and Sool-gui.

The same year a son, Basil, was born to Grand Prince Konstantin Borisovich of Rostov. The same year there was tumult among the Tatars: there were fighting and murders, but in Russia there was tranquility.

In the year 6800/1292. [6794/1282 in *Vozn.,*] Prince Ivan Dmitrievich of Pereiaslavl' [son of Grand Prince of Vladimir], grandson of Aleksandr, gr. grandson of Iaroslav, gr. gr. grandson of Vsevolod, gr. gr. gr. grandson of Iuri Dolgorukii, married the daughter of Prince Dmitrii Borisovich of Rostov, and the wedding took place in the church of the Holy Saviour in Pereiaslavl'.

The same year the cathedral church of St. Saviour in Tver' was adorned with frescoes.

The same year Aleksandr, son of Grand Prince Dmitrii— the latter was the son of Aleksandr Nevskii—died in the Horde.

The same year there were horrifying portents in the skies: at night there were in the sky appearances like military troops, at noon; and so it also appeared at midnight.

In the year 6801/1293. Russian princes went to the Horde to complain about grand Prince Dmitrii Aleksandrovich of Vladimir, grandson of Iaroslav, gr. grandson of Vsevolod. [They were] his junior brother, Prince Andrei Aleksandrovich of Gorodets; Prince Dmitrii Borisovich of Rostov; his brother, Prince Konstantin Borisovich of Uglich; their cousin, Prince Mikhail Glebovich of Gorodets;[98] Prince Fedor Rostislavich of Iaroslavl' and Smolensk, who was father-in-law of Prince Mikhail Glebovich of Belozero; Prince Ivan Dmitrievich of Rostov;[99] and Bishop Tarasius of Rostov. The Khan listened to their complaint and wanted to send to Russia for Grand Prince Dmitrii Aleksandrovich of Vladimir; but then he changed his mind and sent them his brother, Tudan[100] with a multitude of warriors. And so they marched from the Horde with the Tatars against their senior brother, Grand Prince Dmitrii Aleksandrovich, son of Iaroslav: these were his junior brother, Andrei Aleksandrovich, grandson of Iaroslav; Prince Fedor Rostislavich of Iaroslavl', grandson of Mstislav, gr. grandson of Davyd, gr. gr. grandson of Rostislav, gr. gr. gr. grandson of Mstislav and gr. gr. gr. gr. grandson of Vladimir Monomakh. And with them there were other princes. At that time Grand Prince Dmitrii Aleksandrovich was in Pereiaslavl'. When the people of Pereiaslavl' learned of it they all fled, and even Grand Prince Dmitrii Aleksandrovich with his druzhina fled to Volok, and from there to Pskov; and so tumult spread over the entire land of Suzdal'. The Tatar army, which arrived with Prince Andrei Aleksandrovich of Gorodets and Prince Fedor Rostislavich of Iaroslavl', took Vladimir and robbed the [cathedral] church of Vladimir. They even tore out its marvelous copper floor, stole the sacred vessels, and occupied Suzdal', Iur'ev, Pereiaslavl', Dmitrov, Moscow, Kolomna, Mozhaisk, Volok and Uglich Pol'e. Altogether, they captured fourteen cities and devastated the entire land. Thanks to the intercession of God, they did not reach Tver', although a great multitude of refugees gathered in Tver'. They all held council, how to fight the Tatars.

98. This is probably an error and should be Prince Mikhail Glebovich of Belozero, and not Gorodets, as it is mentioned earlier and subsequently; in *Nik.*, it reads Mikhail Glebovich, prince of Gorodets.

99. Son of Dmitrii Borisovich.

100. "Duden'," in the Russian chronicles.

1293   [In the year 6802/1294 in *Laur.*] Grand Prince Mikhail Iaroslavich of Tver', who at that time was journeying from the Khan
of the Golden Horde, knew nothing of this. He passed by Moscow
through the Tatar lines, and then a certain person told him about
this misfortune and guided him along a quiet route. So he attained his grand principality of Tver' in good health, thanks to
the grace of God and the Most Pure Theotokos.

Grand Prince Dmitrii Aleksandrovich with his druzhina
fled to Pskov. The Tatars wanted to march to Novgorod and to
Pskov but the Novgorodians sent their envoys to Khan Duden'
and to all the Tatars. These envoys were Semion Klementich
and Ivan Mikhailovich,[1] and they had a multitude of gifts to beseech the Tatars not to wage war and not to devastate the land.
The latter accepted the numberless multitude of gifts, retreated
to the prairie, to their land, and returned to the Horde.

The same year [6802/1294 in *Laur.*] Prince Fedor Rostislavich of Iaroslavl' became prince of Pereiaslavl', while Prince
Andrei Aleksandrovich of Gorodets became prince of Novgorod.

The same year Takhtamir, son of the Khan, marched from
the Horde to Tver' and caused the people many difficulties.
[6802/1294 in *Laur.*]

In the year 6802/1294. Khan Tokhta became the khan of the
Golden Horde, and he defeated Khan Nagai of the latter horde.[2]

The same year [6801/1293 in *Laur.*] Prince Andrei Aleksandrovich came with Novgorodians from Novgorod to Torzhok
with the intention of cutting off the retreat of his senior brother,
Grand Prince Dmitrii Aleksandrovich.

The same year Prince Fedor Romanovich of Riazan' passed
away.

[FEUDS IN THE LAND OF TVER']

The same year [6801/1293 in *Laur.*] Grand Prince Dmitrii
Aleksandrovich marched from Pskov to Tver', bypassing Torzhok.
His junior brother, Prince Andrei Aleksandrovich of Gorodets,
caught him at the ford but Grand Prince Dmitrii Aleksandrovich

---

1. In *Novg. Kom.*, only "Semion Klimovich."

2. Tokhta's headquarters were in Sarai, on the Volga, while Nagai
roamed near the Balkans, west of the Dnieper river.

succeeded in fording the river. His people did not manage to **1294** carry his treasury over the river, and so his brother, Prince Andrei Aleksandrovich, took all his treasury, captured all his possessions and chased after him with the Novgorodians. The latter escaped to Tver', from whence he sent him [Prince Andrei] Bishop Andrew of Tver', as well as Prince Sviatoslav, with a greeting. Prince Andrei Aleksandrovich obeyed Bishop Andrew and Prince Sviatoslav and returned to Torzhok; and he returned Volok to Novgorod.

Prince Ivan Dmitrievich became prince of Kostroma, while Prince Andrei Aleksandrovich marched from Torzhok to Gorodets and further to Niz.[3] In the meantime, Grand Prince Dmitrii Aleksandrovich went from Tver' to Volok, where he fell ill.

The same year [6803/1295 in *Laur.*] Prince Fedor Rostislavich of Iaroslavl' burned the entire city of Pereiaslavl'.[4]

The same year [6803/1295 in *Laur.*] Grand Prince Dmitrii Aleksandrovich, grandson of Iaroslav, gr. grandson of Vsevolod, gr. gr. grandson of Iurii Dolgorukii, gr. gr. gr. grandson of Vladimir Monomakh, gr. gr. gr. gr. grandson of Vsevolod, gr. gr. gr. gr. gr. grandson of Iaroslav, gr. gr. gr. gr. gr. grandson of Great Vladimir, was shorn to the holy, angelic orders and to the order of *schema*, and then he passed away. His body was taken to Pereiaslavl' and was buried in the church of St. Saviour, and this happened after eighteen years of his rule. His sons were *[Sic!]* Prince Ivan of Pereiaslavl'.

After him, his brother, Andrei Aleksandrovich, became grand prince of Vladimir.

The same year Prince Dmitrii Borisovich of Rostov, grandson of Vasil'ko, gr. grandson of Konstantin, gr. gr. grandson of Vsevolod [Great Nest], gr. gr. gr. grandson of Iurii Dolgorukii, gr. gr. gr. gr. grandson of Vladimir Monomakh, gr. gr. gr. gr. gr. grandson of Vsevolod, gr. gr. gr. gr. gr. gr. grandson of Iaroslav Vladimirich, passed away. After him, his brother, Prince Konstantin Borisovich of Uglich, became prince of Rostov. His son, Prince Aleksandr Konstantinovich, grandson of Boris, became prince of Uglich after him [6801/1293 in *Laur.*], while Prince

3. "Niz" was the Volga-Oka land.

4. Apparently, the people of Pereiaslavl' Zaleskii remained faithful to Grand Prince Dmitrii and were unwilling to accept Prince Fedor.

1294 Fedor Rostislavich, grandson of Mstislav, gr. grandson of Davyd, became prince of Iaroslavl'.[5]

The same year [6803/1295 in *Laur.*] Prince Mikhail Iaroslavich of Tver' married Anna, the daughter of Prince Dmitrii Borisovich of Rostov, and the wedding took place on the day of Holy Archangel Michael in the cathedral church of St. Saviour and was performed by Bishop Andrew of Tver'; and there was great rejoicing in Tver'.

The same year Grand Prince Andrei Aleksandrovich of Vladimir, grandson of Iaroslav, married the daughter of Prince Dmitrii Borisovich of Rostov, Vasilissa.[6]

The same year [6803/1295 in *Laur.*] Basil, Bishop of Riazan', passed away.

The same year [6801/1293 in *Novg. III.*] the Swedes came and built a fortress in the land of Karela.[7]

The same year [6801/1293 in *Novg. III.*] Grand Prince Andrei Aleksandrovich sent Prince Roman Glebovich with the Novgorodians and Iurii Mikhailovich and tysiatskii Andrei toward this Swedish fortress. They arrived there in the week of Praise [of the Most Holy Theotokos][8] and many Novgorodians were killed there by the people from the fortress. And also Ivan Klekovich,[9] a great, brave and glorious man, was shot from the city and many others were wounded. Thereafter, the great thaw came and people and horses were in dire need and barely able to reach home. Many were dead, and Ivan [Klekachevich] died from his wound.

In the year 6803/1295. Grand Prince Andrei Aleksandrovich went to the Golden Horde, to the Khan, with his princess.

The same year [6804/1296 in *Laur.*] all the city of Tver' burned.

5. Actually, Fedor was already prince of Iaroslavl'; see entry under 1277.

6. According to *Laur.* In *Nik.*, "married the daughter of Prince Vasil'ko of Rostov," incorrect.

7. The future city of Keksholm.

8. "Week of Praise:" the fifth week of Lent, when the Great Acathiste, Praise of the Theotokos, is sung during the night of Saturday. Roty, p. 9.

9. In *Novg.*, Ivan Klekachevich.

The same year [6804/1296 in *Laur.*] His Holiness Maxim, **1295**
Metropolitan of Kiev and all Russia, consecrated Simon bishop of
Vladimir, Suzdal' and Nizhnii Novgorod.

[FEUDS AMONG THE SUZDALIAN PRINCES]

In the year 6804/1296. [6807/1299 in *Novg. III.*[There was a
great disturbance among the Russian princes; but at that time there
came from the Horde, from Khan Tokhta,[10] his envoy, Nevrui; and there was a meeting of all Russian princes in Vladimir.
Each of them presented his complaint to the envoy. On one side
were Grand Prince Andrei Aleksandrovich of Vladimir; Fedor
Rostislavich Chernyi of Iaroslavl'; and Prince Konstantin Borisovich of Rostov. On the other side, against them, were Grand Prince
Danilo Aleksandrovich of Moscow, and Grand Prince Mikhail
Iaroslavich of Tver', grandson of Iaroslav; and, together with them,
were the people of Pereiaslval'. It nearly resulted in bloodshed,
but Bishop Simon of Vladimir, Suzdal' and Nizhnii Novgorod
reconciled them, and so they divided the principalities among
themselves, and each went to his own place.

The same year [6805/1297 in *Laur.*] Grand Prince Andrei
Aleksandrovich of Vladimir gathered a large army and wanted to
march against Pereiaslavl', Moscow and Tver', but Prince Mikhail
Iaroslavich of Tver' and Prince Danilo Aleksandrovich of Moscow
gathered a large army against him. They marched and camped
near the Iur'ev field, and so they did not let Grand Prince Andrei
Aleksandrovich march to Pereiaslavl'. At that time the prince
of Pereiaslavl', Ivan Dmitrievich, grandson of Aleksandr [Nevskii],
gr. grandson of Iaroslav,[11] gr. gr. grandson of Vsevolod, gr. gr.
gr. grandson of Iurii Dolgorukii, was in the Golden Horde. Set-
tng out for the Golden Horde, he asked them to guard his patrimony, Pereiaslavl'; and so [both sides] negotiated and were reconciled.

In the year 6805/1297. The church of St. Athanasius was built
in Tver' and was consecrated the same year.

The same year in the principality of Tver', on the Volga, a
fortress was built and named Zubtsov.

---

10. In *Nik.* the Khan is erroneously called "Aleksa."
11. Missing in *Nik.*

1297   The same year Prince Iurii Danilovich [of Moscow], grandson of Aleksandr, gr. grandson of Iaroslav, gr. gr. grandson of Vsevolod, married in Rostov.

In the year 6806/1298. The entrance hall burned under Grand Prince Mikhail Iaroslavich of Tver' and the entire estate of Prince Mikhail Iaroslavich burned. By the grace of God, Prince Mikhail, himself, awoke and, with his princess, jumped out of the window. Albeit the entrance hall was crowded with young princes, the boiars' sons and many guards, no one heard anything. Some of them escaped and the others burned. And so the treasury of the prince and all his possessions burned.

The same year Grand Prince Mikhail Iaroslavich of Tver' fell gravely ill.

The same year there was a great drought and the forests, swamps, marshes and fields burned. There was great need for everything, and many cattle died.

The same year [6807/1299 in *Laur.*] Grand Prince Fedor Rostislavich of Iaroslavl' gathered a large army and marched toward Smolensk against his grand nephew, Prince Aleksandr Glebovich, grandson of Rostislav, gr. grandson of Mstislav, gr. gr. grandson of Davyd, gr. gr. gr. grandson of Rostislav, gr. gr. gr. gr. grandson of Mstislav, gr. gr. gr. gr. gr. grandson of Vladimir Monomakh. He besieged the city, remained there a long time, fought fiercely and returned to Iaroslavl' without taking the city.

In the year 6807/1299. There was a portent in the sky. The sun was terrifyingly encircled.

The same year [7808/1300 in *Laur.*] Clement, Archbishop and lord of Novgorod, passed away and was buried in the chapel of the cathedral church of Holy Sophia.

[METROPOLITAN MAXIM LEAVES KIEV FOR VLADIMIR]

The same year [6808/1300 in *Laur.*] His Holiness Maxim, Metropolitan of Kiev and all Russia, unable to abide the violence of the Tatars in Kiev, left Kiev and the entire population of Kiev scattered. The Metropolitan went from Kiev to Briansk, and from Briansk he went to the Suzdalian land. He came hither with his clergy and with all his possessions, and he settled in Vladimir [becoming bishop of Vladimir], Suzdal' and Nizhnii Novgorod, and other lands which belonged to these cities. He sent Bishop Simon of Vladimir to Rostov and gave him the diocese of Rostov.

The same year the people of Novgorod with their prince,

Boris Andreevich, grandson of Aleksandr, nominated Theoktist, **1299** abbot of the monastery of the Annunciation, to be Archbishop [of Novgorod], provided that the Metropolitan give his blessing. They petitioned him and settled him in the Bishop's estate until they learned where Maxim, Metropolitan of Kiev and all Russia, would reside.

The same year [6808/1300 in *Laur.*] Grand Prince Fedor Chernyi of Iaroslavl', son of Grand Prince Rostislav of Smolensk, grandson of Mstislav, gr. grandson of Davyd, gr. gr. grandson of Rostislav, gr. gr. gr. grandson of Mstislav, gr. gr. gr. gr. grandson of Vladimir Monomakh, gr. gr. gr. gr. gr. grandson of Vsevolod, gr. gr. gr. gr. gr. gr. grandson of Iaroslav, gr. gr. gr. gr. gr. gr. gr. grandson of Great Vladimir, was shorn to the holy, angelic, monastic order and passed away in his holy angelic, monastic order and in the order of the *schema*, and was buried in the church of St. Saviour in Iaroslavl'. After him, there were many miracles and up to now there are many miracles and endless cures performed among all those who come to his grave with faith.

The same year Grand Prince Iaroslav Romanovich of Pronsk passed away.

The same year a son, Dmitrii, was born to Grand Prince Mikhail Iaroslavich of Tver', grandson of Iaroslav.

The same year [6806/1298 in *Novg. III.*] the Germans raided Pskov, burned the suburb, killed many people and besieged the city; but Dovmont, Prince of Pskov, made a sortie and there was an evil battle near the church of Holy Peter and Paul on the shore. And such a battle had never occurred near Pskov, and many people of Pskov were killed. Still, with the aid of God, the people of Pskov defeated and killed the Germans, and the others were trampled. Prince Dovmont of Pskov captured Vilnevich[12] and sent him to Vladimir, to Grand Prince Andrei Aleksandrovich of Vladimir.

The same year Khan Tokhta campaigned for the second time against Khan Nagai and defeated him.

In the year 6808/1300. [6807/1299 in *Novg. III.*] There was a great conflagration in Novgorod and there was a strong wind and a whirlwind. Many holy churches and people burned.

---

12. "Vilnevich" can either be a proper name or designate the people of Vilna.

1300   The same year the German Swedes[13] came in great force to the river Neva. They brought with them very clever craftsmen and a very ingenious battering ram which they got from the Pope of Rome; and they received very strong aid from the Pope. They built a fortress at the mouth of the river Okhta, which they called "Venets Zemli" ["Crown of the Land"]. They fortified it with unbelievably strong fortifications and left in it a commander named Osten' with a large number of special soldiers. Thereafter the commanders returned to their land with the clever craftsmen of the Pope and of the king.

The same year His Holiness Maxim, Metropolitan of Kiev and all Russia, came to Novgorod and to Pskov; with him were Simeon, Bishop of Rostov, and Andrew, Bishop of Tver', With the two bishops—Simeon of Rostov and Bishop Andrew of Tver'—they elevated Theoktist, abbot of the monastery of the Assumption, to archbishop of Novgorod and Pskov. This occurred on the day when Apostles Peter and Paul are remembered. And there was great rejoicing in Novgorod.

The same year in Novgorod they laid the foundation of the stone church of St. Michael in Mikhail Street.

In the year 6809/1301. There were strong winds, many storms and thunder, powerful whirlwinds and terrifying thunderstorms, and lightning, and tremendous rains, so that all the people trembled and became frightened. The clouds were so large that the moats and ravines became like abysses and the winds, with whirlwinds, tore down many churches and many houses to their foundations, ripped off roofs and even destroyed the floors of the great churches. There were so many such misfortunes that it is impossible to count them all.

[PRINCE DANILO OF MOSCOW GOES AGAINST RIAZAN']

The same year Prince Danilo Aleksandrovich of Moscow campaigned against Riazan' and they fought near the city of Pereiaslavl', and Grand Prince Danilo Aleksandrovich of Moscow was victorious and killed many boiars and men and cunningly

13. All Germanic-speaking people were called "German" by the Russians.

caught their prince, Konstantin Romanovich of Riazan'. It was a **1301** betrayal on the side of the boiars of Riazan'. He brought him to Moscow, kept him under arrest but cared for him and rendered him honor because he wanted to have an agreement confirmed by a pledge on the cross. Thereafter he let him go to his patrimony, the grand principality of Riazan'.

The same year [6808/1300 in *Laur.*] Prince Aleksandr Glebovich of Smolensk, grandson of Rostislav, gr. grandson of Mstislav, gr. gr. grandson of Davyd, gr. gr. gr. grandson of Rostislav, gr. gr. gr. gr. grandson of Mstislav, gr. gr. gr. gr. gr. grandson of Vladimir Monomakh, campaigned against Dorogobuzh. Besieging the city, he cut off the water supply and caused the people much misfortune. Prince Andrei of Viaz'ma marched against him toward Dorogobuzh and aided the people of Dorogobuzh. At that time the son of Prince Aleksandr Glebovich of Smolensk was killed at Dorogobuzh, while Prince Aleksandr Glebovich and his brother, Roman Glebovich, were wounded; and in their levy of Smolensk two hundred people were killed.

The same year [6810/1302 in *Laur.*] Grand Prince Andrei Aleksandrovich of Vladimir campaigned with the levies of Vladimir and Novgorod against the Germans [apparently, Swedes!], taking the German fortification of Venets on the river Neva. Burning it, he killed many men; and so, without God's help, all their clever constructions and fortifications were of no avail. As it says in Scripture, "When God does not want to protect a city, it is vain to try to guard it."

The same year [6808/1300 in *Novg.*] the city of Torzhok burned.

[THE GATHERING OF THE PRINCES]

The same year there was a gathering of all the princes in Dmitrov concerning a distribution of principalities, and there was much discussion. Grand Prince Andrei Aleksandrovich of Vladimir, Prince Mikhail Iaroslavich of Tver', grandson of Iaroslav, Grand Prince Danilo Aleksandrovich of Moscow, and Prince Ivan Dmitrievich of Pereiaslavl', grandson of Aleksandr, did not agree to peace in the spirit of Christian love between themselves, so they returned home.

1301   The same year a son, Aleksandr, was born to Prince Mikhail Iaroslavich of Tver', grandson of Iaroslav.

In the year 6810/1302. There was a violent storm and many misfortunes happened to the people. Houses were destroyed, forests were torn down, and people and cattle were killed. The same year there was a portent in the sky. In the west a star appeared having a tail directed down toward the south.

The same year the son of Prince Mikhail Iaroslavich of Tver' underwent the rites of manhood.

[PRINCE DANILO OF MOSCOW INHERITS PEREIASLAVL']

The same year [6811/1303 in *Laur.*] the Grand Prince of Pereiaslavl', Ivan Dmitrievich, grandson of Aleksandr [Nevskii], gr. grandson of Iaroslav, gr. gr. grandson of Vsevolod, gr. gr. gr. grandson of Iurii Dolgorukii, gr. gr. gr. gr. grandson of Vladimir Monomakh, gr. gr. gr. gr. gr. grandson of Vsevolod, gr. gr. gr. gr. gr. gr. grandson of Iaroslav Vladimirich [the Wise], died on the fifteenth day of the month of May. He did not have any children and he was quiet, humble, meek, full of love, and merciful, caring much for the divine churches and greatly respecting the clergy and monks. He loved to speak with them without end and he was a father toward paupers and pilgrims. He was so virtuous that people marvelled at his life. He blessed Grand Prince Danilo Aleksandrovich of Moscow, his uncle, to be prince, in his place, of his patrimony of Pereiaslavl'. This Danilo was the brother of Ivan's father, Grand Prince Dmitrii Aleksandrovich. Being the youngest of Dmitrii's brothers, he was loved by him more than anyone else; and so Grand Prince Danilo Aleksandrovich of Moscow became the prince of Pereiaslavl', where he settled, and assigned there his own namestnik. He cast out from thence his senior brother, Grand Prince Andrei Aleksandrovich of Vladimir.

The same year [6811/1303 in *Laur.*] Grand Prince Andrei Aleksandrovich of Vladimir [and Gorodets] went to the Golden Horde, to the Khan.

The same year [6811/1303 in *Laur.*] Prince Boris Andreevich, grandson of Aleksandr [Nevskii], passed away in Kostroma, on the twenty-fifth day of the month of February.

The same year in Novgorod the foundation was laid for a new Novgorodian stone fortification, called *Detinets.*

In the year 6811/1303. [6812/1304 in *Laur.*] Grand Prince of **1303**
Moscow, Danilo Aleksandrovich, grandson of Iaroslav, gr. grandson of Vsevolod, gr. gr. grandson of Iurii Dolgorukii, gr. gr. gr.
grandson of Vladimir Monomakh, gr. gr. gr. gr. grandson of
Vsevolod, gr. gr. gr. gr. gr. grandson of Iaroslav, gr. gr. gr. gr. gr.
gr. grandson of Great Vladimir, was shorn to holy, angelic orders
and to the *schema*, and passed away on the fourth day of the
month of March; he was buried in the church of St. Archangel
Michael in Moscow, his own patrimony. His children were Iurii,
Aleksandr, Boris, Ivan and Afanasii. After his passing, the people
of Pereiaslavl' wanted his son, Iurii for prince—and did not even
permit him to depart from Pereiaslavl' to go to his father's burial.

The same spring Prince Iurii Danilovich of Moscow, grandson of Aleksandr [Nevskii], gr. grandson of Iaroslav, gr. gr.
grandson of Vsevolod [Great Nest], and his brothers campaigned
against Mozhaisk. Taking it, he captured Prince Sviatoslav,
whom he brought to Moscow.

The same year Grand Prince Andrei Aleksandrovich of Vladimir, grandson of Iaroslav, returned from the Golden Horde,
from the Khan.

[BEGINNING OF THE STRUGGLE BETWEEN MOSCOW AND TVER']

In the year 6812/1304. Grand Prince Andrei Aleksandrovich
of [Vladimir and] Gorodets, grandson of Iaroslav, gr. grandson
of Vsevolod, gr. gr. grandson of Iurii Dolgorukii, gr. gr. gr.
grandson of Vladimir Monomakh, gr. gr. gr. gr. grandson of
Vsevolod, gr. gr. gr. gr. gr. grandson of Iaroslav, gr. gr. gr. gr. gr.
gr. grandson of Great Vladimir, was shorn to the angelic, monastic orders and to the *schema* and passed away on the twenty-
second day of the month of June. They took him to Gorodets and
buried him in the church of St. Archangel Michael. He ruled for
eleven years. After his passing, his boiars, including boiar Akinf,
went to Tver' [to express allegiance] to Grand Prince Mikhail
Iaroslavich of Tver'. [This transfer of allegiance to Tver'] led to
a struggle between two princes over the Grand Principality:
Grand Prince Mikhail Iaroslavich of Tver' and Grand Prince
Iurii Danilovich of Moscow. They both went to the Horde, to the
Khan, to present their grievance, and so trouble arose in all the
cities of the Suzdalian land. Grand Prince of Moscow Iurii Dani-

1304   lovich, with most of his brethren, went to the Horde. He sent his
brother, Boris Danilovich, to Kostroma.[14] There, the boiars of
Grand Prince Mikhail Iaroslavich of Tver' captured him and took
him to Tver'. Furthermore, these boiars of Tver' were awaiting
in Kostroma [also to capture] Grand Prince Iruii Danilovich of
Moscow; but the latter went to the Horde by another route.
Thereupon the Tver' faction dispatched to Great Novgorod the
namestniks [appointed by] Prince Mikhail Iaroslavich of Tver',
doing so vaingloriously and shamelessly; but the people of Novgorod did not care in the least for the latters' vainglory and their
shamelessness, and so they—the namestniks—returned to Tver',
while the Novgorodians sent their troops to Torzhok to guard
Torzhok. The people of Tver', in the meantime, gathered together and also marched thither; but those of Novgorod told
them, "Be patient and wait until the princes return from the
Golden Horde. Then we will elect our prince according to our
own will, according to our ancient custom." And so they departed
in peace.

This year there was a *veche* in Kostroma concerning the
boiars, Davyd Davydovich, Zherebets, and others. And at that
time they killed Zerno and Aleksandr.

The same year [6813/1305 in *Laur.*] in Rostov two very large
bells broke.

The same year Tarasius, Bishop of Rostov, passed away.

STORY ABOUT THE MURDER OF AKINF, BOIAR OF TVER'

Grand Prince Mikhail Iaroslavich of Tver' and Grand Prince
Iurii Danilovich of Moscow, who competed for the Grand Principality [of Vladimir], went to the Khan of the Golden Horde and
there was a great quarrel between them. Prince Ivan Danilovich
ruled in Moscow after the departure of his brother, Iurii [to the
Horde]; but he journeyed from Moscow to Pereiaslavl', since he
was the Grand Prince of Pereiaslavl'. There he secretly received
information from Tver' that the men of Tver' wanted to raid
him in Pereiaslavl'. He asked all his boiars and all the people of

14. Boris Danilovich was sent to Kostroma because that city was without a prince after the death of Prince Boris Andreevich.

Pereiaslavl' to confirm their allegiance to him, and sent to Moscow **1304**
to summon troops. At that time Akinf, boiar of Prince Mikhail
Iaroslavich of Tver', the grandson of Iaroslav, gr. grandson of
Vsevolod, came to Pereiaslavl' fighting against him; this boiar
Akinf was previously the boiar of Grand Prince Andrei Aleksandrovich of [Vladimir and] Gorodets, the grandson of Iaroslav, gr.
grandson of Vsevolod.

Prince Ivan Danilovich marched against him and together
with him were the troops of Pereiaslavl', who were of the same
spirit as he and who fought fiercely. Besides, at that time the army
from Moscow arrived: they also fought extremely fiercely, and
God helped Grand Prince Ivan Danilovich. And so here at Pereiaslavl' Akinf and his son-in-law, Davyd, were killed, and many
other men of Tver' were killed there. Akinf's two sons, Ivan and
Fedor, barely escaped to Tver', where sadness and great grief
spread, while in Pereiaslavl' people rejoiced and were happy, because at that time Prince Mikhail Iaroslavich of Tver' was in the
Golden Horde [so they did not fear him].

[TVER' GAINS THE GRAND PRINCIPALITY OF VLADIMIR]

The same year [6813/1305 in *Laur.*] Prince Mikhail Iaroslavich of Tver' came from the Golden Horde from the Khan to be
the Grand Prince, and he ascended to the throne of the Grand
Principality of Vladimir. When he learned what had happened
to Akinf, he became very grieved.

The same year [6803/1305 in *Vozn.*] Prince Mikhail Iaroslavich, grandson of Iaroslav, gr. grandson of Vsevolod, campaigned
against Moscow, against Grand Prince Iurii Danilovich, grandson
of Aleksandr Iaroslavich, gr. gr. grandson of Vsevolod, and his
brothers. There was much fighting between them, but after a-
while they reconciled.

In the year 6813/1305. There was a portent in the sky. The
same year there was violent thunder and lightning.

The same year [6815/1307 in *Hyp.*] His Holiness Maxim,
Metropolitan of Kiev and all Russia, passed away. This happened
during the fast of St. Phillip on the sixth day of the month of November, when great wondermaker Nicholas is remembered. He
was buried in Vladimir, in the church of the Most Pure Theotokos.

1305   The same year [6814/1306 in *Vozn.*] during St. Phillip's fast, Grand Prince Iurii Danilovich commanded in Moscow that Grand Prince Konstantin Romanovich of Riazan' be killed. He was caught cunningly during the fighting by his father, Grand Prince Danilo Aleksandrovich, son of Iaroslav.

The same year [6814/1306 in *Vozn.*] the brothers of Grand Prince Iurii Danilovich of Moscow left his brother, Grand Prince Iurii Danilovich, and went from Moscow to Grand Prince Mikhail Iaroslavich of Tver'.

The same year in Nizhnii Novgorod, the common people killed the boiars of [late Grand] Prince Andrei Aleksandrovich.

The same year Prince Mikhailo Andreevich[15] returned from the Golden Horde to Nizhnii Novgorod and he killed all those who had participated in the *veche*, as well as those who had killed the boiars. So they drank from their own cup. "As ye judge, so will ye be judged; and as ye measure, thus will ye be measured."

The year 6814/1306. A son, Konstantin, was born to Prince Mikhail Iaroslavich of Tver', son of Iaroslav.

The same year there were heavy rains.

In the year 6815/1307. [6816/1308 in *Novg.*] Grand Prince Mikhail Iaroslavich of Tver' ascended to the throne of Novgorod.

The same year [6814/1306 in *SAof.*] Archbishop Theoktist, lord of Novgorod, gave up his diocese of his own volition because of his illness. He selected a quiet and silent life, going to the monastery of the Annunciation. He blessed his own spiritual father, David, to be archbishop of Novgorod in his stead. The latter was settled in the archbishop's estate after being petitioned and honored, where he was to remain until there should be a Metropolitan of Kiev and all Russia, and then he would go to him to be consecrated.

In the year 6816/1308. Athanasius, Patriarch of Constantinople, consecrated Peter to be Metropolitan of Kiev and all Russia, and the latter was received with great honor by the Patriarch and by the Emperor. The same year His Holiness Peter, Metropolitan of Kiev and all Russia, came from Constantinople and settled in Kiev.

The same year there were famines and epidemics.

---

15. In *Vozn.*, "Iaroslavich," which is quite possible, since Andrei Aleksandrovich's only son, Boris, died in 1302; see entry under 1302.

The same year Prince Vasilii Konstantinovich of Riazan'   **1308**
was killed in the Horde. The same year the Tatars campaigned
against Riazan'.

The same year Grand Prince Mikhail Iaroslavich, grandson
of Iaroslav, gr. grandson of Vsevolod, campaigned for a second
time against Moscow, coming with his entire forces on the day
when the Holy Apostle Titus is rememberd. There was a battle
near Moscow and they caused much evil; and they retreated
without taking the city.

In the year 6817/1309. His Holiness Peter, Metropolitan of
Kiev and all Russia, came from Kiev to Vladimir.

The same year the mice ate the rye, wheat, oats, barley and all
the grain. Therefore everything was very dear, and there was a
very lean summer:[16] there was great starvation in all the Russian
land, horses and cattle died.

The same year Prince Aleksandr Danilovich, grandson of
Aleksandr [Nevskii], gr. grandson of Iaroslav, gr. gr. grandson of
Vsevolod [Great nest], gr. gr. gr. grandson of Iurii Dolgorukii,
gr. gr. gr. gr. grandson of Vladimir Monomakh, passed away.

The same year Prince Konstantin Borisovich of Rostov,
grandson of Vasil'ko, gr. grandson of Vsevolod, gr. gr. grandson
of Iurii Dolgorukii, gr. gr. gr. grandson of Vladimir Monomakh,
passed away; after him his son, Vasilii, became prince.

The same year Prince Vasilii Mikhailovich of Suzdal' passed
away.

The same year in Vladimir His Holiness Peter, Metropolitan
of Kiev and all Russia, consecrated David to be Archbishop of
Novgorod.

The same year Prince Sviatoslav Glebovich[17] chased from
Briansk his nephew, Prince Vasilii, and became Prince of Briansk,
himself. The same year Prince Vasilii of Briansk went to the
Golden Horde, to the Khan, to complain about his uncle, Prince
Sviatoslav Glebovich.

In the year 6818/1310. His Holiness Peter, Metropolitan of Kiev
all Russia, went to Briansk, where he was met by Prince Sviatoslav
in great honor.

16. *Mezenina*—the months of June, July and August.
17. Prince of Smolensk: see *Baumgarten* II—XVII.8

1310   The same year the Tatar army with Prince Vasilii marched against the latter's uncle, Prince Sviatoslav Glebovich of Briansk, and there was a great disturbance in the city of Briansk. Then Metropolitan Peter told Prince Sviatoslav of Briansk, "My son! Either divide the principality with your nephew, Vasilii, or give him all of it. Flee from the city; do not fight." But Prince Sviatoslav Glebovich of Briansk, relying on his power and his bravery because he was very mighty, physically, and very courageous, became overconfident, depending upon the strong troops of Briansk. He responded, "My lord! The people of Briansk will not let me go. They are ready to die for me." And so he did not heed Metropolitan Peter: as it is written, "Disobedient sons will receive vengeance." Also, it is said, "Do not boast of your strength because whosoever relies on his own power will perish." And so Prince Sviatoslav Glebovich marched with a large army against the Tatar army. And so they clashed, and the Tatar arrows darkened the sky like rain. They also fought with lance and saber, and there was an evil battle; and the people of Briansk gave up Prince Sviatoslav Glebovich of Briansk: they were traitors, they cast down their banners and fled. Prince Sviatoslav, however, fought a long while with his court against the Tatars, but was finally killed in battle. Metropolitan Peter locked himself up in church and God protected him from the pagan Tatars; as it is written, "I will save him who is elected by Me from the evil weapon, and I will protect his head in the day of battle."

The same year Theoktist, former Archbishop of Novgorod, passed away in Novgorod, having suffered greatly from his illness, which God sent him for his own salvation; he died in the monastery of the Annunciation of the Most Pure Theotokos and was buried there.

The same year a son, Fedor, was born to Prince Vasilii Konstantinovich of Galich [in the Suzdal' land], the grandson of Boris, great grandson of Vasil'ko.

The same year Prince Vasilii of Briansk marched with Tatars to Karachev, where he killed Prince Sviatoslav Mstislavich of Karachev.

In the year 6819/1311. Prince Dmitrii Mikhailovich of Tver' gathered many troops with the intention of marching against Nizhnii Novgorod; but Metropolitan Peter, whose See was in Vladimir, did not give him his blessing to do this. So he remained

in Vladimir three weeks, gathering a large force; in vain, however,   **1311**
he petitioned Metropolitan Peter for his blessing, and so he let his
troops disperse and they all went home.

The same year Simeon, Bishop of Rostov—earlier in Vladimir,
before he was transferred from Vladimir to Rostov by Metropolitan Maxim of Kiev and all Russia—gave up his diocese of Rostov.

The same year Peter, Metropolitan of Kiev and all Russia,
appointed Prokhor, archimandrite of the monastery of the Saviour
located in Iaroslavl', to be bishop of Rostov.

The same year a conflagration took place in Novgorod and
many holy churches, households and people burned.

In the year 6820/1312. Grand Princess Oksinia, dowager of
Iaroslav Iaroslavich, passed away after having taken the veil as a
nun and having received the *schema*, and she was buried in Tver'.

The same year Peter, Metropolitan of Kiev and all Russia,
deprived Lord Bishop Ishmael of his bishopric of Sarai.

The same year Peter, Metropolitan of Kiev and all Russia,
appointed Barsonophius to be Bishop of Sarai; and the same year
he let him go to Sarai.

The same year Nizhnii Novgorod burned.

In the year 6821/1313. Tokhta, the Tatar Khan [of the Golden
Horde] passed away.

The same year Prince Aleksandr Glebovich of Smolensk,
grandson of Rostislav, great grandson of Mstislav, gr. gr. grandson
of Davyd, gr. gr. gr. grandson of Rostislav, gr. gr. gr. gr. grandson
of Mstislav, gr. gr. gr. gr. gr. grandson of Vladimir Monomakh,
passed away. His sons were Vasilii and Ivan.

The same year Uzbeg, who became Khan of the Golden
Horde, converted to Islam.

The same year Grand Prince Mikhail Iaroslavich of Tver',
as well as Peter, Metropolitan of Kiev and all Russia, went together
to the Horde. They went because Khan Tokhta of the Golden
Horde passed away and the new Khan, Uzbeg, became the ruler.
They had to renew their *Iarlyks*[18] and all the princes and bishops
went to the Horde together for these Iarlyks, each in his own
name. Thanks to God's grace, Metropolitan Peter was held in
great honor by the Khan of the Golden Horde and he was permit-

18. *Iarlyk*: a patent for ruling.

1313 ted to return home quite soon, being greatly honored; and he came to Russia.

The same year the posadnik of Ladoga, together with the army of Ladoga, marched against the Germans.[19] While he was on the march out of the city, the Germans came to Ladoga, took the city and burned it, captured the people and returned home with great booty.

In the year 6822/1314. Prince Vasilii Aleksandrovich of Briansk, grandson of Gleb, great grandson of Rostislav, gr. gr. grandson of Mstislav, gr. gr. gr. grandson of Davyd, passed away.[20]

The same year there were great floods. The same year there was hunger in Novgorod.

The same year the Novgorodians summoned the *veche* because they disliked the namestniks of Prince Mikhail Iaroslavich of Tver', from whom they suffered much offense and abuse. At the time Prince Mikhail Iaroslavich of Tver' was in the Horde and [the Novgorodians] sent for help to Grand Prince Iurii Danilovich of Moscow. The latter secretly contacted Prince Fedor of Rzhev, informing him that he was marching toward Novgorod. Prince Fedor gathered his troops, awaiting further news from Grand Prince Iurii.

The same year Grand Prince Iurii Danilovich of Moscow sent to Novgorod Prince Fedor of Rzhev. The latter came to Novgorod, arrested the namestniks of Prince Mikhail of Tver', who were in Novgorod, and marched toward the Volga with the men of Novgorod. Prince Dmitrii Mikhailovich, grandson of Iaroslav, whose father, Mikhail [of Tver'] was then in the Golden Horde, marched against them with the men of Tver'. He camped opposite them on his side of the river Volga, remaining there for six weeks until it began to freeze. And so the Novgorodians made peace according to their own will and sent for Grand Prince Iurii Danilovich of Moscow, whom they invited to Novgorod. He came to them and became prince of Novgorod, together with his brother, Afanasii.

In the year 6823/1315. Khan Uzbeg of the Golden Horde sent for Grand Prince Iurii Danilovich of Moscow, requesting him to

19. Here, again, are meant the Swedes.
20. Prince Vasilii was from the princely line of Smolensk.

come without delay to the Golden Horde. Prince Iurii left in **1315**
Novgorod his brother, Afanasii Danilovich, and from thence
went to Rostov, and from Rostov on the fifteenth day of March—
the Saturday of St. Lazarus—he set out on his journey to the Khan
of the Golden Horde.

The same year Prince Ivan Mikhailovich of Starodub, grandson of Ivan, great grandson of Vsevolod, passed away.

The same year Grand Prince Mikhail Iaroslavich of Tver' returned from the Khan of the Golden Horde and the Khan's envoys were with him—Taji-Temir and Imar-Khodzha and Indryi.
The same year Prince Afanasii Danilovich, grandson of Aleksandr [Nevskii], great grandson of Iaroslav, marched from
Novgorod toward Torzhok; with him were the boiars of Novgorod but not the common people. When Prince Mikhail of Tver'
heard about this he gathered the entire force of the Niz and, with
Tatars, also advanced toward Torzhok. Prince Afanasii Danilovich and Prince Fedor of Rzhev, with the men of Novgorod,
marched against them and there was a great battle and an evil
slaughter. Many men of Novgorod were killed: the tysiatskiis,
posadniks, boiars and many outstanding people, and many other
Novgorodian men, and they—the dead—were numberless. And
so Prince Afanasii Danilovich and Prince Fedor of Rzhev escaped
to Novgorod with the few remaining. Prince Mikhail Iaroslavich
sent to the Novgorodians, saying, "Turn Prince Afanasii Danilovich and Prince Fedor of Rzhev over to me." The Novgorodians
turned over Prince Fedor of Rzhev but they stood firmly behind
Prince Afanasii Danilovich and gave, on their part, 5,000 gri-
venkas of silver.[21] And so they concluded peace. Prince Mikhail
Iaroslavich of Tver' summoned to him Prince Afanasii Danilovich
and the boiars of Novgorod, and undertook to make an agreement with them according to their old customs; but the Novgorodians were unwilling to contract any new obligations and
therefore he—Prince Mikhail of Tver'—became wroth, arrested
everyone and sent them to Tver'; the other men he sold for whatever price he could get. He sent their horses, their armaments
and weapons. and all their masters, to Tver', destroyed the city
of Torzhok, and assigned his own posadniks to Novgorod; and

21. In *Novg.*, 50,000 grivna of silver.

1315 of his own volition he gave the office of posadnik of Novgorod to Mikhail Klementievich and Ivan Dmitrievich. This happened on the fourth day of February.

The same year Andrew, Bishop of Tver', gave up his diocese and went to the monastery.

The same year His Holiness Peter, Metropolitan of Kiev and all Russia, consecrated Barsonophius to be bishop of Tver'.

The same year the Novgorodians, themselves, went to the Horde for their own purposes but they were caught by the people of Tver' and arrested and brought to Tver'.

The same year Annunciation coincided with Tuesday of Holy Easter Week.

In the year 6824/1316. The people of Novgorod drove the namestniks of Prince Mikhail of Tver' out of Novgorod. The same year the people of Novgorod marched against Torzhok with Prince Afanasii Danilovich. Grand Prince Mikhail Iaroslavich of Tver' gathered a great army and marched against them. There was a great battle and an evil slaughter and Prince Mikhail Iaroslavich of Tver' won the battle. He captured many Novgorodians and killed the others. Prince Afanasii Danilovich barely escaped with a few people to Novgorod, and there was great grief in Novgorod.

The same year the people of Novgorod caught Ignat Beks[22] and threw him off the bridge into the river Volkhov because they believed he was secretly informing Prince Mikhail Iaroslavich of Tver'. The same year the Novgorodians killed Danilo the Scribe.[23] His servant denounced him to the Novgorodians, saying, "My lord Danilo the Scribe maintained friendship with and informed Prince Mikhail Iaroslavich of Tver', and he sent me to him with his letters." And so Danilo the Scribe was killed—he was thrown off the bridge into the river Volkhov.

The same year Grand Prince Mikhail Iaroslavich of Tver' marched toward Volok,[24] campaigning against Novgorod the

22. In *Nik.*, just Besk; in *Novg.*, Ignat Beks.

23. In *Novg.*, Danilko Pischev—i.e., Daniil, son of the Scribe—who was denounced by his servant, who said, "He sent me to Prince Mikhail with letters." And this servant had to kill him on the meadow.

24. "Volok:" in *Nik.* Probably, Volot', a town about forty miles SSW of Novgorod.

Great. The Novgorodians, learning of this, were very aggrieved **1316**
and appealed to Lord God and His Most Pure Mother, repenting
and confessing, and shedding many tears. They assembled a
great army, promising themselves that they would all unite and
stand firm. Lord God and the Most Pure Theotokos heard their
prayers and did not permit the enemy troops to attack them.
Prince Mikhail Iaroslavich of Tver' hurried toward Novgorod but
he travelled through unknown places and unfamiliar routes, and
so he lost his way in the evil forests, in the marshes and among the
lakes before he arrived at Volot'. He stayed there in great grief
and sadness because there was severe famine among them and
they ate leather, the tops of their boots and their leather belts.
Many died of starvation and the remaining ones suffered greatly.
Only some returned, with difficulty, to their homes, coming back
from Volot' not having succeeded in the least and having done all
in vain: without God's help, no one can succeed in anything.

The same year a conflagration started up in the city of Tver'
and over twenty households there burned. They extinguished
the fire only with difficulty.

The same year during the early dawns the moon disappeared, then set without taking its full shape.

[PRINCE IURII OF MOSCOW BECOMES GRAND PRINCE OF VLADIMIR]

In the year 6825/1317. Grand Prince Iurii Danilovich of Moscow came from the Horde to be grand prince. In the Horde he
married Konchaka, sister of the khan of the Great Horde, who received baptism and was named Agafiia.[25] He brought with him
Tatar envoys, named Kavgadyi, Astry Byl and Ostrev, [with] very
strong [troops]. Prince Mikhail Iaroslavich of Tver' took counsel
with the princes of Suzdal'. Amassing strong forces, he marched
against them, meeting them at Kostroma. He camped on the
Volga for a long while. Grand Prince Iurii Danilovich of Moscow
took counsel with Kavgadyi, and he gave up the grand principality
to Prince Mikhail Iaroslavich of Tver'. So Prince Mikhail Iaroslavich returned to his patrimony of Tver', where he laid the foundation of a large fortress, *Kremlenik*.

25. "Agafiia:" In English, "Agatha."

The same year in the month of September, a Saturday, before dinner, a portent appeared in the sky: there was a circle over
the city of Tver' which moved slightly around midnight, and it had
three rays: two toward the east and a third toward the west.

The same year the princes of Suzdal' joined Grand Prince
Iurii Danilovich of Moscow, and these princes marched to meet
him in Kostroma. The other princes also marched to meet him
in Kostroma, and many great forces assembled around him in
Kostroma. They also contacted the Novgorodians, whom they
ordered to march toward Torzhok and to be ready to wage war
against Tver'.

The same year Grand Prince Iurii Danilovich of Moscow,
with Kavgadyi and with numerous Tatar troops, and with the
princes of Suzdal' and other princes, along with large forces,
marched from Kostroma to Rostov. From Rostov he marched to
Pereiaslavl' and from Pereiaslavl' he marched to Dmitrov, and
from Dmitrov to Klin. At the same time the Novgorodians came
to the aid of Grand Prince Iurii Danilovich of Moscow to fight
Prince Mikhail Iaroslavich of Tver'; camping for six weeks at
Torzhok, they discussed [with Iurii] how to march against Tver'.
So the Novgorodians began to campaign in the land of Tver', as
did Prince Iurii Danilovich of Moscow with Kavgadyi, with Tatars
and with the entire force of Suzdal'; taking many prisoners, they
sent them into captivity. They approached the city [of Tver'] as
close as eight versts, and camped there five weeks. All this campaign in the land of Tver' lasted three months.

Kavgadyi's envoys went to Prince Mikhail Iaroslavich in
Tver' with cunning words, and there was no peace. So Kavgadyi
marched with Grand Prince Iurii Danilovich of Moscow, with the
princes of Suzdal' and with all forces toward the Volga, camping
at the crossing of the Volga; and then they campaigned everywhere and marched toward the city of Tver'. When they were
forty versts from Tver' they were met at a place called "Borte-
nevo," by Prince Mikhail Iaroslavich of Tver' and his forces. The
two armies came together and a great battle and evil massacre
ensued. God aided Prince Mikhail Iaroslavich of Tver' and he
won the final victory. Grand Prince Iurii Danilovich of Moscow
fled with a small troop to Novgorod; but his wife, Princess Konchaka, who was the sister of Uzbeg, Khan of the Golden Horde,
was captured. They also captured his brother, Prince Boris Dani-

lovich, and many other princes, boiars and Tatars, and took them   **1317**
to Tver'. Kavgadyi ordered his troops to turn their banners[26] and
he, himself, fled to his camp. This occurred on Thursday, the
twenty-second day of the month of December, in an evening hour
three days before Christmas. On the morrow of the battle, Saturday, Kavgadyi sent to Prince Mikhail Iaroslavich and agreed on
peace with him. He marched to him in Tver' to get his [captured]
soldiers.

Prince Mikhail Iaroslavich of Tver' ordered that Kavgadyi's
Tatars not be killed but be conducted to Tver', and he rendered
great honor to Kavgadyi and to his Tatars, who flattered him, saying, "Now we are yours. We campaigned against you with Prince
Iurii without the Khan's order, and the blame is ours. We fear
the Khan's punishment because we undertook this campaign
and shed much blood." Prince Mikhail Iaroslavich believed them
and presented them with many gifts and released them with
honor. [Konchaka] the wife of Prince Iurii, the sister of Uzbeg,
Khan of the Golden Horde, died in Tver'; some claimed that
Konchaka, the wife of Grand Prince Iurii, sister of the Khan, who
in Holy Baptism was named Agafiia, was poisoned there in Tver'.
Her body was taken from Tver' to Rostov and was buried in the
church of the Most Pure Theotokos in Rostov.

The same winter Prince Iurii Danilovich of Moscow came
with Novgorodians to the ford of the Volga, where he was met by
Prince Mikhail Iaroslavich of Tver'. A battle almost ensued there
but they began to negotiate and they reached peace, confirming
it by a pledge on the holy cross that they should both go to the
Horde. The same winter Prince Mikhail Iaroslavich of Tver' sent
his son, Konstantin, to the Golden Horde.

In the year 6826/1318. A mean envoy named Kokcha came
from the Golden Horde and he killed one hundred twenty people
at the city of Kostroma. Then he marched further and waged war
in the entire Rostov land.

The same winter there was famine among the people of Tver'.

The same year Prince Mikhail Iaroslavich of Tver' sent Aleksandr Markovich to Moscow with an embassy of friendship; but
he was killed by Grand Prince Iurii Danilovich of Moscow; and so

26. Turning the banner was a sign of retreat.

1318 he received a violent death, and there was still greater enmity between them [Tver' and Moscow].

The same year [6827/1319 in *Vozn.*], following the advice of Kavgadyi, Grand Prince Iurii Danilovich of Moscow went to the Golden Horde with many princes, boiars and men of Novgorod. He journeyed to the Horde, conspiring with Kavgadyi. In the meantime, as was related before, Prince Mikhail Iaroslavich sent thither his son, Konstantin.

The same fall, in the month of September, a conflagration started in the city of Tver' and the greater part of the city burned; and six churches burned. They extinguished the fire with difficulty.

The same winter [6827/1319 in *Vozn.*] Prince Iurii Danilovich of Moscow and the initiator of all evil, Kavgadyi, went to the Horde, and the latter began to calumniate Prince Mikhail Iaroslavich of Tver', saying the following to Khan Uzbeg: "Prince Mikhail of Tver' gathered much tribute in the cities and wants to escape to the Germans. He does not intend to come to you and he does not obey your authority." The Khan became wroth and ordered that his son, Prince Konstantin, be arrested and put alone in jail, and be allowed to die of starvation. When this was done, some people told Khan Uzbeg, "If you kill his son, his father will never come to you." And so Khan Uzbeg ordered that his—Mikhail's—son, Konstantin, be released.

The same year Kavgadyi sent a strong Tatar force to ambush Prince Mikhail Iaroslavich of Tver', with the order to put him to death, wheresoever they might find him; but the same year, in the month of August, Grand Prince Mikhail Iaroslavich of Tver' went to the Horde to Khan Uzbeg.

STORY OF THE MARTYRDOM OF PRINCE MIKHAIL OF TVER'[27]

In the year 6827/1319. Grand Prince Mikhail Iaroslavich of Tver' came to the Khan of the Golden Horde, who was camped at that time near the Surozh Sea[28] at the delta of the river Don be-

27. The "Martyrdom of Prince Mikhail of Tver' " was written in 1319-1320, most probably by Abbot Alexander of Tver's *Otrochii* Monastery. V. A. Kuchkin, *Povesti o Mikhaile Tverskom*, Moscow, 1974.

28. "Surozh Sea" was a name for the Azov Sea.

cause the Don flows into this sea, and the sea is called the "Sea of **1319**
Surozh." This occurred on the sixth day of the month of September, when the great miracles of Great Archangel Michael are remembered. According to the custom, he gave presents to all the Tatars, lords and ladies, including the Khan, himself, and his wife. Mikhail remained in the Horde with the Khan for a month and a half. During that time Kavgadyi uninterruptedly calumniated him to the Khan. So the Khan summoned his lords and told them, "You must try Mikhail and Iurii Danilovich [of Moscow], and when you have judged, tell me." The Tatar lords gathered in the court and began to try Mikhail and Iurii. Everyone helped Iurii and put all the blame on Mikhail. Whatsoever Mikhail answered them, they let it pass by their ears. And those depositions which were correct they did not take into consideration but they listened and heeded what had been told by Kavgadyi. And so he became not only Mikhail's prosecutor but also his judge, and he spoke whatsoever was in his mind, convincing everyone to agree with him. So they dispersed and decided to have the sentencing the next week. They told the Khan, "Prince Mikhail Iaroslavich, according to our trial, deserves death; but you, sovereign Khan, should give your final word." Thus they told the Khan of Mikhail's great guilt. The Khan ordered them to repeat the proceeding and to find out everything exactly; but Kavgadyi said, "My Khan! You can rely upon me and my opinion. I know all. According to the decision of those who participated in the trial, Mikhail deserves death. If you want to decide about the sentence, yourself, then Mikhail must appear before you during a trial and answer, being bound. We neither want our great Khan to be offended or your lords to be offended because our offense is your offense and your glory and honor are the life and existence of all of us in the whole Horde." And the Khan told them, "If you want to do so, then you must try him righteously in my court because our Khan's court is supposed to be right. And so try him rightly; and, after making a decision, you will tell me."

And so the next week both princes appeared in the court and Mikhail was brought bound. Everyone listened to the speeches of Iurii and turned their ears away from the speeches of Mikhail. And so they told him the following: "You are proud and do not obey our Khan. You put to shame Kavgadyi, our Khan's envoy; and you fought with him and you killed many Tatars; and you collected the Khan's tribute for yourself and did not give it to the

1319   Khan. You wanted to escape with the treasury to the Germans and you sent your treasury to Rome, to the Pope; and you poisoned the wife of Prince Iurii. You killed many of the Khan's lords and Tatars."

And Mikhail answered the accusations. "I obeyed the Khan and I obey him now; and I worked hard for him; and I turn the tribute over to him; but the Khan's envoy came to me, waging war, and I fought him without wishing it. Thereafter I honored him and gave him gifts, and let him go with great honor and many gifts. I did not poison Prince Iurii's wife; but she died her own death. My brother, Iurii Danilovich, should remember my friendship and concord because when his father was in trouble I helped him, and I am not against him; but he arose against me and he wanted to rule everywhere against our customs; and he developed enmity toward me. Now he wants still more; but I appear here with him according to the will of the Khan and your decision. It will be according to the Khan's wishes and your trial; but now, please, show your grace toward me." Kavgadyi arose and said, "He does not deserve your grace, but he deserves death." And he spoke fiercely, at length, against him; and so all the Tatar lords stood up and said the following to the Khan: "For the second time, Khan, we tell you that according to our judgment, Mikhail deserves death." The Khan told them, "If it be right, so be it." It was a Friday, late evening.

On the morrow, Saturday, the Tatar lords were in court and Mikhail was placed before them bound by ropes. Next to him were seven guards, each from one of the great Tatar lords; and there was an endless number of others. Prince Mikhail Iaroslavich grieved greatly, and some men brought irons, wanting to put them on him; but they only bound his hands with the irons and put an iron on his neck, and bound his arms behind his back. And those who were with him were overcome and driven off.

So on the morrow, Sunday, they put on his neck a great piece of wood, and they took him to follow the Khan at his hunting, and he remained in this painful position for twenty-five days. Thereafter Kavgadyi ordered that he be brought to the marketplace in order to put him to shame and to do him offense, as if he were a thief and criminal; and he said much evil about him, then he [Kavgadyi] spoke the following before many people present, whose number was endless: "The Khan's grace always follows those who are supposed to be punished; but this one deserves death. It is **1319** well and certainly known, according to the Khan's word, and a just court has investigated him. They found out that Prince Mikhail Iaroslavich, because of his evildoings, moved away from the Khan's grace and approached death. Now he is in difficulties and need because soon he will be put to death. Still, in accord with the Khan's grace and His Majesty's command, we have to honor him because he is so close to death."

And so Kavgadyi ordered that his irons be removed and that he be unbound and washed, and that expensive clothing be put on him; and he ordered that he be brought food and all manner of fruit and, also, drink. Mikhail, however, neither touched nor ate anything. There were many people who had gathered, as the sand, and they looked upon all this because at that time people from all lands came thither; and they were [as numerous] as the grass and sand. There were people from Constantinople, Germans, Lithuanians, Russians and many other Orthodox. Seeing this, they shed tears and no one was without tears at that hour. Thereafter Kavgadyi ordered them to take from him the expensive clothing and to put all the original irons back upon him; and so he remained in such destitution for twenty and six days. This happened beyond the river Terek, close to the high mountains of the Ossetians and Cherkess, near the city of Titiakov[29] on the river Sivints near the Iron Gate,[30] near the copper idol, near the golden head of Temir, near the grave of the Bogatyr'.[31]

It was very early, Wednesday, when Grand Prince Mikhail Iaroslavich awoke and summoned his spiritual father, Abbot Mark, because the abbot, two other priests and a deacon accompanied him. He spoke to him, shedding tears and weeping greatly, saying the following: "Three times last night it was shown to me that the day of my death is approaching; but show me your love; remember me in your holy prayers and do not forget me, so that Lord God will remit my sins which I have committed before Him." Thereafter he asked that matins and the hours be celebrated, and

29. Titiakov (in some instances spelled Dadakov): now Vladikavkaz or Ordzhonikidze.

30. Iron Gate: the narrow valley between the Caucasian mountains and the Caspian Sea.

31. "Bogatyr':" these last words may be of folklore (*bylina*) origin.

1319   he followed the service carefully, weeping tearfully and with bitter sighs. Then he asked to begin the rites of holy communion and he, himself, chanted from the books and spoke everything with many tears, and he made his confession to his spiritual father, Abbot Mark.

After divine service he received the Holy and Divine and Life-giving Gifts of Christ, and the guards of the Khan and of the Tatar lords did not interfere with it in any way, in anything that was done according to the Christian law. And so, after divine communion, he embraced his spiritual father, Abbot Mark, as well as all the priests and deacons, and he kissed them and then pitifully, in tears, asked them not to forget him and to remember him in their holy prayers.

He also summoned his son, Konstantin, because his son, Konstantin, also was there. He embraced him, saying, "My son! Follow in all purity the Orthodox faith and respect the divine churches and all the clergy and monks. Do not disdain pilgrims or paupers because they are loved by God."

Then he began to instruct his son concerning his princess and his other sons, about his patrimony, and about everyone who was with him, all of whom were in great grief and great sadness. He told them not to forget the latter and not to abandon them. He also said, "Abide ye here. My soul is sorrowed unto death and the hour of separation is drawing near." [*Math.* 26:38 paraph.] He was covered with tears, as with water. Then he slept for a-while and, awakening, wept again and ordered that the Psalter be brought to him, saying, "My soul is sad and grieves at my forth-coming death, and the hour of separation approaches!" Opening the Psalter, he found the Fifty-Fourth Psalm of David:

"Give ear to my prayer, O Lord;
And hide not Thyself from my supplication.
Attend unto me, and answer me.
I am restless in my complaint and moan
Because of the voice of the enemy,
Because of the oppression of the wicked.
And in anger they persecute me.
My heart is sore pained within me
And the terrors of death are fallen upon me."[32]
And then he read one line after another, shedding tears.

32. In the English text, this is Psalm 55.

Then he also began the chant,

"Most Holy Theotokos!
Do not give me up during my life,
Do not abandon me to the hands of men,
But intercede for me and have mercy upon me.
All my hopes I place upon Thee, Mother of God;
And keep me under Thy protection."

Thereafter he began to repeat the prayer of Jesus, shedding tears, and would say nothing more.[33] When people asked him he would not respond but would only say, "Do not disturb me. My soul grieves before death."

When many hours had passed and he was still repeating the prayer of Jesus, with tears, one of his young pages came to him, saying, "My lord, Grand Prince Mikhail! Kaygadyi is coming from the Khan of the Golden Horde, and with him is Prince Iurii Danilovich of Moscow; and with them is a great multitude of people, and they are coming directly to you." And he asked, "Why are they coming?" And the page cried out, shedding tears, "Oh, my lord, Grand Prince Mikhail! They are going to slay you."

Grand Prince Mikhail Iaroslavich thereupon sent his son, Konstantin, to the Khan's wife, saying, "You promised to help me and, if you can, please help. Now, today, they are hurrying hither, lord Kavgadyi and Grand Prince Iurii Danilovich of Moscow." But before his son managed to reach the Khan's wife, Kavgadyi sent his people ahead of himself to Prince Mikhail's camp. When they arrived they dismounted from their horses at the market place, because there was a great market there and it was as close as a stone's throw. These murderers chased away all his people and his Tatars because there were many Tatars who served him; and everyone wept, shedding tears. The killers caught Prince Mikhail by the piece of wood which was on his neck and they beat him lengthily, and then hanged him on the wall but the wall broke and he jumped up. But several people caught him and threw him to the ground and began to torture him, kicking him with their feet. A certain Ivanets caught him by the ears and began to strike his head upon the ground, telling him, "You like to jump and rush. Now you can jump as much as you want." Then another, named Romanets, approached. He had a great knife and he struck

33. The prayer of Jesus is, "Jesus Christ, Son of God, have mercy upon me, a sinner."

1319   Mikhail with the knife in the ribs on the right side, and then he turned the knife one way and the other. Pushing the knife in, he said, "You are too daring. Drink this good cup." But he, Prince Mikhail, cried out loudly and passed away on the twenty-second day of the month of November. [In 6826/1318 in *Laur.*]

His tent was robbed by the Russians and the Tatars. They also robbed all the Christians and Tatars who were with him and who served him. They tore their clothing from them and pulled them, naked, torturing them as if they were robbers; and, separating them, they put them in irons. Thereafter, lord Kavgadyi and Grand Prince Iurii Danilovich of Moscow approached his body. His—Prince Mikhail's—body was lying, naked, and lord Kavgadyi said to Prince Iurii Danilovich of Moscow, wrathfully, "What is this? Why did you forget? Were you not his senior brother, in the place of his father? And why is his body thrown to the ground, naked, and lies there to be offended by all? Take him and bury him in your land and in his patrimony, according to the custom which you have."

Then Grand Prince Iurii Danilovich of Moscow ordered that the body be taken and placed on a board and covered, and so they put him in a cart, attached it firmly and carried it beyond the river called Adezh, which means "grief." And he commanded two men to guard it. When night came they were seized by fear and great terror and could not stand it. They ran to the camps; and when they returned early, they could not find the body on the board. The board remained, however, attached to the cart, while the body lay at a distance from the cart, the wound toward the earth; and much blood issued from this wound, and the right hand was under his face and his left was on the wound, and he was dressed only in breeches. No one touched this body, although there were an endless number of animals there; but God preserved him, as it is written: "God will preserve all his bones and none of them will be broken; but the death of a sinner will be evil." And so it happened to the accursed Kavgadyi: he did not last one single year, and his accursed life came to an end.

Many believers and even infidels at that time saw two clouds which came over the body of blessed Prince Mikhail, and they came together and parted and they shone as the sun. These people told us of it with tears, and giving many oaths. From thence the body was sent to Mozhcharyk.[34]

34. Mozhcharsk, in some versions.

At that time there were Russian merchants present who wanted to place the body in a church and cover it with a saintly cover; but they were not permitted to do so and the body was put in a barn, under guard. Then others living there saw at night a fiery column extending from the earth to the sky. Others saw a rainbow which bent over the barn in which the body lay.

From thence the body was taken to the town of Bezdezh, and when they drew near the town, many people in the town saw a vision: around the sledge there was a multitude of people with candles and others on horseback with lanterns, riding in the air. And so they brought the body to the town, but the body was not placed in the church, but only in the yard. Two of the guards lay down in the sledge above his body but they were seized by great fear and were thrown out of the sledge and pushed afar off. When they arose and recovered, they went and confessed what had happened to the priests who were there. I heard it from them and I have written it exactly. From thence his body was taken [In 6826/1318 in *Laur.*] to the Russian towns, and little by little he was brought to Moscow. When they carried it to the city of Moscow, they placed his body in the monastery of the church of the Holy Transfiguration; but the people in Tver' did not know about it.

In the year 6828/1320. [6827/1319 in *Novg.*] Grand prince Iurii Danilovich of Moscow became grand prince [of Vladimir] and he brought with him Prince Konstantin Mikhailovich,[35] grandson of Iaroslav, as well as the latter's boiars and squires. He brought them as if they were his captives. Then the news spread rapidly over the land and reached Tver'. When the dowager of Prince Mikhail and her sons, Dmitrii, Aleksandr and Vasilii, heard it they wept greatly and sent to Grand Prince Iurii in Vladimir, asking for the body and praying for it with tears. The same year Prokhor, Bishop of Rostov and Iaroslavl', came to Aleksandr Mikhailovich, asking him to go to Prince Iurii and to abide in concord according to their oath on the cross. He went to him in Vladimir and concluded peace. He persuaded him [Iurii] with many prayers and many tears to give them the body. Taking it up, they bore it to Tver' with the clergy. [In 6827/1319 in *Laur.*]

On the Volga he was met by his sons, Dmitrii, Aleksandr and Vasilii, their mother, Grand Princess Anna, and by Bishop Bar-

35. Prince Konstantin Mikhailovich was the son of the late Prince Mikhail of Tver'.

1320   sonuphius and the entire clergy, who met the body on the boats, with candles and censers. On the shore near the church of Archangel Michael a great multitude of people met the body. And they buried the body in the church of St. Saviour on the sixth day of September.

This body was preserved intact and was not harmed by anything, despite the fact that it had been brought from a far distant land by cart and sledge, and had remained for a time in Moscow; but it had not decomposed and was in all its entirety and uncorrupted.

This Grand Prince Mikhail Iaroslavich, Grandson of Iaroslav, great grandson of Vsevolod, gr. gr. grandson of Iurii Dolgorukii, gr. gr. gr. grandson of Vladimir Monomakh, gr. gr. gr. gr. grandson of Vsevolod,[36] gr. gr. gr. gr. gr. grandson of Iaroslav, gr. gr. gr. gr. gr. gr. grandson of Great Vladimir, was tall of body, very strong and courageous, and his mien was terrifying. He always used, himself, to read divine scripture. He cared for the churches and greatly respected the clergy and monks, and he was very much loved by his boiars and all his subjects. He disliked drunkenness and was desirous of being a monk. He always spoke of the deeds of the martyrs and he, himself, drank this cup for the sake of the Christians. If he had not gone to the Golden Horde, having heard even then of the possible misfortunes for himself, and if he had gone away to other lands, the Tatars would have entered this country, tortured a great many Christians, put them to death and defiled the holy churches. But this blessed Mikhail sacrificed himself for all and died a violent death; and, rejoicing, he came to His Lord Christ in the Heavenly Kingdom. This life ends with death, and had he not died that death, he would nonetheless have died in some other manner.[37]

The same year Prince Aleksandr Mikhailovich of Tver', grandson of Iaroslav, great grandson of Iaroslav, gr. gr. grandson of Vsevolod, gr. gr. gr. grandson of Iurii Dolgorukii, married.

36. Missing in *Nik.*

37. Here ends the story of Mikhail of Tver', which, in *Nik.*, was slightly abridged by the chronicler, especially in the anti-Muscovite descriptions of the original text. See *Rogozhskii letopisets* and *Tverskaia letopis'*. *PSRL XV*, Vols. 39 and 42. Nonetheless, its vivid realism and some anti-Muscovite character were preserved.

The same year [6829/1321 in *Novg.*] Prince Boris Danilovich, **1320** grandson of Aleksandr [Nevskii], gr. grandson of Iaroslav, gr. gr. grandson of Vsevolod, gr. gr. gr. grandson of Iurii Dolgorukii, passed away and was buried in the church of the Most Pure Theotokos in Vladimir.

The same year Prince Konstantin Mikhailovich of Tver', grandson of Iaroslav, great grandson of Iaroslav, gr. gr. grandson of Vsevolod, gr. gr. gr. grandson of Iurii Dolgorukii, married, and the wedding took place in the church of St. Theodore in Kostroma.

The same year Prince Dmitrii Mikhailovich of Tver', grandson of Iaroslav, great grandson of Iaroslav, gr. gr. grandson of Vsevolod, gr. gr. gr. grandson of Iurii Dolgorukii, married. He brought from Lithuania the daughter of Prince Gedimin, and the wedding was celebrated in the church of the Holy Saviour in Tver' by Bishop Barsonuphius of Tver', and there was great rejoicing in the land of Tver'.

The same year an envoy named Bayder came to Grand Prince Iurii Danilovich and caused much harm in Vladimir.

The same year [6827/1319 in *Vozn.* and *Novg.*] Grand Prince Iurii Danilovich sent his brother, Afanasii Danilovich, to Novgorod to rule there. The same year a son, Danilo, was born to Prince Ivan Danilovich. The same year Prince Ivan Danilovich, grandson of Aleksandr [Nevskii], went to the Golden Horde to Khan Uzbeg.

The same year Prince Iurii Aleksandrovich of Rostov passed away.

In the year 6829/1321. A certain Tatar, Taianchar, came with his Jewish tax collector from the Horde to Kashin and caused great distress in Kashin.

The same year on the twenty-sixth of the month of July when St. David of Salonika is remembered, at the third hour of the day the sun disappeared and then became as a two-day-old new moon. Then, an hour later, it became full.

The same year Grand Prince Iurii Danilovich [of Moscow] gathered all the forces of Niz and Suzdal' and wanted to march against Kashin, waging war. Prince Dmitrii Mikhailovich of Tver', however, marched against him toward the river Volga with all his forces, and there the former Bishop Andrew arranged peace between them and each returned home.

1321   The same year after the agreement Grand Prince Iurii Danilovich took the tribute silver from the princes of Tver' but did not
go to meet the Khan's envoy; rather, he went with the silver to
Great Novgorod.

The same year a son, named Lev, was born to Prince Aleksandr Mikhailovich, grandson of Iaroslav, gr. grandson of Iaroslav. The same year Prince Davyd Fedorovich of Iaroslavl', grandson of Rostislav, gr. grandson of Mstislav, gr. gr. grandson of
Davyd, gr. gr. gr. grandson of Rostislav, gr. gr. gr. gr. grandson of
Mstislav, gr. gr. gr. gr. gr. grandson of Vladimir Monomakh,
passed away.

The same year when Prince Iurii [of Moscow] was in Novgorod the Novgorodians had a minor disagreement with him.

In the year 6830/1322. Grand Prince Iurii Danilovich of Vladimir, Moscow and Novgorod made peace with the Novgorodians.
The same year the Germans[38] campaigned, but Grand Prince
Iurii Danilovich of Vladimir and Novgorod marched against
them with the levies of Novgorod, and so some Germans were
killed and some escaped.

The same year Prince Dmitrii Mikhailovich of Tver', grandson of Iaroslav, went to Khan Uzbeg of the Golden Horde and
was received with great honor by the Khan and the latter's lords.
Khan Uzbeg turned over to him the grand principality of Vladimir, which was under Grand Prince Iurii Dmitrievich; but earlier
the same Khan Uzbeg had given the grand principality of Vladimir to Prince Iurii Danilovich of Moscow, taking this grand principality from Mikhail Iaroslavich of Tver'.

The same year Grand Prince Iurii Danilovich marched with
his army and with Novgorodians to Vyborg.[39]

The same year Grand Prince Iruii Danilovich, grandson of
Aleksandr Nevskii, beseeched the Novgorodians to accompany
him to the Horde, and from Novgorod he went to Niz. When he
was in Urdom[40] Prince Aleksandr Mikhailovich of Tver' came
against him, so he fled to Pskov, taking his treasury with him; but
at that time Prince David the Lithuanian was in Pskov; and so

38. The Livonian Order

39. Vyborg—a city in Karelia, land north of the Neva, which was in
the process of subjugation by the Swedes.

40. (?) Location unclear.

from thence the Novgorodians, according to their pledge on the   **1322**
cross, invited him [Iurii Danilovich] to Novgorod. They did so
because they were in difficulties with the Germans, and the Germans waged war in the Novgorodian land. So they began to re-
pair the battering rams, willing to march with Grand Prince Iurii
Danilovich against the Germans; but Prince Iurii Danilovich at
that time had his own troubles because Prince Dmitrii Mikhailovich of Tver' went to the Horde, to Khan Uzbeg, and received
from him the grand principality of Vladimir of Russia.

The same year Prince Dmitrii Mikhailovich of Tver', grandson of Iaroslav, came from the Golden Horde with the charter
from Khan Uzbeg for the grand principality of Vladimir, and
with him was a powerful Tatar envoy, lord Sevenchbuga.

The same year from the Horde came Prince Ivan Danilovich,[41] grandson of Aleksandr, great grandson of Iaroslav, gr. gr.
grandson of Vsevolod, gr. gr. gr. grandson of Iurii Dolgorukii.
With him came a powerful Tatar envoy named Akhmyl. And he
[Akhmyl] caused much evil to the cities of the Niz. He took the
city of Iaroslavl', burned it and captured a great number of people. He summoned Grand Prince Iurii Danilovich to the Horde
to Prince Uzbeg and, himself, went with an endless number of
captives to the Golden Horde.

In the year 6831/1323. Andrew, the former bishop of Tver',
passed away in his monastery of the Holy Theotokos on the river
Shesha, and on the morrow lord Bishop Barsonuphius, with the
Holy Council, brought him to St. Saviour. They chanted over
his body and buried him in the small church of the Holy Presentation of the Holy Theotokos.

The same year in the land of the Bulgars, who are on the
Volga and Kama, a certain Christian from Jerusalem was martyrized, a merchant having great wealth. He, whose name was
Theodore, was very learned in philosophy and debated with them
concerning religion; but these accursed ones could not abide
defeat in debate and on the twenty-first day of the month of April
they martyrized him for adhering to the Orthodox Christian
faith.

---

41. Prince Ivan Danilovich, brother of Iurii Danilovich, later known
as Ivan Kalita ("Ivan Moneybags") because of his ability to accumulate
money.

1323   The same year there was completed and consecrated the stone church in Tver' which was dedicated to St. Theodore, and it was built and adorned by a certain abbot called John of Constantinople. The same year the wife of Khan Uzbeg, by the name of Baialyn, died in the Horde.

In the year 6832/1324. Grand Prince Iurii Danilovich marched with the Novgorodians and the men of Pskov, waging war against the German[42] city of Vyborg. The same year [6831/1323 in *Novg. IV*] the men of Novgorod marched with Grand Prince Iurii Danilovich toward the river Neva and they built a fortress at the mouth of the river Neva on the island of Orekhov. The envoy of the Swedish king came to them and they concluded permanent peace.

The same year [6831/1323 in *Novg.*] the Novgorodians marched with Grand Prince Iurii Danilovich to Zavaloch'e, and they went as far as Ustiug, coming to the river Dvina. Then the envoys of the [Finnic] princes of Ustiug were sent to Prince Iurii and the Novgorodians. They concluded peace according to the old custom and agreed to give tribute to the Horde, according to the old custom.[43]

The same year [6831/1323 in *Novg. IV*] Grand Prince Iurii Danilovich journeyed from the Zavoloch'e to the Horde and he went by way of Great Perm. Then he travelled along the river Kama.

The same year [6731/1323 in *Novg. IV.*] Davyd, lord Archbishop of Novgorod, passed away. The same year the Novgorodians summoned a veche according to their old custom, and they elected as Archbishop a certain Moses, abbot of St. George Monastery, provided the metropolitan give his blessing. And they settled him in the court of the archbishop until the metropolitan should send for him [for his consecration].

In the year 6833/1325. Grand Prince Dmitrii Mikhailovich of Tver', grandson of Iaroslav, went to the Horde.

The same year [6834/1332 in *Novg.*] in Moscow His Holiness Peter, Metropolitan of Kiev and all Russia, elevated Moses to Archbishop of Novgorod.

42. Actually, the Swedish city of Vyborg.

43. *Zavoloch'e:* the region between the northern Dvina and Volga rivers.

The same year Khan Uzbeg sent [Russian] princes to campaign in Lithuania and they committed much evil in Lithuania and came back and returned to the Horde with many captives. The same year Prince Dmitrii Mikhailovich of Tver', grandson of Iaroslav, killed in the Horde Grand Prince Iurii Danilovich of Moscow, grandson of Aleksandr [Nevskii], great grandson of Iaroslav, gr. gr. gr. grandson of Vsevolod [Great Nest], gr. gr. gr. grandson of Iurii Dolgorukii, gr. gr. gr. gr. grandson of Vladimir Monomakh, gr. gr. gr. gr. gr. grandson of Vsevolod [missing in gr. gr. grandson of Great Vladimir. It happened during the fast of St. Philip on the twenty-first day of the month of November when the holiday of the Presentation of the Most Pure Theotokos in the Temple is celebrated. He did it without the Khan's sanction, relying upon the Khan's favor because Khan Uzbeg respected Prince Dmitrii Mikhailovich of Tver'; and therefore the latter, relying on it, killed Grand Prince Iurii; but it did not do him any good because he fell into the Khan's great disfavor, and remained so until the Khan decided what to do. The same year Khan Uzbeg ordered that the body of Grand Prince Iurii Danilovich of Moscow be taken to Russia and be buried in his patrimony of Moscow.

The same year from the Horde came Prince Aleksandr Mikhailovich of Tver' and with him the Tatars, to whom he had to pay tribute.

The same year they brought the body of Grand Prince Iurii Danilovich of Moscow from the Horde, and Metropolitan Peter buried him on the first Saturday of Great Lent in the church of St. Archangel Michael of Moscow.

The same year [6831/1323 in *Novg.*] the Germans [the Livonian Knights] campaigned against Pskov in ships, boats and by horses; besieging the city for eighteen days, they tried to destroy the walls with battering rams and they dug their trenches up to the fortress wall. There was great grief in Pskov.

At that time Prince Davyd returned from Lithuania with his men and he marched against them—the Germans—beyond the river Velikaia, and he captured their battering rams and destroyed their fortifications, killing many of them. At that time Aleksei

1325   Khrabryi,[44] posadnik of Pskov, and many other brave men were killed by the Germans.

The same year there was a great drought and many marshy places dried out and the forests and marshes burned up.

The same year Prince Ivan Danilovich [Kalita] of Moscow went to the Horde.

[METROPOLITAN PETER SETTLES IN MOSCOW]

The same year [6834/1336 in *Laur.*] His Holiness Peter, Metropolitan of Kiev and all Russia, laid the foundation in Moscow on the Square, in the vicinity of his estate, of the first stone cathedral church of the Assumption of the Most Pure Theotokos. And it happened in the presence of Prince Ivan Danilovich [Kalita], grandson of Aleksandr [Nevskii]; and he, himself [the metropolitan], laid the foundation of his grave in the wall, in the vicinity of the altar, where he was later buried and where he remains till now, providing many miracles for those who come to him with faith.

In the year 6834/1326.   Archbishop Moses came from Moscow to Novgorod after being consecrated by Peter, Metropolitan of Kiev and all Russia.

The same year the envoys from Lithuania came to Novgorod. They were brothers of the Lithuanian Prince Gedimin: Voina, Prince Vasilii of Polotsk, and Prince Fedor Rostislavich of Minsk, and they arranged peace with the Novgorodians and the Germans.

The same fall on the fifteenth day of September, when Holy Martyr Nikita is remembered, Khan Uzbeg in the Horde ordered that they kill Prince Dmitrii Mikhailovich of Tver', grandson of Iaroslav, great grandson of Iaroslav, gr. gr. grandson of Vsevolod, gr. gr. gr. grandson of Iurii Dolgorukii, gr. gr. gr. gr. grandson of Vladimir Monomakh, gr. gr. gr. gr. gr. grandson of Vsevolod [missing in *Nik.*], gr. gr. gr. gr. gr. gr. grandson of Iaroslav, gr. gr. gr. gr. gr. gr. grandson of Great Vladimir; and he did this because the latter killed Prince Iurii Danilovich of Moscow. And Khan Uzbeg was very angry with all the princes of Tver', calling

44. Selila Alekseich in *Novg. IV*.

them "traitors, enemies and adversaries." But although he was **1326** angry with them, he gave the grand principality, after [killing] Dmitrii Mikhailovich, to his brother, Aleksandr Mikhailovich. The same day in the same place on the river Kandrakla, on the order of Khan Uzbeg, Grand Prince Aleksandr of Novosil'sk was killed.

The same year Grand Princess Maria was tonsured a nun.

The same year Prince Aleksandr Mikhailovich of Tver' came from the Horde and, with the Khan's permission, he became Grand Prince of Tver'.

The same year [6832/1324 in *Hyp.*] Grand Prince Ivan Danilovich [Kalita—"Money bags"] of Moscow returned from the Golden Horde. The same year a son, Ivan, was born to Grand Prince Ivan Danilovich [of Moscow].

The same year His Holiness Peter, Metropolitan of Kiev and all Russia, the great wonderworker, passed away in the third hour of the night on the twenty-first day of the month of December. He had remained in the Metropolitan See and was shepherd of the divine church for eighteen years and six months; and he was buried in the city of Moscow, in the church of the Most Pure Theotokos, which he, himself, began to build together with his [spiritual] son, Grand Prince Ivan Danilovich, and where, with his own hands, he laid the foundation of his grave. At that time, thanks to divine aid and the help of the Most Pure Theotokos and our prayerful blessed Metropolitan Peter, three people were cured who had been ill with various diseases. Prince Ivan Danilovich of Moscow and Bishop Theodosius of Lutsk participated in his funeral. Prince Ivan Danilovich wept long, as did Bishop Theodosius and the entire Council of clergy and monks, as well as many boiars and common people, recalling his salutary and instructive words. And he was buried in the vicinity of the holy altar in the wall, in the new stone grave; and there were many cures of those who came to him with faith.

ABOUT THE HUMILITY AND FORBEARANCE OF THE SAINT [PETER] AND ABOUT HIS COMING TO THE CITY OF MOSCOW[45]

45. The original *Life* of Metropolitan Peter (1309-1326) was written in 1327, when Metropolitan Peter was canonized. Its author was a

1326   When, by the blessing of the Holy Sprirt, His Beatitude
Athanasius, Bishop of Constantinople, consecrated reverend
Peter, abbot of Ratsk, to be Metropolitan of Kiev and all Russia, he
honored him greatly and let him go to Russia. The latter, thanks
to the grace of God, successfully crossed the sea and arrived in
the Holy See of the Russian Metropolia, according to the statutes
of the Holy Apostles and saintly fathers. He journeyed from city
to city, from towns to villages, with great humility and much
labor, with quietude and meekness, remembering the One Who
said, "In humble hearts, God reposes." And, also, "A humble and
meek heart will not be destroyed by God. I will look to him that
is of poor and contrite spirit, the humble and meek one, that
trembleth at My words." [*Isaiah* 66:2] "Take My yoke upon you
and learn from Me for I am meek and lowly in heart and you
shall find rest unto your soul." [*Math.* 11:29] But the devil could
not abide this because, from the very beginning, he was the enemy
and adversary of humankind and was reluctant to see any salutary
deeds. And he opposed and incited people to oppose his arrival;
but after a certain time the people changed their minds and accepted His Holiness [Metropolitan Peter] and submitted themselves to him.[46] But he—Metropolitan Peter—not only was not
rancorous, he devoted himself wholeheartedly to them, prayed
for them and dedicated himself to his work.

After a certain time the devil, ever envious, approached and
instilled Andrew with envy, him who was the bishop of the diocese of Tver'. The latter had a light mind, even lighter reason, and
was quite earthly, caring primarily for vainglory. He made his
tongue sharp, spreading lawless words about righteous men, and
weaving words of lies and calumny, which he sent to Constantinople to His Holiness and His Beatitude, Patriarch Athanasius.
The latter was very astonished and took them for misinforma-

clergyman from his immediate milieu. Its purpose was to extol Mos-
cow's importance as the Metropolitan's residence and as a political
center. Possibly it was inspired by Ivan Kalita or his closest advisers. In
Nik. there appears a considerably reworked later version of it. V. A.
Kuchkin: *Skazanie o smerti mitropolita Petra, TODRL*, XVIII. See, also,
Makarii, v. 4, pp. 308-312.

46. Here is an obvious reference to Prince Mikhail of Tver' and Andrew, bishop of Tver', who tried to expel Metropolitan Peter, the latter
being on good terms with the Muscovite princes.

tion; but in view of this devil's cunning, he sent one of his clerics **1326** with an epistle, in which he wrote, "Peter, most sacred Metropolitan of Kiev and all Russia! My beloved brother in the Holy Spirit and co-servant of our humility! I am aware that by the selection of the Holy Spirit you were appointed shepherd and teacher of Christ's flock. Now there have arrived from your land and from your confines heavy accusations against you which fill my ears and trouble me. Do your best to investigate it and make it clear and correct." The cleric took this epistle and these words sent by the Patriarch and came to the Russian land.

And so Andrew's calumnies were no longer concealed from His Holiness, Metropolitan Peter. Placing his hopes in God, he said, "We must abide whatsoever is sent by the Lord and then God will show us who is against us." And so, when the cleric sent by the Patriarch came to Russia, a council was summoned in the city of Pereiaslavl' [Zaleskii], to which came God-loving Simeon, Bishop of Rostov, and most reverend Prokhor, still abbot at that time [but who was nominated bishop]. Andrew, Bishop of Tver', was summoned thither because he was the initiator of all these rumors. Prince Mikhail Iaroslavich of Tver' was then in the Golden Horde; but his children, Dmitrii and Aleksandr, as well as many other princes and boiars, and the best of the clergy, abbots, monks and priests were there in great multitude. Then the cleric sent by Patriarch Athanasius presented the letter and the words addressed to His Holiness Peter, before all.

There was a great uproar over this lying and cunning calumny against His Holiness Peter, Metropolitan of Kiev and all Russia. There was much talk and it was nearly unclear what had happened; but His Holiness raised his voice, imitating His Teacher, Christ, when He told Apostle Peter, "Put your sword into its sheath." He was a meek pupil of a Meek Teacher, and he follows Him in all things. And so he said to all of them, "My brethren and my children, beloved in God! I am no better than Prophet Jonas, and because of me there is a great disturbance. Cast me out and the talk will cease. Why do you care so much for me?" But those who argued on behalf of their teacher and good shepherd created a disturbance and decided to investigate the matter in order to ascertain from whence came these false words about our father and our teacher. The evildoer could not hide and it became clear to all that he had calumniated His Holiness

1326   Peter, Metropolitan of Kiev and all Russia; and Andrew's calumny
was disclosed and he was put to shame and defeated by the Council. His Holiness Peter did him no harm, but with words of consolation he taught him, saying, "Abide in the peace of Christ, my
child, Bishop Andrew! You did not do this, but it was done by the
enemy of the human race, the invidious devil. Now, be care-
ful and Lord God will forgive what you did." Thereafter he
preached to the princes, to the whole council of clergy and to the
people, and let them go in peace.

He did more and more, and increased a hundredfold the
talent given him. He added humility to humility and journeyed
unstintingly to all cities and villages, teaching the flock entrusted
to him by God, paying no heed to his weariness or to his illness.
And thus he labored in great patience and helped all in trouble,
paupers and poor, pilgrims and orphans and widows; and he was
for them as a father should be.

At that time there appeared a certain heretic, Seit, who would
unsettle the churches of God and spread sophistications about the
Orthodox faith. He was defeated in a dispute with His Holiness;
but, since he did not submit, he was cursed, and he perished.

And so, journeying through lands and cities, Peter, the man
of God, Metropolitan of Kiev and all Russia, worked and taught
and instructed all. And he came to the glorious city called Moscow,
which at that time was still very small, with far fewer people than
we see in it now. At that time the ruler of this city was pious Grand
Prince Ivan [Kalita], son of Daniil, grandson of blessed Aleksandr
[Nevskii]. When blessed Peter saw him shining in Orthodoxy,
adorned with good deeds, merciful to the poor, honoring the
holy, divine churches and their servants, loving divine writ, hark-
ening to the holy teachings of the scripture, His Holiness loved
him very much and began to reside in the city of Moscow more
than in any other place. He advised and gave good counsel to the
prince, and he advised him to erect a stone church devoted to the
Name of the Most Pure Lady Theotokos and Virgin Mary; and
he prophesied the following [to Grand Prince Ivan Kalita]:

THE SAINT'S PROPHESY

"My son! If you will follow me and build a temple to the Most
Pure Theotokos, and bury me in your city, you will be more glori-

fied than any other princes, and your children and grandchildren **1326**
will rule there, and the city will become more glorious than any
other cities of Russia. And the metropolitans will live there and
they will raise their hands against its enemies; and God will be
glorified in this city; and my bones will be buried there."

The prince listened to these words and accepted them with
great joy, and he began to care for the building of this church.
It was founded, and from day to day was built higher and higher;
and His Holiness, himself, participated in its construction, hurrying to do so. And there was constant spiritual joy between them
both. The prince would listen and honor his spiritual father, as
was prescribed by the Lord, while the Metropolitan enjoyed it
that his pupil heeded him: "One who heeds you heeds Me, and
one who accepts you, accepts Me." And His Holiness cared for
the spiritual and physical needs of his son, the Prince, to whom
he spoke in the same way as did Apostle Peter: "Who can divide
us in our love for Christ?" Such was the holy divine love between
them.

When they began to build the church, His Holiness could
foresee his forthcoming death through divine revelation and he
began to build his own grave with his holy hands, in the vicinity
of the altar. When he completed it, he had a vision announcing
to him that he would depart from this life and would go to God,
Whom he had loved from his infancy. He became filled with joy,
preparing his departure from this vain, quickly-passing life, and
every day would come to the church, celebrate divine service,
pray for the Orthodox emperors and princes and for his spiritual
son—I mean here, Ivan [Kalita]—whom he loved for his piety,
and for the whole pious Christian multitude of the entire Russian
land. And he would mention the dead during his service, and receive Holy Communion. Leaving the church, he would summon
the clergy and the people and instruct them at length, as he was
wont to do for all those who came to him.

From that time he did not cease distributing alms to the
poor, to the pilgrims, to the paupers, monasteries, churches and
priests. And when he learned the hour for his departure from
this world, he summoned a certain Protasii, who had been appointed the city elder by the Prince because at that time the Prince
was not present in the city. This man, Protasii, was honest, pious
and adorned by all good deeds, and he told him, "My child! I
am departing this life and am bequeathing to my beloved son,

1326 Prince Ivan, and to his forthcoming generation, mercy, peace and the blessing of God for ages and ages, because my spiritual son has provided me with peace; and God will render him still more in this world, and he will, as well, then inherit the Eternal Kingdom. And God will not let his forthcoming generation weaken while ruling this place, and the memory of him will spread." And whatsoever he possessed he left to him, willing that it be spent for the construction of the cathedral church. And giving his blessing of peace to all, he began to chant vespers; while the prayer was still on his lips, his soul abandoned his body and he raised his hands to the heavens and he left his body on earth; but his soul ascended to Christ, so desired by him.

[SHEVKAL INVADES TVER']

In the year 6835/1327. A very important envoy, the Tatar lord Shevkal,[47] came to Tver' from Khan Uzbeg in the Golden Horde. He was a cousin of Khan Uzbeg and he wanted to kill the princes of Tver' and, himself, become prince of Tver' and place his own Tatar lords in the Russian cities, as well as to convert the Christians to the Tatar faith. Although he remained a few days in Tver', he caused the Christians much evil; and when a festival day came and he wanted to impose his will in the people's council, Grand Prince Aleksandr Mikhailovich, grandson of Iaroslav, learned of it and summoned the men of Tver'. They armed themselves and marched against him. Shevkal with his Tatars also advanced against him and they both started fighting at dawn, and they fought all day. Only toward evening did Aleksandr with difficulty defeat him. Shevkal ran onto the porch, but they burned the porch and the entire estate of Prince Mikhail, Aleksandr's father, and so Shevkal and the other Tatars burned there. The merchants who had come from the Horde, those who were already there and newcomers who had come with Shevkal

47. "Shevkal" in *Laur.* Instead of Shevkal, *Nik.* writes "Shchelkan Diudenievich". This is a popular folkloristic transformation of Shevkal's name, especialy in the *bylinas.* In the fifteenth-century chronicles (i.e., *Moskovskii svod kontsa XVogo veka. P.S.R.L.* Vol. 24 *a.o.*), it is just "Shchelkan."

and had not fought, all were slain. Some of them were burned **1327** and some were cast into bonfires and burned there.

When Khan Uzbeg of the Golden Horde learned this, he became greatly wroth and grieved and was sad about his cousin, Shevkal. He roared like a lion against the princes of Tver', determined to destroy them all and capture the entire remaining Russian land. He sent to Russia for Prince Ivan Danilovich of Moscow.

The same year Prince Vasilii of Riazan' was killed in the Horde on the order of Khan Uzbeg.

[DEVASTATION OF THE LAND OF TVER']

The same winter Grand Prince Ivan Danilovich of Moscow journeyed to the Khan of the Golden Horde, and the same winter he returned to Moscow; and with him was the Tatar army of Khan Uzbeg with many commanders: Fedor-chuk, Turalyk, Siuga and many other lords of the Horde, and five great *temniks*,[48] as well as Prince Ivan Vasilievich of Suzdal'. In one place it is written that his uncle, Vasilii Aleksandrovich, was with them. On the Khan's order they marched and took the cities of Tver' and Kashin, and took other cities of the land of Tver'. They burned those lands and those towns and took the people into captivity. They devastated Torzhok and its land. They even wanted to march against Novgorod but they did not: Lord God and Holy Sophia protected it. From thence they sent their envoys to Novgorod and the people of Novgorod were so afraid that they sent their own envoys to render them great honor, sending many gifts and five thousand Novgorodian rubles. And so the Tatars returned from thence with many captives and great booty and there was over the entire Russian land great weariness and grief and bloodshed caused by the Tatars.

At that time they killed Prince Ivan Iaroslavich of Riazan' and they killed many Christians and captured others. Only Prince Ivan Danilovich, his city of Moscow and his own patrimony, however, were protected by God from conquest and from the Tatar

---

48. *Temnik*: a commander of a corps consisting usually of ten thousand men.

1327   bloodletting; and so the Tatars returned to the Golden Horde with many captives.

Grand Prince Aleksandr Mikhailovich of Tver', who could not endure the devil's cunning intrigues and the Tatar violence, relinquished the grand principality of Vladimir [and Tver'] and his entire patrimony, and he went to Pskov with his princess and children, and he lived ten years in Pskov. His brothers, Prince Konstantin Mikhailovich of Tver' and Prince Vasilii Mikhailovich of Tver', grandchildren of Iaroslav and great grandchildren of Iaroslav, with their mother and their boiars, returned to Tver', suffering with great grief and sadness. They settled in Tver' in dire poverty and need because the entire land of Tver' was devastated and there were only the forests and impassable wilderness. And all this occurred because of the treachery, cunning and violence of the Tatars. Little by little, they began to gather people and to console their great sadness and grief, and in the holy churches and monasteries there [again] were chanting and divine services.

The same year a son, Andrei, was born to grand Prince Ivan Danilovich of Moscow.

The same year on the fourth day of the month of August the cathedral church of the Assumption of the Most Pure Theotokos was consecrated in Moscow by Bishop Prokhor of Rostov. Its foundation was laid and its construction was undertaken by His Holiness, blessed Peter, Metropolitan of Kiev and all Russia.

THEOGNOST, METROPOLITAN

In the year 6836/1328. His Holiness Isaiah, Patriarch of Constantinople, consecrated a Greek named Theognost to be Metropolitan of Kiev and all Russia.[49] The same year he came to the great See of the Metropolia of Kiev and all Russia; and he journeyed from Kiev to visit many cities; and he came to the city of Vladimir; and in the glorious city of Moscow [he went] to the cathedral of the Assumption of the Most Pure Theotokos and to

49. Metropolitan Theognost, 1328-1353. According to the tradition and following the example of Metropolitan Peter, Theognost resided in Moscow. He greatly contributed to the strengthening of the prestige and influence of Moscow.

the grave of wonderworker Peter. He occupied his See and took   **1328** up residence in his estate. The grace of God and the Most Pure Theotokos were with him, as well as the prayers and blessings of the great wonderworker Peter. The other princes, however, did not find it very sweet to their taste that the city of Moscow became the seat of the metropolitan.

[IVAN KALITA BECOMES GRAND PRINCE OF VLADIMIR]

The same year Grand Prince Ivan Danilovich of Moscow and Prince Konstantin Mikhailovich of Tver', grandson of Iaroslav Iaroslavich, went to the Golden Horde; the Novgorodians also sent their envoy to the Horde, whose name was Fedor Kolesnitsa. Khan Uzbeg received them all with honor and gave the grand principality of Vladimir to Prince Ivan Danilovich, grandson of Aleksandr [Nevskii], gr. grandson of Iaroslav, gr. gr. grandson of Vsevolod [Great Nest], gr. gr. gr. grandson of Iurii Dolgorukii; he gave him, together with Moscow, several other principalities. He gave to Prince Konstantin Mikhailovich, grandson of Iaroslav, gr. grandson of Iaroslav, the grand principality of Tver'; and he accepted the petition of the Novgorodian envoy, Fedor Kolesnitsa, and ordered all of them to get Prince Aleksandr Mikhailovich of Tver', grandson of Iaroslav.

The same year the earth trembled in Novgorod.

The same year Barsonophias, Bishop of Tver', passed away.

The same year the German [Livonian] city of Iur'ev[50] burned entirely, including their temples, which they called "churches"; and their houses fell apart, and two thousand five hundred thirty Germans and four Russian people burned there.

The same year Prokhor, Bishop of Rostov, passed away.

The same year His Holiness Theognost, the Metropolitan of Kiev and all Russia, consecrated Anthony to be bishop of Rostov and Iaroslavl'. The same year Grand Prince Ivan Danilovich, grandson of Aleksandr [Nevskii], came from Khan Uzbeg in the Golden Horde with great honor and with the patent[51] to be Grand Prince of Vladimir. He settled in the Grand Principality

---

50. Also, Dorpat or Tartu.

51. *Iarlyk, pozhalovanie.*

1328   of Moscow, although he received Vladimir and many other principalities from Khan Uzbeg, to have them under Moscow. And so there was great tranquility in the Russian land for forty years, and the Tatars stopped campaigning in the Russian land.

The same year Prince Konstantin Mikhailovich, grandson of Iaroslav Iaroslavich, came from Khan Uzbeg, from the Golden Horde, to be prince of Tver'.

The same year the Novgorodian envoy, Fedor Kolesnitsa, returned from Khan Uzbeg, from the Golden Horde, to Novgorod and there was great rejoicing.

Following Khan Uzbeg's order, Grand Prince Ivan Danilovich of Moscow, grandson of Aleksandr, sent his envoys to Pskov to Prince Aleksandr Mikhailovich of Tver', asking him to go to the Horde. The Novgorodians also sent their own envoys to Pskov to Prince Aleksandr Mikhailovich of Tver', following Uzbeg's order, and asked him [Prince Aleksandr] to go to him [to Uzbeg] in the Horde. His own brother, Prince Konstantin Mikhailovich of Tver', also sent his envoys to him in Pskov about the delay; but he did not want to go to Khan Uzbeg in the Horde, and did not go.[52]

In the year 6837/1329. [In Moscow] the foundation was laid for a stone church of St. John Climacus, which now is under the belfry [called "Ivan the Great"]. The same year a stone church of the Veneration of the Venerable Irons of the Apostle Peter was built.

The same year Khan Uzbeg of the Golden Horde sent his envoys to all the Russian princes requesting that all of them should capture Prince Aleksandr Mikhailovich of Tver' and bring him to him in the Horde.

THE METROPOLITAN

The same year His Holiness Theognost, a Greek, Metropolitan of Kiev and all Russia, arrived in Novgorod.

UZBEG WANTS PRINCE ALEXANDER MIKHAILOVICH

The same year in the German city of Iur'ev an honorable

---

52. In the same annual entry, on pages 196-201, of Vol. 10 of *PSRL*, are several stories about Serbia, Bulgaria and Byzantium. Since they have no bearing on Russian history, those stories, which were taken from the *Chronograph*, are omitted here.

and courageous man, the son of Ivan, was killed.[53] The same
year the accursed enemy, the devil, put it into the minds of the
Russian princes to catch, on the order of the Tatar Khan Uzbeg,
Prince Aleksandr Mikhailovich of Tver', and they tried to do so,
and raised an army throughout all Russia. Grand Prince Ivan
Danilovich [Kalita] went to Novgorod, and with him were the
princes of Tver', junior brothers of Aleksandr Mikhailovich of
Tver', Prince Konstantin Mikhailovich of Tver', and his brother,
Prince Vasilii Mikhailovich of Tver', as well as Prince Aleksandr
Vasilievich of Suzdal'. And they took with them all the men of
Novgorod.

Grand Prince Ivan Danilovich sent his envoy, Luka Protasiev,
to Pskov, to Prince Aleksandr Mikhailovich of Tver', while the
Novgorodians sent, on their behalf, Lord Bishop Moses and
tysiatskii Avraam in order to convince him to go to the Horde to
Khan Uzbeg, saying, "Khan Uzbeg has ordered all of us to find
you and send you to him, to the Horde. Go to him. In this way
you will not draw his wrath upon us all. It is just that you should
suffer for all, than that we should all suffer because of you; and
the entire land would be devastated."

Aleksandr told them, "Indeed, I have to suffer for everyone
with due passion and love, rather than take revenge against those
who were cunning and who plotted against me. This life is of no
importance; we will all disappear and pass into oblivion. Everyone will be given by God whatsoever he deserves for his deeds.
It would be more fitting for you to stay together, brother for
brother, not to betray anyone to the Tatars but fight them, being
united for the sake of the Russian land and the Orthodox Christians. But you act unjustly and bring the Tatars against the Christians and betray your brethren to the Tatars!" And he wanted
to go to Khan Uzbeg, to the Golden Horde; but the men of Pskov
did not permit him to do so, saying:

"Our lord, Prince Aleksandr Mikhailovich! They want to
send you to the infidel khan, to the Horde, who wants to destroy
you so that you not remain alive. Uzbeg sent them his envoys, and
they promised Uzbeg, and they are united in turning you over to
death. Do not go uselessly to the Horde to be given over unto
death; but stay in Pskov, and we will all sacrifice our heads for
you."

53. The name is omitted in *Nik.* but appears in *Novg. III.*

1329   And so all the men of Pskov strongly supported him.

When the princes saw that the men of Pskov stood staunchly for him they began to deliberate, and Grand Prince Ivan Danilovich said, "In case we do not bring Prince Aleksandr Mikhailovich of Tver' to the Horde, all of us will be deprived by Khan Uzbeg of our patrimonies and we will be given over to death, and the Russian land will be devastated." And so Grand Prince Ivan Danilovich with the aforementioned princes and with all the men of Novgorod marched against him, and it was a large army and strong force. They camped in Opochka, and the princes began deliberating among themselves, saying the following: "In case we march against Prince Aleksandr Mikhailovich of Tver', the men of Pskov will stand in all firmness for him, and they all promise to die for him; and the Germans[54] are in the vicinity and they may help him—under these conditions, we can neither drive him away nor capture him!"

And then they began to ask and consult His Holiness, Metropolitan Theognost, that he interdict and excommunicate him [Prince Aleksandr], thus binding him, and send him to Khan Uzbeg. And so Metropolitan Theognost sent his interdiction and his curse upon Prince Aleksandr Mikhailovich of Tver' and on the entire city of Pskov and on their land.

Then Prince Aleksandr Mikhailovich of Tver' said the following to the men of Pskov:

"Brethren and faithful friends! My beloved and brave men of Pskov! I do not want any excommunication or curse from His Holiness upon you because of me, poor and sinful one. I do not wish that, because of me, a sinful wretch, His Holiness should excommunicate and damn you. And in order to avoid breaking my and your oath [of mutual support], I, wretch, will leave you and will go to the Germans and to Lithuania. In such a way Khan Uzbeg and the Russian princes will not cause any hardship for you or your land. And those of my enemies who persecute me and attempt to take my soul from me will not be able to do so."

The men of Pskov summoned a *veche*, wept sorely, and let Prince Aleksandr Mikhailovich of Tver' leave them, according to his will; and they did this with great weeping and tears. He went to the Germans and from thence to Lithuania; and the people of

54. Livonian Knights.

Pskov sent to Grand Prince Ivan Danilovich a petition offering   **1329**
peace and concord. He made peace with them and returned to
Novgorod, and from Novgorod he went to Moscow, and all the
other princes went to their respective principalities.

The same year the Russian princes sent to Khan Uzbeg in
the Golden Horde, informing him of the escape of Prince Aleksandr Mikhailoich of Tver' to the Germans and to Lithuania.

The same year the people of Pskov built themselves a stone
fortress on the Zherava Mountain and named it "Izborsk."

The same year Novgorodian Lord Bishop Moses gave up his
diocese and went to the monastery in Kolomtsa, and took the
schema; and so the Novgorodians remained for eight days without a bishop. Thereupon they selected the priest, Grigorii, of
the church of Kosma and Damian from Kholop'e street, and he
was shorn a monk; and they brought him to the porch of the Bishop's estate. He was given the monastic name, Basil.

ABOUT THE MONASTERY OF ST. DANIEL

The same year His Holiness Theognost, Metropolitan of
Kiev and all Russia, went from Novgorod to the Volynian land,
and from thence to Galich and Zharava, and from thence to Kiev,
The envoys of Grand Prince Ivan Danilovich of Vladimir and
Moscow came thither, asking him to organize a monastery for
himself inside the city of Moscow and to build a church of the
Transfiguration of the Saviour, and to transfer thither from
Zarech'e[55] the monastery of St. Daniel, whose abbot had the
rank of archimandrite. Grand Prince Daniel Aleksandrovich
built this monastery dedicated to his own Christian name and he
was able to enjoy its grace, which shone there as the sun. He [Ivan
Kalita] wanted to transfer it inside the city, near his court, because
he was a great lover of wisdom and sure supporter of the monastic
life. He did not want to be separated from them—the monks—
even for a single hour, neither by day nor by night. And so he
received a blessing from His Holiness Theognost, Metropolitan
of Kiev and all Russia, for everything which was connected with
this deed.

In the year 6838/1330. Temir, son of Uzbeg, died in the Gold-

55. Zarech'e: the region south of the Moscow river.

1330 en Horde. He killed the king of Zagor'e.[56] And Khan Uzbeg
grieved greatly.

The same year Khan Uzbeg honored the bishop of Sarai and
gave him whatsoever he petitioned, so that none could offend
him. The same year the great lord of the Horde, Hassan, was
killed by his wife.

The same year there was a great drought.

The same year Prince Fedor Ivanovich of Starodub, grandson of Mikhail, great grandson of Ivan, gr. gr. grandson of Vsevolod [Great Nest], gr. gr. gr. grandson of Iurii Dolgorukii, was
killed in the Horde.

The same year Prince Vasilii Mikhailovich of Tver', grandson of Iaroslav, great grandson of Iaroslav, gr. gr. grandson of
Vsevolod [Great Nest], married in Briansk.

The same year His Holiness Theognost, Metropolitan of
Kiev and all Russia, came from Kiev to the city of Vladimir in
Volynia. The same year His Holiness Theognost, Metropolitan
of Kiev and all Russia, while in the city of Vladimir in Volynia,
there elevated Theodore to bishop of Tver'.

The same year Grand Prince Ivan Danilovich [Kalita of Mos-
cow], grandson of Aleksandr [Nevskii], great grandson of Iaroslav, gr. gr. grandson of Vsevolod [Great Nest], gr. gr. gr. grandson of Iurii Dolgorukii, with the blessing of his spiritual father,
His Holiness Theognost, Metropolitan of Kiev and all Russia,
built a wonderful monastery near his court in Moscow, and built
there a beautiful church dedicated to the Holy Transfiguration of
Our Lord God and Our Saviour Jesus Christ. He gathered many
monks there and he loved this monastery more than any other,
and would often go thither to pray, in great humility and de-
votion, so that all marvelled at his meekness and piety. He would
distribute alms and everything needed by the monks who lived
there: food, drink, clothing; and he gave them the right to levy
certain taxes, so that they could live without being in need. It
was a very venerable monastery and it received many privileges
and much care from all sides, so that it would not be hurt by anyone. In it was a church which was adorned with holy and venerable icons, holy books, holy vessels and all manner of valuables.

---

56. Zagor'e: the land beyond the mountains—probably, the Caucasus.
It may be either Georgia or Armenia.

The first archimandrite brought thither was Ivan, an imposing man who was very eloquent and wise and who was learned in divine scripture. He was very virtuous and because of his virtues later was consecrated bishop of Rostov. There he successfully cared for the flock entrusted to him by God and he went to God in a very old age.

Some people, following the saying of the old monks, claim that in the beginning it was Grand Prince Danilo Aleksandrovich, grandson of Iaroslav, great grandson of Vsevolod [Great Nest] who built beyond the Moscow river this abbey of St. Daniel; and he built the church which was dedicated to the saint of his own name. After some years his son, Grand Prince Ivan [Kalita], who was very pious and who loved the monks and pilgrims, and whose great piety was very warm, transferred this abbey to the city of Moscow and built it close by him because he wanted to see it often and have joy in it. Therefore he organized such a divine treasure near his place, where all could come on pilgrimage and where it would be a memorial for his future generations. In this way he acquired a great, pious and glorious recompense, especially a glory which would please God, as it is said in the Scriptures: "He chose the blessed part, and it will never be removed from him." And so, being pious and Christ-loving, this prince laid the foundation for a blessed and Christ-loving beginning, and after him, his children and grandchildren and great grandchildren followed him, and did the same. His descendants received the same blessing and glory, and from generation to generation this monastery remained as a blessing from God and His Most Pure Mother: "When the roots are blessed, the branches are also venerable and will not be hurt."

In the year 6839/1331. There was a portent in the sky and the sun became dark. The same year there was a conflagration in Moscow and the entire city of Moscow burned.

The same year [6840/1332 in *Vozn.*] Grand Princess Elena, wife of Ivan Danilovich [Kalita], was tonsured a nun and to the schema, and passed away; she was buried in the church of the Holy Transfiguration of Our Lord God and Saviour, Jesus Christ. The same year Basil, nominated bishop of Novgorod, who already lived in the residence of the lord bishop but was not yet consecrated, laid the foundation of a stone fortification which extended from [the church of St.] Vladimir to [the church of] the Theotokos, and thence to [the church of] Boris and Gleb.

1331   The same year on the twenty-eighth day of May Prince Fedor Vasilievich[57] passed away.

[THE TRIBULATIONS OF BASIL, ARCHBISHOP OF NOVGOROD]

The same year the envoys of Theognost, Metropolitan of Kiev and all Russia, came from Vladimir in Volynia to Novgorod and summoned the nominated bishop of Novgorod, monk Basil, who earlier was [called] priest Gregory,[58] of the church of Kosma and Damian, to go [to Theognost] to be consecrated. He was already shorn a monk on the estate of the lord bishop, was nominated by Novgorod and was supposed to be consecrated. And so monk Basil went from the residence of the lord bishop to Volynia, to be consecrated archbishop of Novgorod by Theognost, Metropolitan of Kiev and all Russia. Together with him went the Novgorodian posadniks, Kuz'ma Tverdislavich, and Efrem Ostafiev, son of a tysiatskii. Since they passed through the Lithuanian land, Prince Gedimin of Lithuania caught them during their journey, and when they were his prisoners they promised him they would cede to his son, Narimont, the Novgorodian districts of Ladoga and the town of Orekhov, as well as the Karelian land, and half of Kopor'e.[59] And this would be his patrimony and belong to his children and grandchildren. Only then were they released. From thence they went to the city of Vladimir in Volynia.

When they arrived in Vladimir in the Volynian land, and came to Theognost, Metropolitan of Kiev and all Russia, on the twenty-fifth day of August, monk Basil was consecrated Bishop of Novgorod in the church of the Most Pure Theotokos. With Metropolitan Theognost there were five bishops: Athanasius of Vladimir and Volynia, Gregory of Polotsk, Theodore of Galich, Mark of Peremyshl, and John of Kholm. At that time a bright star appeared over the church.

About the same time an envoy came from Pskov, from Prince Aleksandr Mikhailovich of Tver', from Prince Gedimin of Lithuania, and from all the princes of Lithuania, to Theognost,

57. Prince of Rostov, son of Vasilii Konstantinovich.

58. Gregory Kalika in *Novg. Kom.*

59. Kopor'e: a town on the Gulf of Finland southwest of present Leningrad, and its district.

Metropolitan of Kiev and all Russia, bowing and petitioning him **1331**
to consecrate a bishop for them in Pskov. They brought him with
them and his name was Arsenius. The people of Pskov did not
care for the supremacy of Novgorod and they intended to have
their own bishop and their own prince. Metropolitan Theognost, however, did not listen to them and did not consecrate them
a bishop for the city of Pskov; and so monk Arsenius, with the
envoys of Pskov, left Metropolitan Theognost and Vladimir in
Volynia with shame.

In the year 6840/1332. [6839/1331 in *Novg. III, Vozn.*]. After
consecrating Basil archbishop of Novgorod, His Holiness Theognost, Metropolitan of Kiev and all Russia, let him and the posadniks of Novgorod go to Novgorod. He—Basil—afraid of the
Lithuanians, marched with his Novgorodian posadniks along the
borders of Lithuania and Kiev, trying to escape from them. Even
Metropolitan Theognost sent a missive after them with one of
his nobles,[60] for him and his posadniks, announcing, "The prince
of Lithuania has sent five hundred Lithuanian men against you
in order to seize you." They began quickly to flee and they escaped from them; but when they approached the city of Chernigov they were caught up with there by Prince Fedor of Kiev and a
Tatar baskak with a small troop of fifty men; but with the Archbishop and posadniks there were six hundred men.

When they received these tidings they fortified their camp,
but more people began to join Prince Fedor and so the Novgorodians took fright and gave a ransom for themselves. Prince
Fedor of Kiev made peace with them, accepted the ransom but
nonetheless after the peace caught an honorable and glorious
man, a protodeacon of the Metropolitan's named Radislav, and
took him to Kiev and from thence sent him to Metropolitan Theognost. But this prince was put to shame by Metropolitan Theognost and was punished by God: all his horses died and he had to
go on foot. Also, Metropolitan Theognost told him, "It is a shame
for a prince to cause injustice, to offend, violate and rob." So the
prince was put to shame by the metropolitan.

Archbishop Vasilii of Novgorod with the posadniks marched
from thence to Briansk, and from Briansk they went to Torzhok
on the third day of the month of November. At that time in Nov-

60. *Boiarskii syn.*

gorod there was great grief about the archbishop and the posadniks because no correct news had been received from them and there were false speeches that the bishop had been seized and the posadniks killed. And that is the reason why there was grief in Novgorod. However, thereafter, thanks to the grace of God and the Most Pure Theotokos, Archbishop Vasilii was protected and saved, as well as all those with him, and they came to Novgorod on the eighth day of November; at that time there were there Prince Ivan Danilovich [Kalita of Moscow], posadnik Varfolomei, and tysiatskii Ostafii. And so the Novgorodians rejoiced, meeting their archbishop and their posadniks.

The same year [6834/1311 in *Vozn.*] Grand Prince Ivan Danilovich [Kalita] went to the Horde and Prince Konstantin Mikhailovich of Tver' accompanied him.

The same year there was a disturbance in Novgorod and there were troublemakers, and they took away the office of posadnik from Fedor Akhmyl and gave it to Zakharii Mikhailovich, and they sacked the estate of Semen Sudakov and his brother, Selifont,[61] taking from them all their estates, wealth and towns.

The same year Grand Prince Ivan Danilovich [Kalita] came from the Horde and he became wroth with the Novgorodians, asking from them [as a fine] silver from beyond the river Kama; and for this [disturbance] he took from the Novgorodians the towns of Torzhok and Bezhetskii Verkh. The same year there was a bad harvest in the Russian land and very high prices, and some people said that this dearness occurred because of the rye.

The same year Prince Konstantin Mikhailovich [of Tver'], grandson of Iaroslav, came from the Horde.

In the year 6841/1333. [6840/1332 in *Sof. V* and *Vozn.*] Prince Aleksandr Vasilievich of Suzdal' passed away.

The same year Basil, archbishop of Novgorod, went to Pskov and there in Pskov he baptised Prince Mikhail, son of Grand Prince Aleksandr Mikhailovich of Tver'.

The same year Prince Narimont Gediminovich, who in holy baptism was named Gleb, came to Novgorod to take over the lands which had been promised to him [by the posadniks and nominated archbishop] when they were in Lithuania travelling

---

61. "Senlifont" in *Novg.*

to Metropolitan Theognost, to the Volynian land, and they gave **1333** him what had been promised.[62]

The same year His Holiness Theognost, Metropolitan of Kiev and all Russia, came to Moscow after having visited Constantinople and the Horde. The same year [6842/1334 in *Laur.*] Grand Prince Ivan Danilovich laid in Moscow the foundation of a stone church of St. Archangel Michael on the square inside the fortress, and the same year its construction was completed and it was consecrated by His Holiness Theognost, Metropolitan of Kiev and all Russia. This occurred on the twentieth of the month of September, when the Holy Martyrs Eustachius Placida and others are remembered.

The same winter [6842/1334 in *Laur.*] in Moscow Grand Prince Ivan Danilovich [Kalita] married his seventeen-year-old son, Semion, bringing as his bride a Lithuanian princess named Augusta, who in Holy Baptism was called Anastasia.

The same winter Grand Prince Ivan Danilovich [Kalita] marched with all the princes and with a great force to wage war against Torzhok. He recalled his namestniks from Novgorod and, himself, settled in Torzhok, waging war in the Novgorodian land from Epiphany to the Council.[63] And so they—the Novgorodians—sent a petition with Archimandrite Laurentius, Fedor Tverdislavovich and Luka Varfolomeev; but he did not listen to their entreaties, did not accept their petition and did not agree to peace, and went to Moscow.

The same year Basil, archbishop of Novgorod, removed the scaffold from the wall of the great cathedral of Holy Sophia [as in *Novg. Kom.*] and, thanks to the Holy Ghost, he built a stone fortification in two years.

The same year an envoy named Saranchuk came from the Horde, from Khan Uzbeg, to Russia, summoning Grand Prince Ivan Danilovich [Kalita]. The same year Grand Prince Ivan Danilovich with Khan Uzbeg's envoy, Saranchuk, went to the Horde, having been summoned by Khan Uzbeg.

62. Districts of Ladoga, Orekhov, Karela and half of Kopor'e, *Novg. Kom.*

63. "Council:" the day of the Council, or the first Sunday of Lent, when the Council of Constantinople is memorialized for restoring veneration of icons.

1334   *In the year 6842/1334.* Grand Prince Ivan Danilovich came from Khan Uzbeg, from the Horde with grants and honors.

The same year Boris, Prince of Dmitrov, passed away in the Horde.

The same year Prince Dmitrii of Briansk came with a Tatar army against Smolensk, waging war against Prince Ivan Aleksandrovich; and after fighting a long while, they made peace.

The same year [6841/1333 in *Novg. IV,* but 6842/1334 in *Novg. Kom.*] the Novgorodians for the second time sent their envoy to Grand Prince Ivan Danilovich [Kalita] and they concluded peace according to the old [tradition]. The same year Basil, Lord Archbishop of Novgorod, went with many presents and honors to Vladimir, to Theognost, Metropolitan of Kiev and all Russia.

In the year 6843/1335. Moses, former Archbishop of Novgorod, started building a stone church of the Holy Resurrection in Derevianitsa, and he founded an honorable monastery there.

The same year Grand Prince Ivan Danilovich [Kalita] marched from Novgorod toward Torzhok. The same year Lithuanians campaigned in the land of Novotorzhok and therefore Grand Prince Ivan Danilovich assembled an army and marched, burning the Lithuanian towns of Otsechin, Riasna and others. And at that time the Lithuanians killed many good Novgorodian men.

The same fall [6844/1336 in *Novg. III,* but 6843/1335 in *Novg. Kom.*] there was a flood, ice and snow in the river Volkhov, and the water was so high that it destroyed fifteen piers. The same year Basil, archbishop of Novgorod, went to Moscow to Grand Prince Ivan Danilovich and was received with honor.

The same year Prince Fedor of Galich passed away.

The same year [6844/1336, *Novg. III.*] Prince Fedor Aleksandrovich of Tver', grandson of Mikhail, great grandson of Iaroslav, came from the Horde, from Khan Uzbeg, and with him came the Khan's envoy, Abdul.

In the year 6844/1336. Grand Prince Ivan Danilovich Kalita went to the Horde to Khan Uzbeg and the same winter he came from the Horde from Khan Uzbeg, with grants and honors for his patrimony.

The same year [6845/1337 in *Laur.*] Anthony, Bishop of Rostov, passed away. The same year His Holiness Theognost, Metropolitan of Kiev and all Russia, consecrated Gabriel Bishop of Rostov.

The same year Prince Aleksandr Mikhailovich of Tver' went from Pskov to Tver' and brought back with him to Pskov his son, Fedor.

The same year Grand Prince Aleksandr Mikhailovich of Tver' began to grieve and sorrow because of his life in Pskov and he said, "In case I should die here, what will happen to my children? All the nations know that I fled from my principality; and should I die here, then my children will be deprived of their right to the principality. Better that I die for the sake of God than live in misfortune." And he sent his boiars to Theognost, Metropolitan of Kiev and all Russia, asking his and the other bishops' blessings and prayers because he decided to go to the Khan in the Horde. He received from Metropolitan Theognost and from all the Russian bishops their blessing and prayers, and he began to prepare himself to go to the Horde with his boiars and his squires.

In the year 6845/1337. [6846/1338 in *Novg. IV.*] A son, Vasilii, was born to Prince Semion Ivanovich [son of Kalita], grandson of Daniil. The same fall there was a great flood.

The same fall Prince Aleksandr Mikhailovich of Tver' went from Pskov to the Horde and, coming to Khan Uzbeg, he told him, "My lord, Autocrat and Khan! I have done you much harm; but I have come to you in order to accept from you death or life, as God directs you. I am ready for everything. In the case, for the sake of God, the Khan's majesty will show me mercy, I will thank God and Your Majesty. In the case you deliver me over to death, then I deserve death, and here is my head before you." Khan Uzbeg marvelled at the sweetness of these words and at his meekness and he told his lords, "Do you see Prince Aleksandr Mikhailovich of Tver'? How he, through humble wisdom, has escaped death?" And everyone marvelled, and Khan Uzbeg

64. The misfortunes and death of Prince Aleksandr of Tver' were written down in a realistic story by one of his supporters and probable eyewitness to his death, most likely a clergyman from Tver'. The whole original story has not been preserved but is known from the *Nik.* text. It was divided, according to the system of the chronicle, into several annual entries under the years 1327, 1329, 1336-1339. Its pro-Tver' and anti-Moscow bias is obvious, but is nonetheless weakened by this division into sections and insertion into the same yearly entries of other historical material. It is discussed in *IRL*(AN)II/I, pp. 103, 106.

1337 rendered him great honor and granted him his patrimony, the grand principality of Tver', and let him go to Russia.

The same year there was a conflagration in Moscow and eighteen holy churches burned.

In the year 6846/1338. Grand Prince Aleksandr Mikhailovich of Tver' came from the Horde, from Khan Uzbeg, to be Grand Prince of Tver', and with him were the [Tatar] envoys, lords Kindiak and Abdul.[65] The same year many boiars abandoned Prince Aleksandr Mikhailovich of Tver' and went to Moscow, to Grand Prince Ivan Danilovich. The same winter Prince Aleksandr Mikhailovich of Tver' sent his son, Prince Fedor, with the [Tatar] envoy, Abdul, to the Horde; but he did not make any agreement with Grand Prince Ivan Danilovich [Kalita] nor was he reconciled with him. The same year Grand Prince Ivan Danilovich of Moscow went to the Horde. The same year the Tatars waged war in Lithuania. The same year in the Horde certain people sorely calumniated Prince Aleksandr Mikhailovich of Tver' to Khan Uzbeg, and they filled the Khan's ears with much bitterness. Khan Uzbeg became very alarmed and, summoning one of his men by the name of Istorchii, told him, secretly, the following words: "Go to Russia and summon hither to me Prince Aleksandr Mikhailovich of Tver', and do not do so with fright and cruelty but quietly and meekly." And the latter went to Russia and did as he had been told, saying, "The Autocrat, Khan Uzbeg, summons you and asks you to come to him, to the Horde, with your son, Fedor; and the Khan will do all according to your will and you will receive from him the grand principality [of Vladimir] and great honor." But Prince Aleksandr had already heard from some people about the Khan's wrath, and he began to contemplate. "In case I go to the Horde, to Khan Uzbeg, I will be delivered to death. In case I do not go to him, to the Horde, his army will come hither and many Christians will be killed and captured, and I will be responsible for it. Better that I, alone, should die for everyone else, since I have to receive the revenge of Lord God and His punishment." And so he began to prepare himself to go to the Horde.

The same year Prince Vasilii Semionovich, grandson of Ivan [Kalita], great grandson of Daniil, gr. gr. grandson of Alek-

65. "Avdul," in *Nik.*

sandr [Nevskii], gr. gr. gr. grandson of Iaroslav, gr. gr. gr. gr.   **1338**
grandson of Vsevolod [Great Nest], gr. gr. gr. gr. gr. grandson of
Iurii Dolgorukii, gr. gr. gr. gr. gr. gr. grandson of Vladimir
Monomakh—the latter being the son of Vsevolod and grandson
of Iaroslav, and great grandson of Vladimir—passed away.

In the year 6847/1339. There was a portent in the church of
St. Lazar', from the icon of the Most Pure Theotokos. Tears
flowed from both the eyes [of the image of the Theotokos], so that
people put two wax vessels underneath. The same year the suburbs of Vladimir burned. The same year there was a portent in
the sky.

The same year [6848/1340 in *Laur.*] Grand Prince Ivan
Danilovich Kalita, grandson of Aleksandr [Nevskii], gr. grandson
of Iaroslav, went to the Horde with two of his sons, Semion and
Ivan; and he sent his third son, Andrei, to Novgorod. When
Grand Prince Ivan Danilovich Kalita came to the Horde, to Khan
Uzbeg, he and his sons were received with great honor by Khan
Uzbeg, and then Khan Uzbeg sent more Tatar [envoys] for
Prince Aleksandr of Tver', Prince Vasilii Davydovich of Iaros-
lavl', grandson of Fedor, gr. grandson of Rostislav; and for the
other princes. Prince Aleksandr Mikhailovich of Tver' sent his
son, Fedor, ahead of himself to the Horde, to Khan Uzbeg. When
Fedor Aleksandrovich learned of the furious wrath of the Khan
at his father, he sent him tidings about everything which he had
heard; but the latter said, "If I should live now, I will nonetheless
die, later; but if I do not go now to the Horde, it will cause the
Khan great wrath, and much Christian blood will be shed." And
so he prepared himself to go to the Horde.

The same year Grand Prince Ivan Danilovich Kalita came
from the Horde, from Khan Uzbeg, to Russia, to his patrimony,
with great grants and honors.

The same year [6848/1340 in *Laur.*] Grand Prince Aleksandr Mikhailovich of Tver' went to the Horde, and at that time
his son, Prince Fedor, was already in the Horde. His mother,
boiars, merchants and better men of the city, and the entire city
shed tears for him and attempted mightily to persuade him not to
go to the Horde, to the Khan: "You are aware that the Khan is
wrathful toward you and wants to execute you. And divine scriptures do not teach one to go in order to deliver oneself over to
death." But he responded, "The Lord says in His Gospel, 'Be not

1339 afraid of them that kill the body, but are not able to kill the soul.'
[*Math*. 10:28] And then He said, 'Greater love hath no man than
this: that a man lay down his life for his friends.' [*John* 15:13, originally quoted in *Laur.*] And the Apostle said, 'through many
tribulations we must enter the Kingdom of God,' [*Acts* 14:22] and
all those who want to live piously, according to Christ, will be
elected. And, also, the Holy Prophets and Holy Apostles and
Holy Patriarchs and reverend fathers who suffered for the sake
of Christ were crowned and won heavenly gifts. Since I issued
from my mother's womb, I have sinned and do not stop sinning:
so how is it possible that I should not suffer in this present rapidly-
passing life? All our life here is but a passing shadow and disappears as smoke, and is as a dream of no importance." And they—
his people—grieved and said, "The will of the Lord be done."
[*Math*. 6:9 paraph.] And so they remained silent.

And he went to the boat with those accompanying him, but a
great wind arose. Although the people were rowing, his boat
went backward, and although they labored, the wind struck them
in the face and their boat was pushed back. Only with great labor
did they cross the Russian land. His brother, Prince Vasilii Mikhailovich, bedridden and badly ill, bewailed Prince Aleksandr
Mikhailovich greatly, and said, "This one is approaching the end
of his life. He was our mentor and the securer of our patrimony,
and the people have been edified by him after this war."

And so they went with him to the Horde, to Khan Uzbeg—
Prince Vasilii Davydovich of Iaroslavl', grandson of Fedor, gr.
grandson of Rostislav, gr. gr. grandson of Mstislav, gr. gr. gr.
grandson of Davyd; and Prince Romanchuk of Belozero. When
they came to the Horde Prince Aleksandr Mikhailovich of Tver'
found there his son, Fedor, and they embraced and shed tears.
The son told him about the Khan's wrath and he answered, "The
Lord's Will will be done." He took many presents for the Khan,
for the Khan's wife, for his lords and for the other dignitaries. He
remained in the Horde for one month with Khan Uzbeg; and
many Tatars who were his friends told him, "The Khan wants to
kill you because you were badly calumniated to him." And he responded to them, "What should I do? If God wants to turn me
over to death, who can help me to escape it?" And he began to
pray diligently and to repent, and he confessed to his spiritual

father; and when the day of Great Martyr Demetrius[66] was approaching, he received the news that he would be killed and would be turned over to a bad death within three days. And he answered, "Lord, Thy Will be done as Thou wantest." And the whole day, grieving, he walked and prayed and sorrowed.

The day came when the Holy Martyrs Terentius and Neonila, and reverend Stephen, the hymnwriter, and Sabbatius and the Holy Martyr Paraskeve—also called *Piatnitsa*[67]—are remembered. He awoke early and asked that matins be chanted. When they began to read David's Psalms,

"Lord! How are mine adversaries increased!

Many are they that rise up.

Many there are that speak of my soul!" [*PS*. 3:1-2]

he asked that the service be interrupted, he approached the icon, made the sign of the cross, and made his devotions before the icon, saying, "Since King David, the Great Prophet of God, the Father, blessed by the Holy Spirit, had so many misfortunes and troubles, why, then, should I not suffer—I, who am so sinful? Lord, Thy Will be done. I am ready for everything and I, greatly sinful, why should I not suffer? Oh, Lord, I am ready for everything for the sake of Thy Holy Name."

Then he ordered that the service be continued according to the rules, and the prayers were read. After a longer while had passed, he sent to the wife of the Khan to find out the news and he, himself, mounted his horse and rode, asking for news of his forthcoming death from those whom he knew and who were his friends. When he learned, verily, that he would be turned over to death at once, he returned to his camp and the news came from the Khan's wife that he would be executed the same hour.

He embraced his son, kissed his boiars, spoke of his patrimony and of his son, and asked for forgiveness of his boiars and his squires and, especially, of his spiritual father, and he forgave them and shed tears for all. Finally, he confessed to his spiritual father about everything, and then he received the Holy and Divine Communion, and so did his son and his boiars and all who were with him: no one expected to remain alive.

66. Oct. 26.

67. *Paraskeve*—"Friday" in Greek, *Piatnitsa* in Russian, Oct. 28.

1339   After a short time his pages came to him, saying, with bitter weeping and many tears, "Lord! Our beloved prince! Berkan and Cherkass, who are sent by Khan Uzbeg to kill you, are already coming." And he raised his arms toward Heaven and began to pray. "Lord! Thy, and not my, Will be done. It will be as according to Thy will, whether I am to live or to die. Be merciful to me and forgive me my sins." And when he had said this and was uninterruptedly shedding tears from his eyes—as did everyone else—the Khan's envoys came to his camp. [6848/1340 in *Laur.*]

He went to meet them with humility, and so he was killed, with his son, Fedor: they cut off their heads. His boiars and squires, however, dispersed, but those who remained there took up their bodies and bore them to Russia.

When they[68] came to the city of Vladimir, they were met by Theognost, Metropolitan of Kiev and all Russia, with the entire Holy Council, and they sang the burial chants and let them go further. His brothers, Prince Konstantin Mikhailovich and Prince Vasilii Mikhailovich, met them in Pereiaslavl'. Gabriel, Bishop of Rostov, and Theodore, Bishop of Tver', also met them in Pereiaslavl' with a procession and they sang the usual burial chants and let them proceed to Tver'. And there, at the Church of St. Michael, the citizens met them, attached their heads and carred them into the city, bringing them to the church of the Holy Saviour. His mother, his brothers, his wife, the princess with his children, and the entire city bitterly bewailed them for a long time; and so the principality of Tver' became deserted [by its prince].

His Holiness Theodore, Bishop of Tver', together with the Holy Council, sang the burial hymns over them and they buried them in the church of the Transfiguration of Our Lord and Saviour, Jesus Christ. And thus did Grand Prince Aleksandr Mikhailovich of Tver' pass away—the grandson of Iaroslav, gr. grandson of Iaroslav, gr. gr. grandson of Vsevolod [Great Nest], gr. gr. gr. grandson of Iurii Dolgorukii, gr. gr. gr.gr. grandson of Vladimir Monomakh, gr. gr. gr. gr. gr. grandson of Vsevolod[69], gr. gr. gr. gr. gr. gr. grandson of Iaroslav, gr. gr. gr. gr. gr. gr. gr. grandson of Great Vladimir. He remained in Pskov for thirteen

---

68. "They"—the bodies of Princes Aleksandr and Fedor.
69. Missing in *Nik.*

years and escaped to Germany and to Lithuania and, finally, re-   **1339**
turned to his patrimony, to Tver'; and he met his death in the
Horde with his son, Fedor, on the order of Khan Uzbeg on the
twenty-eighth day of the month of October, when Holy Martyrs
Terentius and Neonila, and reverend Stephen the Hymnwriter,
and Sabbatius and the Holy Martyr Paraskeve, called *Piatnitsa*,
are remembered.

The same year Khan Uzbeg released from the Horde with
grants, with many honors and with friendship, Prince Semion
Ivanovich and his brothers, Prince Ivan Ivanovich and Prince
Andrei Ivanovich, to return to Russia, to their patrimony. And
they returned to Moscow happily and greatly rejoicing.

The same year Grand Prince Ivan Danilovich Kalita took
from Tver' to Moscow the bell from the church of the Holy Saviour.

The same year on the fifth day of the month of November,
when holy martyr Clement is remembered, they decided to build
and lay the foundation of the fortress of Moscow; and they finished building it the same winter so that it was ready in spring
during Great Lent.

The same year [6848/1340 in *Laur.*], together with Prince
Ivan Ivanovich Korotopol of Riazan', many Tatars came from the
Horde, from Khan Uzbeg, as well as the envoy, lord Tavlubii,
and lord Mengukash, and many other Tatar lords who were sent
by Khan Uzbeg to wage war against Smolensk. At that time
Prince Ivan Ivanovich Korotopol of Riazan' met his cousin,
Prince Aleksandr Mikhailovich of Pronsk, who was going to the
Horde, to the Khan, with tribute. And he caught him and robbed
him and brought him to his city of Pereiaslavl' in the Riazan' land.
There, Prince Aleksandr Mikhailovich of Pronsk was killed by
his brother [cousin], Prince Ivan Ivanovich Korotopol of Riazan'.
Then Prince Ivan Korotopol marched from Pereiaslavl' [in the
Riazan' land] with Tavlubii and other Tatars. Grand Prince Ivan
Danilovich [Kalita] sent his troops with them against Smolensk,
following the Khan's order. And his voevodas were Aleksandr
Ivanov and Fedor Akinfovich. Also, on the Khan's order other
princes marched with the Tatar army against Smolensk. They
were Prince Konstantin Vasilievich of Suzdal', Prince Konstantin
Borisovich of Rostov, Prince Ivan Iaroslavich of Iur'ev, Prince
Ivan of Drutsk, Fedor of Fominsk, and with them the baskaks, as

1339   well as the Mordva princes with men of Mordva. They came to Smolensk, burned the suburb, robbed and burned the lands and towns and, after remaining at the city for several days, the Tatars returned to the Horde with a great many captives and booty, and the Russian princes returned home in good health and sound.

[DEATH OF GRAND PRINCE IVAN KALITA]

In the year 6848/1340. [6849/1341 in *Laur.*]. Grand Prince Ivan Danilovich Kalita was shorn a monk and to the *schema*, and died and was buried in the church of Holy Archangel Michael in Moscow, which he, himself, built. He was the grandson of Aleksandr [Nevskii], great grandson of Iaroslav, gr. gr. grandson of Vsevolod [Great Nest], gr. gr. gr. grandson of Iurii Dolgorukii, gr. gr. gr. gr. grandson of Valdimir Monomakh, gr. gr. gr. gr. gr. grandson of Vsevolod,[70] gr. gr. gr. gr. gr. gr. grandson of Iaroslav, gr. gr. gr. gr. gr. gr. gr. grandson of Great Vladimir. His senior son, Prince Semion ["the Proud"] could not at that time attend his father's burial because he was in Nizhnii Novgorod. His [Ivan Kalita's] sons were Semion, Ivan and Andrei; and he was Prince for eighteen years.[71] The same year [6848/1341 in *Laur.*], Prince Semion Ivanovich and his brothers, Prince Ivan Ivanovich and Prince Andrei Ivanovich, went to the Horde. At that time many princes were in the Horde with Khan Uzbeg.

The same year there was a conflagration in Novgorod and because of the storm and whirlwinds the fury of the fire was so fierce that the flames spread even across the river, and many people were drowned in the river Volkhov. The fire crossed over the Volkhov to the other side, which also burned, including all the wooden and stone churches.

The same year on the Day of the Transfiguration of Christ [August 6] the city of Smolensk burned.

[GRAND PRINCE SEMION IVANOVICH OF VLADIMIR AND MOSCOW]
[1340-1353]

The same year [6849/1341 in *Laur.*] Prince Semion Ivano-

---

70. Missing in *Nik.*

71. This is incorrect. Ivan I Kalita was Prince of Moscow from 1325 to 1340, and Grand Prince of Vladimir from 1328 to 1340.

vich with his brothers, Prince Ivan Ivanovich and Prince Andrei   **1340**
Ivanovich, left the Horde, and Khan Uzbeg conferred on him the
patents to rule the Grand Principalities of Vladimir and Moscow;
and so he ascended to the throne of the Grand Principalities of
Vladimir and of Moscow.

The same year [6849/1341 in *Laur.*] the evil mutineers of
Briansk summoned the veche and killed their prince, Gleb Svia-
toslavich. At that time Theognost, Metropolitan of Kiev and all
Russia, was present, but he was not able to stop them.

[UNREST IN TORZHOK]

The same year [6849/1341 in *Laur.*] Grand Prince Semion
Ivanovich sent his man to Torzhok to levy tribute, but they started
hurting [the people] and using violence. The people of Novotorzhok petitioned Novgorod and the Novgorodian posadniks
sent their boiars with many men; they came unexpectedly and
caught Prince Semion's envoys, Prince Mikhail Davydovich,[72]
Ivan Rybkin, Boris Semionov and others. They, as well as their
wives and their children, were arrested and put in irons, and they
remained under arrest in Torzhok for a month.

Then the Novgorodians sent Koz'ma Tverdislavich to the
Grand Prince, saying the following: "You have not yet become
our prince but your boiars have already inflicted violence!" The
people of Novotorzhok, however, grew fearful [of Prince Semi-
on] and the mob mutinied against the boiars, saying, "Why did
you invite the Novgorodians? They arrested the envoys of Prince
Semion Ivanovich and now all of us may perish." Taking up
arms, the mob came to their estate and released Grand Prince
Semion's envoys from irons and let them depart from Torzhok,
and accompanied them. The Novgorodian boiars escaped to
Novgorod but the estates of the boiars of Novotorzhok were
sacked, their houses were destroyed and their towns were captured and devastated.

The same year [6849/1341 in *Vozn.*] there was a gathering in
Moscow of all the Russian princes and they marched against
Torzhok waging war. They were Grand Prince Semion Ivan-

72. Mikhail Davydovich was Prince of Mologa, of the Iaroslavl' branch
of the princes, and the grandson of Prince Fedor the Black, Prince of
Iaroslavl' and Smolensk. *Baumgarten*, II, xix-7.

1340 ovich, Prince Konstantin of Suzdal', Prince Konstantin of Rostov, and Prince Vasilii of Iaroslavl'; and all the other princes were with them. Even His Holiness Theognost, Metropolitan of Kiev and all Russia, went with them. When they came with strong forces to Torzhok, the Novgorodians arrayed troops against them from their entire land, and they sent Basil, Archbishop of Novgorod, to Metropolitan Theognost to present a petition. They also sent posadnik Iakov and tysiatskii Avraam, together with other boiars, to Grand Prince Semion Ivanovich; and so they concluded peace on the basis of the old, very ancient charters, according to the Novgorodian rights, and they confirmed this agreement between them with an oath on the cross. And they gave to Grand Prince Semion Ivanovich the right to cut the best pine wood[73] from the entire Novgorodian land; and a tribute of a thousand rubles was imposed upon the people of Novotorzhok.

In the year 6849/1341. His Holiness Theognost, Metropolitan of Kiev and all Russia, went to Novgorod with a great many of his clergy, as well as with his servants; but the supplies and many gifts weighted heavily on the Archbishop of Novgorod and the monasteries.

The same year Grand Prince Semion Ivanovich of Vladimir and Moscow sent his namestniks to Novgorod.

The same year Khan Uzbeg of the Horde died, and after him his eldest son, Tinibeg [1341-1342] became Khan of the Horde. He had another son, Dzhanibeg, who killed his junior brother, Khidyr Beg. And therefore his senior brother, Khan Tinibeg, the eldest son of Uzbeg, became angry with him and great hatred arose between them.

[OLGERD, GRAND PRINCE OF LITHUANIA]

The same year Gedimin, Grand Prince of Lithuania, passed away. His children were Narimunt, Olgerd, Iavnut, Keistut, Koriat, Liubart and Monvid. After him, Olgerd became Grand Prince of Lithuania.[74] This Olgerd was extremely wise. He spoke

73. "Best pine wood:" *chernyi bor.*

74. Olgerd, 1345-1377, built Lithuania into a powerful state which extended from the Baltic to the Black Sea. Its population was primarily Russian. Many Russian princes preferred, rather, to be under Olgerd than under the Tatars. This resulted in a certain cultural division of Russia into its eastern (Moscow) and western (Lithuanian) parts.

many languages, and his power and majesty surpassed all. He **1341** was very cautious and did not care for any vain amusements or games, or similar pastimes; but he cared about his dominion day and night. He despised drinking and never drank wine, mead, or any other intoxicating beverages. He particularly hated drinking, and he abstained and was moderate in everything. Therefore he was very wise and had a great mind, and he developed a keen intellect, acquired great wisdom and reason, was able thoroughly to consider everything. Through his cunning he conquered many states and lands and won many cities and principalities for himself. He held great power, and his principality grew more than any other, more than had his father's or his grandfather's.

The same year [6853/1345 in *Vozn.*] Prince Ivan Ivanovich, grandson of Danilo, married the daughter of Prince Dmitrii of Briansk.

The same fall on the day of the Holy Protective Veil of the Most Pure Theotokos [Oct. 27] Olgerd, Grand Prince of Lithuania, came with a strong army to the city of Mozhaisk, occupying districts and towns and burning suburbs. He besieged the city but was unable to take it, and returned. The same year the Lithuanians took Tishinov and returned with many captives.

The same year the Germans [of the Livonian Order] moved into the Lithuanian land and built a new fortress there on the river Pizhva.

The same year young Prince Mikhail Aleksandrovich of Tver', who was the godson of the Novgorodian Archbishop Basil, came to him in Novgorod to learn literacy.

The same year Konstantin, a son of Grand Prince Semion Ivanovich—who was Danilo's grandson—was born, and he died the same day. The same year [6850/1342 in *Novg. III.*] the Germans [Livonian Order], despite the peace, killed several outstanding men of Pskov. The men of Pskov, with Prince Aleksandr Vsevolodich, marched against them and captured Latigoda.

The same year Prince Aleksandr Vsevolodich decided to return home and left [Novgorod]. The same year the Novgorodian Archbishop Basil covered[75] the cathedral of Holy Sophia with lead, had icons painted and built a new altar.

---

75. Probably, "roofed."

1342   *In the year 6850/1342.* Khan Dzhanibeg of the Horde, son of Uzbeg, killed his senior brother, Khan Tinibeg, and himself became Khan [1342-1357]. Previously, he slew his junior brother; and so he became ruler over the Horde and over all its *Ulus*.[76]

The same year Luka Varfolomeev, not heeding the instructions and blessing of Theognost, Metropolitan of Kiev and all Russia, and his own Archbishop Basil of Novgorod, gathered around himself war-loving and cunning men, as well as the serfs of the boiars, and marched with them to the river Dvina, beyond the portage [Volok]. And he built there the fort of Orlets. He ruled the people of the Em' there,[77] and all the land beyond the portage [Volok], and he conquered the land and towns along the river Dvina. Then his son, Ontsyfor, went to the river Volga, and so the father, Luka, remained with only a small troop, and he was killed by the people from beyond the portage [Volok]. When these tidings came to Novgorod the common people grieved for him and they rose up against posadniks Andrei and Fedor Danilovichev,[78] saying, "You sent people to kill Luka;" and they sacked their homes and their towns. The two posadniks escaped to Kopor'e, where they remained not a short while. Thereafter Ontsyfor, son of Luka, came to Novgorod. He petitioned the Lord Archbishop and all Novgorodians, complaining about posadniks Fedor and Andrei, saying, "They sent men to kill my father." And so the Archbishop and people of Novgorod sent Archimandrite Joseph and the boiars for Fedor and Andrei. The posadniks came to Novgorod and began talking to them, shedding tears. "We have never had it in mind or plotted to kill our brother, Luka; and we did not send anyone against him." But Ontsyfor, with Matvei, started to ring the veche bell at the cathedral of Holy Sophia, while Fedor and Andrei rang the veche bell in Iaroslav's court. Ontsyfor and Matvei sent the Lord Archbishop to the veche. Not waiting for the Lord Archbishop to come from the other veche, they attacked Iaroslav's court; but those who were there captured Matvei Kozka and his son, Ignatii. Ontsyfor escaped with his supporters. This occurred before dinner, but

76. *Ulus* originally designated a part of a nomadic horde; later, it meant just a region under the aegis of the Horde.

77. *Em'*: a Finno-Ugric tribe.

78. "Danilov" in *Novg. III.*

after dinner the entire city, with Lord Archbishop Basil and with   **1342**
namestnik Boris, arranged peace between them.

[PSKOV AND OLGERD FIGHT THE GERMANS]

The same year the people of Pskov sent to Novgorod, announcing, "A German army is marching against us. Help us." The Novgorodians gathered their forces and wanted to send troops to help them, but they—the people of Pskov—sent another envoy, who said, "There is no army marching against us and there is peace." And so the Novgorodian troops returned and all went to their own homes. Thereafter, however, the people of Pskov refused to be under Novgorod and under the Grand Prince of Russia, and sent [6869/1341 in *Novg. IV.*] their envoys to Vitebsk, to Grand Prince Olgerd Gediminovich of Lithuania, asking him to help against the Germans, saying, "Our brethren, the people of Novgorod, do not help us."

He—Olgerd—accepted their request and sent his voevoda, Prince Iurii Vitovtovich, ahead of his troops, and then he, himself, marched with his brother, Keistut, with the Lithuanians and with his son, Andrei. And he sent Prince Iurii Vitovtovich with volunteers from Pskov to get some prisoners and information at Novyi Gorodok. He, himself, went between the frontier lines, where he met a large German [Livonian] army advancing against Izborsk. In the meantime, near the river Mekozhitsa the Germans killed sixty men of Pskov, while Prince Iurii Vitovtovich escaped with difficulty to the fortress of Izborsk. The Germans advanced with great forces and with wall-breaking rams, and besieged the fortress of Izborsk; but all of this remained unknown to Olgerd and to Keistut. Olgerd commanded his troops to go on the river in boats, unaware that the German army was already besieging the fortress of Izborsk.

When they crossed the river and camped on the Kamna, Olgerd sent some of his men as advance troops, ahead of the main army; and they caught a prisoner and brought him to Olgerd; he told Olgerd about the large German army and that many of them were besieging Izborsk. Olgerd rapidly ordered a retreat over the river, to march to Pskov, and to fortify the fortress and gather the people in order to prepare the city for siege. With Keistut and

1342 with a small troop Olgerd, himself, went to the swamp of Gram and began to reconnoitre there regarding the German army.

At that time Prince Liubka Voinov, son of the prince of Polotsk, with another man, separated himself from Olgerd and accidentally encountered the vanguard of the German army, unaware that they were the enemy. And so he and his men were killed there. Olgerd became very sad and lamented him greatly.

Izborsk was in a difficult position because of the [siege by the] German army, and they sent to Olgerd, asking aid. He did not want to march against the Germans' main forces but told them, "Remain in the fortress and do not surrender. Fight them. If you don't have any traitors among you, they will be unable to do anything against you; but if I march with my forces against their large army, many people will be killed, and who knows who will win? And so, perhaps, by the grace of God we may win and not so many will be killed. And what would be the purpose of it? But you remain in the fortress and try to do your best united, and then they will never succeed."

The Germans besieged the city for ten days and cut off the water supply from those in the fortress; but they were opposed by divine wrath and so they burnt their camps and their supplies and their battering-rams and fled home, not pursued by anyone. The people of Pskov greatly implored Grand Prince Olgerd Gediminovich to be baptised and to become their prince in Pskov, but he answered them, "I have already been baptised [in the Roman Catholic Church] and I am Christian. I do not want to be baptised for the second time, and I do not want to be your prince." The people of Pskov, however, baptised his son, Andrei, in their cathedral church and they put him in Pskov to be their prince. And so his father, Olgerd Gediminovich, together with Keistut, returned to their own land, while the people of Pskov made peace with Novgorod. The same year the men of Pskov killed three hundred German men.

The same year [6851/1343 in *Novg. III.*] on order of Grand Prince Semion there was built in Gorodishche[79] a stone church of the Annunciation of the Most Pure Theotokos, and it was consecrated by Basil, Lord Archbishop of Novgorod. The same

79. *Gorodishche:* the grand prince's suburban residence near Novgorod.

year there was a conflagration in Novgorod. The same year the **1342**
Novgorodian posadnik, Varfolomei Iurievich, passed away.

The same year Prince Iaroslav of Pronsk came from the
Horde, together with the Tatar envoy, Kindiak, to be prince of
Riazan'. The Tatars came to the land of Pereiaslavl'[80] and Riazan';
but Prince Ivan Ivanovich Korotopol fortified himself in the city
of Pereiaslavl' and fought, them all day. [6851/1343 in *Vozn.*]
At night he fled from the city and so the Tatar envoy, Kindiak,
with Tatars, entered the city and caused the Christians much evil:
some were killed and some were taken captive. And so Prince
Iaroslav of Pronsk settled in Pereiaslavl', in the land of Riazan'.[81]

The same year Grand Prince Semion Ivanovich, grandson
of Danilo, went to the Horde, to the new khan, Dzhanibeg, son
of Uzbeg; before him, Princes Konstantin of Suzdal' and Konstantin of Tver', as well as Konstantin of Rostov, also went altogether to the khan, to the Horde. The same year [6851/1343 in
Novg. III.] Theognost, Metropolitan of Kiev and all Russia, went
to the Horde, to the new khan Dzhanibeg, son of Uzbeg, on behalf of the clergy.

The same year [6851/1343 in *Novg. III.*] Grand Princess
Avdotiia, wife of Prince Vasilii Davydovich of Iaroslavl', passed
away. The same year Theodore, Bishop of Tver', passed away.

The same year [6851/1343 in *Novg. III.*] Grand Prince
Semion Ivanovich, grandson of Daniil, returned from the Horde.
The same year Theognost, Metropolitan of Kiev and all Russia,
came from Khan Dzhanibeg in the Horde. He had gone [thither]
on behalf of the ecclesiastical authorities in order to secure the
iarlyks[82] from the Khan of the Horde for the Metropolitan and
for the bishops, and for their clergy. Some Russian people calumniated Theognost to Khan Dzhanibeg, saying, "He has an
endless amount of income—gold, silver and other wealth—and he
should give an annual tribute to the Horde." And so the khan

80. Pereiaslavl'—now called "Riazan' ", after the Tatar invasion and
destruction of the old Riazan' in 1239 by Batu—became the capital of
the principality of Riazan'. Old Riazan', some thirty-three miles southeast of the present city, was never rebuilt but remains just a site of ruins.

81. In *Nik*: Rostislavl'; obviously a misspelling, this should read
"Pereiaslavl'."

82. *Iarlyks:* The Tatar term for patent, or charter, for the administration of a region or diocese.

1342   asked for an annual tribute from the Metropolitan; but the Metropolitan did not give them any. Then the khan kept him stringently, and then the Metropolitan gave six hundred rubles to the khan, to the khan's wife and to their lords. And so the khan released him and all those who had accompanied him, back to Russia; and he came back to Russia in good health with all his people.

In the year 6851/1343. The entire city of Moscow, including eighteen churches, burned. It was the fourth conflagration in Moscow in the last thirteen years.

The same year Prince Ivan Ivanovich Korotopol of Riazan' was killed because earlier he killed his kin, Prince Aleksandr Mikhailovich of Pronsk, and now he drank the same bitter cup. "And with what judgment you judge him you shall be judged, and with what measure ye mete it shall be measured unto you." [*Math. 7:2*] He received the same sentence as the sentence with which he had sentenced before.[83]

The same year the men of Pskov, with their Prince Ostafii, waged war against the German land [Livonia], and they marched to the town of Medvezhaia Golova, where they fought for eight days. The Germans marched against them and there was an evil massacre, and the men of Pskov won. But a number of their best men were killed, as well as their leading posadniks, Korman, Kirei, Varfolomei, Al'ferii and many other boiars; and an endless number of other good men fell there. And Daniil, posadnik of Pskov, cut off his armour, himself, and barely escaped. This was a terrible loss for the men of Pskov.[84]

83. This is an interesting and rare instance in *Nik.* of the stylistic application of various Russian forms of the same root: *Im zhe bo sudom sudil osudiisia i eiu zhe meruiu meri voz'merisia emu.*

84. This entry about the encounter between Pskov and the Livonian Knights obviously is the result of a misunderstanding of earlier texts. The chronicles of Pskov *(Pskov II.* as well as *Syn.* and *Stroev mss.)* provide a clearer text. When the Germans caught up with the retreating troops of Pskov, in the first encounter they killed seventeen Pskovians; but then the men of Pskov countercharged and killed many Germans, while the survivors fled. In place of "posadnik Daniil" we find in *Pskovian Chronicles* a certain "priest Ruda," who panicked, abandoned his arms and fled to Pskov, bringing there the false news of the defeat of the troops of Pskov and that all the men of Pskov had been killed. *Pskov II, Syn.* and *Stroev mss.*

In the year 6852/1344. Grand Prince Semion Ivanovich, **1344** grandson of Danilo; and his brother, Prince Ivan Ivanovich, grandson of Danilo; and Prince Andrei Ivanovich, grandson of Danilo, went to the Horde. And all the Russian princes at that time were in the Horde.

The same year Prince Iaroslav Aleksandrovich of Pronsk passed away.

The same year they started painting frescoes in two stone churches in Moscow. One was the cathedral church in the residence of His Holiness Theognost, Metropolitan of Kiev and all Russia, where the frescoes were painted and completed the same year by Greek masters. The other church was on the estate of the grand prince. It was the church of the Holy Archangel Michael in which, on order of Grand Prince Semion Ivanovich, the frescoes were painted by Russian masters. Their elders and senior masters were Zakharii, Denisii, Iosif, Nikolai and the rest of their team; and they could not finish it the same year because of the magnitude and many details of the frescoes.

The same year Theodore, Lord Bishop of Tver', built brass doors in the cathedral church of the Holy Transfiguration of Our Lord God and Saviour, Jesus Christ, in Tver'.

In the year 6853/1345. The foundation of the church of the Holy Saviour in Kovaliovo was laid in Novgorod. On the sixth day of September, when the miracles of the Holy Archangel Michael are remembered, there was a very strong wind with snow and the ice on the river Volkhov moved and destroyed seven piers of the large bridge.

The same year the office of posadnik was given to Matvei Varfolomeich.

The same year Anastasia, wife of Grand Prince Semion Ivanovich, took the veil and the schema, and passed away. By birth she was Lithuanian, and her Lithuanian name was Augusta; but in Holy Baptism she was named Anastasia. She was buried in the monastery in the church of St. Saviour in Moscow which she, herself, had ordered to be adorned with frescoes; she supplied the monks who lived there with all manner of goods and she honored them greatly. The same year on order and at the expense of Grand Princess Anastasia, wife of [Grand Prince] Semion Ivanovich, they completed painting the frescoes in the monastic church of the Holy Saviour. Their elder masters and leaders were

1345   Russian by birth but pupils of the Greeks: Goitan, Semion, Ivan, and their pupils and other masters in the team.

The same year Grand Prince Semion Ivanovich, grandson of Danilo, married for the second time: he married Eupraksia, daughter of Prince Fedor Sviatoslavich of Smolensk. The same year his brothers, Princes Ivan Ivanovich and Andrei Ivanovich, the grandsons of Danilo, also married; and so all three brothers married the same year.

The same year Grand Prince of Lithuania Olgerd Gediminovich and his brother, Keistut Gediminovich, unexpectedly raided their senior brothers in Vil'na, Nairimunt Gediminovich and Iavnut Gediminovich. And the people of the city became frightened and Prince Narimunt Gediminovich fled to the Horde to Khan Dzhanibeg, son of Uzbeg, while the other brother, Iavnut Gediminovich, escaped to Pskov and from thence to Novgorod and from thence to Moscow to Grand Prince Semion Ivanovich. There in Moscow he was baptised and named Ivan in Holy Baptism.

The same year Prince Vasilii Davydovich of Iaroslavl' was tonsured a monk and to the schema and passed away, and was buried in the church of St. Saviour in Iaroslavl'.

The same year Prince Vasilii of Murom passed away and was buried in his patrimony of Murom, in the church of the Holy Martyrs, Boris and Gleb, of the monastery on the river Uzhna.

In the year 6854/1346. They completed painting frescoes in three stone churches in Moscow: in the monastery of St. Saviour, in the cathedral of St. Archangel Michael, and in the church of St. John Climacus. The same year in Moscow Grand Prince Semion Ivanovich with his brothers, Ivan Ivanovich and Andrei Ivanovich, had three large bells cast, and two smaller ones. They were cast by master Boris *Rymlianin.*[85] The same year Basil, Lord Archbishop of Novgorod, came to Moscow to invite Grand Prince Vasilii Ivanovich to become prince of Novgorod. Before doing so, he received a blessing from Metropolitan Theognost and he

85. *Rymlianin* means "Roman;" but it is hard to believe that a fourteenth-century Italian would have the purely Russian Christian name of "Boris." It may be that he was originally a Catholic but was re-baptised into Orthodoxy and on that occasion received a new Russian name. In *Musc. late XV C.* this master is called "Borisko."

brought him greetings of honor and gifts [from the Novgorod- **1346** ians[. Metropolitan Theognost blessed him and gave him ecclesiastic vestments with crosses, but he took from him his deacon, Cyril, who surpassed all with his voice and purity of diction. The same year His Holiness Theognost, Metropolitan of Kiev and all Russia, consecrated John, Archimandrite of the monastery of the Saviour, to be bishop of Rostov.

The same year there were severe epidemics in the eastern land: in Ornachi,[86] in Astrakhan', in Syria and in Bezdezh, and in the other cities of those lands; and they spread among the Christians,[87] the Armenians, Franks and Cherkess, as well as to the Tatars and the Abkhazians, and there were no people to bury many.

The same year [6855/1347 in *Novg. III.*] Grand Prince Olgerd Gediminovich of Lithuania with his brother, Keistut Gediminovich, marched toward Novgorod to wage war and they camped at the mouth of the river Pshaga. They sent to the Novgorodians, telling them, "I will meet you. If God helps me, I want to protect myself.[88] Your posadnik Astafii Dvorianinets abused me and made many reproaches to me and called me a 'hound.' " Sojourning there, he started campaigning and occupied the land of the river Shelona up to Golyn, Luga and Sablia, and many districts, towns and places. He campaigned there and captured people, and from Porkhov he received a tribute of three hundred sixty Novgorodian rubles. And then the Novgorodians assembled and marched against him toward Luga. Then they returned rapidly to Novgorod and rang the veche bell in the court of the prince, and they killed posadnik Astafii Dvorianinets, saying, "You are the cause of this fighting. Because of you all our land may be taken into captivity. Who asked you to abuse the king?" And so Astafii Dvorianinets was killed, while Olgerd Gediminovich with his brother, Keistut Gediminovich, and a large number of captives returned to his land.

The same year Grand Prince Semion Ivanovich, grandson of Danilo, sent his wife, Princess Eupraksia, to Volok to her fath-

---

86. Ornachi: a city at the mouth of the Don river, *PSRL XIII*. Bezdezhi, a city on a channel of the lower Volga, now Enotolsk, *PSRL XIV*.

87. "Christians" here denotes "Orthodox."

88. Actually, "my honor."

1346 er, Prince Fedor Sviatoslavich. The same year Grand Prince Semion Ivanovich marched to Novgorod and became prince there on the Day of the Council.[89] He sojourned there three weeks and returned to Moscow.

The same year Prince Konstantin Mikhailovich of Tver' developed dislike toward his princess, Anastasiia, and Prince Vsevolod Aleksandrovich; and he began arresting their boiars and their squires because they levied taxes—silver—from their land beyond human possibilities; and there was great grief among them. Prince Vsevolod Aleksandrovich could not abide this and he left Tver', going to Moscow to Grand Prince Semion Ivanovich.

The same year Grand Prince Konstantin Mikhailovich of Tver' went to the Horde to Khan Dzhanibeg, son of Uzbeg. The same year Prince Vsevolod Aleksandrovich [of Kholm in the Tver' Land] also went to the Horde from Moscow. The same year Grand Prince Konstantin Mikhailovich of Tver' passed away in the Horde. He was grandson of Iaroslav, great grandson of Iaroslav, gr. gr. grandson of Vsevolod [Great Nest], gr. gr. gr. grandson of Iurii Dolgorukii, gr. gr. gr. gr. grandson of Vladimir Monomakh, gr. gr. gr. gr. gr. grandson of Vsevolod, gr. gr. gr. gr. gr. gr. grandson of Iaroslav Valdimirovich.

The same year Prince Vasilii Mikhailovich of Kashin, grandson of Iaroslav, great grandson of Iaroslav, sent his tax collectors from Kashin to Kholm to the principality of Prince Vsevolod Aleksandrovich[90] and they levied taxes from the people of Kholm and then went to the Horde to Khan Dzhanibeg, son of Uzbeg. At that time his nephew, Prince Vsevolod Aleksandrovich of Kholm, was in the Horde and the khan granted him the principality of Tver'. When Prince Vsevolod Aleksandrovich of Kholm learned that his uncle, Prince Vasilii Mikhailovich of Kashin, had levied a tax in his principality of Kholm, he became offended and, with the khan's envoy, departed from the khan and the Horde. In Bezdezh he met his uncle, Prince Vasilii Mikhailovich of Kashin, and he robbed him.[91] Prince Vasilii Mikhailovich of

89. The Council *(Sobor)*, is the Sunday of Orthodoxy, the first Sunday of Lent.

90. Prince Vsevolod Aleksandrovich was the nephew of Vasilii Mikhailovich of Kashin and the son of the late Prince Aleksandr Mikhailovich, who had been killed in the Horde.

Kashin was greatly vexed by the behavior of his nephew, Vsevolod   **1346**
Aleksandrovich of Kholm and Tver', because the latter had received from Khan Dzhanibeg the [iarlyk for the] entire principality of Tver'.

[KING MAGNUS' II LETTER]

In the year 6855/1347. [6856/1348 in *Novg. III.*] Magnus,
King of Sweden [1319-1363], sent his envoys—monks and
priests—to Great Novgorod, telling them, "Summon a council
in a place of your choosing, and gather your theologians to this
council at that place; and I, also, will gather my theologians and
will send them to the council at that place so that they can discuss
the faith, as it is in the Scriptures; and thus we will learn whose
faith is better. In the case your faith is true and right, I will convert to your faith; but if our faith should be found true and right,
according to the Scriptures, then you must convert without any
doubts to our faith. Thus we will be together in unanimity, in
peace, in spiritual love and in concord. And we will be united in
our blessed decisions, and we will be dreaded by our enemy. If
you do not want to do thus, I will wage war against you with all my
forces." Lord Bishop Basil with the Novgorodians answered Magnus, King of Sweden, "If you want to find out whose faith is better,
just and right, send your people to Constantinople to the Patriarch, because we received this true faith from the Greeks, and we
adhere to the laws of the Greek church, which we received from
them; and we do not want to argue with you about the faith. If,
between us and you, there should be any manner of offense, then
you must advise us of it; and so you should send to us concerning
your problems and you should settle all justly; and we will settle
everything justly with you, in concord, in agreement and in peace;
but we do not become involved in disputes, arguments or accusations about the faith and will have no argument with you."
And so the King stared and ceased his long speeches; and his
proud theologians were silenced by that short and wise speech of
the Lord Bishop.[92]

91. Actually, he took away the tax that belonged to him.

92. A similar text of the letter of King Magnus Erikson (1319-1363) is
in *Novg.* under the year 1348 and in *Musc. late XV C. PSRL.* XXV, under
y. 1347. See also *King Magnus' Testament* under the year 1352, for additional commentaries.

1347   The same year the Germans [Livonian Order] waged war against Lithuania. There was great fighting and the Germans killed twenty thousand Lithuanians.

The same year there was a great flood, such as never was before.

The same year Grand Prince Semion Ivanovich, grandson of Danilo, married for the third time. He married Princess Mariia, daughter of Grand Prince Aleksandr Mikhailovich of Tver'; [his boiars] Andrei Kobyla[93] and Andrei Bosovolkov went to Tver' for her. The same year His Holiness Theognost, Metropolitan of Kiev and all Russia, held a council concerning some spiritual problems[94] of his spiritual son, Grand Prince Semion Ivanovich [*Gordyi*, "the Proud"], and therefore they sent to Constantinople to receive the Patriarch's blessing. The same year His Holiness Theognost, Metropolitan of Kiev and all Russia, consecrated Nathaniel bishop of Suzdal'. The same year Grand Prince Semion Ivanovich, grandson of Danilo, went to the Horde.

In the year 6856/1348. A son, Danilo, was born [6855/1347 in *Vozn.*] to Grand Prince Semion Ivanovich. The same year Grand Prince Semion Ivanovich, grandson of Danilo, came from the Horde from Khan Dzhanibeg, son of Uzbeg. He came with great honors and grants, and with him was his brother, Prince Andrei Ivanovich.

The same year in Moscow in the metropolitan cathedral church of the Most Pure Theotokos, thanks to the mercy of God and the Most Pure Theotokos, and thanks to the prayers of holy wonderworker Peter, the later metropolitan of Kiev and all Russia, a certain widow was cured from her grave illness: her hands were crooked and bent inward toward her chest. She received the remission of her sins and was cured, and she returned home in good health, glorifying God and the Most Pure Theotokos and Her prayerful holy wonderworker Peter, late metropolitan of Kiev and all Russia.

The same year [6857/1349 in *Vozn.*] Grand Prince Olgerd Gediminovich of Lithuania sent his brother, Koriat, and others,

93. Andrei Kobyla was one of the ancestors of the later Romanov dynasty.

94. Probably about the Prince's previous divorce and his third marriage.

to the Horde to Khan Dzhanibeg, son of Uzbeg, asking for help[95]   **1348**
against Grand Prince Semion Ivanovich. When Grand Prince
Semion Ivanovich received these tidings he sent Fedor Glebovich
to the Khan in the Horde, and with him his officials,[96] Fedor
Shubacheev and Amin, complaining of Olgerd and sending the
following message: "Olgerd has devasted all your *ulus*[97] and has
taken everyone with him into captivity.[98] Now he wants to take all
of us into captivity, and so your *ulus* will be devastated to the end.
Then, becoming powerful, Olgerd Gediminovich will march
against you." When the Khan heard that Olgerd had devastated
his *ulus* and taken people into captivity from them and wanted to
march against him, he became as wrathful as fire and he turned
over the Lithuanian envoys to the Grand Prince's officials: they
[Olgerd's envoys] were Olgerd's brother, Koriat, and those others with him; and they were taken to Moscow by the Khan's envoy,
Totui. Following the Khan's orders, his envoy, Totui, turned over
Koriat, Olgerd's brother, and those Lithuanians accompanying
him, to Grand Prince Semion Ivanovich.

The same year [6855/1347 in *Sof. V* and *Vozn.*] Magnus,
King of Sweden, sent his envoys to Basil, Lord Archbishop of
Novgorod,[99] and to the posadniks of Novgorod, and to everyone
[in Novgorod], saying, "Send your theologians to the Council so
they can argue about the Faith, according to the Scriptures.
When they come to a decision according to the Scriptures, we will
all be of the same faith. If you do not want this, then I will wage
war against you, calling God to my aid." Basil, Lord Archbishop
of Novgorod, and all the Novgorodians, answered him, "Many,
many years ago our forefathers received their faith from the
Greeks, and it is the true and right one. Our forefathers, grandfathers and fathers preserved this faith, and so do we, following

95. Actually, seeking alliance.

96. *Kilichei*—officials in the service of a prince.

97. *Ulus*: a Mongol word for a region, or part of the state. Each of the
four surviving sons of Genghis Khan had their own *ulus*.

98. Here is meant the conquest of southwestern Russia by Olgerd.

99. An expanded version of the text in the year 1347. In *Musc. late
XV C, Sof. V* and *Vozn.* 1347, but 1348 in *Novg. III*. The difference
in dating probably resulted from different calendar systems (New Year
on March 1 in Old Russian, and Sept. 1 in Byzantine) by the earlier
chronicle writers.

1348 the canonic laws according to the Greek laws which we received from the Greeks. We do not want to argue with anyone because we know that our faith is the true and right one which we received from the Greeks. And it is just and right, and we observe its laws. If you want to argue about the faith, then send your people to Constantinople to the Patriarch, and he will answer you. In the case there should be any offense from us toward you, then you must advise us of it; and if there should be any offense by you to us, we will also advise you, and thus we will abide peacefully and without trouble, according to all truth." And they sent to the king tysiatskiis Avraam and Koz'ma Tverdislavich, because at that time the king was on the island of Berezovo. When they came to Orekhovets, the people of Orekhovets did not let tysiatskii Avraam depart from then; but Koz'ma went to the king, and the king told him, "There is no offense between us; but let us be united in the Faith and be in unity, in good counsel, of the same mind, and live in concord and peace. If you do not do so as I suggest, I will wage war against you." The people of Orekhovets prepared their fortress for a siege and the king besieged the city: and some of whom he took captive he managed forcefully to baptise into his faith, and he sent his other troops on raids. The men of Novgorod sent Ontsyfor Lukin against his raiders, and they killed five hundred raiding Swedes. King Magnus, however, because of treachery, took the town of Orekhovets and he rebaptised many into his faith. Some, however, did not obey him; he took a ransom and took with him beyond the sea tysiatskii Avraam and eleven other best men; but he let the namestnik of Narimunt and his people leave the town of Orekhovets. At the fortress, though, he left his troops, and fortified it still better.

The Novgorodians sent to Grand Prince Semion Ivanovich, asking him to come to their aid. Grand Prince Semion Ivanovich marched as far as Torzhok; but then they returned because the messenger from the Horde came to him there, announcing the Khan's wishes and desires: a message of benevolence, that he turn over Koriat, Olgerd's brother, to Prince Semion. And so he returned to the city of Moscow, and in his place he sent to Novgorod his brother, Prince Ivan Ivanovich, Prince Konstantin Borisovich of Rostov, and Ivan Okinfovich; and, together with them, he sent his voevodas and large troops. When the Prince [Ivan Ivan-

ovich] came to Novgorod and learned that the Swedes[100] had al-   **1348**
ready taken the town of Orekhovets and had strengthened its
fortifications, he did not march against the Swedes but left Novgorod and went back to the Niz, not heeding the entreaties of the
Lord Archbishop and the requests of the Novgorodians. However, the Novgorodian posadnik, Fedor Daniilovich, with the
namestniks of Prince Semion Ivanovich and with all the levies of
Novgorod and Pskov and of the entire Novgorodian land, gathered together, marched against the town of Orekhovets, and killed
there some Swedes at that town; but there, also, was killed their
voevoda, Liudek. Therefore the Novgorodians held council
whether they should not besiege the city for a longer while, but
the people of Pskov did not want to remain there. The Novgorodians then told them, "It was agreed that our posadniks should
not be in your city of Pskov, and that they should not try anyone
there; [we also agreed] that only our archbishops may interfere
with Pskov's problems; and that Novgorod should not call the people of Pskov to arms; and that neither our nobles of Novgorod
nor the bailiffs of Novgorod nor the clergy of Holy Sophia nor
the investigators nor the heralds [should interfere in the affairs
of Pskov]. The people of Pskov are our brethren and the city of
Pskov is the junior brother of Novgorod; but you rapidly forgot
this agreement and this concord, and you want neither to endure
with us nor to fight the enemy. If you insist on it, then go home at
once by night, so that the enemy should not rejoice and say,
'There is discord among them.' " The Pskovians, however, left
at noon, sounding trumpets, drumming drums and playing flutes.
Seeing this, the Germans [Swedes] laughed, but the Novgorodians
became angry. They gathered the men from the entire Novgorodian land, received many supplies, built fortifications and decided to continue longer besieging the city. The Swedes in the
city began to weaken because they did not have enough grain
supplies, and there was great grief among them. Seeing this, the
Novgorodians set fire to the town and so the Swedes were burned
there and some of them were killed. Those who remained alive
were taken to Moscow to Grand Prince Semion Ivanovich. The

100. For the word, "Swedes," the chronicles used either *Svei* or
Nemtsy. The word, *nemtsy*, is just a generic word for all Germanic-
speaking peoples, including the Scandinavians.

1348 Novgorodians besieged the city from the Day of the Assumption of Our Lady until the Day of the Council,[1] until they burned the city.

The same year Temir, a lord from the Horde, came waging war against the town of Alekshin, the town of holy wonderworker Peter, Metropolitan of Kiev and all Russia. They burned the suburbs and returned to the Horde with a great number of captives. The Lord, however, delivered His servants from those who offended them and He avenged them with His true trial: his [Temir's] own Tatar servants killed him in the Horde the same year, and in such a way the accursed one perished with his children.

The same year a certain man by the name of Ivan was cured—one of his eyes was diseased—in the cathedral church of the Most Pure Theotokos, at the burial place of holy wonderworker Peter, Metropolitan of Kiev and all Russia.

The same year Prince Vsevolod Aleksandrovich of Kholm came from the Khan in the Horde with great honors and the patent to be Prince of Tver', and with him was the [Khan's] envoy. His uncle, Prince Vasilii Mikhailovich of Kashin, also came from the Horde to Kashin and discord arose between them. It was a heavy burden for the people of Tver' and therefore many people of the land of Tver' left the principality because of this discord.

The same year the Germans killed Prince Narimunt Gediminovich and, with him, several princes, voevodas and a great number of Lithuanians.

The same year there was a fierce struggle in the principality of Tver' between Grand Prince Vsevolod Aleksandrovich of Kholm—who, by the Khan's patent, had become Grand Prince of Tver'—and his uncle, Prince Vasilii Mikhailovich of Kashin, grandson of Iaroslav. Bloodshed nearly ensued between them.

In the year 6857/1349. Olgerd Gediminovich, Grand Prince of Lithuania, sent [6858/1350 in *Vozn.*] his envoys to Grand Prince Semion Ivanovich of Moscow, with gifts and petitions requesting peace and the preservation of the life of his brother, Koriat Gediminovich, as well as the latter's boiars and the latter's Lithuanian guard. Grand Prince Semion Ivanovich agreed upon

1. "Day of the Council" *(Sobor)*: the first Sunday of Great Lent.

the peace and concord offered and let Olgerd's brother, Koriat   **1349**
Gediminovich, go to his brother, together with his boiars and his
Lithuanian guard.

The same year the King of Krakow[2] seized the Volynian land
by deceit and he converted the churches of the Greek faith into
ones of the Latin faith.

The same year Theodore, Lord Bishop of Tver', arranged
peace and concord between Prince Vasilii Mikhailovich of Kashin
and Grand Prince Vsevolod Aleksandrovich of Tver', and they
both wept in amity and peace. And so Vsevolod Aleksandrovich
gave up the Grand Principality of Tver' to his uncle, Prince
Vasilii Mikhailovich of Kashin, and they both kept their patrimonies—Prince Vasilii Mikhailovich kept Kashin and Prince
Vsevolod Aleksandrovich kept Kholm. And so to the throne of
the Grand Principality of Tver' came Vasilii Mikhailovich of
Kashin, grandson of Iaroslav, great grandson of Iaroslav, gr. gr.
grandson of Vsevolod, gr. gr. gr. grandson of Iurii Dolgorukii;
and they confirmed unanimity, good counsel and unity by a
pledge on the cross.[3] Grand Prince Vasilii Mikhailovich came
to Tver' to be grand prince there, and so he started to live in peace
and great concord quietly and meekly, with his nephew, Prince
Vsevolod Aleksandrovich of Kholm. And people began to gather
in their cities, in their lands and throughout all the land of Tver',
and the population increased and everyone rejoiced with great
joy.

The same year Theodore, Lord Archbishop of Tver', had
frescoes painted on the altar walls of the cathedral of the Holy
Saviour in Tver'.

The same year Grand Princess Maria, dowager of Grand
Prince Dmitrii Mikhailovich of Tver', who was killed with his
son, Fedor, in the Horde, passed away.

The same year His Holiness Theognost, Metropolitan of
Kiev and all Russia, came from Volynia [to Moscow]. The same
year a son, Mikhailo, was born to Grand Prince Semion Ivanovich
[of Moscow] and he was baptised by Metropolitan Theognost.

2. Krakow was the capital of Poland.

3. According to tradition in the Russian dynasty the uncle, as repre-
sentative of the senior line, was supposed to rule before his nephew,
especially in the main principality.

1349   The same year [6858/1350 in *Vozn.*] Prince Liubart Gediminovich of Volynia sent his envoys to Grand Prince Semion Ivanovich requesting in marriage his niece, the daughter of Prince
Konstantin Borisovich of Rostov, and he [Prince Semion] agreed
that the daughter of his sister should marry him. The same year
[6858/1350 in *Vozn.*] Grand Prince Olgerd Gediminovich of
Lithuania sent to Moscow to Grand Prince Semion Ivanovich requesting in marriage the latter's sister-in-law, the daughter of
Grand Prince Aleksandr Mikhailovich of Tver', whose name was
Uliana. He took counsel with his spiritual father, His Holiness
Theognost, Metropolitan of Kiev and all Russia, and gave his
agreement that he [Grand Prince Olgerd] should marry his
sister-in-law, Uliana.

The same year there was an epidemic among the people of
the land of Polotsk.

In the year 6858/1350. Prince Konstantin Vasil'evich of Suzdal' laid the foundation of a stone church in Novgorod.

The same year Grand Prince Semion Ivanovich [6859/1351
in *Vozn.*] with his brothers, Prince Andrei and Prince Ivan, went
from Moscow to the Horde to Khan Dzhanibeg, son of Uzbeg. He
returned with his brother from the Horde with grants and great
honors rendered him by the Khan.

The same year a stone chapel of the church of St. Saviour in
Moscow was completed.

The same year [6859/1351 in *Vozn.*] on the twelfth day of the
month of October a son, Dmitrii [later called "Donskoi"] was
born to Prince Ivan Ivanovich.

The same year [6859/1351 in *Vozn.*] Prince Konstantin of
Suzdal' went to the Horde.

The same winter [6859/1351 in *Vozn.*] a son, Ivan, was born
to Prince Semion Ivanovich. The same winter in Tver' Grand
Prince Semion Ivanovich gave his daughter in marriage to Prince
Mikhail Vasilievich of Tver'.

The same year [6859/1351 in *Vozn.*] Grand Prince Vasilii
Aleksandrovich of Riazan' passed away. The same year Theognost, Metropolitan of Kiev and all Russia, became ill.

In the year 6859/1351. A woman who was gravely ill and had
had paralysed legs and arms for two years was cured in Moscow
in the Metropolitan cathedral church of the Most Pure Theotokos, thanks to divine mercy and the grace of the Most Pure
Theotokos and to the prayers of holy wonderworker Peter, late

Metropolitan. When she was brought into the church of the Holy **1351**
Theotokos to the grave of holy wonderworker Peter she was
cured at once and she went home quite well, glorifying Lord God,
the Most Pure Theotokos and Their prayerful holy wonderworker Peter, late Metropolitan. The same year His Holiness
Theognost, Metropolitan of Kiev and all Russia, gave his blessing
to Bishop Daniil to continue as bishop in Suzdal'—he had been
excommunicated before, but now he recovered his former bishopric and was honored with the great and holy position of bishop.

The same year Prince Iurii Iaroslavich of Murom rebuilt his
patrimony, the city of Murom, which was devastated long ago, in
the time of the first princes; and he built his estate there in the fortress; and also his boiars, magnates and the common people built
their homes there. And he restored the holy churches and a-
dorned them with icons and books.

The same year there was a violent tempest which destroyed
the churches and the houses.

The same year [6858/1350 in *Novg. III.*] a stone church of St.
Flore and St. Laur was erected in Novgorod; and then in Kholop'e
street a stone church of St. Cosma and St. Damian was built; and
a third stone church, dedicated to St. John Chrysostom, was built
by posadnik Iurii Ivanovich. The same year [6858/1350 in
Novg. III and *Kom.*] the men of Novgorod fought in Livonia, and
returned with many captives. The same year Novgorodian envoys went to the town of Iur'ev [6858/1350 in *Novg. III* and *Kom.*]
in Livonia and agreed on peace with the Germans [of Livonia];
also, they traded those Swedes of the Swedish king whom they
had taken in Orekhov, alive, for their tysiatskii Avraam, Koz'ma
Tverdislavich, and the others whom Magnus, King of Sweden,
had taken beyond the sea. The same year [6858/1350 in *Novg. III*
and *Novg. Kom.*] they elected Ontsifor Lukin to the office of posadnik of Novgorod.

The same year [6858/1350 in *Novg. III* and *Novg. Kom.*] the
Novgorodian Lord Archbishop Basil built a stone palace. The
same year [6858/1350 in *Novg. III*] the Novgorodians chased from
Novgorod to Pskov posadnik Fedor and his brothers, Mikhail,
Iurii and Andreian, and they sacked their homes and also sacked
all Prus'kaia street; but they departed Pskov for Kopor'e.

At the same time Prince Iurii Vitovtovich was killed at Izborsk.

The same year [6858/1350 in *Novg. IV*] an epidemic broke

1351 out among the people, and this happened by the designs of God because He has His designs for every creature, those acting to the benefit and salvation of men. He expects us to appeal to Him and repent our evil deeds which we commit sinfully and uninterruptedly. Caring for our salvation, He sends [as a warning] to us sometimes famine, sometimes epidemics, sometimes war, sometimes various illnesses, sometimes misfortunes, grief and sadness. It is written in Scripture that "through many tribulations we must enter the Kingdom of God." [*Acts.* 14:22] "And many sorrows shall be to the wicked." [*PS.* 32:10] "And many afflictions to the righteous; but Our Lord delivereth them, finally, out of them all." [*PS.* 33:20] As soon as we abandon our lawless ways and repent our sins, He will turn aside His wrath, will forgive our trespasses, and will grant us His blessings. And He will be merciful and destroy our enemies, provided we live according to His Commandments and do His will. "God is nigh unto all them that call upon Him." [*PS.* 114:18]

In the year 6860/1352. [6859/1351 in *Novg. IV.*] Grand Prince Semion Ivanovich [Gordyi] with his brothers, Prince Ivan and Andrei, and other princes, gathered a strong force and campaigned against Smolensk; when they reached Vyshgorod on the river Porotva, the envoys from Olgerd Gediminovich, Grand Prince of Lithuania, came to him bearing many gifts and suggesting peace. He did not disdain Olgerd's offer and agreed to peace, and let the envoys depart in peace; but he moved toward the Ugra river, wanting to go toward Smolensk. And the envoys from Smolensk came to him. He remained eight days on the river Ugra, sent his envoy to Smolensk and, achieving peace, he returned to Moscow.

The same year the Khan's envoy, Akhmat, came from the Horde to Prince Vasilii Mikhailovich of Tver', bringing him a *yarlyk* in his name. Thereafter, Grand Prince Vasilii Mikhailovich of Tver' developed dislike for his nephew, Prince Vsevolod Andreevich of Kholm, remembering the latter's robbery at Bezdezh; and he began to injure him and to offend his boiars and squires—and thus, because of the devil's plots, distrust and discord arose among them.

[THE PLAGUE] **1352**

The same year there was an extremely violent plague in the city of Pskov and throughout all the land of Pskov, and death would come very fast. A man would start to spit blood and the third day he would die; and the dead were everywhere. So all the people began to think about their souls. Wealthy people would give to the holy churches and monasteries towns, lakes, fishing places and their estates. In this way they sought to cleanse themselves from their sins and win eternal memory, according to the Scripture: "Through alms and faith, sins will be cleansed." So they would cleanse their souls through confession, penitence and tears, remembering the end of this quickly-passing life.

The priests were unable even to bury the dead because in one night before matins they would bring twenty, even thirty, dead persons to the church, and so the memorial service, as well as the prayers for remittance—a charter remitting sins—were served for all at once. This charter is to be given individually to everyone—to men and to women. And so they buried five or ten persons in the same grave, and thus it happened in all the churches. There was no place to bury the dead because everywhere there were new graves, and therefore the dead were buried far away from the church. There were weeping and wailing among all the people because everyone expected the other would pass away, and expected death for himself, and they would distribute their possessions to the poor and to the paupers. And no one would have a debt paid back because one would die as soon as he would contract a debt.

Many people were willing to help the dying, but the diseased would die so fast, and the merciful person would then run off. People were in awe of God and remembered the forthcoming hour of death, which none can escape; and therefore they helped the diseased and dying, and would cover them, take them away and bury them. Neither rank nor importance can halt death, which bares its all-devouring teeth to all.

Some people said that this epidemic came from the Indian land and from the land of the Sun City.[4] The people of Pskov

4. Indeed, this plague—called the "Black Death" in Western Europe—was brought by gypsies from India. It was the time of the Great Plague throughout all Europe.

1352   tearfully sent their envoys to Novgorod, asking Basil, Lord Archbishop of Novgorod, to give them his blessing; and Lord Archbishop Basil listened to their prayers and went to them in Pskov and gave them his blessing. Then he went from them to Novgorod, and on the third day of the month of June he died, on his way [to Novgorod], on the river Uza. He was brought to Novgorod and was buried in the big chapel of the cathedral of Holy Sophia. He remained in his bishopric for twenty-one years, four months and two days.

Then the Novgorodians sent to Moscow to His Holiness, Metropolitan Theognost, asking him to give his blessing to the old, retired Archbishop Moses to be bishop of Novgorod, and he gave his blessing to their former archbishop, Lord Moses of Novgorod, to be on the See of the Holy Archbishopric of Christ. The same year there was a very severe plague in Novgorod and in the entire Novgorodian land. By the will of God, a distressing, terrifying and sudden death came upon people, and it lasted from the Day [of the Dormition] of Our Lady [August 15] to Christmas. And a great, numberless multitude of good people died. And this happened not only in Novgorod; but it was so in all lands. He whom God wanted would die, and whomsoever God wanted to keep was preserved. So people became filled with the fear of God and spent their remaining days and years in chastity and without sin.

The same year there was a very violent plague in Smolensk, Kiev, Chernigov, Suzdal' and the entire Russian land. It was a terrifying, sudden and fast death, and there were fear and great trembling among all people. In the city of Glukhov not a single person survived. All died, and the same occurred in Belozero.

The same year Prince Vsevolod Aleksandrovich of Kholm sent his princess back to Riazan'.

The same year they erected a stone church in Nizhnii Novgorod. The same year:

THE TESTAMENT OF MAGNUS, KING OF SWEDEN[5]

"I, sinful Magnus, King of Sweden, called 'Gregory' in Holy Baptism, leaving this rapidly passing life, do bequeath my broth-

5. Magnus II became King of Sweden at the age of three in 1319. In 1363 he was deposed by the feudal lords of Sweden because of his un-

ers, children and my entire Swedish land to live in peace and con- **1352**
cord and to avoid all sort of cunning, injustice, arrogance, drinking and all the devil's games. Do not offend or use force against
anyone, and do not trespass your oath on the cross. Do not trespass an agreement or oath on the cross with the Russian lands because you will not gain any material benefits but your soul will
perish. Once our prince, Master Birger,[6] wanted to wage war a-
gainst them and entered the river Neva; but then on the river
Izhora he encountered Prince Aleksandr Iaroslavovich [Nev-
skii], and the latter pursued him and defeated his troops. Thereafter my brother, Lord Moskalka, entered the river Neva and built
a fortress on the river Okhta, where he settled a great many of his
Swedes, and returned.[7] But Grand Prince Andrei Aleksandrovich went thither, took the fortress and killed the Swedes. Thereafter we had peace with Russia for forty years, and we also later
made peace for forty years with Grand Prince Iurii Danilovich,

stable and unpredictable behaviour as a ruler. He died in exile in 1374
in Norway, where his son, Haakon VI, was King (1343-1380). In 1348
Magnus undertook his campaign against Novgorod but was defeated.
This Novgorodian victory over their powerful neighbor became reflected in this apocryphal *Testament* of Magnus, which, as a matter of fact,
is just a product of Novgorodian patriotic and political literature. Several events from Magnus' life and Swedish history mentioned in the
Testament are historically correct and, most probably, were taken into this
Novgorodian writing from the so-called *Swedish Rhymed Chronicle of the
XV Century*. There were always Swedish merchants in Novgorod who
could have access to this chronicle. The date of writing of this Novgorodian work is unclear but it was included, at least in part, before the
writing of *Nik.*, in the *Sof. PSRL* Vol. V (written before 1481) and the
Muscovite Late XV c. Chronicle, PSRL Vol. 25, p. 178. See also Rydzevskaia,
E. A., *Drevniaia Rus' i Skandinaviia, XIV to XVI Centuries*, Moscow, 1978,
pp. 124-127.

6. See item under the year 6749/1241 concerning *Jarl* (Earl), not
Master or Prince, Birger's attack on the Novgorodian lands in 1240-41,
and Aleksandr Nevskii's victory.

7. Lord Moskalka, Novgorodian transliteration of the Swedish
Marskalk—Marshall, a high dignitary of the court. Here is meant Marshall Torgils Knutson, who campaigned against Novgorod in 1300 and
built the fortress of Landskron on the Neva river, where is now the city of
Leningrad (Petersburg). He was not a brother of King Magnus. Prob-
ebly, the word, "brother," is used to designate a kinsman or person of
the same nation.

1352 and we divided the lands and the waters, and we signed charters and attached our seals.

"Thirty years later I, sinful King Magnus, without taking counsel, waged war with the help of the entire Swedish land because I wanted to capture them—the Russians—because they were unwilling to accept our faith. And I took many captives and I converted them into our faith; and I took their fortress of Orekhov,[8] where I put my men, and I retreated beyond the sea; but then the Novgorodians came. They took their town of Orekhov and killed my men.

"Unaware of this, one year later I went thither with an army and I received the tidings that Novgorodian forces were near Orekhov; and so I went toward the fortress of Kopor'e and spent the night there. The tidings came to me in that place that the Novgorodians were on the border of our lands, so I escaped beyond the sea. A fierce storm arose and there were such waves that we could not use the sails due to them. I took fright and trembled, and I was overcome by fear because I saw that my armies' ships were destroyed by the sea waves and sank. Many of my troops drowned in the mouth of the Narva river,[9] and I returned to my land with but a few men, the remnants of my army.

"Since that time the wrath of God overcame our Swedish land: there were famine, plague, fratricidal feuds and, because of my many sins, God took away my senses and I remained in my palace a year, chained to the wall with an iron chain; and so I was incarcerated in my palace.

"Then my son, Haakon,[10] came to me from the Murman [Norway] land, and he delivered me from the palace and gazed upon me, and he saw that I was quite blackened and dried out, and my eyes looked like two deep holes, and my arms and legs were extremely thin, my skin and my muscles adhered to my bones, I could hardly speak and my voice was like that of a sick bee. All those who saw me shed tears of grief. My son, for grief,

8. Apparently this is a modified version of the story of Orekhovets (Orekhov, Oreshek), reported under the year 6856/1348, a fortress on the Neva river near Lake Ladoga. Later called Schluesselburg, now Petrokrepost'.

9. Nerova in *Nik*.

10. Sakun in *Nik*. Magnus' son Haakon VI, King of Norway, 1355-1380.

beat his head upon the ground, grieving and shedding tears over   **1352** me.

"Then my son took me to his land of Murman [Norway] and I boarded a ship, and such a strong tempest arose that we were not able even to see our ships and sails because of the waves; and so all my men were drowned. I myself, remained on the bottom of the ship for three days and three nights, and Lord God sent the wind to bring me to the Polnaia river. The monks who were there took me from the boards and brought me into the monastery of the Holy Saviour, and they put black vestments upon me and tonsured me a monk and to the schema. And so God let me live for three days and nights.

"All this was brought upon me by Lord God because of my vanity and my ambitions and my pride and my cunning, because there is no other man in this world who is as proud, cunning and sin-loving as I; and therefore I suffered badly. On many occasions I trespassed my oath on the cross and I raided the Russian land; but Lord God stilled me and I suffered sorely and unbearably.

"Now I bequeath you, my brothers, my children, and the entire Swedish land, not to care for cunning, for injustice, or for the perishable vanity of this world because everything disappears like smoke as does a dream, and passes by like a shadow. Do not employ violence and do not wage war against the Russian land; do not trespass your oath on the cross because you will perish. And whosoever will attack the Russian land or trespass his oath on the cross will be punished by God, Who will send fire and water upon him, just as He punished me for my lawlessness, for my cunning, for my ambitions and my pride and my violence and my mercilessness, and for all manner of evil which I have committed. And all this the Lord God did by His Divine Providence for the sake of my salvation."

The same year a son, Semion, was born to Grand Prince Semion Ivanovich.

The same year on the sixth day of the month of December, when our holy father, wonderworker St. Nicholas, is remembered, His Holiness Theognost, Metropolitan of Kiev and all Russia, consecrated his successor, monk Alexis bishop of Vladimir. He loved him greatly and kept him at his court as his successor. During his life he consecrated him lord Bishop, and he blessed

1352   him to be in his place on the great See of the Metropolia of Kiev
and all Russia after his own passing away. Thereafter he took
counsel with his spiritual son, Grand Prince Semion Ivanovich
[the "Proud"], grandson of Danilo, and with his brothers,
Prince Ivan Ivanovich and Prince Andrei Ivanovich, as well as
with the boiars and magnates.

And they sent envoys to Constantinople. The envoys of
the Grand Prince were Dementii Davydovich and Iurii Vorob'ev,
and the envoys of the Metropolitan were Artemii Korob'in and
Mikhailo [the "Pockmarked"], the Greek. They told them [to
tell the Patriarch of Constantinople] not to consecrate as Metropolitan of Russia anyone other than the reverend elder Alexis,
because he was the main assistant of His Holiness Theognost,
Metropolitan of Kiev and all Russia, and because he was greatly
virtuous and honorable. The same year monk Theodorit was
consecrated by the Patriarch of Tyrnov and came to Kiev.[11]

In the year 6861/1353. [6860/1352 in *Novg. III.*]. His Holiness Theognost, Metropolitan of Kiev and all Russia, passed away
on the eleventh day of the month of March, and he was buried
in his tomb on the thirteenth day of the same month. At the burial were Alexis, Bishop of Valdimir, who had been his main assistant; Athanasius, Bishop of Volynia; and Athanasius, Bishop of
Kolomna; and the entire Holy Council. He was buried in the
chapel of the Veneration of the Irons of Holy Apostle Peter in
the cathedral church of the Most Pure Theotokos in Moscow,
and his grave was in the same wall with wonderworker Peter,
late Metropolitan of Kiev and all Russia. And then the same
week Prince Ivan and Prince Semion, two sons of Grand Prince
Semion Ivanovich, grandson of Danilo, passed away, and they
died the same week as Metropolitan Theognost.

[DEATH OF GRAND PRINCE SEMION IVANOVICH]

And then, six and one half weeks after his death and after
forty days of memorial services for him, on the twenty-sixth day

11. Tyrnov: a city in north central Bulgaria. During the second Bulgarian "Tsarstvo" (empire), 13th-14th centuries, Tyrnov became the
capital of Bulgaria and residence of the Patriarch of Bulgaria. In 1383
the Turks conquered Tyrnov and put an end to the second "Tsarstvo"
and to the Bulgarian Patriarchate. *Izvory za bolgarskaia istoriia*, Sofia
1959-1960, Vols. I-II.

of the month of April Grand Prince Semion Ivanovich passed   **1353**
away. He was the grandson of Danilo, great grandson of blessed
Aleksandr [Nevskii], gr. gr. grandson of Iaroslav, gr. gr. gr.
grandson of Vsevolod [Great Nest], gr. gr. gr. gr. grandson of
Iurii Dolgorukii, gr. gr. gr. gr. gr. grandson of Vladimir Monomakh, the latter being the grandson of Vsevolod Iaroslavich,
grandson of Vladimir; he was buried in the church of St. Archangel Michael in his patrimony of Moscow. He was prince for
thirteen years, and he lived, altogether, for thirty-eight years.
The same year [his brother] Prince Andrei Ivanovich passed
away. He was the grandson of Danilo, great grandson of Aleksandr, gr. gr. grandson of Vsevolod, gr. gr. gr. grandson of
Iurii Dolgorukii; and he died on the third day after forty days of
memorial services for his brother, Grand Prince Semion Ivanovich. And he was buried in Moscow in the same church of St.
Archangel Michael on the sixth day of the month of June.

The same year a son, Prince Vladimir, was born to the late
Prince Andrei Ivanovich, and this happened after forty days of
memorial services for his father, Prince Andrei Ivanovich.

[GRAND PRINCE IVAN II IVANOVICH OF MOSCOW]

The same year the [Russian] princes went to the Horde to
Khan Dzhanibeg, son of Uzbeg, and they argued there about the
succession to the Grand Principality of Vladimir. They were
Prince Ivan [II] Ivanovich, grandson of Danilo [Prince of Mos-
cow], and Prince Konstantin Vasilievich of Suzdal'. At the same
time the people of Novgorod sent their envoy, Semion Sudakov,
to the Horde to Khan Dzhanibeg, asking him to assign Prince
Konstantin Vasilievich of Suzdal' to become Grand Prince of
Vladimir; but the Khan gave the Grand Principality of Vladimir
to Prince Ivan Ivanovich [of Moscow], the brother of [late]
Grand Prince Semion Ivanovich. The Novgorodians remained
one and a half years in discord with him, but no evil occurred.

The same year the envoys sent by the late Grand Prince
Semion Ivanovich and His Holiness, the late Theognost, Metropolitan of Kiev and all Russia, returned from Constantinople:
they were Dementii Davydovich and Iurii Vorob'ev; and the
Metropolitan's [returning] envoys were Artemii Korob'in and
Mikhailo [the "Pockmarked"] the Greek. They were sent to the
blessed and melodious Philotheus, Oecumenical Patriarch, and

1353   to his spiritual son, Emperor John Kantakuzen. From thence they brought a message from the Patriarch and Emperor for Alexis, Lord Bishop of Vladimir, to go to the Patriarch, to Constantinople, to be consecrated Metropolitan by him, by the Patriarch.

The same year during St. Peter's Fast, on the twenty-second day of the month of July, the people of Riazan' took Lopasna. Prince Oleg Ivanovich was at that time very young and he and his namestnik, Mikhail Aleksandrovich, were captured and were taken to Riazan'. He remained there in great hardship but later was ransomed and he returned home.

The same year, thanks to Theodore, Bishop of Tver', a gilt cross was placed over the church of St. Saviour in Tver'. Then [one] was placed on the church of St. Demetrius and on the church of the Holy Presentation.

The same year Moses, Archbishop of Novgorod, sent his envoys with gifts and great expressions of honor to the blessed and melodious Philotheus, Oecumenical Patriarch in Constantinople, and to the latter's spiritual son, Emperor John Kantakuzen. He asked the Patriarch's blessing and help for Novgorod against the offenses of the Metropolitan. The same year a stone church of St. Simeon was erected in Novgorod.

In the year 6862/1354. Prince Ivan Ivanovich, grandson of Danilo, came from the Horde, from Khan Dzhanibeg, son of Uzbeg, who gave him the Grand Principality of Vladimir. At that time all the princes of Russia were in the Horde and all of them were permitted to return to their patrimonies. The same winter [6861/1353 in *Laur.*], on the twenty-fifth of the month of March, the day of the Annunciation of the Most Pure Theotokos, Grand Prince Ivan Ivanovich (II) ascended to the throne of the Grand Principality of Vladimir. The same year the city of Moscow burned, and thirteen churches burned there.

The same year [6863/1355 in *Novg.*] confusion arose in the hierarchy of the Russian church, such as never happened before: the Patriarch of Constantinople consecrated two Metropolitans, Alexis and Roman, to the Metropolia of the entire Russian land, and there was great enmity between them.[12] Envoys from both

12. Actually, the Patriarch of Constantinople consecrated one Metropolitan—Alexis—for eastern Russia, with the title, "of Kiev and all

of them came from Constantinople to Tver', to Theodore, Bishop   **1354**
of Tver'. Everywhere was great hardship for all the clergy. The
same year [6863/1355 in *Novg. III.*] His Holiness, blessed Metropolitan Alexis, came from Constantinople to Moscow; and, also,
Metropolitan Roman left Constantinople for Russia.

The same year Prince Konstantin Vasil'evich of Suzdal'
married his son, Boris, to the daughter of Olgerd Gediminovich,
Grand Prince of Lithuania.

The same year [6863/1355 in *Novg.*] three stone churches
were erected at Novgorod: one, dedicated to the Miraculous Ap-
parition of the Holy Theotokos, was in Il'ina Street. Another,
dedicated to St. Demetrius, was in Liubianitsa. But the third, of
the Forty Martyrs, collapsed. At that time the people caught fish
on the shore of the Volkhov with their own hands.

In the year 6863/1355. [6862/1354 in *Novg. III.*] Prince
Dmitrii Fedorovich of Starodub passed away and was buried in
his patrimony in Starodub. Then his brother, Prince Ivan Fedorovich, went to the Khan in the Horde.

The same year [6862/1354 in *Vozn.*] Prince Fedor Glebovich
assembled many troops and marched with his army against Murom, against Prince Iurii Iaroslavich. And he drove him from the
city of Murom, entered the city and, himself, ascended to the
throne of the principality of Murom. And the people of Murom
were very glad to have him and stood for him and went with him
to the Horde. One week after his departure Prince Iurii Iaroslavich returned to Murom and, gathering the remaining men of
Murom, also went with them to the Horde, to the Khan, to receive a decision from him. There was a great dispute between
them [Fedor and Iurii] before all the lords of the Horde and the
principality of Murom was given to Prince Fedor Glebovich.
Also, Prince Iurii Iaroslavich was turned over to Prince Fedor
Glebovich, who kept him in a strong jail where he suffered many
hardships, and from these hardships and deprivations he passed
away.

The same year Grand Prince Ivan Ivanovich [of Moscow]
came to an agreement with Prince Konstantin Vasil'evich of Suz-

Russia," and another one—Roman—without a clearly defined title, for
western Russia (Lithuania). Since Kiev was also under Lithuanian control, and the borders of both Metropolitan dioceces were not determined, this led to real confusion in ecclesiastic affairs.

1355 dal'. The same year [6862/1354 in *Vozn.*] Prince Konstantin Vasil'evich of Suzdal' passed away after being tonsured monk and to the schema, and he was buried in Nizhnii Novgorod in the church of the Holy Saviour erected by him. He ruled for fifteen years, protecting his patrimony honorably and fearsomely a- gainst stronger princes and the Tatars. The same winter his son, Prince Andrei, went to the Horde to Khan Dzhanibeg, son of Uzbeg, with gifts. The Khan honored him and gave him his patri- mony and the throne of his father, of the principalities of Suzdal', Nizhnii Novgorod and Gorodets.

The same year the people of Novgorod came to an agree- ment with Grand Prince Ivan Ivanovich, grandson of Danilo.

The same year [6860/1352 in *Novg. III.*] an envoy of the lord and Bishop of Novgorod returned from Constantinople from His Holiness, Patriarch Philotheus, and from the latter's spiritual son, the Byzantine Emperor John Kantakuzen. He brought with him charters having golden seals, about the taxes for ordination, about the ecclesiastic taxes of the bishops, and other various rules; he also brought to Lord Archbishop Moses of Novgorod church vestments with embroidered crosses and a blessing for the entire city of Novgorod. The same year Lord Archbishop Moses erect- ed a stone church of St. Michael on Skovorodka. The same year [6862/1354 in *Novg. III.*] the office of posadnik was given to Alexis, brother of Dvorianinets.

In the year 6864/1356. Grand Prince Ivan Ivanovich, grand- son of Danilo, gave in marriage his daughter in Lithuania to the son of Koriat, grandson of Gedimin.

The same year John, Bishop of Rostov, passed away. The same year His Holiness, Alexis, Metropolitan of Kiev and all Rus- sia, consecrated Ignatius Bishop of Rostov. The same year His Holiness Alexis, Metropolitan of Kiev and all Russia, consecrated Basil Bishop of Riazan' and Murom. The same year His Holiness, Metropolitan Alexis, consecrated Theophilact Bishop of Smo- lensk. The same year His Holiness, Metropolitan Alexis, con- secrated John Bishop of Sarai. The same year Metropolitan Alexis went for the second time to Constantinople; but Metro- politan Roman had gone to Constantinople before him. And the same year there was great discord between them there.

The same year Ivan, son of [the prince of] Sviiazhsk, with the

help of the Lithuanians, occupied Rzhev. The same year Olgerd   **1356**
Gediminovich occupied Briansk and Smolensk, and he took prisoner the son of Prince Vasilii of Smolensk.

The same year Prince Ivan Fedorovich came with honor
from the Khan of the Horde and he ascended to the throne of his
patrimony, Starodub. The same year Prince Andrei Konstantinovich of Suzdal' returned from the Horde, from the Khan, having
been honored there and having received the yarlyk.[13]

The same year His Holiness, Metropolitan Alexis, returned
from Constantinople after being honored by the Patriarch,
bringing the Patriarchal blessing for the entire Russian land; but
Metropolitan Roman also came from Constantinople from the
Patriarch to rule the church in the Lithuanian and Volynian
lands.

The same year Irinchei and the merchants of Surozh came
from the Horde to Moscow. The same year Prince Vasilii came
with a iarlyk from the Horde, from the Khan, and became prince
of Briansk. After remaining there but a short while he passed
away, however, and a rebellion of evil people occurred in Briansk,
and there were troubles and the devastation of the city. Thereafter the Grand Prince of Lithuania took over Briansk. The same
winter on the third day of the month of February, at night when
the bell began to ring for matins in Moscow, tysiatskii Aleksei
Petrov of Moscow was killed. His murder was fearsome and no
one knows or could comprehend by whom or why he was killed.
He was found murdered, lying on the square, at a time when the
bells announced matins. And some people said that there was a
secret conspiracy by the boiars or by someone else; and so he was
killed in the same way as Grand Prince Andrei Bogoliubskii was
killed by the Kuchkovichs. There were grave disturbances in
Moscow because of this murder. The same winter some leading
boiars of Moscow departed for Riazan' with their wives and children, and that was the last occasion to travel.[14]

In the year 6865/1357. Dzhanibeg, son of Uzbeg, Khan of the
Horde, occupied the kingdom of Tabriz.[15]

13. Charter for the Principality of Suzdal'.

14. The "last occasion to travel": when, because of the snow, it was
possible to leave Moscow.

15. Tabriz: in Persian Azerbaidjan.

1357   [DISCORD IN THE LAND OF TVER']

The same year Alexis, Metropolitan of Kiev and all Russia, journeyed from Moscow to Vladimir, whither to him with his complaints came Prince Vsevolod Aleksandrovich of Kholm, grandson of Mikhail, great grandson of Iaroslav, gr. gr. grandson of Iaroslav, gr. gr. gr. grandson of Vsevolod. He complained against his uncle, Prince Vasilii Mikhailovich of Tver', because of offenses which the latter caused him despite their agreement. Prince Vasilii Mikhailovich of Tver', following the Metropolitan's counsel, sent his men to Grand Prince Ivan Ivanovich of Moscow agreeing on peace and concord with Grand Prince Ivan Ivanovich, grandson of Danilo. Then, together with Theodore, Bishop of Tver', he went to Metropolitan Alexis in Vladimir. There were many discussions between them but they could not agree on peace and concord.[16]

An envoy came from the Horde, from Taidula, wife of Khan Dzhanibeg, to blessed Alexis, Metropolitan of Kiev and all Russia, inviting him to come to her in the Horde to visit her because of her illness. He prepared everything needed for the journey; and at that time a candle started burning by itself in the Metropolitan cathedral church of the Most Pure Theotokos at the grave of St. Wonderworker Peter. He [Alexis] with the Holy Council served a church service, divided this candle and distributed it with a blessing to the people; and then, the same day, he left for the Horde. Thanks to the mercy of God, of the Most Pure Theotokos and the great wonderworker Peter, he cured the Khan's wife, Taidula; and then he was rapidly permitted to return because at that time enmity and great discord arose in the Horde. At the same time an envoy named Itkar was also sent to Moscow in order to question all the Russian princes. The same year [another] envoy of the Khan, by the name Koshak, came from the Khan to Russia.

[THE MURDER OF KHAN DZHANIBEG]

During the same year the discord did not cease in the Horde but only increased. At that time there was in the Horde a certain

16. That is, between Prince Vasilii of Tver' and his nephew, Prince Vsevolod of Kholm.

Tovlubii, an army commander and one of the lords of Khan   **1357**
Dzhanibeg, son of Uzbeg. He was clever and cunning and he was
enjoined by Satan, and he wanted to rule the entire Horde and all
lands. He began to whisper in the ear of Berdibeg, son of Dzhanibeg, praising and flattering him and saying, "The time has come
for you to become khan and for your father to give up his rule."
So, little by little, he started advising him to kill his father, Dzhanibeg, son of Uzbeg, and he drew many lords of the Horde into
his conspiracy, promising each that he would be given something.
And so the accused khan's son, Berdibeg, cunningly approached
his father with his advisors, the lords of the Horde, and he strangled his father, Dzhanibeg, son of Uzbeg. This Khan Dzhanibeg,
son of Uzbeg, was very kind toward Christians and he gave many
privileges to the Russian land; but [supreme] judgment struck
him because he had killed his own brothers, and now he had to
drink the very same cup. His son, Berdibeg, ascended after him
to rule over the Horde, and he killed twelve of his brothers. He
was instructed by this accursed lord, his teacher and supporter,
Tovlubii, to kill his father and his brothers; but later he, himself,
perished, together with his advisors.[17]

The same year His Holiness, Alexis, Metropolitan of Kiev
and all Russia, thanks to the mercy of God and the Most Pure
Theotokos, returned whole and hearty from the Horde. The
same year all the princes went to the Horde, to the new khan,
Berdibeg, son of Dzhanibeg. And thus did Prince Vasilii Mikhailovich of Tver', with his nephew, Prince Vsevolod Aleksandrovich of Kholm; but they did not go together because there
were enmity and discord between them. Prince Vsevolod Aleksandrovich of Kholm went to the Horde by way of Pereiaslavl',
but there the namestniks of Grand Prince Ivan Ivanovich did
not allow him to pursue his journey, and he went to Lithuania.

In the year 6866/1358. Grand Prince Ivan Ivanovich, grandson of Danilo, came from the Horde, and he asked two of his
boiars who had left him for Riazan', to return to him. They
were Mikhail and his son-in-law, Vasilii Vasil'evich.[18]

17. This was the beginning of what the Russians called the "Great
Trouble" *("Velikaia zamiatnia")* in the Horde, which severely under-
mined its power and prestige.

18. Both were members of one of the influential Muscovite boiar
families, Vel'iaminov. Vasilii, who died in 1374, had become in 1358 the

1358   The same year Prince Vasilii Mikhailovich returned to Tver' from the Horde. The same year a son, Ivan, was born to Prince Mikhail Aleksandrovich [of Kashin, in the land of Tver']. The same year a great envoy, son of the Khan, named Momat [Muhammad?] Khodzha, came from the Horde to the land of Riazan', and he sent to Moscow to Grand Prince Ivan Ivanovich, grandson of Danilo, concerning the borders of the land of Riazan', in order to establish inviolable and unchangeable boundaries of this land. Grand Prince Ivan Ivanovich did not let him come to his patrimony, and thus it happened to him. But soon, shortly, this Khan's son, Momat Khodzha, was quickly summoned to the Khan in the Horde because some calumny about him was told to the Khan. He became involved in a great conspiracy because at that time a favorite of the Khan's was killed. And so he escaped to Ornachi,[19] where he was caught and taken by the messenger of the Khan, and he was killed there on the Khan's order.

The same year Prince Aleksandr, son of Mikhail Aleksandrovich of Tver', grandson of Mikhail, great grandson of Iaroslav, passed away in the monastery of Holy Sophia where he was living with his grandmother, Grand Princess Sophia.

Grand Prince Fedor Aleksandrovich of Kholm,[20] grandson of Mikhail, great grandson of Iaroslav, journeyed from Lithuania to the Horde.

The same year the troops of Tver' and Mozhaisk took Rzhev and drove out the Lithuanians. The same year Theodore, Bishop of Tver', installed brass doors in the church of St. Saviour which was on his estate.

The same year Prince Vasilii Mikhailovich of Tver' sent his envoys, Grigorchuk and Korei, to the Khan, to the Horde, to complain of his nephew, Prince Vsevolod Aleksandrovich, [of Kholm]. There the Khan and his wife turned over Prince Vsevolod Aleksandrovich of Kholm to his uncle, Prince Vasilii Mikhailovich of Tver'. And there were many hardships for Prince Vsevolod Aleksandrovich from his uncle, Prince Vsevolod Mi-

last tysiackii of Moscow. His father, Vasilii, also served as tysiackii under Ivan Kalita. Soloviev, Vol. III.

19. A city in the delta of the Don.

20. Apparently, this should read "Vsevolod Aleksandrovich of Kholm." See the end of the entry under the year 1357.

khailovich. And, also, there were hardships, confiscations and robberies of the estates of his boiars and squires; and, also, the common people suffered from these confiscations.

The same winter after Epiphany His Holiness, Metropolitan Alexis, journeyed to Kiev with Theodore, Lord Bishop of Tver', because of the dissension between the princes of Tver' [that is, between Mikhail and Vsevolod]. His Holiness, Metropolitan Alexis, however, convinced him [to return] and instructed him, telling him to abide there in great love and patience because Lord God would do His Will howsoever He wants. And so he let him go with great love from Kolomna back to Tver' to the cathedral of St. Saviour.

The same year Prince Ivan Andreevich passed away. The same year the people of Novgorod agreed among themselves and pledged on the cross that they would not use the devil's game and would not break barrels.

[THE DEATH OF IVAN II]

In the year 6867/1359. Pious, Christ-loving, meek, quiet and merciful Grand Prince Ivan II Ivanovich passed away, after being tonsured monk and to the schema. He was the grandson of Danilo, great grandson of Aleksandr [Nevskii], gr. gr. grandson of Iaroslav, gr. gr. gr. grandson of Vsevolod, gr. gr. gr. gr. grandson of Iurii Dolgorukii, gr. gr. gr. gr. gr. grandson of Vladimir Monomakh, the latter being the son of Vsevolod Iaroslavich and grandson of Vladimir. And he was buried in his patrimony in the city of Moscow, in the church of St. Archangel Michael, and he remained Grand Prince for six years.[21] His sons were Dmitrii and Ivan.

The same year Prince Andrei Konstantinovich, grandson of Vasilii, erected a stone church of St. Archangel Michael in his patrimony in Nizhnii Novgorod.

The same year Khan Berdibeg, son of Dzhanibeg, grandson of Uzbeg, was killed by his accursed favorite, Tovlubii,[22] a dark and powerful prince, together with other of the Khan's advisors. And so he drank from the same cup which he had given his father and his brothers. After him, Khan Kul'pa ruled in the Horde—he

21. Grand Prince Ivan Ivanovich died of the plague.
22. Probably, "Tovlu-Beg."

1359 ruled only six months and five days, and he did much evil. Divine justice did not suffer him and he was killed, with two of his sons, Mikhail and Ivan, by Nevruz.[23] And so, after Kul'pa, Khan Nevruz became Khan of the Horde. Prince Andrei Konstantinovich, grandson of Vasilii, was in the Horde at this troubled time, and he was barely saved by God from a bitter death at pagan hands. The same year all Russian princes went to the Horde to the new Khan Nevruz, petitioning the Khan to confirm their rights to their principalities. He arranged peace among them and gave the principalities to them so that each should know his own principality and not trespass. And so he distributed the patrimony of each and let them return home in peace and honor. And so each of them returned to Russia to his own patrimony in peace and concord.

The same year Moses, Archbishop, lord of Novgorod, gave up the rule over the diocese of Novgorod, and entered a monastery. The Novgorodians summoned a veche and they brought to the porch of the Bishop's estate Monk Alexis, who earlier was the Bishop's key bearer. The same year Theodore, Bishop Tver', ordained Monk Alexis deacon and then priest. The same year Theodore, Bishop of Tver', laid a marble floor in his cathedral church of St. Saviour.

The same year Prince Ivan Aleksandrovich of Smolensk, grandson of Gleb, gr. grandson of Rostislav, gr. gr. grandson of Mstislav, gr. gr. gr. grandson of Davyd, gr. gr. gr. gr. grandson of Rostislav, gr. gr. gr. gr. gr. grandson of Mstislav, gr. gr. gr. gr. gr. gr. grandson of Vladimir Monomakh, son of Vsevolod Iaroslavich, who was the grandson of Vladimir, passed away. After him his son, Sviatoslav, became prince of Smolensk.

The same year Prince Vsevolod Aleksandrovich of Kholm [in the land of Tver'], grandson of Mikhail, great grandson of Iaroslav, went to Lithuania.

The same year the people of Smolensk fought at Belaia. The same year Olgerd Gediminovich, Grand Prince of Lithuania, came with his army to Smolensk and took the city of Mstislavl', placing

23. It seems that Ivan and Mikhail, the sons of Khan Kulpa, were Christian. It is possible that their conversion to Christianity, and possibly their father's, was the cause for a Moslem reaction and conspiracy against them by the nobles of the Horde. Nevruz is also spelled Naurus, in the Russian chronicles, including *Nik.*

there his own namestniks. The same year Grand Prince Olgerd   **1359**
Gediminovich sent his son, Andrei, with strong forces, to Rzhev.
He took the city and placed his namestniks there.

In the year 6868/1360. His Holiness, blessed Metropolitan
Alexis, returned to Vladimir and Moscow from Kiev. Metropolitan Roman came suddenly and shamelessly to Tver' but he did
not in love approach His Holiness, Metropolitan Alexis. He could
achieve nothing that he wanted or planned in Tver' and Theodore,
Bishop of Tver', did not see him or honor him. So he remained a
short time in the lands of Tver', gathering what he needed from
the princes, from the boiars of Tver' and from some others, and
then he returned to Lithuania.

The same year Prince Vsevolod Aleksandrovich of Kholm
came from Lithuania and he agreed on peace and concord with
his kin. And his uncle, Prince Vasilii Mikhailovich, gave him a
third of their patrimony, and so they divided the lands among
themselves. Prince Vsevolod Aleksandrovich of Kholm rendered
great honor to Metropolitan Roman, giving him many gifts, and
ordered that he be accompanied to Lithuania in honor.

The same year Grand Prince Olgerd Gediminovich of Lithuania went to Rzhev to see the city.

[DMITRII OF SUZDAL' BECOMES GRAND PRINCE]

The same year the princes of Suzdal' went to the Horde to
Khan Nevruz. They were Prince Andrei Aleksandrovich of
Suzdal', grandson of Vasilii; and his kinsman, Prince Dmitrii
Konstantinovich. They were received with honor by Khan Nevruz,
and the Khan gave the Grand Principality of Vladimir to Prince
Dmitrii Konstantinovich of Suzdal'. This was done contrary to
the tradition of their fathers and grandfathers.[24] Previously,
the Khan gave the Grand Principality of Vladimir to his senior
brother, Prince Andrei Konstantinovich of Suzdal'; but he did not
want to accept it and so Prince Dmitrii Konstantinovich of Suzdal'
received the Grand Principality of Vladimir, and he left the Horde
and the Khan with this grant and with honor, accompanied by the
Khan's envoy. He came to the Grand Principality of Vladimir
one week before the Fast of St. Peter, on the twenty-second day

24. According to tradition, the Grand Principality of Valdimir was
in the hands of the Prince of Moscow, sometimes of Tver', and very rarely in the hands of other princes.

1360 of the month of June, and this was contrary to their fathers' and grandfathers' tradition. When he was in Vladimir [6867/1359 in *Novgorod III.*] His Holiness, Metropolitan Alexis, consecrated Alexis Archbishop of Novgorod.

The same year Grand Prince Dmitrii Konstantinovich [of Suzdal'] sent his envoys and namestniks to Novgorod. The Novgorodians received them with honor and let his namestniks remain in Novgorod. The same year Semion Andreevich erected a stone church of St. Theodore in Theodore Street in Novgorod.

The same year there was a terrifying portent in the sky. Some clouds of the color of blood moved across the sky.

The same year Theodore, Bishop of Tver', had frescoes painted in the small church of the Presentation of the Most Pure Theotokos in Tver'.

[KHAN KHYDYR]

The same year there came from the Orient a certain Khydyr, Khan of the Horde beyond the river Iaik [now Ural], to conquer the Horde of the Volga.[25] And there was a conspiracy among the lords of the Volga [Golden] Horde, and they began secretly to contact Khydyr, Khan of the Horde beyond the Iaik, conspiring against Nevruz, their Khan of the Volga Horde. Their secret conspiracy grew into a strong action and fighting ensued. Nevruz, Khan of the Volga [Golden] Horde, was turned over by his lords to Khan Khydyr of the Horde beyond the Iaik. And so he was killed, with his son, Temir. At that time they also killed Taidula, the dowager of Khan Dzhanibeg, as well as those lords of the Horde who supported or counselled Nevruz, Khan of the Volga Horde. Among them were the descendants of Mual Buzin [?], and a great many Tatars were killed. So, after the death of Nevruz, Khan of the Volga Horde, Khydyr, Khan of the Horde beyond the Iaik—who came from the Orient—became Khan of the Volga Horde; and great trouble continued in the Horde.

The same year Prince Dmitrii Borisovich came from the Horde, from the Khan, and he was given the charter for the

25. This Khan Khydyr was apparently also a descendant of Genghiz Khan, and of the latter's son, Dzuchi; but he belonged to the line which ruled in present Kazakhstan. The center of the Golden Horde was Sarai, on the Volga.

principality of [Northern] Galich. The same year Prince Kon- **1360**
stantin of Rostov returned from the Horde with honor and with
the charter for the entire principality of Rostov. The same year
freebooters came from Great Novgorod to Zhukotin and killed
a multitude of Tatars and took their wealth. Because of this
robbery the Christians in Volga Bulgaria were robbed by the
Tatars.

The same year the lord of Zhukotin[26] went to the Khan in
the Horde and petitioned the Khan, asking the Khan to protect
him from the freebooters because they would kill and rob uninterruptedly. Khan Khydyr sent three envoys to Russia: Urus,
Ka'in Beg and Altyn Beg. He sent them to the Russian princes,
asking them to catch the robbers and send them to him. A meeting of all the princes was summoned in Kostroma. They were
Grand Prince Dmitrii Konstantinovich of Vladimir; his senior
brother, Grand Prince Andrei Konstantinovich of Nizhnii Novgorod; and Prince Konstantin of Rostov. They caught the robbers and they turned them over to the Khan's envoys with all
their booty, and so they sent them to the Horde.

The same year Theodore, Bishop of Tver', retired from his
diocese and went to the Otroch' monastery. The same year there
was a plague in Pskov.

In the year 6869/1361. There was a portent in the sky: the
moon disappeared and the sky was the color of blood. The same
year Grand Prince Dmitrii Ivanovich of Moscow, grandson of
Ivan [Kalita], great grandson of Daniilo, gr. gr. grandson of
Aleksandr [Nevskii], went to the Horde to Khan Khydyr, and
divine mercy protected him because he left the Horde before
the Great Troubles [*Velikaia zamiatnia*] occurred there. As soon
as he left the Horde very grievous troubles started in the Horde.
The same year Russian princes went to the Horde, to Khan
Khydyr. They were Grand Prince Dmitrii Konstantinovich of
Suzdal' and his senior brother, Grand Prince Andrei Konstantinovich of Nizhnii Novgorod; and Prince Konstantin of Rostov;
and Prince Mikhail of Iaroslavl'. During their sojourn in the
Horde there were Great Troubles there. Khan Khydyr was
killed, although he was quiet, meek and peaceful: he was killed

26. Zhukotin (in Turkic, *Dzhuke Tay*: a very rich trade city in the
Volga Bulgars' land.

1361 together with his younger son, Kutlui, by his senior son, Temir Khodzha. And so Temir Khodzha, Khydyr's senior son, became Khan of the Horde of the Volga.

The same year His Holiness Alexis, Metropolitan of Kiev and all Russia, went to Tver' and consecrated Basil, abbot of the Monastery of the Saviour, Bishop of Tver'. The same year there were portents in the sky. The sun disappeared and then the moon became the color of blood.

[RISE OF MAMAI]

The same year Mamai, the army commander[27] of the Horde, became hateful toward his Khan. Since he was very powerful, he rose up against his Khan, Temir Khodzha, son of Khydyr, and he brought troubles to the entire khanate of the Volga. He accepted a certain Abdul as his khan, and fracas and great dissension continued in the Horde.[28]

At that time Grand Prince Andrei Konstantinovich of Nizhnii Novgorod travelled from the Horde to Russia, and during his trip he was attacked by a Tatar lord, Reti Khodzha. God, however, aided Prince Andrei Konstantinovich of Nizhnii Novgorod, and he came in good health to Russia. At that time many Russian princes escaped from the Horde; but the princes of Rostov escaped only after being robbed. Temir Khodzha, son of Khydyr, Khan of the Horde beyond the Volga, escaped over the river Volga, but he was killed there; he remained Khan just one month and seven days, and he drank from the same cup which he had given his father, Khydyr, and his junior brother, Kului, to drink from. Thereafter, Lord Mamai crossed the river Volga with strong forces, toward the Volga's high [western] bank; and with him was the entire Horde; and their Khan was named Abdul. Then, a third Khan, by the name Kildibeg—who claimed to

27. *Temnik*: a commander of *t'ma*—10,000 men; and also an army commander.

28. Mamai: an army commander in the Golden Horde. Not being a descendant of Chenghiz Khan, he could not, himself, become Khan of the Horde. During the so-called "Time of Discord" in the Horde (1356-1380) when some twenty-five khans came to power and were overthrown and killed, he became *de facto* ruler of the Horde. After his defeat by the Russians in 1380 he was also defeated by Tokhtamysh, Khan of the Horde beyond the Volga river. He escaped to Kafa in Crimea, where he was killed. Grekov, B. D., and Iakubovskii, A. Iu., *Zolotaia Orda i ee Padenie*, Moscow-Leningrad 1950.

be the son of Dzhanibeg and grandson of Khan Uzbeg—laid claim   **1361**
to power, wanting to become Khan of the Volga Horde; he killed
many people but was, himself, finally killed. Then the lords of
Sarai fortified Sarai and proclaimed a certain Amurad, brother of
Khan Khydyr, Khan. In the meantime Bulat Temir, a noble of the
Horde, occupied the land of the Bulgars, conquered all the cities
and all the lands along the Volga, and took control over the entire
Volga route. Another noble of the Horde, named Togai—he
from Bezdezh[29] and from Naruchad[30]—occupied the entire
region and became independent over there; many other nobles of
the Horde also became independent. Among them there were
great famine and troubles and great discord, and they did not
cease from waging war among themselves, and they fought and
shed blood. In this way, God sent His wrath against them, being
merciful toward their servants, the humble Orthodox Christians.

The same year the Lithuanians campaigned in the lands of Tver'.

The same year Lord Mamai fought Khan Amurat and other
nobles of the Horde.

In the year 6870/1362. Between Lord Mamai and Khan Amurat
there was fierce fighting for the Volga. The same year Khan Amurat
unexpectedly raided Lord Mamai, and he killed many of his Tatars.
At that time in the Volga Horde were two khans: Khan Abdullah,
who was Khan of Mamai's Horde—who was proclaimed Khan by his
own lord and commander Mamai in his Horde; and another Khan
named Amurad, with the nobles of Sarai. And so these two Khans
and these two Hordes had little peace between them because they
fought incessantly and had feuds and fighting between them.

That year Grand Prince Dmitrii Ivanovich of Moscow, grandson of Ivan [Kalita], gr. grandson of Danilo, gr. gr. grandson of
Aleksandr [Nevskii]; and Grand Prince Dmitrii Konstantinovich
of Suzdal', grandson of Vasilii, gr. grandson of Mikhail, gr. gr.
grandson of Andrei, struggled between themselves over the
Grand Principality of Moscow[31] and they sent their officials[32] to
the Horde to Khan Amurad, and they brought the charter for the

29. Bezdeth, cith on the lower Volga.

30. Naruchad: a Finnic Mordva tribe and town (present Narovchat),
PSRL Vol. XXV, p. 439.

31. This should read, "Grand Principality of Vladimir."

32. *Kilicheis*: officials or messengers, Tatar.

1361 Grand Principality from Khan Amurad to Grand Prince Dmitrii Ivanovich of Moscow. And it passed according to the tradition of their fathers and grandfathers. And so Prince Dmitrii Konstantinovich left Vladimir and went to Pereiaslavl', where he became prince. The same winter Grand Prince Dmitrii Ivanovich with his brother, Prince Ivan Ivanovich, grandson of Ivan Kalita, gr. grandson of Danilo, with Prince Vladimir Andreevich, grandson of Ivan, great grandson of Danilo, gr. gr. grandson of Aleksandr, gathered a large number of troops in their patrimony and they marched to the city of Pereiaslavl' against Prince Dmitrii Konstantinovich of Suzdal', grandson of Vasilii, gr. grandson of Mikhail, gr. gr. grandson of Andrei. The latter escaped from Pereiaslavl' to the city of Vladimir, and from thence he fled to Suzdal' to the land of his father and grandfather, after having remained grand prince of Vladimir slightly more than two years.

THE REIGN OF GRAND PRINCE DMITRII IVANOVICH [DONSKOI][33]

[*6870/1362*].   Grand Prince Dmitrii Ivanovich, grandson of Ivan [Kalita], great grandson of Danilo, together with his brother, Prince Ivan Ivanovich, grandson of Ivan Kalita, great grandson of Danilo, and with Prince Vladimir Andreevich, grandson of Danilo, marched with all their forces from Pereiaslavl' [Zaleskii] to Vladimir, where Dmitrii Ivanovich ascended to the throne of the Grand Principality of Vladimir—the throne of his father and grandfather. He was only eleven years old; but in mind and energy, he was older than anyone else. And he resided three weeks in Vladimir, thereafter returning to Moscow, where he disbanded his army.[34]

The same year Roman, Metropolitan of Lithuania and Volynia, passed away. The same year, on the fifth day of the month of January, Moses, the former Lord Archbishop of Novgorod, passed away, and was buried in the church of Archangel Michael in Skovorodka. He was shepherd of the divine Church, and remained on his See for eight years. The same year Daniel, Lord

33. Beginning of Volume XI of *PSRL*.

34. The *de facto* ruler for the youthful grand prince was Metropolitan Alexis, who governed with the assistance of the old Muscovite boiar families.

Bishop of Suzdal', passed away. The same year Athanasius, Lord   **1362**
Bishop of Kostroma, passed away.[35]

In the year 6871/1363. Grand Prince Dmitrii Ivanovich, grandson of Ivan, great grandson of Danilo, marched from Moscow to
Vladimir, and together with him were his brother, Prince Ivan
Ivanovich, grandson of Ivan, great grandson of Danilo, and with
another of his kinsmen, his cousin—Prince Vladimir Andreevich,
grandson of Danilo. There, the envoy of Abdullah, Khan of
Mamai's Horde, brought him the *iarlyks* for the Grand Principality
of Vladimir. The Grand Prince rendered honor to the envoy,
gave him gifts and let him return to Khan Abdullah of Mamai's
Horde, while he, himself, journeyed from Vladimir to Pereiaslavl'.

The same year Khan Amurat, brother of the late Khan Khydyr,
as well as his nobles of Sarai, learned that the envoy of Khan
Abdullah of the Horde of Mamai had brought to Grand Prince
Dmitrii Ivanovich the *yarlyks* for the Grand Principality of
Vladimir, and he fell into a rage. At that time Prince Ivan of
Belozero was in Amurat's Horde, and therefore Khan Amurat sent
Prince Ivan of Belozero to Russia, and with him he sent his envoy,
Ilyak, with thirty Tatars, to present his *iarlyk* for the Grand Princi-
pality of Vladimir to Grand Prince Dmitrii Konstantinovich [of
Suzdal']. When they arrived in Suzdal' and went to Prince Dmitrii
Konstantinovich they were received by him with honors and joy.
The same year Prince Dmitrii Konstantinovich of Suzdal', grand-
son of Vasilii, great grandson of Mikhail, gr. gr. grandson of Andrei,
went from Suzdal' to Vladimir to become Grand Prince there.
With him were Ilyak, the envoy of Khan Amurat, with thirty
Tatars, and Prince Ivan of Belozero; this occurred because at
that time Prince Ivan of Belozero came from Amurat's Horde with
the envoy, Ilyak, and thirty Tatars. And so Prince Dmitrii Konstantinovich of Suzdal' for the second time ascended to the throne
of the Grand Principality of Vladimir. When Grand Prince Dmitrii
Ivanovich, grandon of Ivan, with his brother, Ivan Ivanovich,
grandson of Ivan, and their kinsman—their uncle, Prince Vladimir
Andreevich—learned of this, they assembled strong forces and
waged war against him and against the city of Vladimir. And so

35. They were victims of the plague, known in the West as the "Black
Death."

1363 they chased him from Vladimir, and he fled to Suzdal', having ruled in the Grand Principality of Vladimir exactly twelve days. Grand Prince Dmitrii Ivanovich marched after him to Suzdal' and stayed with strong forces near Suzdal', devastating everything around. Then Prince Dmitrii Konstantinovich made peace with him and went from Suzdal' to Nizhnii Novgorod to his senior brother, Andrei Konstantinovich, while Grand Prince Dmitrii Ivanovich, having imposed his will on him, returned to Vladimir. Also, he imposed his will over Prince Konstantin of Rostov.

The same year [6870/1362 in *Laur.*] Grand Prince Dmitrii Ivanovich chased Prince Ivan Fedorovich of Starodub from the principality of Starodub. Then all the princes, fearing for their principalities, went to Nizhnii Novgorod to Prince Dmitrii Konstantinovich.

The same year Grand Prince Vasilii Mikhailovich of Tver' marched, fighting, against his nephew, Prince Mikhail Aleksandrovich, against the city of Mikulin; but then they made peace and agreed on concord. The same year the Lithuanians took Korsheva. The same year Grand Prince Olgerd Gediminovich of Lithuania campaigned in Siniaia Voda and Beloberezh'e.

The same year Prince Vasilii Vasil'evich of Kashin passed away. He was the grandson of Mikhail, great grandson of Iaroslav, gr. gr. grandson of Iaroslav, gr. gr. gr. grandson of Vsevolod, gr. gr. gr. gr. grandson of Iurii Dolgorukii, gr. gr. gr. gr. gr. grandson of Vladimir Monomakh, gr. gr. gr. gr. gr. gr. grandson of Vsevolod Iaroslavovich, the latter being a grandson of Vladimir.

The same year in Nizhnii Novgorod, after the Eucharist in church, there was a portent: when Lord Bishop Alexis of Suzdal' with his cross blessed Grand Prince Andrei Konstantinovich of Suzdal', Nizhnii Novgorod and Gorodets, myrrh at once began to issue from the cross, and the people marvelled.

In the year 6872/1364. There was a bad plague in Nizhnii Novgorod and in its entire land, as well as along the rivers Sara and Kisha and in the neighboring lands and estates. People spat out blood and their glands would hurt one day or two or three; and thereafter they would die. Thus did it last, days and nights, and the living could not even manage to bury the dead because every day fifty or a hundred people, or more, would die.

That year there was a terrible noise and loud thunder over the cathedral church of Tver', and there were many portents, and there were terrifying lightning and tornadoes.

The same year Princess Anastasiia came from Lithuania **1363**
with her granddaughter, who was Olgerd's daughter; and she
was baptised in Tver'. For the sake of this baptism His Holiness,
Metropolitan Alexis, came to Tver'.

The same year there was a plague in Pereiaslavl' [Zaleskii],
and the disease was like this: first of all, a man would have the
feeling that he had been struck with a bear spear between his
shoulders, or in the chest against his heart, or between his shoulderblades. Then the man would fall ill and spit blood. A fiery
fever would burn him and destroy him, and then he would sweat
greatly, and then he would shake; and thus would he lie ill a day
or two; and only a few of them would live three days; and thus
they would die. Those who had the sickness of the glands, however, looked different because some would have boils on their
necks, others on their thighs, and some on their chests, some
under their cheekbones, some on their shoulderblades. And so
every day sometimes seventy, sometimes a hundred, and sometimes one hundred and fifty people would die. Thus it happened
not only in the city of Pereiaslavl' but also in the districts and
towns and monasteries of the principality of Pereiaslavl'. The
first city hit by the plague was Nizhnii Novgorod, whither it came
down the river Volga from Bezdezh. From Nizhnii Novgorod
it moved to Riazan' and Kolomna, and from thence to Pereiaslavl', whence it went to Moscow; and thus it spread over all cities:
to Tver', to Vladimir, to Suzdal', to Dmitrov, to Mozhaisk, to
Volok [Lamskii], and to all the cities did this bad and fearsome
plague spread. Alas! Alas! Who can report such a fearful and
sad story? In Belozero not one single man survived. And there
was great grief throughout the entire land, and the land became
devastated and overgrown with forests, and everywhere there
was an impassable wilderness. And they would bury seven and
even ten, even twenty, people in the same grave.[36]

The same winter Prince Ivan Ivanovich, called "the Junior,"
brother of Grand Prince Dmitrii Ivanovich, grandson of Ivan
[Kalita], great grandson of Danilo, gr. gr. grandson of Aleksandr
Nevskii, gr. gr. gr. grandson of Iaroslav, gr. gr. gr. gr. grandson
of Vsevolod [Great Nest], gr. gr. gr. gr. gr. grandson of Iurii
Dolgorukii, gr. gr. gr. gr. gr. gr. grandson of Vladimir Mono-

36. This was the continuation of the bubonic plague, the Black
Death of the West.

1364 makh—the latter being the son of Vsevolod Iaroslavich, who was the grandson of Vladimir—passed away and he was buried in Moscow in the church of St. Archangel Michael, which is on the Square.

The same year Grand Prince Andrei Konstantinovich of Suzdal', Nizhnii Novgorod and Gorodets, was tonsured a monk. This prince was very religious and highly virtuous.

The same year there was a bad drought throughout the whole country, the air was filled with smoke and the [dry] earth burned.

In the year 6873/1365. His Holiness Alexis, Metropolitan of all Russia, laid the foundation of a church within the fortified part of the city of Moscow. It was named in honor of the miracle performed by Archistrategos (Archangel) Michael in the city of Colossae in Chona. Therefore the church and the monastery are called "of the Miracle."[37]

The same year there was a portent in the sky. The sun was the color of blood; and black spots were on the sun, and fog remained half of the summer. Then there was great heat, and it was so hot that the forests and marshes burned, and the rivers dried out. Some watering places dried out completely and everyone was terrified, alarmed and greatly aggrieved.

The same year [6872/1364 in *Vozn.*] the meek, quiet, humble and most virtuous Grand Prince Andrei Konstantinovich of Suzdal', Nizhnii Novgorod and Gorodets passed away. He was shorn a monk and to the schema, and was buried in the church of the Holy Saviour in Nizhnii Novgorod, where his father, Grand Prince Konstantin Vasil'evich, was also buried. He was the grandson of Vasilii, great grandson of Mikhail, gr. gr. grandson of Andrei, gr. gr. gr. grandson of Aleksandr [Nevskii], gr. gr. gr. gr. grandson of Iaroslav, gr. gr. gr. gr. gr. grandson of Vsevolod ["Great Nest"], gr. gr. gr. gr. gr. grandson of Iurii Dolgorukii, who was the son of Vladimir Monomakh—the latter being the son of Vsevolod Iaroslavich, grandson of Vladimir.

The same year Prince Vasilii [called "Kirdiapa"], the son of Prince Dmitrii of Suzdal', grandson of Konstantin Vasil'evich, went to the Horde.

The same year there was a conflagration in Moscow because there was great drought and great heat; and at that time a storm

37. Colossae: a city in Phrygia, in n.w. Asia Minor.

with a tornado arose, spreading fire everywhere, and many people were killed and burned, and everything burned up and disappeared. It was called "the Great Fire," which started near
the Church of All Saints and which spread everywhere, carried
by the wind and the tornado.

The same year there was a plague in Tver' and in Rostov.

The same year Prince Konstantin [of Rostov] passed away,
together with his wife and his children. And so did Lord Bishop
Peter and Grand Princess Nastasiia, wife of Aleksandr, and
Avdotiia, wife of Konstantin; and also, Prince Semion Konstanti-
novich. The latter bequeathed his patrimony and domains, as
well as those of the Princess, to Prince Mikhail Aleksandrovich.
Then Sophia, wife of Prince Vsevolod, passed away; and then
Prince Vsevolod Aleksandrovich, himself, as well as his brother,
Prince Andrei Aleksandrovich, and the latter's wife, Princess
Evdokiia. And many boiars and outstanding merchants[38] and
men died; and then Prince Vladimir Aleksandrovich passed
away; and fear seized everyone. The same year [6872/1364 in
Vozn.'] Grand Princess Aleksandra, the dowager of Ivan Ivano-
vich, took the veil and the schema, receiving the monastic name,
Maria; and she passed away and was buried in the monastic
church of the Holy Saviour in Moscow, in the lateral chapel.[39]

The same year Prince Dmitrii Konstantinovich of Suzdal',
grandson of Vasilii, great grandson of Mikhail, gr. gr. grandson
of Andrei, gr. gr. gr. grandson of Aleksandr Iaroslavich [Nev-
skii], came to Nizhnii Novgorod to be grand prince there. He
went thither with his mother, Elena, and with his Lord Bishop
Alexis of Suzdal', Nizhnii Novgorod and Gorodets; but his junior
brother, Prince Boris Konstantinovich, grandson of Vasilii,
did not want to turn over to him the principality of Nizhnii Novgorod.

The same year an envoy came from the Horde, from Bairam
Khodzha and from Assan, the Khan's wife. And he assigned the
principality of Nizhnii Novgorod to Boris Konstantinovich,
grandson of Vasilii, great grandson of Mikhail, gr. gr. grandson
of Andrei Aleksandrovich. But that year [6872/1364 in *Vozn.*]
Prince Vasilii Kirdiapa of Suzdal', son of Dmitrii, grandson of

38. *Gosti:*—the top strata of the merchantry.
39. It was still the same plague (Black Death) which started in 1346.

1365   Konstantin, great grandson of Vasilii, came from the Horde of
Khan Azis, and with him came the Khan's envoy, named Urus-
Manda. The latter brought the *iarlyk* for the grand principality
of Vladimir to Prince Dmitrii Konstantinovich of Suzdal'. The
latter, however, did not want to accept it and relinquished the
grand principality of Vladimir to Grand Prince Dmitrii Ivanovich of Moscow. He requested the latter [6873/1365 in *Vozn.*]
to send a troop to Nizhnii Novgorod to fight his junior brother,
Prince Boris Konstantinovich. Grand Prince Dmitrii Ivanovich
sent him his envoys in order to arrange peace and divide the
patrimony between them, but Prince Boris did not acquiesce.

[ABBOT SERGIUS GOES TO NIZHNII NOVGOROD]

The same year Metropolitan Alexis took the dioceses of
Nizhnii Novgorod and Gorodets from Bishop Alexis of Suzdal'.
At the same time reverend Sergius, Abbot of Radonezh, came from
Grand Prince Dmitrii Ivanovich, from Moscow to Nizhnii Nov-
gorod, to Boris Konstantinovich, asking him to come to Moscow.
But the latter did not listen to him and did not go to Moscow. The
reverend Abbot Sergius, following the order of Metropolitan
Alexis and Grand Prince Dmitrii Ivanovich, closed all the churches
[in Nizhnii Novgorod]. Then Grand Prince Dmitrii Ivanovich
sent troops to Dmitrii Konstantinovich, who was the senior brother,
to fight his junior brother, Boris Konstantinovich. Prince Dmitrii
Konstantinovich also assembled a sizable force in his patrimony
of Suzdal' and marched, waging war, toward Nizhnii Novgorod.
When he arrived in Berezhie he was met there by his junior
brother, Boris Konstantinovich, with the latter's boiars. Boris
bowed and submitted to him, suing for peace and relinquishing
his claims to the principality. Prince Dmitrii Konstantinovich did
not disregard his brother's petition and request, agreed with him
on peace and divided with him the principalities of Suzdal', of
Nizhnii Novgorod and of Gorodets. Prince Dmitrii Konstantinovich, himself, became Prince of Nizhnii Novgorod, while he gave his
junior brother the principality of Gorodets.

The same year [6872/1364 in *Vozn.*] Alexis, Bishop of Suzdal',
passed away.

The same year Tagai, a lord of the Horde, came after the
trouble in the Horde, to Naruchad, and he became the lord of
Naruchad. Thereafter he wanted to fight against Russia and he

assembled all his forces and the forces of the land of Naruchad. He   **1365**
marched with a sizable army into the land of Riazan'. Marching
secretly and unexpectedly upon Riazan', he took the city of Perei-
slavl' Riazanskii.[40] He burned it, occupied all lands and towns, and
took many captives. Thus, having heavy booty, he marched slowly
toward the prairie. Prince Oleg Ivanovich of Riazan', however, with
his kinsmen, Vladimir of Pronsk and Tit of Kozel'sk, gathered their
forces, marched after him, caught up with him near a place called
"Shishevskii Forest" on the river Voina. There was a very fierce
battle and fight, and great slaughter, and many were killed on both
sides; but God aided Prince Oleg Ivanovich of Riazan' and his kinsmen, Vladimir of Pronsk and Tit of Kozelsk; and the proud Tagai,
lord from the Horde, who was the ruler of the land of Naruchad,
became very frightened, trembled greatly and grew bewildered,
not knowing what to do, seeing that all his Tatars were killed.
And so, weeping, shedding tears and scratching his face with grief,
he escaped with difficulties, with a small troop.

The same year [6872/1364 in *Novg. III.*] the leading merchants
[*Gosti*] and the other merchants and common people of Torzhok
erected a stone church of the Holy Transfiguration to the Glory of
Christ God, the Most Pure Theotokos, and for the sake of their
own salvation. The same year [6872/1364 in *Novg. III.*] Alexis,
Bishop of Novgorod, built over the gate of the monastery of St.
Anthony a stone church of the Meeting of the Lord in the Temple.[41]
The same year, with the blessing of Lord Bishop Alexis, they started
building in Pskov a stone church of the Holy Trinity, and they
built it on the old foundation.

The same year there was a portent in the church of the Holy
Apostle Peter in Slavna on the icon of the Most Pure Theotokos, on
which dew appeared.

The same year there was a plague in Pskov. The same year
there was a violent plague in Torzhok.

In the year 6874/1366. There was a portent in the sky. There
was a great plague in the city of Moscow and in all the lands of
Moscow. The same year there was a very great plague in Volok.

40. Pereiaslavl' Riazanskii, now Riazan', became the capital of the
Riazan' land after the Mongol invasion, during which the ancient city of
Riazan' was completely destroyed.

41. The holiday of the Meeting of the Lord in the Temple (February 2), where He was met by righteous Simon. Luke 22-39.

1366   The same year there was a very great plague in Lithuania. The same
year there were drought and extreme heat; and there was smoke in
the air, and the earth burned and grain was very dear everywhere;
and there was great famine throughout the land, people dying because of it.

The same year there was a rupture in the peace among the
princes of Tver': Prince Vasilii Mikhailovich, Prince Eremei, and
their cousin, Prince Mikhail Aleksandrovich. They argued concerning the division of the patrimony of Prince Semion Konstantinovich. The same year with the blessing and on the order of the
Metropolitan, Lord Bishop Basil made a decision concerning them,
and he exculpated Prince Mikhail Aleksandrovich.

[THE USHKUINIKS]

The same year Novgorodian freebooters[42] came from Novgorod the Great, and there were two hundred *ushkui* with them.
They went down the river Volga and killed a great multitude of
Tatars and Armenians in Nizhnii Novgorod. They also killed
many Tatar and Nizhnii Novgorodian merchants, their wives and
children, sacking their merchandise and hacking their boats to
pieces.[43] They set fire to everything and moved to the river Kama.
So, moving on the Kama, they fought the Bulgars, killing many of
them.

The same year in Great Novgorod there was built in Riaditina
Street a church dedicated to the Holy Trinity. The same year the
young nobles from Great Novgorod, without asking the counsel of
the Novgorodian elders, formed a warring band. Their voevodas
were Osip Varfolomeevich, Vasilii Fedorovich, Aleksandr Avak-
umovich. They returned to Novgorod the same year with great
booty. Because of their raids Prince Dmitrii Ivanovich became
wroth with the Novgorodians, broke the peace agreement with
them, saying, "Why did you go a-robbing and a-killing my best
merchants?" The same winter the people of Grand Prince Dmitrii
Ivanovich caught the Novgorodian boiar, Vasilii Danilovich,

42. Freebooters: *Ushkuiniki*, Novgorodian river freebooters who
organized vast robbing expeditions, sometimes of several thousand men,
travelling on riverboats called *ushkui*.

43. Seven types of boats are mentioned but there are no contemporary English equivalents for these terms.

together with his son, Ivan, while he was returning from the   **1366**
Dvina; he was not on guard, being unaware [of them, the men of
the Grand Prince].

The same winter on the eighteenth day of the month of January
Grand Prince Dmitrii Ivanovich married Evdokiia, the daughter of
Grand Prince Dmitrii Konstantinovich of Suzdal' and Nizhnii
Novgorod; their wedding took place in Kolomna. The same winter,
having taken counsel with his cousin, Prince Vladimir Andreevich,
and with his senior boiars, Grand Prince Dmitrii Ivanovich decided
to build a stone fortress of Moscow; and what they determined
upon, they carried out. The same winter they started carting stone
into the city.[44]

The same year Prince Mikhail Aleksandrovich of Tver' started
building a new town of Gorodok on the Volga.

In the year 6875/1367. Theodore, the former Lord Bishop
of Tver', passed away in the Otroch monastery and was buried
in the small church dedicated to the Presentation of the Most
Pure Theotokos; his burial place was the same as Bishop Andrew's.

The same year Grand Prince Dmitrii Ivanovich laid the
foundation of the stone fortress of Moscow, and the work on it
continued without interruption. He brought all the Russian
princes under his will, and he intended to handle in the same
manner those who did not obey him, including Prince Mikhail
Aleksandrovich of Tver'; and therefore Prince Mikhail Aleksandrovich departed for Lithuania. On behalf of Prince Vasilii
Mikhailovich and his son, Mikhailo, as well as Prince Eremei,
Lord Bishop Vasilii [of Tver'] was summoned to Moscow by
the bailiffs of the Metropolitan to appear before the court of the
Metropolitan because he made an unjustified judgment concerning the patrimony of Prince Semion. And so Lord Bishop Basil
was fined heavily by this court, and so were the common people
of Tver' who were involved in the [litigation of the] patrimony
of Prince Semion. Prince Vasilii, together with his princess,
his son, Prince Mikhail, and Prince Eremei, as well as with the
entire force from Kashin—came to the land of Tver' and caused

44. Thereafter, in the *Nik.* text there is found, unexpectedly, in the
same annual entry, a story about Prince Andrew of Cyprus which is not
related to Russian history; therefore this story is omitted here.

1367   there much offense and multitudinous hardships for many people, sacking their property and selling much of it without mercy. He marched to the city [of Tver'] with his troops, as well as with the Muscovite troop of Grand Prince Dmitrii Ivanovich, which he had brought with him. Thanks to Divine Intercession they did not take the city, but returned, having campaigned in many districts and towns; and a large number of people were taken into captivity. The Muscovite troops, as well as the troops from Volok, which campaigned in the Tver' land, devastated the towns on this side of the Volga as well as the ecclesiastic estates of the Tver' diocese of the Holy Saviour. They took everyone captive and burned and devastated everything.

[MORE FEUDS IN TVER']

The same fall on the twenty-seventh of the month of October Prince Mikhail Aleksandrovich of Tver' returned from Lithuania with his own army. He captured the wife of Prince Eremei, and his boiars, and the wife, boiars and squires of his uncle, Prince Vasilii Mikhailovich. He marched with his army and with Lithuanian troops to the city of Kashin, where, in the town of Andreevskoe, he was met by the envoys of his uncle, Prince Vasilii Mikhailovich, and of Lord Bishop Vasilii of Tver'. And Lord God and the Most Pure Theotokos stilled his fierceness and put mercy into his heart, giving him a blessed idea and a blessed thought. And so, in that place he agreed on peace and concord with his uncle, Prince Vasilii Mikhailovich of Kashin, as well as with Grand Prince Dmitrii Ivanovich of Moscow; and there was great peace and concord between them, and he released the envoys with honor. And their boiars and all their magnates, as well as their great merchants and simple merchants, and all the working people and all people descended from Adam rejoiced greatly.

This happened because we are all descendants of the tribe of Adam, be we emperors, princes, boiars, magnates, great merchants, merchants, craftsmen or working people. There is just one race and tribe of Adam; but, forgetting this, they fight, hate, gnaw and bite each other, forgetting and shunning God's commandment to love one's neighbors as oneself. And so Prince Eremei arrived and made peace with Prince Mikhail Aleksandrovich and Prince Mikhail Aleksandrovich showed him his great amity, allowing his wife, the Princess, to return to him [from **1367** captivity]. In winter, around Epiphany, Prince Mikhail Vasilievich of Kashin also came from his father, Vasilii Mikhailovich, and agreed on peace with Prince Mikhail Aleksandrovich. And Prince Mikhail Aleksandrovich of Tver' made peace and agreed on concord with Grand Prince Dmitrii Ivanovich of Moscow. The same year Prince Eremei renounced his pledge on the cross to Prince Mikhail Aleksandrovich of Tver' and went to Grand Prince Dmitrii Ivanovich in Moscow.

The same year Bulat Temir, a lord of the Horde who had strong forces and who fought victoriously in many battles, gathered many troops and marched into the land and principality of Nizhnii Novgorod, and he campaigned in the districts and towns of Prince Boris Konstantinovich. Then Prince Dmitrii Konstantinovich of Suzdal' and Nizhnii Novgorod, together with his brothers, Prince Boris Konstantinovich and Prince Dmitrii Konstantinovich,[45] as well as their children, gathered a large army and marched against him; and he fled beyond the river Piana. Going thither, they massacred the Tatars who were there and drowned other Tatars in the river Piana, while the remaining Tatars were killed in the chase. And so Bulat Temir, a lord of the Horde, pursued by divine wrath, escaped with but a small troop to the Horde, where he was killed by Khan Azis.

The same year in the town of Gorodok, in the monastery of St. Lazar', lightning killed monks and nuns, as well as many people in the neighboring towns.

[NOVGOROD MAKES PEACE WITH MOSCOW]

The same year the people of Novgorod sent petitions and gifts to Grand Prince Dmitrii Ivanovich of Moscow, asking for peace, and he concluded peace with them according to the tradition of old, and he released with the envoys their boiar, Vasilii Danilovich, and his son, Ivan; also, he sent his namestniks to Novgorod, and so there were peace and concord. The same year posadnik Ontsifor of Novgorod passed away. The same year in Slavnaia

---

45. Probably, Prince Dmitrii Konstantinovich of Dorogobuzh; Baumgarten, table IX.

1367   Street in Novgorod a stone church was erected, dedicated to the holy and supreme Apostle Peter.

The same year the Novgorodians were in disagreement with the people of Pskov, and therefore the Germans[46] from Vilnevichi invaded and fought around the fortress of Izborsk. They devastated all the lands and towns of Pskov up to the river Velikaia, then they crossed the river Velikaia, came to the city of Pskov, burned the suburb, occupied and burned the neighboring towns and lands, but did not succeed in taking the city. At that time in the city were neither Prince Aleksandr nor posadnik Pantelei[47] nor any other courageous men. But thereafter the people of Pskov were joined by the Novgorodians and campaigned against the Germans. Many Novgorodian men, however, as well as men of Pskov, were killed. At that time the brave Novgorodian, Zakharii Davydovich, and all in his troop with him, were killed. Also killed was Selilo, the famous voevoda of Pskov. A numberless host of Germans were likewise killed.

The same year Grand Princess Nastasia, widow of Andrei Konstantinovich of Nizhnii Novgorod, took the veil of the holy angelic and monastic order.

In the year 6876/1368. There were portents and terrifying thunder on Maundy Thursday. The thunderstorm and lightning set fire to the cathedral church of the Holy Archangel Michael in Gorodets, as well as to the church of the Holy Archangel Michael in Suzdal', burning many churches in other cities. The same year a star appeared with a tail.[48]

The same year Prince Andrei Olgerdovich of Polotsk campaigned in Khovrach and Rodno.

The same year Prince Vladimir Andreevich, grandson of Ivan, great grandson of Danilo [cousin of Grand Prince Dmitrii Donskoi] campaigned in the land of Rzhev and took the city.

[TVER' AND LITHUANIA AGAINST MOSCOW]

The same year Grand Prince Dmitrii Ivanovich, grandson of Ivan [Kalita], great grandson of Danilo, gr. gr. grandson of blessed

46. The knights of the Livonian Order.
47. Leontii, in *Novg. III.*
48. Oviously, a comet.

Aleksandr [Nevskii], together with his spiritual father, His Holi- **1368**
ness Alexis, Metropolitan of Kiev and all Russia, invited with love
to Moscow Prince Mikhail Aleksandrovich of Tver'. When he
arrived, however, they presented accusations against him and so
there was an open trial, according to the laws, and he was arrested.
Those boiars who had come with him were seized and were incarcerated in various places. Remaining under arrest, they were
held in great hardship while Prince Mikhail Aleksandrovich of
Tver' was incarcerated in the Gavshin estate. Thereupon, after
awhile, suddenly and unexpectedly the Tatars came from the
Horde: [*viz.,*] Lord Karach, and Oaidar with Tutekash; and when
they [Grand Prince Dmitrii and his advisors] learned of this they
grew doubtful, held counsel and pondered. Then they released
[Prince Mikhail and his boiars] to go home, after having received
from him a pledge of peace on the cross.[49] Prince Mikhail Aleksandrovich of Tver' was very upset about this happening, dis-
liking all this, and he was greatly disturbed. Considering this a
treason, he became hateful, and broke the peace with Grand Prince
Dmitrii Ivanovich. Full of wrath, he complained primarily of the
Metropolitan, saying, "I had such love and faith, especially in the
Metropolitan, and he rendered me shame and offense." Then
they [the Muscovite government] took from Prince Mikhail
Aleksandrovich the town of Gorodok, which was part of Prince
Semion's patrimony, and together with Prince Eremei, they put
their namestniks there.

The same year Prince Vasilii Mikhailovich of Tver' passed
away in Kashin; he was the grandson of Iaroslav, great grandson of
Iaroslav, gr. gr. grandson of Vsevolod ["Great nest"], gr. gr. gr.
grandson of Iurii Dolgorukii, gr. gr. gr. gr. grandson of Vladimir
Monomakh, gr. gr. gr. gr. gr. grandson of Vsevolod, gr. gr. gr.
gr. gr. gr. grandson of Iaroslav Vladimirovich. The same year
Sofia, the dowager of Grand Prince Dmitrii Iaroslavovich of Tver',
passed away.

The same year Grand Prince Dmitrii Ivanovich, grandson of
Ivan [Kalita], great grandson of Danilo, gr. gr. grandson of Aleks-

49. The text is corrected here according to the *Late XVth C. Musc.
Codex, PSRL XXV*, because in *Nik.* the sentence is unclear. Apparently,
Prince Dmitrii, then about eighteen, and his advisers, Metropolitan
Alexis and the boiars, were frightened by the Tatars' appearance and
the latters' support of the Prince of Tver'.

1368 andr [Nevskii], gathered many troops and sent them against Grand Prince Mikhail Aleksandrovich of Tver'; but Grand Prince Mikhail Aleksandrovich of Tver' escaped to Lithuania to his brother-in-law, Grand Prince Olgerd Gediminovich of Lithuania, and he began to incite him and advise him how to attack Grand Prince Dmitrii Ivanovich in Moscow. He wanted to take revenge and protect himself, and he implored and petitioned him with tears, and instructed his sister to do likewise.

Olgerd accepted his words with pleasure and, particularly, heeded the entreaties of his wife, Uliana, the sister [of Prince Mikhail Aleksandrovich] and daughter of [late] Aleksandr Mikhailovich of Tver'. Then, the same autumn, Grand Prince Olgerd Gediminovich of Lithuania mustered a large army and marched to wage war against Moscow, against Grand Prince Dmitrii Ivanovich. With him were his brothers, Keistut Gediminovich, Keistut's son, Vitovt—who at that time was young and not yet glorious—and the sons of Olgerd, as well as all Lithuanian princes, Grand Prince Mikhail Aleksandrovich of Tver' and the army of Smolensk.

[OLGERD WARS AGAINST MOSCOW]

Olgerd Gediminovich had the habit of not allowing anyone to know of his intentions or whither he meant to dispatch his army, or for what reason he assembled troops. Even his military commanders and the entire army were unaware whither they marched. No one knew, neither his people nor other people nor his merchants nor foreign merchants. He kept his counsel himself, so that no word should leave his land concerning whomsoever he intended to battle or whatsoever manner of cunning he planned. In such a way he conquered many lands and subjected many cities and countries. He did so not so much by force as by acting with wisdom; therefore, everyone was in awe of him, and he surpassed very many others in majesty and wealth.

Consequently, Grand Prince Dmitrii Ivanovich knew nothing concerning Olgerd's military plans against Moscow before the latter appeared at his borders.

As soon as Grand Prince Dmitrii Ivanovich learned of the approaching troops of Olgerd Gediminovich he ordered that messages be sent to all cities and to his entire principality, urging

them to gather their troops. His warriors did not have time to   **1368**
come from distant places, but he assembled those at hand and sent
them as a vanguard against Olgerd. He gave their command to
Dmitrii Minin and to the voevoda of his uncle, Prince Vladimir
Andreevich, whose name was Akinf Fedorovich, also called
"Shuba." The troops of Moscow, Kolomna and Dmitrov were
under them.

When Olgerd moved into the confines of the Muscovite land,
first of all, he began to raid the border places, burning, sacking
and slaying. Then in an encounter he killed Prince Semion Dmitrievich of Starodub, called "the Nettle" [*Krapiva*]. This occurred
in the region called *Kholokhla*. Then in Obolensk he killed Prince
Konstantin, son of Iurii, grandson of the blessed Grand Prince
Mikhail of Chernigov, great grandson of Vsevolod, gr. gr. grandson of Sviatoslav, gr. gr. gr. grandson of Oleg, gr. gr. gr. gr. grandson of Sviatoslav, gr. gr. gr. gr. gr. grandson of Oleg, gr. gr. gr.
gr. gr. gr. grandson of Great Vladimir.[50] Then he moved to the
river Trostna, where he defeated the vanguard of Grand Prince
Dmitrii Ivanovich, Moscow's advance troops; and on November
twenty-first, the day of the Presentation of the Most Pure Theotokos,
a Tuesday, he killed all their princes, voevodas and boiars.

When Olgerd became aware that Grand Prince Dmitrii
Ivanovich had had no time to assemble a large army and was,
himself, preparing the city of Moscow for siege, then Olgerd be-
gan to move faster and, unexpectedly, advanced on Moscow.
Arriving there, he took a position near the city of Moscow, and
Grand Prince Dmitrii Ivanovich ordered that the suburbs of
Moscow be burned, while he, himself, prepared the city for siege.
He did this together with his spiritual father, His Holiness,
blessed Alexis, Metropolitan of Kiev and all Russia; with his uncle,
Prince Vladimir Andreevich, grandson of Ivan, great grandson of
Danilo, gr. gr. grandson of blessed Aleksandr; and with all his
boiars and all his men.

Olgerd stayed three days near Moscow, not taking the city but
causing much evil there. He burned everything and captured an

50. The lineage of the descendants of Prince Mikhail of Chernigov
is indistinct because, according to Serbian and Hungarian sources, his
sons escaped with him to Hungary, where they remained, becoming the
lords (Herzogs) of Machva, in the region now called "Banat."

1368 uncountable number of people, whom he took into captivity, also taking all the cattle with him. All this occurred for our sins, and never before did such evil befall Moscow from Lithuania. Indeed, the Tatars perpetrated much evil; but never had it come about from Lithuania—and it was an all-destructive curse. This campaign of Olgerd's took place forty-one years after Fedorchuck's invasion.[51] The same year Prince Vladimir Andreevich of Moscow, grandson of Ivan, great grandson of Danilo, went to the aid of the people of Pskov. He was there from the day of the Council[52] to St. Peter's day. The same winter Grand Prince Dmitrii Ivanovich relinquished Gorodok and all parts of Prince Semion's patrimony to Prince Mikhail Aleksandrovich of Tver'; and he allowed Prince Eremei to return to Tver'.

The same winter Prince Mikhail Vasilievich of Kashin, grandson of Mikhail, great grandson of Iaroslav, ordered that the monastic church of the Most Pure Theotokos be torn down and transferred into the city, and that this holy place be destroyed; and he even ordered that the bones of the monks, who had been buried there long ago, be broken in their graves. The same year, however, Prince Mikhail Vasil'evich of Kashin, grandson of Mikhail, great grandson of Iaroslav, as well as his princess, became ill with an unknown and woeful disease. He, himself, was saved by God, but his princess, Vasilissa, passed away on the twentieth day of the month of April. Thus, Prince Mikhail Vasil'evich took fright and was sorely fearful at his own doing. He implored Lord Bishop Basil and the entire Holy Council of the clergy to forgive him. Lord Bishop Basil enjoined him not to destroy that place to the end; he heeded the Lord Bishop and built a small church there, dedicated to the Most Pure Theotokos. Later, however, even this church was destroyed. The same year there was a bad famine in Tver'.

The same year the Germans [of the Livonian Order] waged war against Izborsk. The bishop [of Riga], himself, accompanied them, as well as the grossmeisters and the commanders; but the

51. "Fedorchuk's invasion" denotes here the Tatar's punitive expedition of 1327, led by a certain Fedorchuk; see the entry under the year 1327.

52. Sunday before Lent. St. Peter's day: most likely, here is meant June 29, when the Holy Apostles Peter and Paul are remembered.

people of Pskov assembled and marched against them. The Ger-   **1368**
mans, unable to take the fortress, returned home.

In the year 6877/1369. The Germans took the Lithuanian
city of Kovno.

The same year Prince Liub of Smolensk passed away.

The same year Prince Boris Konstantinovich of Suzdal',
grandson of Vasilii, great grandson of Mikhail, gr. gr. grandson
of Andrei, erected in Gorodets a cathedral church dedicated to
St. Archangel Michael.

The same year they built a wooden fortress in Tver' and
plastered it with clay.

The same year the Novgorodians campaigned against the
Swedish city of Oreshek. Not succeeding in taking it, they returned home. The same year Novgorod the Great burned, including the fortress, the court of the Lord Bishop, Holy Sophia,
the Narva section and the carpenters' section; and many people
burned. The same year they laid the foundation for a stone church
of St. Basil in Iaryshkina Street [the street of court scribes], and
another church to St. Eupatius in Rogatets. The same year the
Novgorodians and people of Pskov marched against a new German [Livonian] fortress, but they did not succeed at all and many
of them were killed, so they retreated.

The same year Grand Prince Dmitrii Ivanovich laid the
foundation of a fortress in Pereiaslavl' [Zaleskii], and in one year
this wooden construction was completed.

The same year Prince Mikhail Vasil'evich of Tver', grandson
of Mikhail, great grandson of Iaroslav, went to Moscow to complain to Metropolitan Alexis about his bishop, Basil, of Tver'.

The same year Olgerd Gediminovich, Grand Prince of Lithuania, campaigned against the Germans and took many captives.

The same year the troops of Moscow and Volok [Lamskii]
campaigned in the land of Smolensk.

In the year 6878/1370. Mamai, a lord of the Horde, put Ma-
mat Sultan as Khan of his Horde.

The same year Grand Prince Dmitrii Ivanovich gathered
many troops and sent them to campaign against the city of Briansk.

The same fall Prince Dmitrii Konstantinovich of Suzdal' and
Nizhnii Novgorod gathered many warriors and sent his brother,
Boris Konstantinovich, and his son, Prince Vasilii Dmitrievich,

1370 together with the Khan's envoy, named Achi-Khodzha, to campaign against Prince Hassan of the [Volga] Bulgars, who are now called the "people of Kazan'." Hassan, Prince of Kazan', sent his envoy to meet them, with his petition and many gifts; they accepted the gifts and they put Sultan, son of Saltan Bak, to rule there and they returned to Nizhnii Novgorod to Grand Prince Dmitrii Konstantinovich, grandson of Vasilii, great grandson of Mikhail, gr. gr. grandson of Andrei, gr. gr. gr. grandson of Aleksandr [Nevskii].

The same fall there was much rain and many floods.

The same winter in Nizhnii Novgorod there was a huge snow avalanche from a high hill which is on the Volga behind the church of the Holy Annunciation, and snow buried households with people.

The same year three days after Our Lady's Day,[53] Grand Prince Dmitrii Ivanovich proclaimed that he renounced his pledge on the cross to Prince Mikhail Aleksandrovich of Tver'; and the same night there was such terrifying thunder that even the earth shook. Because of this end to the peace, Prince Mikhail Aleksandrovich of Tver' went to Lithuania. Then Grand Prince Dmitrii Ivanovich sent a large army into the land of Tver' and ordered a campaign against Tver', ordering that the land and towns be burned and the people captured. So, having campaigned there, they returned home with many captives.

In the year 6879/1371. On the third day of the month of September Grand Prince Dmitrii Ivanovich with strong forces marched, himself, into the Tver' land. He took the city of Zubtsev in the Tver' land, burned everything and captured everyone; he also took Mikulin, another city there, and also burned and captured. And he burned and captured all lands and towns in the land of Tver', burning and devastating everything. He took into captivity a large number of people and brought them back, taking their wealth and cattle to his own land; and so Grand Prince Dmitrii Ivanovich returned to Moscow with great wealth and booty, filling his land with much cattle while very much humbling the people of Tver'. When Prince Mikhail Aleksandrovich of Tver', who at that time was in Lithuania, received word of this he be-

---

53. Our Lady's Day—the holiday of the Presentation of the Virgin Mary in the Temple—November 21.

came greatly saddened and grieved. He went from Lithuania to **1371** the Horde, to Mamai, where he was given by the Khan an envoy named Sari Khodzha, was granted by the Khan a *yarlyk* for the Grand Principality of Vladimir, and went to Russia.

When Grand Prince Dmitrii Ivanovich received word of this he became greatly upset and placed guards along all routes, intending to catch him. They searched at length for him but could not find him because he [the Prince of Tver'] received word from Moscow informing him [of this]. So he fled to Lithuania, to his brother-in-law, Grand Prince Olgerd Gediminovich, beseeching him to protect him; also, he entreated his sister, Uliana, wife of Olgerd Gediminovich and daughter of Aleksandr, asking and instructing her to persuade Olgerd and to require him to wage war against Moscow, against Grand Prince Dmitrii Ivanovich.

A TERRIFYING PORTENT

The same fall there were many portents in the skies: for many nights people saw a manner of pillars in the sky, and the sky was red as blood: the sky was so red that the earth and the snow were as red as blood, and this happened many times. The earth, water and homes all looked bloody, even before it snowed. And when it snowed, the ground, covered by snow, looked like blood, and people walking about looked as red as blood; but as soon as one would enter a house or church he no longer looked red in the least. This portent presaged forthcoming great grief— invasion, war and bloodshed, fratricidal feuds and blood-letting. And so it happened. On the twenty-fifth day of the month of November, the same winter, during St. Phillip's fast Grand Prince Olgerd Gediminovich of Lithuania marched with a great army against Grand Prince Dmitrii Ivanovich. With him were his brother, Keistut Gediminovich, many Lithuanian princes, Prince Mikhail Aleksandrovich of Tver' and Prince Sviatoslav Ivanovich of Smolensk with their forces.

First of all they marched to Volok [Lamskii] and burned the suburbs, capturing everyone; but they were unable to take the fortress so they stood at the fortress of Volok for three days. At that time Prince Vasilii Ivanovich of Bereza was wounded at the fortress of Volok: while he was standing on the bridge before the fortress, suddenly an unnoticed Lithuanian pierced the bridge

1371 from below with his lance, striking and wounding him. He was very badly injured and so he was at once tonsured a monk and passed away. This prince was very brave and well known for his victories. He loved priests and clergymen and he wanted to die in holy orders; and his desire was not denied him by God.

Then Olgerd marched from Volok, campaigning and capturing, and came to Moscow on the sixth day of the month of December, on the very day of St. Nicholas. He burned everything around the city, including the suburbs, and stood at Moscow for eight days but could not take the city. At that time Grand Prince Dmitrii Ivanovich remained, besieged, in the beleaguered city of Moscow while His Holiness Alexis, Metropolitan of Kiev and all Russia, was then in Nizhnii Novgorod. In the meantime Prince Vladimir Andreevich gathered forces and camped at Peremyshl', preparing for battle. Moreover, Prince Vladimir Dmitrievich of Pronsk came to him with his forces and then the army of Grand Prince Oleg Ivanovich of Riazan' also arrived.

Olgerd campaigned everywhere, burning and killing; having taken many captives, he wanted to return to his own land. Hearing, however, that great forces were prepared to do battle, he took fright and became fearful and began to sue for peace. So Grand Prince Dmitrii Ivanovich agreed on an armistice with him until St. Peter's day, although Olgerd desired permanent peace; also, Olgerd wanted Prince Vladimir Andreevich to marry his daughter, and this came to be. Thus, agreeing on peace, he retreated from Moscow, having spent eight days at the city of Moscow; and he returned to his land, marching very cautiously, looking about everywhere, fearing pursuit. Prince Mikhail Aleksandrovich also made peace with Grand Prince Dmitrii Ivanovich and went to Tver'.

The same year Olgerd Gediminovich, Grand Prince of Lithuania, waged war against the Germans and caused the German land much harm.[54] He returned home with many captives.

This winter was very warm and the snow disappeared completely before the Tuesday of the fast, and no snow remained anywhere. During the late harvest, however, snow covered the crops, and therefore even in those places in which the Lithua-

54. "German land" denotes either the Teutonic Order, later called "East Prussia," or the Livonian Order.

nian army did not campaign the people harvested as late as the   **1371**
Great Fast, after the snow had disappeared.[55] And the snow
disappeared everywhere by Tuesday of St. Theodore's week.[56]
The same winter, spring lasted very long.

The same spring Prince Mikhail Aleksandrovich went to
the Horde. The same year he returned to Tver' with a *yarlyk* for
the Grand Principality from the Khan, from the Horde of Mamai.
With him was the Khan's envoy, Sari Khodzha, and they went to
Tver' along the Volga; but Grand Prince Dmitrii Ivanovich of Moscow brought the boiars and common people in all the cities to
pledge on the cross not to accept Grand Prince Mikhail Aleksandrovich of Tver'. Do not let him be prince of Vladimir." And
he, himself, with his cousin, Vladimir Andreevich, remained with
his army at Pereiaslavl'.

Prince Mikhail Aleksandrovich, who called himself "Grand
Prince," having received that title from the Khan of the Horde,
tried to enter the capital city of Vladimir and wanted to ascend
to the throne of the Grand Principality, but the people of Vladimir did not accept him or allow him to ascend to the throne; and
so he retreated. The Tatar, Sari Khodzha, sent his Tatars and
a boiar of Prince Mikhail's to Grand Prince Dmitrii Ivanovich,
summoning him to Vladimir [to attend Prince Mikhail Aleksandrovich's receipt] of the *yarlyk*. But he, Dmitrii, replied,
"I will not go to attend the *yarlyk* [ceremony] and I will not let
[Mikhail Aleksandrovich] into the land of the principality of
Vladimir. And you, envoy, have an open path!" Moreover, he
[Dmitrii] sent to Sari Khodzha his expressions of friendship,
asking him to come; but the latter did not want to come to him
because he loved honors and gifts, and therefore he gave the
yarlyk to Prince Mikhail Aleksandrovich of Tver', to be Grand
Prince with the Khan's permission. Then, in amity and con-
cord, he departed from him; but he went from Mologa to Moscow, to Grand Prince Dmitrii Ivanovich. [Learning of this]
Prince Mikhail Aleksandrovich marched from thence back to
Bezhetskii Verkh and, fighting, arrived in Tver' on the twenty-
third day of the month of May.

55. Unclear, repetitious sentences. "Great Fast" in this case is most
likely either Lent or the so-called "Nativity," or pre-Christmas, fast,
November 15—December 24.

56. St. Theodore's week is the first week of Lent.

1371   The same year Grand Prince Mikhail Aleksandrovich of Tver' sent his son, Ivan, to the Horde, while the Khan's envoy, Sari Khodzha, remained in Moscow with Grand Prince Dmitrii Ivanovich, receiving from him honor and gifts. Having accepted the gifts he returned to the Horde, praising and lauding Grand Prince Dmitrii Ivanovich and stressing his good conduct and humility. He greatly respected him because he was grateful to him.

Then Grand Prince Dmitrii Ivanovich, himself, together with Prince Andrei of Rostov, also went to the Horde, and the fifteenth day of the month of July he crossed the river Oka. His Holiness, Metropolitan Alexis, accompanied him to Oka, prayed for him, gave him, his boiars and squires his blessing and let them go in peace; and then he returned to the city of Moscow. In the meantime the envoys of the Grand Prince of Lithuania came to discuss peace and concord, and also to betroth Prince Vladimir Andreevich to Olgerd's daughter, named Elena.

The same year Grand Prince Dmitrii Ivanovich of Moscow arrived at Mamai's Horde, where he payed his respects to Lord Mamai, to the Khan, to the Khan's wife and to the Khan's lords; he was again granted the Grand Principality of Vladimir and was greatly honored by the Khan and by his lords. And so he went home with great honor and with the *yarlyk* for the Grand Principality of Russia.

He—the Khan—also sent a message to Prince Mikhail Aleksandrovich [of Tver'], saying, "We granted you the Grand Principality and we gave you troops and forces to become Grand Prince; but you did not accept our troops or our forces and you said that you would become Grand Prince by yourself. Now you may abide with whomsoever you want, and do not expect our help."

The same year Prince Mikhail Aleksandrovich of Tver', fighting, took Kostroma, Mologa, Uglich Pole and Bezhetskii Verkh, and he placed his namestniks there.

The same year a Metropolitan named "German" came from Jerusalem to the Russian land looking for alms in order to pay his debts to the Saracens.

The same year the freebooters—"Ushkuiniks"—from Great Novgorod took Kostroma.[57]

57. *Ushkuinik*: See footnote under the entry for the year 1366.

The same year there was a portent on the sun. There were **1371** black spots on the sun which looked like nails and there was such deep darkness that people could not see two yards ahead of them. Many people would fall, hitting their faces, or bump their heads against each other, and birds in the air could not see but would fall to the earth from the air, striking men's heads. And so the beasts—such as bears, wolves, foxes and others—which could not see would walk into the towns and cities, mixing with people.

There was a bad drought and great heat, and it was so warm that people took fright and trembled. Many rivers dried up and even the marshes dried out and would burn, and the earth burned, and there was fear and trembling. Grain was very costly, and there was famine throughout the whole land.

The same year Prince Dmitrii Konstantinovich of Suzdal' and Nizhnii Novgorod, grandson of Vasilii, great grandson of Mikhail, erected a church of St. Wonderworker Nicholas in Nizhnii Novgorod.

The same year there was a conflagration in Novgorod the Great.

The same year the people of Novgorod made peace with the Germans.[58]

In the year 6880/1372. Grand Prince Dmitrii Ivanovich of Moscow returned from the Horde to Moscow, having received many honors there and, again, the charter [*yarlyk*] for the Grand Principality [of Vladimir]. Thus did he strengthen his position in the Grand Principality and put his enemies to shame. Together with him came the Khan's envoy and many Tatars. He also brought with him from the Horde Prince Ivan Mikhailovich of Tver', for whom he paid a ransom in the Horde: he gave for him ten thousand rubles, which is one *t'ma* of rubles.[59] And he brought him to Moscow. There he was taken [into custody] by Metropolitan Alexis and he remained in the court of Metropolitan Alexis not a short time, until his ransom was paid.

The same year the men of Novgorod[60] took the city of Iaroslavl'.

58. That is, they made peace with the Livonian Order.

59. *T'ma*: a Russian borrowing from Mongolian, for "ten thousand."

60. "Men of Novgorod:" probably, the Novgorodian ushkuiniks, river freebooters who moved very rapidly in their boats (ushkuis). Sometimes they raided in bands of several thousand men, pillaging both Russian and foreign cities and caravans.

1372   The same fall Grand Prince Dmitrii Ivanovich sent an army to Bezhetskii Verkh, where they killed Nikifor Lych', the namestnik of Prince Mikhail Aleksandrovich; and they sacked the lands of Tver'.

[MOSCOW AGAINST RIAZAN']

The same winter on the fourteenth day of December, before Christmas, Grand Prince Dmitrii Ivanovich sent his troops against Riazan', against Prince Oleg Ivanovich of Riazan'. His voevoda was Prince Dmitrii Mikhailovich of Volynia, as well as many other voevodas with strong forces. Prince Oleg of Riazan' also gathered many troops and marched against them. But the people of Riazan' are staunch, fierce, haughty, proud, full of confidence, ambitious and sure of themselves; and so, in their haughty minds they became feebleminded and mindless like monsters; and they told each other, "Do not take any armour with you, nor shields, nor lances, nor sabers, nor arrows; but take only ropes, strings and cords with you, with which you will rope the men of Moscow because they are weak, fearful and lacking in strength." Our [Muscovite] men, however, were humble and relied on Lord God, the Most Pure Theotokos, and the great wonderworkers because they knew that God helps the meek. He gives victory not to the strong but to the weak, and He does not offend humble and meek hearts.

And so since Lord God saw the humility of Moscow as well as the pride of the men of Riazan', He gave victory to the men of Moscow and brought down the men of Riazan'. It was according to the word of the most wise Solomon: "God resists the proud and bestows His blessing upon the humble." Therefore he who is haughty will be humbled and the humble will be helped. And David says, "Neither the King will be saved by his great armies nor the giant but will be saved by his strength." And in another place, he said, "[The Lord] removes the strong from the throne and sets the humble upon it." So the men of Moscow, with humility and hope and meek hearts, called God to their aid and they met the men of Riazan' at Skornishchevo.

There was a fierce battle and an evil massacre. The men of Riazan', waving their ropes, strings and cords, did not succeed in the least and fell dead like sheaves and were slaughtered like pigs.

And so the Lord helped Grand Prince Dmitrii Ivanovich and his **1372** warriors, who defeated the men of Riazan', while Prince Oleg Ivanovich of Riazan' barely escaped with a few men of his retinue. And Prince Dmitrii Vladimirovich of Pronsk ascended to the throne of the Grand Principality of Riazan'.

The same winter a son, Vasilii, was born to Grand Prince Dmitrii Ivanovich. The same winter Prince Vladimir Andreevich, grandson of Ivan [Kalita], great grandson of Daniilo, gr. gr. grandson of blessed Aleksandr [Nevskii], married the daughter of Grand Prince Olgerd Gediminovich of Lithuania, who in Holy Baptism was called Elena.

The same winter Prince Oleg Ivanovich of Riazan' chased from the principality of Riazan' Prince Vladimir Dmitrievich of Pronsk and, himself, again became Grand Prince of Riazan'. He also captured his brother-in-law, Prince Vladimir Dmitrievich of Pronsk, and forced him to obey him.

The same year Prince Mikhail Aleksandrovich of Tver' sent his nephew, Prince Dmitrii Eremeevich, and his voevodas to campaign in Kistma and they captured Andrei, Davyd and Boris, the children of Ivan Tishanor, who were voevodas of Kistna; and they brought them to Tver' to Grand Prince Mikhail Aleksandrovich.

The same year Prince Mikhail Vasilievich of Kashin, grandson of Mikhail, great grandson of Iaroslav, sent to Moscow to make peace with Grand Prince Dmitrii Ivanovich and he also gave up his pledge on the cross given to Grand Prince Mikhail Aleksandrovich of Tver'.

The same year when His Holiness, Metropolitan Alexis, was concluding the service of the divine liturgy, a young man was cured at the grave of holy wonderworker Peter, Metropolitan of Kiev and all Russia. His hands had been bent to his chest and he could not speak. Then he began to speak and he extended his arms; and therefore Metropolitan Alexis ordered that the bells be rung, celebrated a thanksgiving service and praised Lord God, the Most Pure Theotokos and the Lord's holy servant [Metropolitan Peter].

The same year Grand Prince Mikhail Aleksandrovich of Tver' campaigned against Dmitrov, imposed an indemnity on the city, burned the towns, villages and settlements, captured boiars and common people, and brought them to the city of Tver'. At the same time Grand Prince Mikhail Aleksandrovich of Tver' un-

1372 expectedly sent the Lithuanian army against the city of Pereias-lavl'. It was the army of Prince Keistut Gediminovich, brother of Olgerd, of Prince Andrei Olgerdovich of Polotsk and of Prince Vitovt Keistutovich, Prince Dmitrii of Drutsk, and many other princes, with great forces. They received an indemnity from the city of Pereiaslavl', burned the entire suburb, campaigned and burned lands and towns and took men into captivity. They also received an indemnity from the city of Kashin, as well as from the towns and villages, and they took everyone into captivity. Thus Grand Prince Mikhail Aleksandrovich of Tver' forced his kinsman to obey his will and pledge to him on the cross. From thence Keistut marched, bypassing Torzhok, but Prince Mikhail Aleksandrovich of Tver', who marched with him, took Torzhok and placed his namestniks there while the Lithuanian army returned home with many captives.

The same year in Nizhnii Novgorod in the church of St. Savior a large bell rang three times by itself.

The same year Prince Dmitrii Konstantinovich of Suzdal' and Nizhnii Novgorod laid the foundation of a stone fortification in Nizhnii Novgorod.

The same year a stone church of St. Nicholas was erected in Rusa.

The same year Prince Boris Konstantinovich built a fortification on the river Sura and named it "Gurmyzh."

[NOVGOROD FIGHTS FOR TORZHOK]

The same year in Great Novgorod a stone church of St. Saviour was erected in St. Elias Street. The same year during St. Peter's Fast the men of Novgorod marched to Torzhok and their posadniks and boiars let the people of Novyi Torzhok pledge on the cross; and they deported the namestniks of Prince Mikhail Aleksandrovich of Tver', and they also killed the merchants of Tver', sacked their estates, killed many other people of Tver' and burned their homes. Thereafter they built a very strong fortress with forts, gathered strong forces and prepared to fight Prince Mikhail Aleksandrovich of Tver'.

On the thirty-first day of May Prince Mikhail Aleksandrovich of Tver' marched toward Torzhok with his army, came to the city just in the middle of dinner and sent his people to them with humility because his men of Tver' had been beaten and sacked:

"I do not want anything from you; only let me have my namest- **1372**
niks in Torzhok." The men of Novgorod, however, did not heed
this and marched against him from the fortress into the field to
fight him. There was a fierce battle and Prince Mikhail Aleksandrovich of Tver' won it: at that time were killed the voevodas of
Novgorod—posadnik Aleksandr Abbakumovich, Ivan Timofee-
vich, Ivan Shakhovich, Grigorii Shchebelkovich, Timofei Daniilovich, Mikhail Groznyi, Denisei Vislov, and, with them, many
others who also were killed. The men of Novgorod were seized
by great fear and fled from the battlefield to Novgorod, some of
them fleeing to the city of Torzhok; and so many of them were
killed and others were captured.

And [Prince Mikhail] burned the suburbs from the side
of the field. Then a strong wind started blowing toward the city
and the fire spread over the entire city; so the people of Novyi
Torzhok fled from the city with their wives and children, straight
into the hands of the men of Tver', while some of them burned,
some were asphyxiated in the church of St. Saviour.

And so there was great lamentation by the people of Novgorod because their heroes were killed or captured and their
brave and strong men fell, struck down not only by swords but
also by the wrath of God just as in ancient times Jerusalem was
taken because of divine wrath. The fortress of Jerusalem was
fortified with three stone walls, and the men of the city were
brave and strong and each man could make a sortie against a hundred brave men and return to the city without wounds. When,
however, once Emperor Titus of Rome besieged the city, seven
brave men of Jerusalem made a sortie from the city of Jerusalem
and cut seven paths through the numberless regiments of the
forces of Titus of Rome, doing so as far as to Titus, Emperor of
Rome, himself. And rivers of blood flowed. Then what was the
purpose of their strength? Although they were able even to
move mountains, still without divine help they could not succeed
in the least. Divine wrath descended upon them and they all
fell and all were killed: the strong and the brave fell and perished.
And likewise every army, without God's aid, can not succeed in
the least.[61]

61. These details of Emperor Titus' taking of Jerusalem are taken
from *The Judaic Wars* by Josephus Flavius. *Cf.* Old Russian translation
in Meshcherskii, M. 1958.

The same year Grand Prince Olgerd Gediminovich of Lithuania, incited by Prince Mikhail Aleksandrovich of Tver', marched with great forces against Grand Prince Dmitrii Ivanovich of Moscow. At Liubutsk on the twelfth day of the month of June they were met by Prince Mikhail Aleksandrovich of Tver'; but Grand Prince Dmitrii Ivanovich gathered strong forces, led them against them and met them near Liubutsk. First of all the men of Moscow chased the vanguard of Olgerd, defeating it, and there arose such panic in the Lithuanian army that even Olgerd Gediminovich, himself, fled and hid behind a ravine. Both sides prepared for battle but between them was this ravine, which was very steep and deep and was covered with a thick forest; therefore they could not come together in battle. So they stayed there many days, made peace and returned home.

In the year 6881/1373. Prince Vladimir Andreevich went to Novgorod the Great and remained in Novgorod from the holiday of the Protective Veil of the Theotokos till St. Peter's Day, when he departed. The same year they dug a moat around the fortress of Novgorod.

The same year Grand Prince Dmitrii Ivanovich sent his officials to the [Golden] Horde with many gifts and there Prince Ivan, son of Prince Mikhail Aleksandrovich of Tver', was turned over to them; and they brought him to Moscow, where he was held in dire straits. The same winter at Christmas Prince Mihail Vasilievich of Kashin renounced his pledge on the Cross to Prince Mikhail Aleksandrovich of Tver' and went to Moscow, from whence he journeyed to the Horde. The same winter Prince Vladimir Dmitrievich of Pronsk passed away. The same winter Prince Eremei of Tver' passed away. The same winter Bishop Vasilii of Tver' passed away.

The same year there was a disturbance in the Horde and many lords of the Horde killed each other; and with them a numberless multitude of Tatars were slain. And thus did Divine Wrath fell upon them because of their lawlessness.

The same year the men of Novgorod who were in Tver' under arrest in the dungeon, dug a passage under the wall of the dungeon and escaped from Tver'. The same year Prince Vasilii Mikhailovich of Kashin came from the Horde to Kashin.

The same year the Tatars from Mamai's Horde campaigned   **1373**
against Riazan', against Grand Prince Oleg Ivanovich of Riazan',
burning his towns, killing many people and capturing others;
and they returned with a great number of captives. Therefore
Grand Prince Dmitrii Ivanovich of Moscow assembled all his
forces and camped on the shore of the river Oka while his cousin,[62] Prince Vladimir Andreevich, who had come to him from
Nizhnii Novgorod, joined him on the shore of the Oka, and they
did not let the Tatars enter [the Russian land] and they remained
over the entire summer.

The same year Grand Prince Mikhail Aleksandrovich of
Tver', with the aid of the men of Tver', of the districts and of
Novyi Torzhok, dug a moat along the earthen wall of the city of
Tver'; and they built another earthen wall from the river Volga
to the river Tmaka.

The same year Prince Mikhail Vasilievich of Kashin, grandson of Mikhail, great grandson of Iaroslav, gr. gr. grandson of
Vsevolod, gr. gr. gr. grandson of Iurii Dolgorukii, gr. gr. gr. gr.
grandson of Vladimir Monomakh, gr. gr. gr. gr. gr. grandson
of Vsevolod—the latter being the son of Iaroslav Vladimirovich—
passed away. His son, Prince Vasilii, in agreement with his
grandmother, Princess Elena, and with his boiars of Kashin,
went to Tver' to Grand Prince Mikhail Aleksandrovich of Tver',
petitioning him and submitting to him. Thereafter the same
year, some days later, thanks to God's mercy, peace and concord
came about between Grand Prince Mikhail Aleksandrovich of
Tver' and Grand Prince Dmitrii Ivanovich of Moscow. The
latter released Prince Ivan [son of Grand Prince of Tver'] with
love from Moscow to Tver', while Grand Prince Mikhail Aleksandrovich of Tver' recalled his namestnik from the Grand Principality [of Vladimir]. Peace ensued and the Christians were
released from irons. The people rejoiced greatly, while their
enemies were put to shame.

In the year 6882/1374. His Holiness Alexis, Metropolitan
of Kiev and all Russia, consecrated Dionysius, Archmandrite
of the monastery of the Caves, to be Bishop of Suzdal'.

The same year the men of Nizhnii Novgorod slew Mamai's
envoys and, with them, one and a half thousand Tatars, while

62. Uncle in *Nik.*

1374   their elder, named Saraika, was captured and taken to Nizhnii Novgorod, together with his guards.

The same year the robber-*ushkuiniks* gathered ninety *ushkui* boats and marched to the Niz beyond Viatka, which they plundered. Thereafter they occupied the land of the Bulgars, who are now called the people of Kazan'. They wanted even to burn their city, but accepted a ransom of three hundred rubles. From thence they broke into two parties: fifty *ushkui* boats went down the Volga toward Sarai while the other forty *ushkui* boats went up the Volga, reaching Obukhov. They plundered all the lands beyond the river Sura and around Marokvash. Then they crossed the Volga, burned all the boats and marched overland by horse to Viatka. On their way they plundered a great many towns and districts along the river Vetluga.

[ST. SERGIUS FOUNDS A MONASTERY IN SERPUKHOV]

The same year Prince Vladimir Andreevich laid the foundation of an oaken fortress in his patrimony of Serpukhov. He gave to his people and to all the merchants a reduction of taxes and several privileges, and as namestnik of the fortress he appointed his *okol'nichii*, a certain Iakov Iurievich, called "Novosilets." The very same year this Prince Vladimir Andreevich decided to build a monastery in his patrimony of Serpukhov because this prince loved the religious and the clergy. At that time in his patrimony, in the place called "Radonezh", there lived a servant of God and holy man named Sergius, the Abbot, who laid the foundations of many monasteries, was the father of many monastic brotherhoods and was very famous—concerning which there are many witnesses.[63] Prince Vladimir Andreevich succeeded in persuading him to go from Radonezh to Serpukhov to lay the foundation of the monastery, and he—Sergius—went from Radonezh to Serpukhov and found a place where it was fitting and convenient to build a monastery. He prayed and with his own hands laid the foundation of a church dedicated to the Name of the Most Pure Theotokos; and this happened on the ninth day of December when Holy Anna conceived the

---

63. St. Sergius of Radonezh was the most revered saint of Russia. See, further on under the year 6900/1392, the *Vita of St. Sergius*.

Holy Theotokos.[64] After blessing the prince, the reverend Abbot   **1374**
Sergius returned to his monastery in Radonezh; but Prince Vladimir Andreevich continued to care for the monastery founded in Serpukhov; and he built the monastic buildings, made the arrangements for the cells and furnished the monastery with all necessities, icons, books and holy vessels. This was to be a communal monastery.[65] The first abbot of this monastery was Athanasius, the pupil of the reverend Sergius, Abbot of Radonezh. He became abbot because Prince Vladimir Andreevich asked for him. He remained abbot of this monastery for several years and then, for the sake of God, he gave up his abbey and went to Constantinople. There he bought his own cell, gave his share of the endowment and remained in silence together with the holy elders; and then, at a very advanced age, he passed to God.

The same year the last tysiatskii of Moscow, Vasilii Vasil'evich Veliaminov,[66] passed away after being tonsured a monk and to the schema. And he received the monastic name of Barsonuphius, and they buried him in the monastery of the Holy Theophany.

The same year on the twenty-sixth day of the month of November, when St. Olympius the Stylite and St. Martyr George are remembered in the city of Pereiaslavl', a son, Iurii, was born to Grand Prince Dmitrii Ivanovich.[67] He was baptised by the reverend Sergius, Abbot of Radonezh. On this occasion there were present Grand Prince Dmitrii Konstantinovich of Suzdal', father-in-law of Grand Prince Dmitrii Ivanovich of Moscow, with his Grand Princess, his brothers, his children and his boiars. And so there was a great assemblage in Pereiaslavl'.

The same winter in the month of February Metropolitan Alexis came to Tver' and on Thursday of the week of the Holy

64. According to the Orthodox Christian tradition, the mother of the Virgin Mary was a pious woman named "Anna."

65. In the Orthodox church there are communal monasteries in which everything belongs to the monasteries and the monks may have nothing of their own. There are also monasteries in which the monks have the right to possess their own property.

66. The position of tysiatskii—army commander—was hereditary in the Veliaminov family.

67. "George" in Russian is "Georgii" or "Iurii."

1374   Cross[68] he consecrated Euthemius Bishop of Tver'. This was on the day when the Forty Holy Martyrs are remembered.[69] He departed Tver' for Pereiaslavl' [Zaleskii] with Cyprian, the Patriarch's envoy.

That summer it was very hot and there was great heat. During the entire summer there was not a single drop of rain. The horses, cows, sheep and other cattle died in great numbers. Thereafter a bad plague came upon the people of the entire Russian land.

Grand Prince Dmitrii Ivanovich of Moscow broke the peace with the Tatars and with Mamai, and at that time there was a bad plague in Mamai's Horde.

The same year Prince Vasilii Mikhailovich of Kashin, grandson of Vasilii, great grandson of Mikhail, gr. gr. grandson of Iaroslav, fled from Tver' to Moscow to Grand Prince Dmitrii Ivanovich.

The same year the Lithuanians waged war against the Tatars of Temir Mirza and there was a great battle between them.

In the year 6883/1375. Grand Prince Dmitrii Konstantinovich [of Nizhnii Novgorod] commanded that the Tatar guards of lord Saraika be separated. Saraika, however, fled to the Bishop's estate, together with his guards, set fire to the Bishop's palace and started shooting at the people. Many were wounded, some were killed; and then he attempted to shoot the Bishop, and one arrow even pierced the mantle of Bishop Dionysius; but Lord God preserved him. Then the people gathered and killed Saraika and his guards.

The same year the Tatars of Mamai's Horde campaigned and took Kashin, burned it and killed boiar Parfenii Fedorovich. They campaigned in the whole land beyond the river P'iana, plundering and burning, and they slew many and led others into captivity.

The same year the reverend Abbot Sergius fell gravely ill. He became bedridden during the second week of Lent; but then he arose from bed on the day of St. Stephen. Thereafter, though,

68. The week of the Holy Cross begins the third Sunday of Lent.

69. The commemoration of forty-two, not forty, martyrs of Amorium is celebrated on March 6. Liturgical Calendar, p. 31.

he remained again bedridden and was gravely ill all spring and   **1375**
summer.

No one should wonder that the righteous are stricken by
griefs and afflictions sent by God because it is written, "There
will be many afflictions upon the righteous and the Lord will deliver them from all of them." We are to attain the Heavenly Kingdom after much grief; and although the sinful are often healthy
and have much joy, not suffering in this world from grief or sadness, yet torments are prepared for them in the future age. If
the sinful, however, suffer in this world then God will forgive
them many of their sins. The righteous who suffer have their
crowns prepared by Lord God, as well as unspeakable glory in
Heaven.

[THE RUSSIAN PRINCES' CAMPAIGN AGAINST TVER']

The same year during Great Lent Ivan Vasilievich, grandson of Vasilii Veliaminov, son of a tysiatskii, escaped from Moscow to Tver' with a certain Nekomat of Surozh.[70] He went with
many lies and cunning words to Grand Prince Mikhail Aleksandrovich of Tver'. Prince Mikhail of Tver' at once sent him to
the Horde during St. Theodore's week while he, himself, went
to Lithuania during the week of the Holy Cross.[71]

He remained in Lithuania a short time and then returned to
Tver'. Shortly thereafter, on the fourteenth day of the month of
July, Nekomat of Surozh returned from Mamai's Horde, from
Mamai, with the latter's envoy, Achi Khodzha, to Tver', to Grand
Prince Mikhail Aleksandrovich of Tver'; and he brought him
the charter [*yarlyk*] for the Grand Principality of Vladimir.
Grand Prince Mikhail Aleksandrovich of Tver' the same day sent
a message to Moscow to Grand Prince Dmitrii Ivanovich an-

70. Apparently this Ivan Veliaminov felt frustrated at not having
been appointed tysiatskii after the death of his father, in whose family
this position was hereditary. Nekomat Surozhanin, a prominent trader
from Surozh (now Sudak) in Crimea, was probably a Central Asian
Nestorian Christian well versed in diplomatic intrigues. From his further actions it can be seen that he played the role of Mamai's agent with
Prince Mikhail of Tver'. (Prokhorov, 39.)

71. St. Theodore's week: an early week in March when three St.
Theodores are remembered, March 4 and 6. (Prokhorov, 134).

1375 nouncing that he had given up his oath on the cross, and he sent his namestniks to Torzhok and his troops to Uglich Pole. Thereafter in Tver' on the twenty-seventh day of the same month in the church of the Protective Veil of the Most Pure Theotokos a candle began to burn by itself before an icon. And then, the same month on the twenty-ninth day—a Sunday—the sun disappeared early in the morning.

[ALL-RUSSIAN CAMPAIGN AGAINST THE PRINCE OF TVER']

The same year Grand Prince Dmitrii Ivanovich of Moscow gathered all his troops. He was joined by all the Russian princes and he marched to Volok [Lamskii], whither all the Russian princes came to him.[72] Among them were his father-in-law, Grand Prince Dmitrii Konstantinovich of Suzdal', with his son, Prince Semion, brother-in-law of Grand Prince Dmitrii Ivanovich; and his brothers, Prince Boris Konstantinovich of Gorodets; and Dmitrii Konstantinovich, junior, of Suzdal', called "Nogot'." There also came at that time Prince Vladimir Andreevich, the cousin of Grand Prince Dmitrii Ivanovich; Prince Andrei Fedorovich of Rostov; Prince Vasilii Konstantinovich of Rostov; and the latter's brother, Prince Andrei Konstantinovich; with them there were also Prince Ivan Vasilievich of Smolensk; Prince Vasilii Vasil'evich of Iaroslavl'; and his brother, Prince Roman Vasil'evich of Iaroslavl'; Prince Fedor Romanovich of Belozero; Prince Vasilii Mikhailovich of Kashin; Prince Fedor Romanovich of Belozero; Prince Fedor Mikhailovich of Mologa; Prince Andrei Fedorovich of Starodub, Prince Roman Mikhailovich of Briansk; Prince Roman Semionovich of Novosil'sk, grandson of Grand Prince Mikhail of Chernigov, great grandson of Vsevolod, gr. gr. grandson of Sviatoslav, gr. gr. gr. grandson of Oleg, gr. gr. gr. gr. grandson of Sviatoslav, gr. gr. gr. gr. gr. grandson of Iaroslav, gr. gr. gr. gr. gr. gr. grandson of Great Vladimir; Prince Semion Konstantinovich of Obolensk, grandson of Iurii, great grandson of Mikhail of Chernigov, with his brother, Prince Ivan Konstantinovich of Tarussa; and many other princes with all their forces.[73]

72. It seems that all the Russian princes were upset at the Prince of Tver's alliance with the Tatars and Lithuanians, their most dangerous enemies, and decided to root out this treason in the very heart of Russia.

73. During this campaign against Tver' most Russian princes—about twenty of them—joined Moscow and *de facto* accepted Muscovite

They all were greatly distressed at Grand Prince Mikhail Aleksan-   **1375**
drovich of Tver' and they said, 'How many times has he summoned the armies of his son-in-law, Grand Prince Olgerd Gediminovich of Lithuania, to invade Russia? How much harm has he
caused the Christians? And now he has allied himself with Mamai,
with the latter's Khan and with all Mamai's Horde! This Mamai
breathes hatred for us and if we let them join forces they will defeat us all!"

So they marched with large forces from Volok [Lamskii]
toward Tver', and on the twenty-fourth day of the month of October they started campaigning in the land of Tver'. They took
the city of Mikulin, as well as all the surrounding places, which
they burned. Grand Prince Mikhail Aleksandrovich, however,
prepared himself for siege in the city of Tver', and so Grand
Prince Dmitrii Ivanovich of Moscow, with all his forces, quar-
tered for four weeks at the city of Tver'. He burned all the suburbs, campaigned and burned all the districts and towns and took
all their property, and his men killed many [people of Tver']
and led others into captivity. He [Dmitrii] also encircled the city
of Tver' with his own countervolutions and built two bridges
over the river Volga. Then Grand Prince Dmitrii Ivanovich
sent for the men of Novgorod. The Novgorodians honored
Grand Prince Dmitrii Ivanovich because they wanted to avenge
the offense which they had received [from the prince of Tver']
in the city of Torzhok. Now, roaring, they came fiercely in four
or five days and they, also, camped at the city of Tver', determined
to get their own booty; and they caused the people of Tver' much
evil. All these forces stormed the city: they moved up wall-bat-
tering rams, burned the others and killed many people. On this
occasion Semion Ivanovich Dobrynskii was killed.

And so they fought for many days, campaigning and burning throughout the whole land. They took the forts of Zubtsov
and Belgorod. Grand Prince Mikhail Aleksandrovich of Tver',

leadership. This was a major step toward the unification of Russia. Besides Tver', only three princes—of Riazan', Pronsk and Mozhaisk—
did not join Moscow. After this victorious campaign even Tver' promised to fight on the side of Moscow against the Tatars. Still, in 1380 Tver'
did not help Dmitrii. Kuchkin, V. A., "Russkie kniazhestva . . . " in *Kuli-
kovskaia Bitva*, Moscow 1980, p. 101; and *Dogovornye i dukhovnye gramoty
velikikh i udel'nykh kniazei*, Moscow-Leningrad 1950, p. 26.

1375   however, did not sue for peace because he expected help from Mamai and from Lithuania, for his son-in-law, Grand Prince Olgerd Gediminovich, had promised to send him forces. Indeed, they drew near Tver'; but, hearing that Grand Prince Dmitrii Ivanovich had besieged Tver' with innumerable forces, they took fright and ran back. When Grand Prince Mikhail Aleksandrovich of Tver' received tidings of this and learned that he could expect no help from anywhere—and, because of his weariness and because all the Russian land had arisen against him—he sent lord Bishop Euthemius with his senior and leading boiars to Grand Prince Dmitrii Ivanovich, petitioning for peace and proclaiming his decision to submit. The latter saw that he, the prince of Tver', was surrendering and therefore he did not want the city's destruction or Christians' bloodshed, and he made peace with him entirely according to his own will. So they made peace, signed the charters, and retreated from the city; and everyone went home.

[THE RAIDS OF THE USHKUINIKS]

When Grand Prince Dmitrii Ivanovich was besieging Tver' the Novgorodian freebooter ushkuiniks in seventy ushkui boats, under the command of Prokofii and Smolianin, marched along the river Kostroma to the river Volga. Altogether there were two thousand of them, and they camped and prepared themselves for battle at the city of Kostroma. The men of the city marched against them from the city and prepared for battle; their voevoda was also their namestnik. Altogether there were about five thousand men of Kostroma. The Novgorodian freebooters—ushkuiniks—numbered only two thousand. Seeing the multitudes of men from Kostroma, however, they divided their men into two troops, sending one secretly through the forests. These bypassed and struck the men of Kostroma from the rear, while the other half attacked from the fore.

Pleshcheev, voevoda of Kostroma, took fright and fled, and all the men of Kostroma did likewise at a run; but many of them were captured alive. Entering the city, they—the ushkuiniks—plundered everything, remained in the city the whole week, found all the hidden treasure and took what they could with them; what they could not take, they burned or cast into the river Volga. And they led many Christians into captivity, with their wives and children.

From Kostroma they went to Nizhnii Novgorod, also burned   **1375**
that city and killed some, leading others into captivity. Descending the river Volga, they turned into the river Kama, plundered
there, returned, went to the land of the Volga Bulgars where now
is the city of Kazan' and sold their captives there. From thence
they went further down the Volga toward Sarai, plundering and
killing the Christian merchants on their way. And so they came
to Astrakhan', where they sold their other captives. Salchei, the
ruler of Astrakhan', flattered them, rendered them honor and
gave them supplies. They started to revel, however, and soon became dead drunk. The men of Astrakhan' killed them all, not
leaving a single one alive; and they carried off their booty. Their
commander, Prokofii, and the other commander, Smolianin,
together with all their men, met such an end. "By whatsoever
measure ye mete, it shall be measured unto you." [*Math. 7:2*]

[MAMAI ATTACKS NIZHNII NOVGOROD AND SMOLENSK]

The same year Mamai's Tatars campaigned against Nizhnii
Novgorod, asking, "Why did you campaign against Grand Prince
Mikhail Aleksandrovich of Tver'?" And so they campaigned in
the entire land of Nizhnii Novgorod and returned to the Horde
with many captives. The same year Grand Prince Olgerd Gediminovich of Lithuania waged war against Smolensk, saying,
"Why did you campaign against Prince Mikhail of Tver'?" And
so they campaigned in the entire land of Smolensk, took many
captives, occupied many towns of the land of Smolensk, took
the people into captivity and returned home. The same year
Mamai's Tatars raided the city of Novosil', saying, "Why did you
fight Tver'?" And so they devastated the entire land of Novosil'
and returned home with many captives.

[KEISTUT'S DAUGHTER MARRIES THE PRINCE OF TVER']

The same year Maria, the daughter of Keistut of Lithuania, was brought to marry Prince Ivan Mikhailovich of Tver',
and she was baptised by lord Bishop Euthemius of Tver' in the
holy church of the Elevation of the Cross; the next day Prince
Ivan Mikhailovich was married in the cathedral church of the
Holy Saviour by lord Bishop Euthemius of Tver'. The marriage
of his son, Prince Ivan, was a great joy for Grand Prince Mikhail
Aleksandrovich of Tver'.

1375   The same year the Karela Semidesiatskaia built a new fortress.[74]

[THE STRIGOL'NIKS]

The same year the Novgorodians threw the heretics—*strigol'niks*[75]—into the river Volkhov, saying, "It is written in the Gospel: 'But whosoever shall cause one of these little ones that believe on me to stumble, it is profitable for him that a great millstone be hanged about his neck and that he be sunk in the depth of the sea.' " [*Math.* 18:6; also *Lk.* 17:2]

In the year 6884/1376. Grand Prince Dmitrii Ivanovich of Moscow marched with his army beyond the river Oka in order to prevent the raids of Mamai's Tatars.

The same year in Novgorod the river Volkhov ran upstream for seven days against the normal current. And this happened likewise for the third year.[76]

[NOVGOROD AND ARCHBISHOP ALEXIS]

The same year the Novgorodian Lord Archbishop Alexis retired of his own will and went to Derevianitsa. The Novgorodians became greatly offended by this and sent to Metropolitan Alexis in Moscow, asking and petitioning him to convey his word to Novgorod to their Lord Archbishop Alexis to prevent him from giving up the diocese of Novgorod; and they [the envoys] brought the Metropolitan's blessing to Lord Archbishop Alexis and to all Novgorod. Then the Novgorodians summoned the veche in Iaroslav's court and sent a petition to the Lord Archbishop with Ivan Prokofievich, namestnik of the Grand Prince with posadnik Iurii Ontsiforovich, tysiatskii Aleksei and many boiars and outstanding men. And he—Alexis—took the Metropolitan's blessing and the Novgorodians' petition into consideration.

74. Karela: a Finnic tribe in the northern Novgorodian land around lakes Ladoga and Onega, and present southern and eastern Finland. *Semidesiatskaia*: "of Seventy towns," or "Seventy tribes". The exact location is no longer known.

75. *Strigol'niks*: a heretical movement in Novgorod and Pskov in the late fourteenth century. They denied the hierarchical structure of the church and several sacraments. Kartashev, 484-489; Kazakova, 34 ff.

76. Probably the Volkhov's running upstream at Novgorod was caused by heavy precipitation and the flooding of the lower Volkhov basin.

The same year the Novgorodian Lord Archbishop Alexis   **1376**
journeyed from Novgorod to Moscow, to Alexis, Metropolitan of
Kiev and all Russia; and the posadniks of Novgorod accompanied
him. They sojourned a fortnight in Moscow with Metropolitan
Alexis, who let them return with his blessing and in peace, and they
returned to Novgorod with joy.

The same year Grand Prince Dmitrii Ivanovich of Moscow
sent his uncle, Vladimir Andreevich, to Rzhev with troops. He
besieged that city three days, burning the suburb, but did not take
the city.

The same year there came two certain archdeacons from
Constantinople, important officials: the name of one was George,
the name of the other was John.

The same winter Grand Prince Dmitrii Konstantinovich of
Suzdal' sent his children, Prince Vasilii and Prince Ivan, against
the Bulgars, who now are called the "people of Kazan'." Grand
Prince Dmitrii Ivanovich of Moscow also sent his voevoda, Prince
Dmitrii Mikhailovich Volynskii. They drew near Kazan'[77] on the
sixteenth day of the month of March. The people of Kazan' made a
sortie against them from the city, shooting from bows and cross-
bows. Others sent thunder from the city, which frightened the
Russian army.[78] Others made a sortie on camels, thus frightening
the Russians' horses. God helped the Russian princes, however,
and they succeeded in chasing them back into the city. Thereafter
the Kazan' rulers, Hassan and Mahmet Sultan, petitioned the
Grand Prince and gave to Grand Prince Dmitrii Ivanovich of Moscow a ransom of one thousand rubles. They also gave Grand
Prince Dmitrii Konstantinovich of Suzdal' and Nizhnii Novgorod a
thousand rubles, and three thousand rubles to the voevodas and
troops. So having imposed their will they [the Russians] appointed their own official[79] and their own customs officer, and they returned to their homes.

[ECCLESIASTIC VISITORS FROM THE NEAR EAST]

The same year a certain Metropolitan by the name of Marko
came from the mountain of Sinai to the Russian land for the sake

77. Kazan': Actually, the city of "Bulgar," now called "Kazan'."

78. This is the earliest mention in the Russian chronicles of gun-
powder. The Bulgars' guns were probably of Chinese origin.

79. In *Nik.*, the Tatar term, *doroga,* is used for "official."

1376   of alms. The same year a certain archimandrite, by the name Niphontus, came from Jerusalem, from the monastery of the Holy Archangel Michael which is located in Jerusalem. He came to the Russian land for the sake of alms, and thanks to these alms he became the Patriarch of Jerusalem.

[CYPRIAN]

That year Metropolitan Cyprian, appointed to the Metropolia by Philotheus, Patriarch of Constantinople, came to Russia from Constantinople. Grand Prince Dmitrii Ivanovich did not accept him and told him, "We already have Metropolitan Alexis. Why do you want to assume the position of a Metropolitan who is still alive?" So the latter journeyed from Moscow to Kiev, and remained in residence there.[80]

The same year there was a plague in Kiev.

[THE DEATH OF OLGERD]

In the year 6885/1377. Grand Prince Olgerd Gediminovich of Lithuania passed away; after him there arose scarcities, disturbances and troubles throughout the entire land. This Olgerd Gediminovich was not the sole son of his father. He was not even

---

80. Cyprian was a Greek-educated Bulgarian. He was consecrated by the Patriarch of Constantinople to be Metropolitan of Russia for several reasons. First, Constantinople wanted the very aged Metropolitan Alexis—who died a year and a half later at the age of 85—to be replaced by their own candidate and not by a Russian, in order better to control the Russian church and to receive more money from it. Then, it was a step toward the preservation of Orthodoxy among the Russians of Lithuania, who formed at least ninety percent of the inhabitants of that country; indeed, the Lithuanian princes, fearing Moscow, were unwilling to recognize the authority of Metropolitan Alexis and therefore the Orthodox population in Lithuania remained without leadership. A Grecized Bulgarian was in a better position, in this regard. After the death of Alexis, without the consent of Grand Prince Dmitrii, Cyprian came to Moscow but Dmitrii refused to accept him and Cyprian returned to Kiev. He went again to Moscow in 1381 and this time was accepted by the Grand Prince. The following year, however, after the sack of Moscow by Tokhtamysh, Dmitrii asked Cyprian to leave Moscow. Only in 1390 was he accepted by the new Grand Prince, Vasilii Dmitrievich, as Metropolitan of Moscow and all Russia, and he resided in Moscow until his death in 1406.

the first son of Gedimin but only the second after the eldest. All **1377**
these brothers were numerous and their names were (1) Nari-
mant, (2) Olgerd, (3) Iavnut, (4) Keistut, (5) Koriat, (6) Liubart,
(7) Monvid. But among all his brothers, Olgerd surpassed all in
power and position because he did not care for drinking; he was
never, himself, drunk; he did not drink wine; he did not like any
games and disliked all things which were not fitting to power and
the structure of government. He was always high-minded and
very restrained; therefore, he was reasonable, loved wisdom, was
strong, very manly and he accumulated much wisdom. Through
cunning he conquered many countries and lands, winning for
himself many cities and principalities; and he preserved very strong
power. In this way his rule grew, and none of his brothers, nor his
father, Gedimin, nor his grandfather, achieved so much as he.

Olgerd Gediminovich had twelve sons. From his first wife he
had five. From his second, the Uliana princess of Tver', he had
seven. These are the sons of his first wife: (1) Andrei, (2) Dmitrii,
(3) Konstantin, (4) Vladimir, (5) Fedor. From his second wife,
Uliana of Tver', there were (1) Koribut, (2) Skirgailo, (3) Iagailo,
(4) Svidrigailo, (5) Korigailo, (6) Mingailo, (7) Luvgen. He distributed cities and principalites to them but the seniority and the
throne of his grand principality he gave to his son, Iagailo, who was
born from Uliana of Tver'. He loved him more than any other
son, and therefore he chose him from among his brothers and
entrusted to him his throne of the grand principality of Lithuania.

This Iagailo possessed the entire Lithuanian land but after
four years he married, taking to wife the queen [Jadwiga] of the
Polish land, who had neither father nor mother. Because of her he
became king of the Polish land. And so, for the sake of his wife,
Iagailo was named king of the Polish land, and this was the reason
why he was king.

Olgerd Gediminovich also had a daughter, Feodora, who
was born from his wife from Tver'; and he married her to Prince
Sviatoslav Titovich of Karachev, grandson of Mstislav, great
grandson of the blessed great martyr, Mikhail of Chernigov, who
was killed because of his Orthodox faith by the impure Khan Batu.
So this Sviatoslav was the gr. gr. grandson of Vsevolod, gr. gr.
gr. grandson of Sviatoslav, gr. gr. gr. gr. grandson of Oleg, and
gr. gr. gr. gr. gr. grandson of Sviatoslav, and gr. gr. gr. gr. gr.
gr. grandson of Iaroslav, son of Vladimir.

1377   Another son of Tit, Andrian of Zvenigorod, married Elena, daughter of the Lithuanian Prince Gamant. This Andrian was also a grandson of Mstislav of Karachev, great grandson of great martyr Mikhail of Chernigov, gr. gr. grandson of Vsevolod, gr. gr. gr. grandson of Sviatoslav, gr. gr. gr. gr. grandson of Oleg, gr. gr. gr. gr. grandson of Sviatoslav, gr. gr. gr. gr. gr. gr. grandson of Iaroslav Vladimirovich. Tit's third son, Prince Ivan of Kozelsk, grandson of Mstislav of Karachev, married the daughter of Grand Prince Oleg Ivanovich of Riazan'. He was also grandson [sic!] of the great martyr, Grand Prince Mikhail of Chernigov.[81]

The same year Prince Fedor, son of Andrian of Zvenigorod, killed many Tatars. This Prince Fedor of Zvenigorod, son of Andrian, grandson of Tit, great grandson of Mstislav of Karachev, gr. gr. grandson of Mikhail of Chernigov, was very tall in stature, valiant against the enemy, and very strong and mighty.

Olgerd gave the glorious and great city of Kiev to his son, Vladimir; but after Olgerd's death, Skirgailo took the city of Kiev away from his brother and captured [Prince] Vladimir, himself, sending him to Kopyl, where the latter died. After him, Skirgailo became Prince.

The same year, on the twenty-third day of the month of April when the great and holy martyr, St. George the Victor, is remembered, there was a portent in the sky. The moon was partly covered and there were rays in the form of a cross emanating from it.

81. This genealogy of these descendants of Prince Mikhail of Chernigov is not confirmed by any other source. According to the Serbian and Hungarian sources, two of Prince Mikhail's sons settled in southern Hungary in the region called "Machva" (now, "Banat"), and they did not return to Russia. Prince Mikhail's *Life* mentioned only his grandson, Prince Boris Vasil'kovich of Rostov, the son of Michael's daughter, Maria, and none of his sons. The very names of these so-called great grandsons of Mikhail—Tit and Andrian—are altogether very uncommon names among fourteenth-century Russians. Most probably, these princes were not certain of their background, especially as to the number of generations between Prince Mikhail of Chernigov (1180?-1246) and themselves. This text was compiled still later, in the fifteenth or sixteenth century, and so errors could easily be committed. See, also, fn. 50.

[THE BATTLE OF THE P'IANA RIVER]

The same year a certain Tatar lord by the name of Arapsha escaped from the Blue Horde beyond the Volga and came to Mamai's Horde, which was on the Volga. This Lord Arapsha was extremely fierce, a great warrior, very courageous and strong, but he was of short stature. In his valor, however, he defeated many, and he intended to raid against Nizhnii Novgorod. Grand Prince Dmitrii Konstantinovich of Nizhnii Novgorod and Suzdal' sent his messenger to Moscow to his son-in-law, Grand Prince Dmitrii Ivanovich. Grand Prince Dmitrii Ivanovich gathered many soldiers and went with them to Nizhnii Novgorod to aid his father-in-law, Grand Prince Dmitrii Konstantinovich. There were no tidings, however, of Lord Arapsha, and therefore Grand Prince Dmitrii Ivanovich returned to Moscow, leaving his voevoda to hold the position with the men of Vladimir, Pereiaslavl', Iur'ev, Murom and Iaroslavl'. Then some people began to say that the Tatars were in the prairie and that Lord Arapsha was hiding in certain places unbeknownst to the Russian princes and voevodas; and they did not reckon with this. Grand Prince Dmitrii Konstantinovich of Nizhnii Novgorod and Suzdal', however, later sent his son, Prince Ivan, and Prince Semion Mikhailovich, and with them he sent his voevodas and his troops, as well as many voevodas and troops of Grand Prince Dmitrii Ivanovich of Moscow.

It was a very large army and it crossed the river P'iana with a great multitude of soldiers. Then they received word that Lord Arapsha was hiding in Wolves' Waters [*Volchie Vody*] and they began to rejoice in anticipation of great booty. Then they received other tidings, but with this, also, they did not reckon or take it into consideration, saying, "None can withstand us." And so they began to walk and ride in coats and shirts and they put their armour on the vehicles, wrapped in sacks. And they did not prepare their bear lances, maces or lances, and some of these weapons were not even yet in order; and they were not even wearing their shields or helmets.

And thus they rode about, letting their coats fall from their shoulders and unfastening them because they were as sweaty as if in the bath, for it was very hot weather. They very much loved drinking, and wheresoever they found beer, mead and wine they

1377 would drink beyond all limits; and they would ride, drinking, saying to each other, "Each of us can fight a hundred Tatars; and, surely, none can withstand us." Their princes, boiars, lords and voevodas were in good spirits and rejoiced, drank and hunted just as at home. And they boasted and spoke highly of themselves, forgetting the wisdom of humility because the Lord gives grace to the humble and because we are all merely the grandchildren of Adam.

And they boasted in their pride, but Lord God humbled their pride. And so, at that time the princes of Mordva unexpectedly brought a Tatar army from Mamai's Volga Horde against our princes, while our princes were quite negligent, thinking of nothing as if they had had no tidings. Our men came as far as Para, aware of nothing, while the Tatars noticed them and rapidly divided their army into five regiments, and quite unexpectedly struck our army in the rear, flaying, slashing and slaying with their lances. Our men did not manage to act—and what could they do, for they were unaware of anything? And so our men fled toward the river P'iana, unable to do anything although earlier they had boasted that they were all-powerful. The Tatars followed them, striking, and they killed Prince Semion Mikhailovich.

A great multitude of princes, boiars and magnates fell under the sharp swords of the Ishmaelites. Prince Ivan Dmitrievich rode rapidly to the river P'iana, trying in vain to escape, rushing forward on horseback into the river P'iana, and he drowned. Together with him a multitude of princes, boiars, lords, voevodas, squires and soldiers also drowned in the river P'iana, and others were slain by the sons of Hagar. All were seized by great fear and horror, and they fled, wearied.

So the sons of Hagar jubilated with great joy, caught an endless number of captives and, pitching their tents, they trumpeted [their victory] on the bones of the Christians and marched to raid Nizhnii Novgorod. Since Grand Prince Dmitrii Konstantinovich was unable to withstand them in battle because all his army was annihilated, he fled to Suzdal'. This evil event occurred on the second day of the month of August when the first martyr, Archdeacon Stephen, is remembered. It happened on a Sunday in the sixth hour of the afternoon. And so they came raiding to Nizhnii Novgorod, while the inhabitants of Nizhnii Novgorod

tried to escape in boats on the Volga, toward Gorodets. The **1377**
Tatars arrived at Nizhnii Novgorod early in the morning on the
fifth day of the month of August, a Wednesday, when the memory
of the holy martyr Eusignius is celebrated. They captured the
remaining people and burned the city, churches and monasteries;
and so thirty-two churches burned in that city. They departed
from the city on Friday, captured people in the district and towns,
and burned everything. And, with a multitude of captives, they
returned home.

The same year the aforementioned Lord Arapsha of the
Volga Horde came to raid and he sacked the land beyond the
river Sura, burning everything, and he withdrew with captives.

The same year in the month of August, Prince Vasilii Dmitrievich came to Nizhnii Novgorod from Suzdal', and he sent his
boiars to the river P'iana, commanding them to bring back the
body of his brother, Prince Ivan Dmitrievich. They did as ordered and Grand Prince Vasilii, his brother, wept greatly over his
body, and so did his boiars and all the people. They buried him
with funeral chants on the twenty-third day of the month of August, in the stone church of the Holy Saviour on the right side of
the narthex.

The same year the Mordva came unexpectedly, raiding a-
long the Volga. They sacked the land of Nizhnii Novgorod,
robbed and killed a multitude of people and captured others.
The remaining districts and towns had already been burned by
the Tatars, and they returned home. Prince Boris Konstantinovich pursued them with a few troops and caught up with them at
the river P'iana: they took fright at divine wrath and fled beyond
the river P'iana. Those who did not succeed in crossing the river
were either slain or drowned.

The same year in the monastery of St. Anthony in Novgorod,
Archimandrite Savva passed away. The same year in Novgorod
they erected in the carpenter quarters a stone church dedicated
to the holy martyrs, Boris and Gleb.

In the year 6886/1378. There was a portent on the sun.

The same fall Lord Arapsha of the Volga Horde killed many
Russian merchants and robbed them of their wealth. The same
fall Lord Arapsha came raiding to Riazan'. He did much evil and
returned home.

The same winter it was very cold and there were continual

1378 freezes; many people and cattle died. Only in a few places was it possible to find water, for because of the great freezes there was no water in the marshes, lakes or rivers.

[CAMPAIGN AGAINST THE MORDVA]

The same winter Grand Prince Dmitrii Konstantinovich of Nizhnii Novgorod and Suzdal' for the second time sent his brother, Prince Boris Konstantinovich, and his son, Semion, to campaign against the Mordva. Grand Prince Dmitrii Ivanovich of Moscow also sent his troops, under voevoda Fedor Andreevich Svibla, with them. Arriving, they began to fight in the land of the Mordva. They sacked their districts, towns, settlements and winter quarters, killed the men and captured their women and children, and devastated the entire land. Those men who remained alive were brought to Nizhnii Novgorod, and some of them were executed there, while dogs attacked the others on the ice of the Volga.

THE STORY ABOUT ALEXIS, METROPOLITAN OF ALL RUSSIA

The same winter on the twelfth day of the month of February when our holy father, Meletius, Patriarch of Great Antiochia, is remembered, a Friday, after morning prayer, His Holiness Alexis, Metropolitan of Kiev and Russia, passed away, being at an honorable and venerable age. This blessed Metropolitan Alexis was born from the illustrious boiars of Chernigov. At that time by the will of God the city of Chrenigov as well as its entire diocese—so to say, its entire land—was often captured by the barbarians [that is, Tatars]. Therefore his father, Fedor, and his mother, Maria, left their native land, the city of Chernigov, and went to the most famous city of Moscow. While they resided there, this blessed one was born to them.

At that time the Grand Principality of Vladimir was under Grand Prince Mikhail Iaroslavich of Tver', grandson of Iaroslav, great grandson of Vsevolod, gr. gr. grandson of Dolgorukii; and it was the time of the rule of His Holiness Maxim, Metropolitan of Kiev and All Russia. This occurred before the killing of boiar Akinf of Tver', who had campaigned in Pereiaslavl' against Prince Ivan Danilovich [Kalita], grandson of Aleksandr [Nevskii], great grandson of Iaroslav, gr. gr. grandson of Vsevolod [Great Nest].

But he, himself, drank the cup of death: it is Akinf and his son-in- **1378**
law, Davyd, who were killed at Pereiaslavl'. This Akinf was the
boiar of Prince Andrei Aleksandrovich of Gorodets, grandson of
Iaroslav, great grandson of Vsevolod, and he served his lord,
Prince Andrei Aleksandrovich of Gorodets, until the latter's
death. After the latter's death, he departed for Tver' to serve
Prince Mikhail Iaroslavich. This Grand Prince Mikhail Iaroslavich of Tver' and Grand Prince Iurii Danilovich of Moscow,
grandson of Aleksandr, great grandson of Iaroslav, both went to
the Horde, having litigation about the Grand Principality of Vladimir. But boiar Akinf wanted to be in the good graces of his
prince and did what the latter wanted. Therefore he marched
with the troops of Tver' toward Pereiaslavl' against Prince Ivan
Danilovich of Pereiaslavl', grandson of Aleksandr, great grandson of Iaroslav. He, himself, however, was killed and with him
many of his troops.

Blessed Alexis was seventeen years older than Grand Prince
Semion, son of Ivan Danilovich [Kalita], grandson of Aleksandr,
great grandson of Iaroslav. Alexis was the godson of Prince Ivan
Danilovich, when the latter was not yet grand prince, and at Holy
Baptism he was given the name, Eulepherius. While still a child
he learned how to read and, grown, he was of good morals.

When he turned twelve years of age, according to some Divine plan—because God cared for him—it happened that he was
catching birds with a net. While watching it he fell asleep. While
he was sleeping he heard a voice which said, "Alexis! What are
you doing? From now on you will catch the souls of people."
The blessed one awoke from his sleep and, seeing no one, he was
astonished and full of awe. He began to ponder: "Why did I receive a new name?" because he was called "Alexis." From that time
on he began to stay mostly in quietude and contemplation, and
since he was unable to understand [the meaning of that voice],
he told no one about it.

His father, mother and brothers asked him:

"Why are you so sad and why do you remain in silence and
hold books in your hand at all times, and study them? Why do
you not address a single word to us? It is the way of life of a monk,
not that of a man of the world. Who told you to live a monastic
life? Why do you weary yourself with fasting and thirst? Do not
afflict yourself because you may become ill, and then we will be sad
and grieve. Just tell us who incited you thus."

1378   The blessed one consoled them but nonetheless maintained his abstinence. He would not play with the boys and would depart from all manner of chatter and laughter; he continued to observe silence, fasting and the reading of divine scripture, and he would always walk in quietude and humility.

When he became twenty years old he developed with all his soul love for Lord God and he tried to follow all His Commandments, and he decided to be tonsured a monk. He left his father and mother, brothers and sisters, his relatives and friends. He abhorred the thought of marriage and any sort of worldly passion but only worked for the sake of God, telling himself, "I would rather remain in the house of the Lord than live in the sinful towns." When he was over twenty years of age or slightly more, he went to the monastery of the Theophany, and there he was tonsured to the holy angelic monastic orders and was given the name, Alexis, which had been earlier told him by God when he had been catching birds with a net in the wilderness. And so he started to live an austere life, fasting and waking, with prayers, humble emotions and tears, and he learned all the Old and New Testaments.

To this monastery of the Theophany there once came from Radonezh a very spiritual and ascetic monk, Monk Stephen. This Stephen was known for his spiritual and strict manner of life: he was the brother of the blessed Abbot Sergius of Radonezh, who built the monastery to the Lord in Radonezh, and they had the same father and mother. And so monk Stephen, together with Alexis, both lived the monastic life. They were always together in church, standing together, singing together about their love for God, and were always humble. In the same monastery of the Holy Theophany there was a certain Gerontius, an outstanding and illustrious monk, renowned for his ascetic life. He remained there together with Stephen and Alexis in great spiritual love for God and in great humility.

Theognost, Metropolitan of all Russia, loved them verily and invited them to him, offering them spiritual support, rest and consolation, respecting them greatly. Later, Metropolitan Theognost, Metropolitan of all Russia, appointed elder Stephen abbot of this monastery of the Holy Theophany, and so Stephen became abbot of the monastery of the Theophany, as well as the spiritual councilor of Grand Prince Semion [the Proud], son of Ivan Dani-

lovich Kalita, grandson of Aleksandr Nevskii; and, also, the spir-   **1378**
itual councilor of tysiatskii Vasilii, the latter's brother, Fedor, and
of the other senior boiars, and of many other people. Everyone
loved him because of his exemplary way of life and his humility.

Thereafter, His Holiness Metropolitan Theognost of all
Russia took the elder, Alexis, from the monastery of the Holy
Theophany to his court and appointed him his vicar, to help him
and discuss with him in a just way [the work] of the clergy, according to the holy rules.

The reverend elder Alexis remained at the court of Metropolitan Theognost for twelve years and three months, and altogether he was monk forty years.

Later, on the sixth day of the month of December, Metropolitan Theognost consecrated him Bishop of Vladimir, desiring
that he become Metropolitan after him. He did so because he loved
him verily for his virtues. The reverend Alexis remained Bishop
four years, performing his sacred duties, until Metropolitan Theognost passed away. After the passing of Theognost he was u-
nanimously elected by the council, the bishops and Grand Prince
Ivan [the Second], the son of Ivan [Kalita], grandson of Danilo,
great grandson of Aleksandr [Nevskii], as well as by the boiars,
magnates and all the people. By God's will and because of this
election he was to go to the Patriarch of Constantinople for consecration as Metropolitan. Although he did not want to go to be
consecrated in Constantinople, he was nonetheless consecrated
there by the blessed Patriarch Philotheus to be Metropolitan of
Russia. Upon returning from Constantinople to his Metropolitan See in Russia he was received with joy by all Russian Orthodox.

He ascended to his See, bearing in mind the words of the
Gospel: "To whom much is given, from him much will be re-
quired." "The servant who learned the will of his lord and did
not do it will be greatly punished." And he always kept this in
mind, where great duties were concerned; and he added labor
unto labor, and he was the light and the image for all, according
to the words of God: "Let your light shine before men so that they
may see your good works and glorify Your Father, Who is in
Heaven." [*Matt.* 5:16]

Then the blessed one resolved to erect a church and to establish a community monastery, saying, "It is my promise to God.

1378   Once while I was journeying by ship from Constantinople it happened that a great storm arose and vast waves struck the vessel. We all became afraid for our lives and each of us prayed. I gave the Lord this promise: I would build a church dedicated to the saint who is remembered on that day when we should reach a haven. From that moment the wind and storm at sea ceased and it grew quite silent. We reached a quiet haven on the sixteenth day of the month of August. Therefore I promised to build a church dedicated to the Icon of Our Lord and Saviour, Jesus Christ, not Made by Human Hand, and to establish a community monastery.[82]

Thus speaking to those with him he approached blessed Sergius, whom he told the following: "Now I want," he said, "to fulfill my vow." Blessed Sergius answered him, "What you want to do is a good and blessed deed. Whatever you request from us, we will help you do and not cause any hindrance." The Metropolitan told him, "I want to appoint your pupil, Andronik, to be the abbot of this monastery."

The reverend Sergius answered, "As you wish, so do." And so holy Alexis gave sufficient alms to this monastery and gathered the brethren. Taking with him monk Andronik, he departed from the monastery [of St. Sergius] and came to the city of Moscow.

In the city of Moscow on the river Iauza he found a place fitting to establish a monastery, and so, with the help of Lord God and the Most Pure Theotokos, he erected a church in the name of the Image of Christ not Made by Human Hand, which he had brought with him from Constantinople. He adorned it with gold and pearls and placed it in the church of this monastery, where it remains until now. And he gave the abbey all provisions which they might need there, and endowed it with towns, [fishing] waters, and lands. The reverend Abbot Sergius visited this abbey, approved and blessed the place, and then returned to his own monastery, which was in Radonezh.

After a certain time holy Alexis, Metropolitan of Russia, journeyed to Nizhnii Novgorod, where he erected a church dedi-

---

82. This icon, the Mandilion of the ancient Christian tradition, was an Image of Christ, an impression of His Face on linen made by Himself and presented to Abgar IV, King of Edessa in Asia Minor.

cated to the Most Pure Theotokos, to Her Most Honorable and **1378** Glorious Annunciation, and organized a community monastery there and endowed it with towns, waters and lands, supplying it with all needed things. And he adorned this church of the Annunciation of the Most Pure Theotokos with all beauty. Then in that same Nizhnii Novgorod he baptised the son of Prince Boris Konstantinovich, grandson of Vasilii, great grandson of Mikhail, gr. gr. grandson of Andrei. In holy baptism he gave him the name of Ivan, and he was received with great honor by Grand Prince Boris Konstantinovich. Grand Prince Boris gave this monastery of the Annunciation of the Most Pure Theotokos all necessities, all manner of goods, and real estate; and this monastery in Nizhnii Novgorod up to now is the monastery of the Metropolitan, who disposes of all necessities, and it is protected by the grace of Christ, of the Most Pure Theotokos, and by the prayers of the holy wonderworker Alexis. From thence he travelled to the city of Vladimir, where, on the river Kliazma, he established a communal monastery and erected a church in it dedicated to the Holy Great Emperor Constantine, equal to the Apostles. And he supplied it with all necessities and endowed it with towns and with sufficient means. And this monastery is preserved up to now with all its endowments by the grace of Christ, the Most Pure Theotokos and the holy wonderworker Alexis.

Because of his virtues and his holy activities, his glory spread not only in Christian countries but also to the infidel Tatar lands. At that time Taidula, wife of Khan Dzhanibeg of the Horde, suffered from sore eyes, and in the year 6865/1357 an envoy of this khan's wife, Taidula, came from the Horde to blessed Alexis, Metropolitan of all Russia, asking him to visit her because she knew him as a holy and wise man who is heard by God, and that when he asked something of God, God would grant it him. He prepared everything needed for the journey and began to celebrate a healing service in the cathedral church of the Most Pure Theotokos. During the service, a candle began to burn of itself at the grave of the holy wonderworker, Peter. He, Alexis, after chanting the service with the entire holy council, divided this candle into pieces and distributed them to the people as his blessing. He also took some of this wax candle with him, with blessed water, and went to the Horde, to the khan's wife, Taidula. The khan's wife saw him in a dream dressed in the vestments of Arch-

1378   bishop, and also his priests, likewise dressed in holy vestments; and therefore this khan's wife, Taidula, had made for him and for all his clergy those same holy vestments as she had seen in her dream. When Khan Dzhanibeg of the Horde heard of the saint's arrival, he, Dzhanibeg, son of Uzbeg, went to meet him, together with his son, Berdibek, and with his other sons, lords and magnates, and met him with great honor. And so it was fulfilled as it is written in the Scripture: "The lion and the lamb will lie down together."

The blessed one celebrated a healing service and ordered that they light the wax candle which had begun to burn of itself. Then he blessed the khan's wife, Taidula, with holy water and she recovered her sight at once. When Khan Dzhanibeg and the other Tatars saw this, they were greatly astounded and they rendered praise and honor to the holy one, gave many gifts to him and to his clergy and squires, and let them return to Russia.

At that time there were great troubles and dissension in the Horde. When the holy one returned to his See in Russia he was praised and admired by everyone, and all considered him a great man before God.

He remained on the holy Metropolitan See of all Russia many years, teaching the word of God, caring for piety, forbidding the the people to commit injustice, consecrating bishops and presbyters. The bishops consecrated by him were (1) Ignatius, Bishop of Rostov; (2) Basil, Bishop of Riazan'; (3) Theophilact, Bishop of Smolensk; (4) John, Bishop of Sarai; (5) Parphenius, Bishop of Smolensk; (6) Philemon, Bishop of Kolomna; (7) Peter, Bishop of Rostov; (8) Theodore, Bishop of Tver'; (9) Nathaniel, Bishop of Briansk; (10) Athanasius, Bishop of Riazan'; (11) Alexis, Bishop of Suzdal'; (12) Alexis, Bishop of Novgorod and Pskov; (13) Basil, Bishop of Tver'; (14) Daniel, Bishop of Suzdal'; (15) Matthew, Bishop of Sarai; (16) Arsenius, Bishop of Rostov; (17) Euthemius, Bishop of Tver'; (18) Dionysius, Bishop of Suzdal'; (19) Gerasimus, Bishop of Kolomna; (20) Gregory, Archbishop of Chernigov; (21) Daniel, Bishop of Smolensk. Those are the bishops who were consecrated by him.[83]

83. It may be added here that Metropolitan Alexis was the actual regent during the youth of Grand Prince Dmitrii, and thereafter remained until his death the most influential man in the Muscovite administration.

ABOUT THE MONASTERY OF THE MIRACLES   **1378**

At God's revelation he established an abbey within the city of Moscow, wherein he erected a stone church dedicated to Saint Archistrategos Michael in honor of the most illustrious miracles of this Archistrategos.[84] And he built there a chapel dedicated to the Most Pure Theotokos in honor of Her Most Honorable and Glorious Annunciation. He adorned this church with many beautiful things—icons, books frescoes, golden holy vessels and with other beautiful things. He established this abbey as a communal monastery, and it exists to this day; and he endowed it with many towns, houses, people, lakes, fields and places, and supplied it with everything which was needed [by it]. Not only did he give the church the above-mentioned gifts and endow it with the aforementioned endowment, but he also ordered that he be buried in this monastery. And so it happened: up to now his grave is in this monastery, in the right side of the altar upon entering the church. And his holy body has cured many people who have come to him with faith. He built this monastery twelve years before his passing.

When the holy one saw that he was becoming wearied from age and that his end was approaching, he summoned to him from Radonezh the reverend Abbot Sergius. When the latter arrived they spoke and Metropolitan Alexis ordered that a cross containing the relics of the saints, adorned with gold and pearls, be brought, and he gave it to St. Sergius. The other bowed humbly, saying, "Forgive me, great Archbishop of Christ, but since my youth I have never worn gold, and therefore in my old age I still want to remain in poverty." The Metropolitan told him, "My child, I know this, and I know your attitude; but obey me and accept this as my blessing." And so, with his own hand he put this golden cross with relics of the saints and adorned with gold and pearls onto St. Sergius, as if it were a manner of consecration.

Thereafter he wanted to speak with him, and he said, "Reverend Sergius, are you aware why I summoned you, and of all that I want to speak to you about?" The reverend Sergius answered, "How can I know, if you have not told me?" Then St.

---

84. This monastery became known later as Chudovskii Monastery, Monastery of Miracles.

1378   Alexis said, "Now, I see that I am approaching my end. I want, during the remainder of my life, to find a man who would be able to be the shepherd of the flock of Christ. I have selected you to rule according to the True Word, and everyone wants you and requests it of me. First, you will be consecrated Bishop, and after my passing you will ascend to my See." The reverend Sergius told him, "Excuse me, great Archbishop of Christ, what you say is beyond my abilities. Who am I? I am the most sinful and worst of men. But I pray you, you should not speak of this either to me or to anyone else because no one is able to persuade me that I should become [Metropolitan]."

Seeing that the other was unbending, St. Alexis, seeing him inflexible, did not insist on speaking of this with him because he feared that the other would grieve and would retreat into an internal desert, and that he would lose such a light of faith. He consoled him with spiritual words and let him return to his monastery with honor, peace and love.

Blessed Metropolitan Alexis, although he was at a very advanced age and was exhausted, still would not cease teaching the Divine Word and showing them the way to repentance. When he was nearing his end, he was serving the holy liturgy and had received Holy Communion, and was praying for the Grand Prince and for all the princes, boiars, soldiers and all the people. He gave his last embrace and, on the twelfth day of February, a Friday, during matins, he departed to the Lord into the endless ages. Because of his great and final humility the saint had instructed that he not be buried in church but outside the church, behind the altar, and he had indicated the place. When his passing became known, all the princes, magnates, monks and bishops hurried to him with tears, and weeping. The Grand Prince was astonished at his final humility and, after discussing it with the bishops, they buried him in the church, in the chapel of the Annunciation of the Most Pure Theotokos, where his honorable relics remain up to now and whither those seeking a cure come to him with faith.

His funeral was attended by Grand Prince Dmitrii Ivanovich, grandson of Ivan [Kalita], great grandson of Danilo, gr. gr. grandson of Aleksandr [Nevskii], gr. gr. gr. grandson of Iaroslav, by [Dmitrii's] uncle, Prince Vladimir Andreevich, grandson of Ivan, great grandson of Danilo, gr. gr. grandson of Aleksandr;

by Prince Vasilii, son of Grand Prince Dmitrii, grandson of Ivan **1378**
(II), great grandson of Ivan [Kalita], gr. gr. grandson of Danilo,
who at that time was six years old—and by the latter's brother,
Prince Iurii, son of Dmitrii, grandson of Ivan, great grandson of
Ivan, gr. gr. grandson of Danilo, who at that time was three years
old.

Burning with the desire and love to work for the Lord, this
blessed Alexis gave up this lay world when he was twenty years
old, or slightly more. He was tonsured a monk in the monastery
of the Theophany, and he lived a considerable period of time in
this monastery. From thence Metropolitan Theognost took him
to his court, where he remained a vicar for twelve years and three
months. Theognost also consecrated him during his life to be
bishop of Vladimir, and he remained bishop four years. After
the death of Theognost he was consecrated in Constantinople by
the blessed Patriarch Philotheus. At that time he was sixty years
of age. He remained Metropolitan twenty-four years [1353-
1378]; and altogether he lived eighty-five years.

His body remained in this grave for sixty years. In the year
6939/1431, during the rule of Grand Prince Vasilii Vasil'evich
and His Holiness Photius, Metropolitan of Kiev and all Russia,
the top of that church collapsed during the holy liturgy, and although the priest had not yet left the altar, he was unhurt. Then
they wanted to clear this place and started digging in order to
build a new stone church. While they were digging they found
the holy body of Alexis, Metropolitan of Kiev and all Russia, and
[his body and] even his vestments were intact. This happened
the twentieth day of May. When the church was erected they
buried his holy body in the church. His grave was placed on the
right side of the chapel of the Annunciation of the Most Pure Theotokos and it remains there to the present day, and emanates a
cure to everyone who comes to him with faith.

STORY ABOUT MITIAI[85]

After the passing of blessed Alexis, Metropolitan of Kiev
and all Russia, there ascended to his bishop's See and to his posi-

85. The original "Story about Mitiai" was written by Metropolitan
Cyprian (1389-1406) who understandably disliked Mitiai, Dionysius and
Pimen, his competitors for the Muscovite Metropolitan See. No degree
of impartiality, therefore, should be expected in his presentation of

1378   tion a certain archimandrite named Mikhail, also called "Mitiai."
In an uncommon, strange and unusual way he donned the vestments of Metropolitan [before being consecrated bishop] and
put on his head the white mitre of the Metropolitan, as well as
[donned] the mantle of the Metropolitan with the embroidered
rays and tablets, as well as [took] the Metropolitan's golden cross
adorned with the relics of the saints, with gold and with pearls.
And he took the Metropolitan's golden staff as well as the Metropolitan's seal, and the rest, and thus did he put himself into the
position of Metropolitan.

Earlier, before this happened, Grand Prince Dmitrii Ivanovich asked Metropolitan Alexis to bless this archimandrite Mitiai
to be his successor as Metropolitan of all Russia; but Alexis was
unwilling to do so because Mitiai had only recently become a
monk and therefore had not yet developed the [monastic] virtues. According to the words of the Apostles, "An ignorant man
may become proud and may enter into sin and the net of the
devil." And, also, the same Apostle said, "Those are first to be
tempted, and although then they try to serve, they are not chaste."

This archimandrite Mitiai had recently become a monk, and
he had to pass through all the difficulties of the life of a monk and
to learn about good deeds and behavior. "If God is willing He
will do this for him; but I am not satisfied with it." The Grand
Prince importuned long and tried to persuade Alexis to bless
Mitiai to be his successor on the Metropolitan See; sometimes he
would, himself, come to the Metropolitan in order to beseech
him and sometimes he would send his cousin, Prince Vladimir
Andreevich, or would send his boiars. But Alexis would say, "I

events. Some historians considered Cyprian a defender of Constantinople's interests—that is, of both the Emperor and the Patriarch. Some
others believe that Cyprian defended primarily the autonomy of the
Russian church from state power. In the present writer's opinion,
Cyprian's works show rather that he—Bulgarian in origin, Byzantine by
training, and a participant in Balkan church affairs—was, primarily,
a capable opportunist who cared for himself. He often contradicts himself in his writings, but still he was firm in his opinion that the church
should be independent from princely political power. *Russkaia istori-
cheskaia biblioteka*, Vol. 6, Nos. 20, 26. Golubinskii, II, pp. 21-262 and
297-356. Prokhorov, *"Povest' o Mitiae,"* pp. 15-65; Waldenberg, pp. 145-
156. In general an able writer, Cyprian mostly defends his own attitude, the
interests of the Metropolitan See, and of the Patriarch of Constantinople.

am not satisfied to give him my blessing; but in the case Lord God **1378** and the Most Pure Theotokos, and His Holiness, the Oecumenical Patriarch, select him, then I would give him my blessing."

After the passing of Alexis, archimandrite Mitiai took over [still not being a bishop] the high office of Metropolitan of all Russia and he did so in a very unusual way, thus provoking unanimous indignation. Everybody was exasperated by him—priests and monks—and looked with stupefaction at each other but did not dare to say anything because whatsoever he said or taught had power behind it. And so everyone would say to himself, "My lord, what is this new occurrence?" because, not yet consecrated by the Oecumenical Patriarch and the Holy Council [to be bishop] he dared, himself, to ascend to this high and supreme See. He lived at the court of the Metropolitan, he would sit and preside in the place of the Metropolitan, and he would appear in the white mitre and mantle which pertained to the rank and dignity of Metropolitan. He assumed the Metropolitan's sacristy and the boiars of the Metropolitan had to serve him; and the Metropolitan's acolytes would cocelebrate with him, and whenever he made any movement, all would appear with him. Everything which was befitting to the rank of Metropolitan was rendered unto him, and he had the glory, dignity, rank and position of Metropolitan. All these Mitiai held and ruled. He made judgments in court and collected taxes, tithes and duties. And he began to persecute the priests, monks, abbots, archimandrites and bishops, and he would sentence and fine many of those who would not agree with his authority, not heeding anyone because he was very bold and spoke clearly and threateningly. The bishops, archimandrites, abbots, monks and priests would sigh because of him, and many of them he put into irons and punished, bending them with his power in such a way that no one dared to resist him.

We should now learn who this archimandrite Mitiai was, and from whence he came by birth. This archimandrite Mitiai was a son of the priest, John, from Shetilov, which is located on the river Oka, and then this Mitiai was one of the priests in Kolomna. He had a high and heavy stature, was tall and strong; he had very powerful, wide shoulders. His beard was straight and long. His face was handsome and in his appearance he surpassed all. His speech was easy, with good diction and very loud. His voice was very beautiful and he pronounced words and speeches in a sono-

1378   rous and sweet way. He was very learned and had a good knowledge of books, and quite an ability for interpreting Scripture.
His reading was sweet and wise, and he was very well versed in
books and knew how to discuss them. No one knew as much as he.

He had a very attractive manner of celebrating the church
service, was clever in business and in judgments, and in his opin-
ions he was elegant and wise. His words and speech were very
clear and he never stuttered; his memory was excellent and he
knew the old stories, books and parables, both spiritual and from
everyday life, so that none was so glib as he. Therefore he was
selected by the desire and love of Grand Prince Dmitrii Ivanovich
to be his spiritual father and guardian of the seal. And so this
priest, Mitiai, became the confessor of Grand Prince Dmitrii
Ivanovich and guardian of the Seal, which he would carry with
him.

The boiars and lords would come to him for confession, and
Mitiai was greatly honored and praised by the Grand Prince and
by all. He had the majesty of a king, and he had many servants
and pages, and he was in such a position and of such importance
for many years—praised and honored more than anyone else.
Every day he would change his costly church vestments and would
appear in very precious robes which astounded everyone because
no one wore such vestments. No one changed his costly and bril-
liant clothes as often as this priest, Mitiai. Everyone honored him
as if he were a king. And what else can be said? No one was so
honored and praised as he because he was the spiritual father of
the Grand Prince and he could command as he wanted. For
many years he had this position, and everyone loved him.

Then archimandrite John, called "Nepeitsa" ["Sober"], of
the monastery of the Saviour, a very humble, meek and quiet
man, attained an advanced age and—for the sake of God and,
also, because of his age and weariness—humbled himself and left
his position of archimandrite, and went to his cell, where he remained in silence. And there was no archimandrite in this monastery of the Saviour after Nepeitsa, and the monks and the monastery were in great need of a leader. Then people started looking
about, who should become archimandrite of the monastery of
the Saviour after Ivan Nepeitsa? This monastery was inside the
city of Moscow, and people began speaking of one and of another;
but the Grand Prince wanted to put Mitiai there because he loved

him very much, and he also was loved by the boiars. When Mitiai **1378** heard this, he did not want it [to become a monk and abbot]; but the Grand Prince spoke to him with spiritual tenderness and humility: "Don't you see that Metropolitan Alexis has become very old? After him, you will become Lord Metropolitan of all Russia. Now, accept the tonsure to monk, and then you will become archimandrite of the monastery of the Saviour, and remain my spiritual father as before, and everyone will obey you." This priest, Mitiai, did accordingly. The Grand Prince attained what he wanted, and so that one was elected and accepted.

Soon thereafter Mitiai was supposed to be tonsured, but he was unwilling to do this; rather, he was forced to come to the monastery of St. Saviour. When he came to the church of St. Saviour, they sent for archimandrite Elyseus of the monastery of the Miracles. Archimandrite Elyseus, called "Chechetka," came at once and tonsured priest Mitiai into the holy angelic orders in the church of the monastery of the Holy Saviour, which is in the city. And so, before dinner he was, first, a lay priest, and then, monk; while after dinner, however, he was already archimandrite. Before dinner, he arrived as a lay priest and became tonsured to the monastic orders; but after dinner, he was already the commander, pastor and teacher.

This Mitiai remained archimandrite of the Metropolitan monastery of the Saviour for two years, but after the passing of Metropolitan Alexis he gave up his monastery, upon the advice of the Grand Prince and the latter's boiars, came to the court of the Metropolitan and, in an arrogant manner and without hesitation, took [command of] the highest and supreme See of this land. And then, just as befits a Metropolitan, he assumed all the possessions of this See and collected the taxes throughout the entire Metropolia, the special collections on the day of St. Peter and of Christmas, and all the income and tithes which pertained to the Metropolitan. And so he lived and commanded.

He decided to go to the Patriarch of Constantinople to be consecrated there but he changed his mind and began to tell the Grand Prince, "It is written in the apostolic rules that two or three bishops may consecrate another bishop. Even in the rules of the Church Fathers, it is written thus. Therefore, five or six Russian bishops may come together and they may consecrate a bishop to head this Metropolia." When Grand Prince Dmitrii Ivanovich

1378 and his boiars learned about his, they also wanted to do thus and they summoned the Russian bishops.[86]

When they came together, they received a blessing from Mitiai; but then came Dionysius, Bishop of Suzdal', who was independent and who opposed the Grand Prince, saying, "Who taught you to change the rules? It is not supposed to be thus." Mitiai, the Metropolitan-elect, understood that he was shamed and that his intention could not be realized, so this Mitiai was embarrassed and began to vacillate. But besides that, some evilminded people who wanted them to quarrel began to denounce the Metropolitan-elect, Mitiai, to Bishop Dionysius of Suzdal', and Dionysius, to Mitiai.

Thereafter, Metropolitan-elect Mitiai sent to Bishop Dionysius of Suzdal', saying, "Why did you not come and bow to me and receive my blessing when you came to the city [of Moscow]? You did not render me honor and you disdain me as though I were the least man. Do you know who I am and that I have power over you and over the entire Metropolia?"

Bishop Dionysius of Suzdal' became disturbed, went to him and said, "You sent for me, saying that you have power over me; but you have no power over me [because you have not yet been consecrated bishop]. As a matter of fact, you were supposed to come to me to bow and to receive a blessing from me, since I am a bishop and you are just a priest. If you have power in the Metropolia to judge and to trade, then you must make judgments according to the truth, and you must test everything according to the testimony of the Divine Books. Who is more important, the bishop or the priest?"

And Mitiai said, "You called me a priest! But I do not consider you even to be a priest. Now, only wait till I return from the Patriarch of Constantinpole." And there was an argument and bad words between them. When Grand Prince Dmitrii Ivanovich learned of this, he became indignant at Bishop Dionysius. Mitiai remained in the court of the Metropolitan of Moscow for one year and six months, ruling over everyone as if he were a consecrated Metropolitan.

86. There have always been tendencies in national Orthodox churches—especially in the Bulgarian, Serbian, etc.—to win independence from the Patriarch of Constantinople. In fact, there has never been one central supreme power in the Orthodox Church, as in the Roman Catholic.

In the meantime, Bishop Dionysius of Suzdal' expressed his   **1378**
intention to go to Constantinpole because he wanted to see himself
on the Metropolitan See. This did not remain concealed from
Mitiai, who reported it to the Grand Prince and advised him to
forbid Dionysius to go to Constantinople. "He should not go
thither because he will make hindrances to my consecration."
The Grand Prince ordered that Dionysius be kept by force but,
seeing that he might be forcibly restrained [from going to Con-
stantinople], Dionysius outwitted Grand Prince Dmitrii Ivanovich, telling him, "Let me out and let me go home so that I can
live according to my own will, and I will not journey to Constantinople without your permission; and the reverend Abbot Sergius
of Radonezh will vouch for this to you."

The Grand Prince listened to him, believed his words and
was ashamed that such a person [as Sergius of Radonezh] should
become involved in this, and he released Dionysius, Bishop of
Suzdal', on the condition that he not journey to Constantinople
without the permission of the Grand Prince and that Sergius of
Radonezh vouch for him.[87]

Mitiai did not trust Dionysius, Bishop of Suzdal'; even the
other referred to the reverend Abbot Sergius of Radonezh, because Mitiai learned that Sergius had advised Metropolitan Alexis
not to give his blessing to him [Mitiai] to be Metropolitan of Russia. Now, Mitiai thought that the reverend Abbot Sergius of
Radonezh was of the same mind as Dionysius, Bishop of Suzdal',
and that neither wanted him to be invested as Metropolitan. So
he was very angry at both of them and became greatly wroth.

And, indeed, the reverend Abbot Sergius said, "I ask Lord
God with a most humble heart not to let Mitiai ruin this holy place,
our holy monastery, or drive us forth from hence without any
fault on our side, as he boasts."

Dionysius departed to Suzdal' but from Suzdal' he went to
Nizhnii Novgorod; and then, without losing time, and despite
his promise, he escaped by boat on the river Volga to Sarai, and
from Sarai he went to Constantinople, breaking his promise to
the Grand Prince and betraying the reverend Abbot Sergius, who

87. Sergius of Radonezh, who enjoyed the respect of all the Russians, considered that Mitiai overstepped the bounds of power of a tem-
porary caretaker of the Metropolitan See.

1378 had vouched for him. The Grand Prince was dolefully saddened, while Mitiai became embarrassed and indignant about Dionysius, and about the reverend Abbot Sergius, because he thought that both Sergius and Dionysius were in agreement and did not want him to be consecrated Metropolitan.

Grand Prince Dmitrii Ivanovich liked Mitiai above all, honored him as his father and heeded him with great pleasure, more than anyone else, and he insisted on his going to the Patriarch in Constantinple to be consecrated Metropolitan. Mitiai began to prepare for his journey and asked the Grand Prince to give him blank charters—or, so to say, blank letters—which would not be written but would be sealed with the seal of the Grand Prince. Then, upon arriving in Constantinople and having in supply such blank charters, sealed by the seal of the Grand Prince but with no written text, he would write in the charter whatsoever he might require. The Grand Prince gave him such blank charters sealed with his seal and told him, "Have them. In the case you are in need or should be without money and should require a loan of one thousand pieces of silver or more, these charters will be my debt, certified with my seal."

In the year 6887/1379 Mitiai set out on his journey to Constantinople to be consecrated Metropolitan: he travelled from Moscow to Kolomna, then, on the twenty-sixth day of the month of July, from Kolomna he crossed the Oka on his way to Riazan'. He was given a farewell with great honor and great respect by the Grand Prince, himself, by the latter's children, by his boiars, by all the bishops of Russia, all archimandrites, abbots, priests, monks, merchants and leading citizens and a large number of people who accompanied him for quite a part of the road.

With him there went to Constantinople three archimandrites: (1) John, Archimandrite of St. Peter, who was the head of the communal life monasteries in Moscow: (2) Pimen, Archimandrite of Pereiaslavl' from Goritsa; (3) Martin, Archimandrite of Kolomna. Then there were Dorofei, Guardian of the Seal; Sergei Azakov; Stefan Vysotskii; Antonii Kop'e ("the Lance"); Aleksandr, a Muscovite archpriest; Davyd, the archdeacon who was usually called "Dasha the Muscovite"; Macarius, abbot of the monastery in Musolinsk; Gregory, deacon of St. Saviour; Gregory, deacon of the Monastery of the Miracles; and many others—abbots, presbyters, deacons, monks, the clergy of Vladimir, the outstanding

men of the court of the Metropolitan; the regular servants—or, **1378**
so to say, the Metropolitan's best servants; the Metropolitan's
treasurers; and his boiars.

Then there were the boiars of the Grand Prince: the leading
boiar was Iurii Vasilievich Kochevin Oleshenskii, who was at the
time the Grand Prince's main envoy and who was supposed to be
the senior elder of the embassy. Then there were the boiars of
the Metropolitan: Fedor Sholokhov; Ivan Artem'ev Korob'in; the
latter's brother, Andrei; Never Barbin; Stefan Il'in Klovynia;
the interpreter, Vasilii Kustov; and another interpreter [by the
name] Buil. And there was really a very large group of them.

They crossed the Riazan' land in peace and tranquility and
then they came to the Horde in the former land of the Polovets,
in the land of the Tatars. And while they were crossing the land
of the Horde, Mitiai, with all who accompanied him, was received
by Mamai. And Mamai kept him for awhile in his place and then
let him go in peace and tranquility, and even ordered that he be
given an escort. So they crossed in peace and tranquility the
whole Tatar land, came to the Sea of Kafa and then boarded
ships.[88] From thence they crossed over the depths of the ocean
[that is, the Black Sea], and when they were so close to Constantinople that they could already see the city, Mitiai suddenly became ill on the ship and passed away at sea.

Some people claim that this ship remained in the same place
and could not move from it either one way or another, while very
many other ships passed her on one side and the other, but only
that one ship was in dire need, as happened to Jonah. Once when
Jonah was in his ship the sea became very turbulent and the boat
started sinking. When Jonah was thrown into the sea the storm
ceased and the boat did not sink. [Jonah I, 3-12.] Now it happened in the same way: a long as Mitiai was on board, the water
would not permit the ship to advance; but when the body of Mitiai
was removed from the ship, the ship was freed and moved further, whithersoever it wanted [cf. Johah; 4-5]. They put Mitiai
into a wooden barge and brought him, dead, to Galata.[89]

88. Kafa, or Caffa: now Feodosiia, a port in Crimea which at that
time was the main Genoese trade center for all southeastern Europe.

89. Galata is the southeastern part of Constantinople (Istanbul),
southeast of the Golden Horn and the port. It was primarily a section for
Italians, mostly Genoese and other foreigners.

1378   After Mitiai's death, his companions became greatly disturbed. They were upset and hesitant, as if drunk, and there was much disagreement and dissension among them. Some wanted Archimandrite John of St. Peter in Moscow to be consecrated Metropolitan. The others wanted Pimen of Pereiaslavl', who was from Goritsa. There was much talk concerning all this and the boiars were for Pimen, Archimandrite of Pereiaslavl'. John grew very angry and told them, "I will tell you frankly that you have done an injustice before God and the Grand Prince!" From this time on the others sought a convenient moment to destroy him and conspired, but he learned of it and told them, "Why are you so distraught? Are you not afraid to do evil?" And they laid their hands on him and arrested him, put him in irons and kept him hungry, wanting to throw him into the sea. In such an evil situation was John, Archimandrite of St. Peter in Moscow, a very eloquent and learned man of great virtue. And they did thus to him because he was not of the same mind with Pimen and the boiars.

Then they decided that he should not be put to death, and in this way their anger against John, Archimandrite of St. Peter in Moscow, was abated and ceased.

And so Pimen, with the boiars, investigated the treasury and the treasures from Mitiai's sacristy, and found there the above-mentioned blank charters with the Seal of the Grand Prince, on which nothing was written. They sought the counsel of their companions, and wrote on one of these parchments a text which said, "From Grand Prince of Russia to the Emperor and to the Patriarch! I send to you Pimen. Please consecrate him Metropolitan because he is the only one whom I could find [fitting to be Metropolitan] in Russia and we could find no other."

This charter was read before the entire Holy Council and the Emperor, and then the Emperor and the Patriarch responded to the Russians, saying, "The Russian prince writes in vain concerning Pimen. In Russia there already is a ready Metropolitan: this is Cyprian. He was consecrated long ago by His Holiness Philotheus, the Oecumenical Patriarch, and we will send him to the Russian Metropolia and we will not consecrate any other."

Then the Russians, thanks to one of those [blank] charters, took a loan on interest in the name of the Grand Prince from the Franks and the Moslems, and from that day on this debt grew so fast that it amounted to more than twenty thousand rubles of **1378** silver. In this way they could give bribes, and they gave bribes on the one hand and on the other. None could say exactly how many gifts of bribes there were, but in this way they succeeded in satisfying everyone.

And so the Emperor and the Patriarch began to question Pimen and those with him and afterwards, they deigned to consecrate Pimen Metropolitan of Russia, saying, "Oh, Russians! Whether you speak the truth or untruth, we act in the right way and perform in the just way and speak the truth, and we have faith in you." In such a way His Holiness Nilus, Patriarch of Constantinople, invested Pimen Metropolitan of Russia.

Very soon, tidings came to Grand Prince Dmitrii Ivanovich that, "Your Mitiai passed away at sea near Constantinople, and Pimen has become Metropolitan."

Some people said of Mitiai that he had been strangled; some others said that he was drowned in the ocean because neither the bishops nor the archimandrites nor the abbots nor the priests nor the monks, nor any of the boiars, nor the common people wanted to see Mitiai become Metropolitan. Only the Grand Prince desired this. And so Grand Prince Dmitrii Ivanovich became very grieved and saddened at the passing of Mitiai, and he did not want to accept Pimen, and said, "I did not send Pimen to be invested Metropolitan; but I sent him only to accompany Mitiai. What happened to Mitiai, I do not know, only God knows, and God will judge this injustice. From them I hear about the consecration, but I do not accept Pimen, and I do not want to see him." And since Metropolitan Pimen with the people accompanying him were delayed in Constantinople, the Grand Prince sent his spiritual father, Theodore, Abbot of the monastery of St. Simon, to Kiev, inviting Metropolitan Cyprian to come to Moscow. And the envoys went to Kiev during Great Lent to bring Metropolitan Cyprian.

THE COMING OF CYPRIAN FROM KIEV TO MOSCOW

Cyprian came from Kiev to Moscow in 6888/1380,[90] on a

90. This arrival of Cyprian occurred not in May, 1380, but May 23, 1381. This error on the part of the chroniclers originated already in *Sokrashchenyi letopisnyi svod 1493 goda, PSRL* 27, p. 251.

1378   Thursday of the sixth week after Easter, the very day of the holiday of the Ascension of Christ. And they began to ring all the
bells and people gathered, and a great multitude flowed. From
everywhere came archimandrites, abbots, priests and monks;
there was a great ringing, and the whole town moved, with wives,
infants, children, babes at the breast, and they went far from the
city to meet him. And the Grand Prince, himself, met him far
from the city with his children and all the boiars, with great honor
and much love, with faith and humility. Returning to the city,
they entered the church and Cyprian crossed himself before all
the icons and said a *Te Deum*, and he enjoyed spiritual love. There
was great exaltation on this day for the Grand Prince and the
Metropolitan, and everyone rejoiced and became gay in joy and
great gladness, and they distributed large alms to pilgrims and
the poor, and they glorified Christ-God, to Whom is the glory,
forever and ever. Amen.

Thereafter, when seven months had passed, in the year
6889/1381 [6884/1376 in *Vozn.*] the news came to the Grand
Prince that Metropolitan Pimen was coming across the prairie
from the Horde from his journey from Constantinople to Russia,
to his Metropolia. The Grand Prince did not want to accept him
and became angry at his senior boiar, Iurii Vasilievich Kochevin
Oleshenskii. When Pimen arrived in Kolomna the Grand Prince
sent his men to him and ordered them to remove Pimen's white
mitre and to put him in gaol; he ordered that they put in irons in
various places his guards, councillors, advisers and his clergymen.
They took from him all the regailia of Metropolitan and all the
treasury, and assigned a bailiff to him, a certain boiar named Ivan
Grigoriev, son of Churila, called "Dranitsa." And they took
Pimen from Kolomna to Okhna to prison, bypassing Moscow;
from Okhna they went to Pereiaslavl'; from Pereiaslavl', to Rostov; from Rostov, to Kostroma; from Kostroma, to Galich; from
Galich, to Chukhloma. He remained in Chukhloma for one year,
and from Chukhloma he was taken to Tver'. The earth is of the
Lord, as well as all its corners! Here is the end of the story about
Mitiai, Pimen and the others.

PRINCESS VASILISA THEODORA

The same year Princess Vasilisa, dowager of Prince Andrei
Konstantinovich of Nizhnii Novgorod, better known under her

monastic name of Theodora, passed away. She was buried in the
nunnery of the Holy Conception which she established, herself.
She was from Tver' by birth: her father was Ivan Kiasovskii and
her mother was Anna, and she was born in the year 6839/1331
when Andronik was Emperor of Byzantium, Callistus was Patriarch of Constantinople, Uzbeg was Khan of the Horde, Ivan Danilovich was the Grand Prince of Russia and Theognost was the
Metropolitan of Russia.[91] When she was still young she learned
all letters, the Old and New Testaments, and desired to become
a nun; but her parents opposed her, and when she was twelve
years old they married her to Prince Andrei Konstantinovich of
Suzdal' and Nizhnii Novgorod. When she was married she did
not care for this vain life but she adhered to fasting, abstinence,
prayer and alms, and she mortified her body with a strict life:
under her fair dress she wore a hair shirt on her body.

When, thirteen years later, her husband, Prince Andrei
Konstantinovich, passed away, having been tonsured a monk,
she buried him in the same church of the Holy Saviour in which
was buried his father, Konstantin. After her husband's passing
she was tonsured to monastic orders by archimandrite Dionysius
of the Monastery of the Caves, and she received the monastic
name of Theodora; she divided all her wealth, gold, silver and
pearls among the churches, monasteries and the poor, she liberated all her serfs and joined the nunnery of the Conception,
which she, herself, had established. She abode in great silence
and lived by the work of her hands. She had a severe and hard-
working life of fasting and prayer, of reading Divine Scripture,
and of emotional tenderness and tears.[92] Many women, and widows
of princes and boiars, and young girls—altogether, one hundred
and ten of them—became nuns in her nunnery. They all lived
the life of community, adhering to it strictly and staeadfastly.
When she grew old she did not relent in her ascetic feats but
passed to God after a strict and wonderful life. She passed to
God, Whom she had loved from her youth and to Whom belongs
the glory unto the ages of ages. Amen.

91. Inaccurate. Andronik was emperor in Byzantium 1328-1341;
but Callistus was Patriarch 1350-1384. Uzbeg ruled 1313-1341 and
1355-1363.

92. In the Orthodox monastic tradition, emotional praying with
tears is considered a high spiritual achievement.

1378

[NIZHNII NOVGOROD IS RAIDED BY THE TATARS]

The same year[93] the Tatars of the Volga Horde of Mamai raided Nizhnii Novgorod, when the prince was not there. The people of this land dispersed, the citizens abandoned the city and fled beyond the Volga. At that time Prince Dmitrii Konstantinovich came from the city of Gorodets and, seeing that the city had been taken by Mamai's Tatars, he sent them a ransom for the city; but they did not accept the ransom and burned the city. So for men's sins the church of the Holy Saviour, together with its beautiful floor and beautifully constructed doors adorned with gilt copper, burned. From thence the Tatars marched further, campaigning, gathered many captives and devastated all the Berezovo Pole [Birch Field], and the entire district.

[THE BATTLE OF VOZHA]

The same year lord Mamai of the Volga Horde sent his lord Begich to wage war against Grand Prince Dmitrii Ivanovich of Moscow, but the Grand Prince assembled strong forces and marched against them beyond the river Oka into the Riazan' land. They met the Tatars in the Riazan' land on the river Vozha, being separated from them by this river Vozha. After a few days the Tatars crossed the river Vozha onto this side and attacked at a trot, yelling at the top of their voices at Grand Prince Dmitrii Ivanovich; but he stood firmly against them with his troops. Then Prince Andrei of Polotsk attacked them from one side; from the other side they were attacked by Prince Danilo of Pronsk while Grand Prince Dmitrii Ivanovich struck them from the fore. The Tatars at once ran off beyond the river Vozha, abandoning their lances, whilst our men followed after them, flaying, slaying, striking them with lances and cutting them in half. They killed a great many of them and the others were overrun in the river. It was late in the evening and the Tatars fled all the night long. The next morning there was heavy fog and only late, after dinner, could our men follow them; but they realized that those had fled too far. In the prairie they came across the abandoned camps of the Tatars, their tents, their possessions and their carts, in which was an endless amount of goods. So they took all the Tatars' wealth and rejoiced, and all returned home with booty and joy.

93. 6887/1379 in *Novg. III.*

In this battle the Tatars killed Dmitrii Monastyrev and Nazar **1378**
Danilov, the son of Kusak, while among the lords of Mamai there
were killed Hadji Bey, Kovyrgui, Karabuluk, Kostruk and Be-
gichka. This battle occurred on the eleventh day of the month
of August, when the holy martyr, Deacon Euplus, is remembered—a Wednesday, late in the evening.

In this battle with Begich[94] which took place on the river
Vozha, the Russians captured the priest of tysiackii Ivan Vasilievich, who came from the Horde.[95] This tysiackii Ivan Vasilievich
had been in Mamai's Horde and had created much disturbance.
With this priest they found a bag of evil, poisonous herbs. He
was interrogated, punished and sent to prison on Lake Lache,
where Daniel the Prisoner used to be.[96] After this battle on the
river Vozha Mamai's Tatars fled, pursued by divine wrath, and
they went to the Horde, to their Khan. They reported, however,
not to their Khan but to lord Mamai, who had sent them. They
did thus because at that time their Khan in the Horde was not
actually ruling at all. He dared not do anything without lord
Mamai, and all the power was held by lord Mamai. This lord
Mamai ruled over everything in the Horde. His name resounded
like the name of the Khan, and this action [of Begich's] was initi-
ated by Mamai. We can truly say that all—the name, the glory
and the deed—was Mamai's.

ABOUT THE RAIDS OF THE RIAZAN' LAND BY MAMAI

6887/1379. When Lord Mamai viewed the destruction of his
troops and saw that some of his lords, magnates and *alpauts*[97] had
been killed and that many had perished, he grew sad, grieved greatly and became very wrathful. The same fall, in the year 6887/1379
[6886/1378 in *Vozn.*] in the month of September Lord Mamai

94. In 6887/1379 in *Novg. IV*.

95. Ivan Vasilievich was not tysiackii but the son of the last tysiackii
of Moscow, Vasilii Veliaminov. See entry under 1375 and the note concerning Veliaminovs.

96. While in prison on this Lake Lache, Daniel the Exile, or Prisoner, wrote his famous missive, or letter, to his prince, imploring that he
be freed and aided by the prince. See *Zenkovsky*, S., *Medieval Russia's
Epics, Chronicles and Tales*, 2nd ed., p. 279.

97. *Alpauts*: sons of the nobles of the Horde. They formed the
Khan's guard, or shock troops.

1379 gathered his remaining forces, assembled a great number of troops and, swiftly and unexpectedly, went campaigning and raiding in the Riazan' land.

Grand Prince Oleg Ivanovich of Riazan' was not aware of this at all, and when the Tatars marched into his land he did not have time to gather [troops], and did not resist them with arms. He did thus because he had no time to be prepared, and he fled to this [northern] bank of the river Oka, abandoning his cities. The Tatars marched into his land, took the town of Dubok, burned it and burned the city of Pereiaslavl' [the captial of Riazan'], as well as all the other cities, districts and towns. They took a great many captives and returned home, having devastated the Riazan' land.

After the Tatars retreated Oleg of Riazan'—seeing his land devastated and burned, and all his wealth and property taken by the Tatars—became sad and grieved greatly. Only a few people escaped captivity by the Tatars, and those began to return and rebuild their homes in the Riazan' land because the entire land had been ravaged and burned by fire.

The same year in the month of September Prince Semion, son of Grand Prince Dmitrii Ivanovich, passed away.

[KEISTUT'S MURDER]

The same year [6886/1378 in *Vozn.*] there was a great mutiny in Lithuania and they—the princes—rebelled and killed Grand Prince Keistut Gediminovich, together with his boiars and his squires; and they accepted the rule of Iagailo Olgerdovich as their grand prince. Vitovt, the son of Keistut Gediminovich, escaped to the Germans, from whence he caused the Lithuanian land much evil.[98]

PORTENT

The same winter during St. Philip's fast, on the fifth day of the month of December, Sunday, at early dawn there was a portent in the sky. The moon became obscured and turned bloody, and it stopped in one place. And then light began to appear from the south, while the east darkened. Thereafter, the moon recovered its customary light.[99]

98. "To the Germans:" that is, to the Order of the Teutonic Knights in Prussia.

99. Probaby, it was an eclipse of the moon.

The same winter [6885/1377 in *Novg. IV*; 6886/1378 in *Novg.*   **1379**
III and *Vozn.*] Andrei Olgerdovich escaped from Lithuania to
Pskov and from thence to Moscow. He was greeted by Grand
Prince Dmitrii Ivanovich with open arms.

[BISHOP DIONYSIUS TRAVELS TO CONSTANTINOPLE]

The same year Dionysius, Bishop of Suzdal', sailed by boat
to Constantinople, down the river Volga toward Sarai. The account of this was written down earlier, in the tale of Mitiai.[100]
Since Dionysius was quarrelling with Mitiai and himself aspired
to the Metropolitan See, Grand Prince Dmitrii Ivanovich forbade
him to go to Constantinople in order to prevent him from hinder-
ing Mitiai's consecration as Metropolitan. But Bishop Dionysius
outwitted Grand Prince Dmitrii Ivanovich, promising him not to
go to Constantinople, and caused the reverend Abbot Sergius to
vouch for him to the Grand Prince. Then, however, he escaped
to Constantinople on the river Volga, toward Sarai, by boat.
When Grand Prince Dmitrii Ivanovich learned that Bishop Dionysius had betrayed him and decieved his surety, the reverend
Abbot Sergius, and had escaped down the Volga to Sarai and
from thence to Constantinople, then he [the Grand Prince]
grieved and allowed Mitiai, archimandrite of the monastery of
St. Saviour, to go to the Patriarch of Constantinople to be there
consecrated Metropolitan of all Russia. Mitiai went overland
from Moscow to Kolomna, from Kolomna to Riazan' and from
Riazan' to Mamai's Horde.

At that time in Mamai's Horde there was a khan, but he had
no power by comparison with Mamai, and was khan in nothing
but the title. Even this title, however, was meaningless because all
glory and all the actions were Mamai's. There was much trouble
in the Horde and many Tatar lords had killed each other, lost
their heads and died at sword's points. Thus, little by little, the
Horde's great power was wasted away.

Mamai detained Mitiai in the Horde for awhile and then let
him go. He crossed all the Tatar land in peace and tranquility
because Mamai ordered some of his Tatars to escort him. He
attained the sea at Kafa and let Mamai's Tatars accompanying
him return to Mamai. So Mitiai with his people boarded a ship

100. See the annual entry under 1378.

1379   and sailed on the sea. When he was so near to Constantinople that all of the city of Constantinople could be seen, Mitiai fell ill on the ship and passed away. He was buried in Galata. Thus it passed according to Scripture: "It depends not upon man's will or his efforts but upon God's mercy." Indeed, Grand Prince Dmitrii Ivanovich wanted, and Mitiai went, and both sought to achieve their purposes; but they did not succeed in the least because it was not God's Will, and He is the Only One Who determines fate.

The same year at the summons of Grand Prince Dmitrii Ivanovich the venerable Abbot Sergius established a monastery on the river Dubenka at Sromyn. He erected there the church of the Dormition of the Most Pure Theotokos. He brought thither from his monastery of the Holy Trinity an abbot, Leontius by name. The church was consecrated on the first day of the month of December, and he brought together the monks, and the monastery was provided with all necessities. Grand Prince Dmitrii Ivanovich provided the means for endowing it with all necessary supplies to the glory of Christ, Our God, and His Most Pure Mother Theotokos, doing so for the salvation of his soul and for the preservation of his dominion.

[THE LITHUANIAN CAMPAIGN]

The same winter Grand Prince Dmitrii Ivanovich assembled many men and sent his cousin, Prince Vladimir Andreevich, with troops. Accompanying the latter were Prince Andrei Olgerdovich of Polotsk, Prince Dmitrii Mikhailovich of Volynia, and many other voevodas, boiars and lords. He let them march on Friday, the ninth day of the month of December, against the Lithuanian land.[1] They marched and took the cities of Trubchevsk and Starodub, and campaigned in many other lands and possessions, and they returned home with great wealth. But Prince Dmitrii Olgerdovich of Trubchevsk did not fight or raise his arm against the Grand Prince; rather, with great humility he marched out of the city, together with his princess, children and boiars. He came to Moscow to serve Grand Prince Dmitrii Ivanovich and he became his service prince and accepted the customary agreement. The Grand Prince gave him an agreement and a service position, and

1. December 9, 6887, was a Friday, according to the March calendar, and a Thursday, according to the September calendar. *PSRL* XI, p. 45.

accepted him with great honor and love, and granted him the   **1379**
city of Pereiaslavl' with all its taxes.

The same winter the men of Viatka campaigned in the Arsk
land[2] and they killed the robbers-ushkuiniks, capturing their commander, Ivan Riazanets, the son of Stanislav, whom they killed.

[THE END OF THE LAST TYSIATSKII'S SON]

The same year tysiatskii Ivan Vasilievich left the Horde;[3]
he was outwitted and caught in Serpukhov and brought to Moscow.
On the thirtieth day of the month of August, Tuesday, when the
holy martyr Felix is remembered,[4] before dinner at the fourth
hour of the day tysiatskii Ivan Vasilievich was executed. He was
beheaded by sword on Kuchkovo Field near the city of Moscow
on the order of Grand Prince Dmitrii Ivanovich. Great crowds
were present and many shed tears for him, saddened over his
honor and majesty: indeed, Satan scattered his evil nets from the
very beginning of time over many sons of man, and filled them
with treacherous pride and injustice, and taught them to fight
each other, to envy and not to obey authority. The Apostle said,
"It is not a man who commends himself who is accepted, but the
man whom the Lord commends." And, "Every man shall abide
in the state to which he is called." And, "Let all men, rulers, subjects, masters and slaves abide in humility and love. For to abide
in humility and love is to fulfill the whole law." And, "Love covereth
a multitude of sins." [I Peter 4:8]. And, "God is love; and he
that abideth in love abideth in God, and God abideth in him."
[I John 4:16]. And, "Love each other. Fear God. Honor the
king. Servants, obey in all things your masters according to the
flesh; not only those kind and gentle but also those who are over-
bearing." [John 3 and Col. 3: 22, rephrased.] In these words is
the true grace, and let through all this Christ Our God be glorified, to Whom be the glory forever and ever. Amen.

In the year 6888/1380. The Feast of the Annunciation fell
on Easter Day, and this occurred before—eighty-four years ago;

2. Arsk land: the land of the Finnic tribe of Ar, located between the
river Volga and the land of Viatka.

3. See the annual entries under 1375 and 1378 concerning Ivan
Vasilievich Veliaminov, the last Tysiatskii's son.

4. St. Felix is remembered on July 6, not August 30; but August 30,
6887, was nonetheless a Tuesday. *PSRL* XI, p. 45.

1380   and the Feast of the Annunciation will again be on Easter Day eighty years hence less one year.

The same year in Kolomna a stone church which had nearly been completed collapsed, and it had been built by Grand Prince Dmitrii Ivanovich.

The same year on the fifteenth day of the month of July the cathedral church of the Holy Trinity was consecrated at the city of Serpukhov, and it was erected by Prince Vladimir Andreevich, grandson of Ivan Kalita, great grandson of Danilo, gr. gr. grandson of Aleksandr [Nevskii], gr. gr. gr. grandson of Iaroslav, and his ancestor was Iurii Dolgorukii.

[THE VICTORY ON THE DON]
THE EDIFYING TALE OF THE MIRACLE WHICH OCCURRED WITH THE HELP OF GOD AND HIS MOST PURE MOTHER THEOTOKOS AND THANKS TO THE PRAYERS OF THEIR HOLY SERVANT AND WONDERWORKER METROPOLITAN PETER OF ALL RUSSIA, AND OF THE REVEREND WONDERWORKER ABBOT SERGIUS AND OF ALL THE SAINTS, WHEN GRAND PRINCE DMITRII IVANOVICH WITH HIS COUSIN, PRINCE VLADIMIR ANDREEVICH, AND ALL THE RUSSIAN PRINCES PUT PROUD LORD MAMAI TO SHAME ON THE RIVER DON, CHASED AWAY HIS VOLGA HORDES AND SLEW HIS HORDES, TOGETHER WITH ALL THEIR IMPURE FORCES.[5]

The impure and proud Mamai, Lord of the Volga Horde, ruled over the entire Horde, and he slew many lords and khans

---

5. One of the major events of Russian history, this first important victory over the Tatars in 1380 on the river Don became reflected in several literary and historical works. Probably the earliest—from the late fourteenth century—is the very poetic and most celebrated *Zadonshchina (The Happenings Beyond the Don)*, written by Sofoniia of Riazan' in the late fourteenth century. More popular, preserved in a larger number of copies, was *Povest' o Mamaievom poboishche*, which provides a more detailed description of the battle. Later this victory was mentioned in all other Russian chronicles of the time. The version in *Nik.* was written after 1520 by some sophisticated ecclesiastic editor of this chronicle. In most of those works the number of Russian troops is considerably exaggerated. In any case, it could not have been four hundred thousand, as is mentioned in most descriptions. Vernadsky, in his *History of Russia*, Vol. III, believes that there were about thirty thousand Russian troops. Cherepnin, in *Istoriia S.S.S.R.*, Vol. II, Moscow, 1966, p. 9, estimates that the Russians numbered between 100,000 and 200,000 warriors. Mamai's troops were of about the same size as the Russians'.

In the text of *Nik.*, Metropolitan Cyprian is mentioned on several occasions as a person who gives his blessing to Grand Prince Dmitrii to fight the infidels. This is obviously an error because Cyprian arrived

and he set up a khan according to his own will. He was, however, **1380**
in great confusion, and everybody distrusted him because he
killed many lords and nobles in his Horde. He even killed his
own khan, and although he had a khan, this khan of the Horde
was ruler in name only, for it was he, himself, who was ruler and

in Moscow only in May, 1381. (See the footnote under the annual
entry for 1378.) There was no metropolitan in Moscow at that time because the Patriarch of Constantinople had consecrated *three* bishops to
the same Metropolitan See, to the See of Kiev and all Russia, thus creat-
ing considerable confusion and angering Grand Prince Dmitrii. None
of these three was in Moscow in August-September, 1380. It is hard to
determine who ascribed to Metropolitan Cyprian an important role in
taking the decision to resist the Tatars, despite the fact that Cyprian was
not in Moscow at that time. As a matter of fact, the earliest report on
the battle of Kulikovo Pole as we find it in the *Suzdal'skaia letopis'*, *PSRL*,
V. I, Col. 536, and which probably is the oldest report on the battle, is
just over a hundred words in length. Thereafter a number of writers,
probably with the help of participants of the battles, expanded this version, and a large number of versions of this battle, including *Zadonshchina* and others appeared.

Cyprian, himself, was a writer and it is possible that he, himself,
in order to increase his prestige, added his name to the story of the
battle. In one of the earliest tales about the battle of Kulikovo Pol'ie in
the so-called *Skazanie*—which, in the opinion of literary historians, was
created in the early part of the first quarter of the fifteenth century—
Cyprian is only mentioned as a church leader who encouraged and
blessed Dmitrii Donskoi to fight the Tatars. (*Povesti o kulikovskoi bitve*,
Moscow, 1959, pp. 43-76; and *Istoriia russkoi literatury 10-ogo–17-ogo vv.*,
Moscow, 1980, pp. 231-240.) In *Moskovskaia letopis' 1493 goda*, *PSRL*,
Vol. XXVII, p. 251, Cyprian is also mentioned as being in Moscow in
1380. *Nik.*'s report of the battle is based largely on the *Skazanie*, which is
to some extgent fictionalized, especially as an exchange of messages and
speeches. (Kartashev, Vol. I, p. 331; Tikhomirov, M. N. and Dmitriev,
L. A., eds. *Povesti o Kulikovskoi bitve*, M., 1959, p. 346, 407, 410.) Another
important point to elucidate in *Nik.* is the role of Grand Prince Dmitrii
in opposing and fighting Mamai. According to the earlier XIV-XV
century text, he decided to go against the Tatars, led the army and defeated Mamai. Although his army had considerable casualties, he was
unwounded but his armour was badly damaged. Later chronicles, especially *Novg. Fifth Chron.*, which was one of *Nik.*'s sources, created a
different version of the battle, according to which, after the battle, Dmitrii was found unconscious. In view of Novgorod's inimical attitude toward Dmitrii, it is hardly astonishing that such a version was written.
Some Novgorodian authors even wrote that Novgorod sent troops to
help other Russians in the fight against Mamai, although no such troops
were ever sent.

1380   master of all. When he learned that the Tatars loved their khan he became afraid that the khan would assume the power from him. Therefore he killed him and all who were faithful to him and those who loved him.

He became wroth at Grand Prince Dmitrii Ivanovich and his cousin, Prince Vladimir Andreevich, and Prince Danilo of Pronsk because they defeated in the Riazan' land on the river Vozha his friend and favorites, his lords and his nobles. He grieved greatly and scratched his face and rent his garments, saying, "Woe is me! Woe is me! What have the Russian princes done to me? They have put me to shame and dishonored me. And they have exposed me to scorn and to ridicule. How can I escape this humiliation and dishonor?" He sorrowed greatly, weeping and mourning, and pondered what he should undertake. His advisors and councillors attempted to console him, saying, "Do you see, our great lord and still greater Khan? Your Horde has grown exhausted and its power is weakened. Yet you still possess untold wealth and very vast treasure. You can also hire the Franks, Circassians, Ossets and others, and thereby raise a great army and avenge the blood of your princes and nobles, your friends and favorites. Already, you have done thus to Prince Oleg of Riazan': you have burned all his cities and towns, you have devastated all his land, you have taken all his people into captivity; and this will you do likewise to Prince Dmitrii of Moscow."

The impure and proud Lord Mamai listened to his councillors and rejoiced greatly, pondering how to obtain great spoils. Over-proud, he elevated himself in his own mind with greatest arrogance, wishing to be a second Batu and to conquer the whole Russian land. He began to inquire concerning events of yore—how Khan Batu had conquered all the Russian land and had ruled over all the Russian princes, how he had prepared this. Inquiring and learning from everyone what had actually happened, he began in his madness to boast and brag, feeling himself superior to all. He likened himself in his mind to the ancient King Nebuchadnezzar of Babylonia, or to Titus, Emperor of Rome, who conquered Jerusalem, or to Khan Batu, who conquered the entire Russian land and all countries and commanded over all the nations and hordes: such thoughts did Mamai ponder in his madness. He cajoled and bribed everyone with gifts so that they would be with him and be ready to fight Russia, particularly Grand Prince Dmitrii Ivanovich of Moscow.

Because of his cajoling and gifts, Tatars from many lands   **1380**
flocked to him. He gave abundantly to all, and sent to many
countries, hiring Franks, Circassians, Ossets and many others.
He gathered a great army and marched against Grand Prince
Dmitrii Ivanovich, roaring like a lion and growling like a bear,
being proud as a demon. Crossing the river Volga with all his
forces, he came to the mouth of the river Voronezh, and there
he halted and roamed with his host. He had a great many troops,
and therefore he was no longer called by all who were with him
"Great Lord Mamai," but "Great Khan Mamai." His pride was
great and his ambitions were beyond all bounds.

At that time Prince Oleg of Riazan' learned that Mamai was
roaming on the river Voronezh within the confines of the land of
Riazan', with the intention of marching against Grand Prince
Dmitrii Ivanovich. And this Oleg, Prince of Riazan', sent his envoy
to the impure Khan Mamai with expressions of great honor and
with vast gifts, and he sent him a message, in which he wrote:

"To the Free Great Sovereign of the East, Khan of khans,
Mamai! Your vassal and liegeman, Oleg, Prince of Riazan' en-
treats you humbly. I have heard, my lord, that you want to go to
fight your servant, Prince Dmitrii of Moscow; and now, Most Illustrious Khan, the time has come: his gold and wealth are abundant.
This Prince Dmitrii is Christian: when he hears your name and
learns of your wrath, he will run away to distant places, either to
Great Novgorod or to the river Dvina,[6] and then all the wealth of
Moscow will be yours. Only have mercy upon me, your servant,
Prince Oleg of Riazan'. I also remind you, Khan, that although we
are both your servants, I still serve you in humility and obedience,
while he is proud and disobedient toward you. I, your liegeman,
have endured many offenses at the hands of this Prince Dmitrii.
And this, oh Khan, is not all. When, being offended by him, I
threatened him with your name of Khan, he paid me no heed and
even appropriated my city of Kolomna. Oh, my Khan, I pray and
bow to you concerning all of this to punish him for usurping what
belongs to others."

This Prince of Riazan' also sent to Grand Prince Iagailo Olgerdovich of Lithuania, telling him,

"Oh, Grand Prince Iagailo of Lithuania! I write to you with

6. At that time the northern Dvina river was beyond the northern
boundary of Moscow and its appanage princes.

1380 great joy. I know that for a long while you have intended to drive
out Prince Dmitrii of Moscow and to assume Moscow. Now, the
time has come because Great Khan Mamai is marching against him
with large forces: let us join him. I have sent him my envoy, render-
ing him honor and providing him with many gifts. You, likewise,
should send him your envoy, also, with honor and gifts; send him
your message, which you know how to write better than I."

Iagailo hearkened to this and was pleased, and praised and
thanked his friend, Oleg, Prince of Riazan', highly lauding him;
and he dispatched his envoy to Mamai with rich gifts and with
entreaties and petitions, and he wrote him:

"To the Free Great Sovereign of the East, Khan Mamai!   I,
Prince Iagailo of Lithuania, your liegeman, by your favour entreat
you humbly and bow to you! I have heard, my lord, that you want
to frighten your liegeland and your servant, Prince Dmitrii of
Moscow. Therefore I supplicate you, my Khan! I know what manner of great offense Prince Dmitrii of Moscow has caused your
servant, Prince Oleg of Riazan'. He likewise causes me many
abuses! Therefore we both entreat you, Most Illustrious Free
Khan, to punish him so that he cause no more injustice. When you,
yourself, Khan, come hither and view our meekness and his
arrogance, then you will see the difference between our meekness
and the rudeness of Grand Prince Dmitrii of Moscow."

But Prince Oleg of Riazan' and Iagailo of Lithuania thought
thus: "When Prince Dmitrii gets tidings of the name of the Khan
[and of his arrival], as well as of our allegiance to the latter, he
will flee from Moscow to some distant places, either to Novgorod
or to the river Dvina, and then we will ascend to the throne of
Moscow and Vladimir. When the Khan comes, we will meet him
with rich gifts and entreat him that he, the Khan, should return
to his land, while we, in accord with the Khan's will, will divide the
Principality of Muscovy into two: one part will go to Vilna
[Lithuania], the other to Riazan'. Then he [Mamai] will give to
us and to our descendants the charters that we might rule these
lands."

Thus did they think in their madness, forgetting what was
said: "If thou deviseth evil unto thy neighbor, it will befall thee,
too." And also, it was said, "Deviseth not evil unto thy neighbor
and diggeth not a pit for him lest God send thee a worse misfortune." [*Proberbs* 26:28]

The envoys of Oleg of Riazan' and of Iagailo of Lithuania **1380** went to Khan Mamai with gifts and letters; Khan Mamai received these gifts with gladness, had the letters read out to him and dismissed the envoys with honor.

He wrote thus to Iagailo, Prince of Lithuania and to Oleg of Riazan':

"If you seek the land of my liegeman, the land of Russia, I will grant all of it to you, my liegemen and vassals; but for the sake of my majesty, you have to give me a faithful pledge and meet me with all your forces, wheresoever that may be. I do not need your help because I want to conquer [the Russian land] with my own forces in the same manner as ancient Jerusalem was conquered by Nebuchadnezzar, King of Babylon, by Antioch, King of Antioch, and Titus, Emperor of Rome. Yet, for the sake of the offenses [which you have suffered from Dmitrii] and your honor, my majesty agrees to defend [deliver] you, my vassals, from violence and affronts. I will assuage your grief, provided you observe your oath and remain faithful allies. And then my liegeman, Prince Dmitrii of Moscow, will doubtless take fright at my mere name and will run off to distant and impassable places. Then, my vassals, your names, also, will be honored in those lands, while the honor of my name will be magnified. And the dread of my majesty will protect and rule my lands. I will not allow anyone to be offended without my majesty's permission. It is beneath the dignity of me, so great a Khan, to capture and defeat him on my account. In view of my majesty as great khan and my innumerable forces, with all my strong and couragous warriors, it behooves me not to defeat him just because he is no more than my vassal and my servant, and because he should fear me. It behooves me, however, to achieve victory in the same manner as great, powerful and glorious kings: as Alexander of Macedon, who defeated Darius, King of Persia, and Pore, King of India. Such a victory would be worthy of my majesty, and then my majesty will be glorified in all lands. Tell this for me to your princes [Oleg and Iagailo], who are my faithful vassals and my liegemen."

The envoys returned and reported all that they had been told by Mamai. And they, mad ones, rejoiced at this, Mamai's vain promise, not realizing that God gives power to whomsoever He wants, and forgetting what the Lord says: "For what shall a man be profited, if he shall gain the whole world, and forfeit his soul?"

1380   [Math. 16:26] For this life and kingdom are but transient, passing from generation to generation, from one land to another; and an evildoer will be tormented throughout the ages, for it availeth him not howbeit he gaineth the whole world. Thus were they deceived by their own madness, seeking wordly and passing prey in the manner of beasts.

Then Grand Prince Dmitrii Ivanovich in Moscow received the tidings: "Lord Mamai of the Volga Horde is no longer called 'Lord,' but 'Great and Powerful Khan,' and now he is as far as the river Voronezh, where his great forces roam, and intends to go against you, waging war." Therefore Grand Prince Dmitrii Ivanovich became greatly saddened and grieved, and he went to the cathedral church and fell tearfully before the icon of the Most Pure Theotokos, painted by Luke, the Evangelist. And he also venerated the grave of the great Wondermaker Peter, Metropolitan of all Russia, and he received a blessing from his spiritual father, Cyprian, Metropolitan of all Russia, whom he told of Mamai's invasion.

This same year Metropolitan Cyprian again came from Kiev to Moscow because he came first to Kiev, having, several years earlier during the life of [Metropolitan] Alexis, been consecrated in Constantinople to be Metropolitan of Russia. At that time he wrote to Grand Prince Dmitrii Ivanovich of Moscow, saying: "The Patriarch consecrated me Metropolitan of all Russia." The Grand Prince, however, responded to him, "We already have Metropolitan Alexis, and we will receive no other because of him." Then Cyprian sent letters to Novgorod and Pskov, and they answered him in the same manner. And so he lived in Kiev until the passing of the blessed Metropolitan Alexis.

After the passing of [Metropolitan] Alexis, Grand Prince Dmitrii wanted to see Mitiai, archimandrite of the monastery of the Saviour, on the Metropolitan See of Moscow; and this Mitiai was installed in the residence of the Metropolitan; then he went from Moscow to Constantinople, there to be consecrated Metropolitan by the Patriarch. He was bade an honorable farewell by the Grand Prince and his boiars; but shortly before arriving in Constantinople he passed away. Among those accompanying Mitiai was Pimen of Goritsa, Archimandrite of Pereiaslavl'. When he saw that Mitiai had passed away he schemed about the Metropolia of Russia, having in readiness all the means which had been sent with Mitiai. And so he succeeded in being consecrated by the **1380** Patriarch of Constantinople as Metropolitan of Russia. These tidings rapidly reached the Grand Prince of Moscow; but the Grand Prince did not want him and said, "I sent Pimen to serve Mitiai, not to become Metropolitan." So in the month of March he sent to Kiev his spiritual father, Theodore, Abbot of the Monastery of St. Simeon, for Metropolitan Cyprian, to render him great honor and to invite him to come to Moscow.

So Cyprian came to Moscow from Kiev on Thursday of the sixth week after Easter, on the holiday of the Ascension of Christ. Together with his children and his boiars and all people, the Grand Prince came out in state to meet him with great honor. Soon thereafter tidings came concerning the invasion by the accursed Mamai, and the Metropolitan told his spiritual son, "Determine exactly what is transpiring and gather troops, so as not to be taken unaware."[7]

And he, Dmitrii, assembled troops and a very large host, being united in great concord and great humility with all the Russian princes and with all the appanage princes under him. Then he sent unto his cousin, Grand Prince Mikhail Aleksandrovich of Tver', asking for help, and the latter rapidly sent him his own forces under his cousin, Prince Ivan Vsevolodich Kholmskii, grandson of Aleksandr, great grandson of Mikhail, gr. gr. grandson of Iaroslav Iaroslavich. He, Dmitrii, also sent for his cousin, Prince Vladimir Andreevich, who at that time was in his patrimony in Borovsk and who straightaway came to Moscow, to the Grand Prince. Then there came new tidings that Mamai, full of wrath, verily was moving in great force.

The Grand Prince was saddened, grieved greatly and, in his bedchamber, approached the icon of Our Lord which hung at the head of his couch. He prayed, saying,

"Our most Merciful and Manloving Lord and Master, God, Jesus Christ! I, Thy servant and wretched sinner, dare to pray to Thee in my grief! For upon Thee, O Merciful Lord and God, do I cast my sorrow! Do not unto us as Thou didst unto our forefathers when Thou broughtest upon them wicked Batu! O Lord, since those days have fear and trembling been with us! And do not,

---

7. As mentioned before, Cyprian came to Moscow on his own initiative but was immediately requested by Grand Prince Dmitrii to depart.

1380   oh Lord, once again raise Thy wrath against us to the end! I am aware, My Lord, that because of me Thou mayest wish to lay waste our entire land. Verily, I have sinned against Thee more than any other man! But grant me Thy mercy, My Lord, for the sake of my tears!"

Praying thus, he departed from his bedchamber, taking with him his cousin, Vladimir Andreevich, and went to his spiritual father, Cyprian, Metropolitan of all Russia, whom he told, "It is true, my father, that the impure Mamai is wrathful and is marching against us with a great host." The Metropolitan comforted and encouraged him, saying, "Do not worry about this, my lord and beloved son. Many are the afflictions of the righteous but the lord delivers him from them. And it is said: The Lord has chastised me sorely; but He has not given me over to death. And God is our refuge and strength, and well-proved help in trouble. Tell me, my son, the truth: in what does your guilt consist toward him [Mamai]?" The Grand Prince replied, "I have examined myself in all strictness, my father, but I am not guilty in anything toward him. I pay him according to the agreement confirmed with him; but I am guilty in nought toward him."

While they spake thus, the Tatars, Mamai's envoys, came unexpectedly to Moscow, to Grand Prince Dmitrii, demanding the same tribute from him as used to be paid in the time of Uzbeg and Uzbeg's son, Dzhanibeg, but contrary to the [last] agreement concluded between them [between Dmitrii and Mamai]. The Grand Prince paid him according to the agreement but Mamai wanted the same tribute as had been paid under the khans of old. The Grand Prince, however, did not want to pay that much. Mamai's envoys spoke insolently and said that Mamai was encamped in great strength in the prairie beyond the river Don.

The Grand Prince related all this to his spiritual father, Cyprian, Metropolitan of Russia, and the latter said,

"Do you see, my beloved lord and son in God? By God's will and because of our sins he is marching to capture our land; but you, Orthodox princes, should satisfy this infidel with four times greater tribute so that he become quiet, meek and humble. If he will not, however, become appeased and satisfied, Lord God will subdue him. It is said in the Scriptures, 'The Lord resisteth the proud but giveth His grace to the humble.' [James 4:6]. And so it happened to Basil the Great of Caesaria.[8] When the evil **1380** apostate, Emperor Julian, marched against the Persians and wanted on his way to destroy his city of Caesaria and put all its people to the sword, then Great Basil prayed to God together with all the Christians there, collected much gold and went to give it to Emperor Julian in order to assuage his fury. Seeing Julian's proud heart, however, God sent His holy warrior, St. Mercurius, against him, ordering him to put him to a cruel death. And so the accursed Emperor Julian was killed by the power of God. For thus did Our Lord command Christians to act with humble wisdom, for it is said in the Gospel, 'Be wise as serpents and harmless as doves.' [Math. 10:16] The serpent's wisdom is the following: when it falls into a snare and is beaten and struck by someone, then it turns its body to the blows and wounds, but with all its power it protects its head. And so should the Christian do, in the Name of Christ. When a Christian is pursued, injured, beaten, tortured, he yields up everything he has: gold, silver, wealth, honor and power; and in extremity he even permits his body to be wounded, but he still protects his head because Christ is there, and the Christian faith is there, and one can be saved for the sake of love for Him and for His faith. And the Lord wisely commanded how to deal and to act: when your persecutor requires your wealth, property, gold and silver, give it him; and when he wants your honor and glory, give them up to him. But when he would deprive you of your faith, resist firmly and protect it with utmost care. And so, my lord, collect as much gold and silver as you can, send it to him, try to justify yourself before him and appease his fury."[9]

Grand Prince Dmitrii Ivanovich listened to his spiritual father, Metropolitan Cyprian of all Russia, and, heeding his advice, dispatched his envoy, chosen for this purpose, whose name was Zakharii Tiutchev, giving him two interpreters who knew the Tatar tongue and providing them with much gold and silver, and he sent him to Khan Mamai. Arriving in the Riazan' land, this

8. St. Basil the Great, 330-379, Bishop of Caesaria in Asia Minor, was one of the leading early Church Fathers.

9. This is a fictionalized later interpolation. As mentioned earlier, Cyprian was not even in Moscow in 1380.

1380 envoy received the tidings that Oleg, Prince of Riazan,' and Iagailo, Prince of Lithuania, had become allies of Khan Mamai, and therefore he secretly dispatched a fast runner to the Grand Prince in Moscow.

When the Grand Prince learned of this, he grew sad and grieved greatly. Taking his cousin, Prince Vladimir Andreevich, he went to his spiritual father, Cyprian, Metropolitan of all Russia, and told him that Iagailo, Prince of Lithuania, and Oleg, Prince of Riazan', had become Mamai's allies against us. But the Metropolitan told him, "My beloved lord and son in Christ! What manner of affront have you caused them?" Grand Prince Dmitrii Ivanovich shed tears and said, "My father, I have sinned and I am not worthy even to live. But as far as they are concerned, I have not trespassed in any way the agreements made by our fathers; and you should know, my father, that I am satisfied with the confines of my dominion and do not seek the land of anyone else. I did not cause them any offense and I do not know why they have risen against me."

The Metropolitan told him, "If this is so, then do not grieve or worry. Our Lord is your Protector and Helper because the Lord loves the truth and the Lord acts according to the truth, and the truth protects from death. Do not behave unwisely, so that they not attack you unaware. But gather troops from all parts of the land in meekness, humility and love, and ask all men to assemble, and the army will grow. Thus you will not resist him only with humility, but with strength, besides; you may frighten him, and then you will defeat and instill with fear all those who are against you."

The Grand Prince sent his envoys to all the principalities in humility and meekness, gathering all the men into the army; and he set aside his grief and his sadness of heart, casting them before God and His Most Pure Mother, and the holy wonder-worker Peter, and all the Saints. For God does as He wants, and who can resist the Lord's will? It behooves us to ask for the remission of our sins and for His mercy, and He will do all that is needed for our salvation. And so the Grand Prince distributed alms to all the monasteries, churches, pilgrims and poor, and soon calm spread throughout the land.

When, once, the Grand Prince with his cousin, Prince Vladimir

Andreevich, and with all the princes and voevodas assembled **1380**
there, were banqueting at the house of Mikula Vasilievich, there
came the tidings that Mamai wanted to march without delay
against Grand Prince Dmitrii Ivanovich. Then he and his cousin,
Prince Vladimir Andreevich, together with his other princes and
voevodas, took counsel and determined to send into the prairie
a strong reconnoitering party. He sent thither with this avant
guard his tried men-at-arms, Rodion of Rzhev, Andrei Volosatyi,
Vasilii Tupik, and other staunch and courageous men. He commanded them to take with all precautions a position on the Bystr-
aia or Tikhaia Sosna rivers, and ordered them to draw near the
Horde and catch a Tatar prisoner who might provide some word
as to the true intention of Mamai.

Grand Prince Dmitrii Ivanovich, himself, at the same time
sent fast runners with messages to all the principalities, asking
everyone to be prepared to come to the onset against the Tatars,
and that all should assemble in Kolomna on the thirty-first day
of the month of July, when the just St. Eudocimus is remembered;
while he, himself, began to arm and prepare those princes who
had come by that time. And they gathered a large army.

But no new tidings were forthcoming because those scouts
sent into the prairie stood still; and there was no word from them.
Then the Grand Prince sent other scouts into the prairie: Kliment
Polenin, Ivan, the son of Sviatoslav, Grigorii Sudok and others
with them, instructing them to return soon. But they encountered
Vasilii Tupik, who was conducting a Tatar prisoner to the Grand
Prince. This one avouched that the Khan, verily, was moving
to the attack against Russia and had made an alliance with Oleg,
Prince of Riazan', and with Iagailo, Prince of Lithuania; and that
the Khan was in no haste but was abiding until autumn, when the
Lithuanians were to join him.

So Grand Prince Dmitrii Ivanovich learned exactly that Lord
Mamai was, indeed, marching with large forces, and he hastened
to encourage and embolden his cousin, Prince Vladimir Andreevich, and the other princes, boiars and voevodas so that they
might be firm and bold confronting the Tatars. In one voice,
they all exclaimed, "We are ready to endure, in the name of Christ,
for the Christian faith, and [to avenge] your offenses!" And he
commanded that all men be in Kolomna on the fifteenth day of

1380 the month of August, the feast of the Dormition of the Most Pure
Theotokos, and that it would there be determined who should be
the voevoda of what regiment.

Very many [men-at-arms] came to Moscow to the Grand
Prince from all lands [of Russia]. There came the princes of
Belozersk, strong and valiant in battle; and, with their troops,
there came Prince Fedor Semionovich, Prince Semion Mikhailovich, Prince Andrei of Kem', Prince Gleb of Kargopol and
Tsydon'; there came the princes of Andom; and, also, there came
the princes of Iaroslavl', with all their forces: Prince Andrei and
Prince Roman Prozorovskii, Prince Lev Kurbskii, Prince Dmitrii
of Rostov, the princes of Ust-Iug, and many other princes and
voevodas with large forces.

The Grand Prince decided to visit the monastery of the Lifegiving Trinity, [where abode] the reverend Abbot Sergius; and
receiving the blessing of his spiritual father, Cyprian, Metropolitan of Russia, he went thither and came to the monastery on the
eighteenth day of the month of August, when the martyrs, St.
Florus and St. Laurus, are remembered. He wanted to return
quickly because more tidings were arriving forthwith telling of
Mamai's invasion; but reverend Father Sergius persuaded him to
break bread in his refectory, and he said, "May Lord God and the
Most Pure Theotokos give you help. The time has not yet come
for you to receive the crown of victory in eternal rest, but numberless eternal crowns of death's repose are being prepared for
others." Then he ordered that holy water be brought, and when
they arose from table in the refectory he blessed [the Grand
Prince] and sprinkled him with the holy water, saying, "Render
gifts and pay homage unto the impure Mamai so that God sees
your meekness, and then He will exalt you and He will defeat
Mamai's untamed ferocity and pride." And the Prince said, "All
this I have already done unto him, my father, but he only magnifies
himself with even greater pride." The reverend Father Sergius
said, "If so, then final defeat anad devastation shall be his doom,
while you will be bestowed with mercy, help and glory from Lord
God, His Most Pure Theotokos and His Saints."

The Grand Prince bethought himself to ask that Peresvet
and Osliabia be given to him because they were very stalwart and
skilled at commanding regiments. And he said, "Father, give
me the two warriors of your monastic host, the two brethren,

Peresvet and Osliabia. For these two are renowned to all as great   **1380**
warriors and valorous fighters [bogatyri], skillful in the arts of
war and weaponry."

The reverend Sergius ordered them to prepare in all haste
for military deeds and they, with all their hearts, obeyed the
reverend Sergius because they never disobeyed his injunctions.
In place of their perishable armour, he provided them with an
imperishable one: the cross of Christ, which was emblazoned on
their schemas,[10] and he ordered them to wear these on their heads
instead of helmets, and to fight staunchly for Christ against His
enemy. And, transmitting them to Grand Prince Dmitrii Ivanovich, he said, "My Prince! Here are my men-at-arms, whom you
requested. I have instructed them to be with you in all possible
danger in this tumultuous and trying time." He added, "Peace
be with you, my beloved brethren in Christ, Peresvet and Osliabia!
Behave as courageous warriors of Christ, for the time of your
action has come!" And he blessed them with the Cross and sprinkled the Grand Prince and these two monks of his, Peresvet and
Osliabia, with holy water, as well as all the princes, boiars and
voevodas, telling the Grand Prince, "God will be Your Protector
and Helper and He will vanquish and put down your enemy, and
will glorify you." The Grand Prince received a blessing from the
reverend abbot, and his heart rejoiced because the reverend
Sergius told him, "God will be Your Protector and Help, and He
will defeat your enemies and exalt you." Bearing this in his mind
as a treasure unknown to anyone, and concerning which he spoke
no word to anyone, the Grand Prince went to the city of Moscow
and received a blessing from his spiritual father, Cyprian, Metropolitan of Russia, telling only him what had been said by the reverend Sergius. The Metropolitan said, "Tell no one of this until
God provides you with His blessing."

The Grand Prince quickly concluded his preparations, went
to the cathedral church and prostrated himself before the image
of the Most Pure Theotokos, which had been painted by the Evangelist Luke, asking for Her aid against the enemy. Then he went
to the grave of holy wonderworker Peter, falling before it with
tears, and prayed also for his aid and protection against the ad-

10. In this case, *"schema"* denotes the monastic cowl, which, in form,
resembles a helmet.

1380 versaries and for the defeat of their pride and of their ferocity. Having prayed thus, he returned to his spiritual father, Cyprian, Metropolitan of all Russia, asking for absolution and for his blessing. The Metropolitan gave him absolution, blessed and crossed him with the Holy Cross and sprinkled him with holy water. Also, he sent many priests and deacons with holy crosses and with holy water to the gates of St. Nicholas, St. Florus, and Sts. Constantine and Helen[11] to bless everyone so that each warrior would be blessed by them and would be sprinkled with the holy water. In the meantime the Grand Prince went to the holy church of St. Michael the Archistrategus, crossed himself before the icons, prayed at the graves of his parents, took leave of them and crossed himself.

He departed from the church, mounted his horse and rode to Kolomna; he sent his cousin, Prince Vladimir Andreevich, by the Brashev road, and he sent the princes of Belozero with their warriors by the Bolvanovka road. The Grand Prince, himself, took the road to Kotel with large forces. Before him the sun warmed them, while from behind, a gentle, still refreshing breeze fanned them. The troops were divided among these routes because they could not all get into the same one. The Grand Prince took with him as eyewitnesses ten important merchants of Surozh because of their knowledge. Whatever God should want to occur, they would be able to speak of it in far distant lands because they travel from one land to another and they know everyone in the Hordes and in the Frankish lands. There was also another reason for this. In the case something might be needed, they would be able to do as was their habit.[12] Their names were Vasilii Kapitsa, Sidor Elferiev, Konstantin, Kuz'ma Kaveria, Semion Antonov,

11. St. Constantine and St. Helen: Constantine the Great, 285-337, emperor of Rome and founder of the city of Constantinople, in 311 A.D. proclaimed Christianity as one of the major religions of that empire and terminated the persecution of Christians. He became Christian, himself, before his death. His mother, Helen, a Celtic Brittanic princess, according to Christian tradition found the Cross on which Christ was crucified. Both are considered equal to the Apostles.

12. Surozh: Now, Sudak, in the Crimea, Surozh was another important trade center with Byzantium, the Near East and the Mediterranean lands. In the last sentence there is probably a reference to the financial power of these merchants of Surozh.

Mikhail Salarev, Timofei Vesiakov, Dmitrii Chernoi, Dementii   **1380**
Salarev and Ivan Shikh.

The Grand Prince arrived in Kolomna on Saturday, the twenty-eighth day of the month of August, when our reverend Father Moses, the Ethiopian Moor, is remembered. Before the Grand Prince's arrival many voevodas had already gathered there, and they met the Grand Prince on the Severka river, while Bishop Gerasimus of Kolomna welcomed him with [a procession of] crosses at the city gate.

The Grand Prince ordered that on the morrow, Sunday, early in the morning, all the princes, boiars and voevodas should ride into the field, and he appointed voevodas to each force. The Grand Prince, himself, took into his force the princes of Belozersk with their warriors, who were highly daring and valiant. To the right-hand force he assigned his cousin, Vladimir Andreevich, and gave him the troops of the princes of Iaroslavl', with their warriors. To the left-hand force he assigned Prince Gleb of Briansk. In the vanguard he assigned Dmitrii, son of Vsevolod, and Vladimir, also son of Vsevolod. Mikula Vasilievich was assigned to be voevoda of the troops of Kolomna; Timofei Voluevich, to the troops of Vladimir and Iur'iev; Ivan Rodionovich Kvashnia, to be voevoda of the troops of Kostroma; Andrei Serkizovich, to those of Pereiaslavl'. Under Prince Vladimir Andreevich, the voevodas were Danilo Belous, Konstantin Kanonovich, Prince Fedor of Elets, Prince Iurii of Meshchera, and Prince Andrei of Murom.

Having assigned [thus] the regiments, the Grand Prince entered the church, prayed to the Lord, Our God, to the Most Pure Theotokos and to all the saints, and received a blessing from Gerasimus, Bishop of Kolomna, after asking him, "Father, give me the blessing to go against the Tatars." Gerasimus, Bishop of Kolomna, blessed him and his entire host to wage war against the impure Tatars.

The Grand Prince marched from Kolomna with large forces and, arriving, he camped at the mouth of the Lopasna river, where it flows into the Oka. There came to him his chief voevoda, Timofei Vasilievich, grandson of tysiatskii Vasilii Veliaminov, with many troops which had remained in Moscow.[13]

13. Apparently, the treason of Ivan Vasilievich Veliaminov—see

1380   Then he hearkened to the tidings and ordered them to cross the river Oka by boats. Warning each detachment, he enjoined them, "As you march through the Riazan' land let none lay hand on anything or take anything from anyone, or touch so much as a hair." In Moscow he left his voevoda, Fedor Andreevich, to remain there and care for his spiritual father, Cyprian, Metropolitan of all Russia, with his wife, Grand Princess Evdokiia, and with his sons, Vasilii and Iurii. On Sunday all his host crossed the river Oka; on the morrow, Monday, he crossed it, himself; but he was concerned because he had not enough footmen. Therefore he left his chief voevoda, tysiatskii Timofei Vasilievich, at Lopasna, commanding him that when some foot or horse troops would arrive, he should lead them forthwith to join him, and that none of these troops crossing the Riazan' land should touch anything or take anything from anyone. Then he commanded that his forces be counted [so as to learn] how many there were [in his host], and there were over two hundred thousand of them.[14]

When, in Moscow, the Metropolitan, Grand Princess Evdokia and the inhabitants of all the cities, and all the people heard that the Grand Prince with all the princes and with the entire host had crossed the Oka river into the Riazan' land and had marched to battle, everyone began to worry and fret, asking with tears, "Why has he gone beyond the Oka? Even if he is spared by God's grace, still many of his poor warriors will perish." Everyone grieved at this, shedding tears disconsolately.

As soon as Prince Oleg of Riazan' learned that Grand Prince Dmitrii Ivanovich of Moscow had crossed the river Oka and was marching with all his forces against Mamai, he became alarmed and said, "What is he doing and wherefrom could he amass such forces? We hoped that he would flee into outlying places—to Great Novgorod or toward the river Dvina. And now he is marching against such a powerful Khan! But how can I give tidings to my friend, Grand Prince Iagailo Olgerdovich of Lithuania? They [the commanders of Dmitrii's army] will not allow us to communicate because they have occupied all the routes." And his boiars

the end of the annual entry under 6887—did not undermine the position of the rest of the Veliaminov family.

14. The number of Russian soldiers has been exaggerated, even by chroniclers contemporary to this battle, as well as later. See the comments in the introduction to this tale, and Fn. 5.

and lords told him, "Our lord! We heard this fifteen days ago **1380** but we feared to tell you. It is said that in his dominion there is a monk by the name of Sergius who has the gift of prophecy from God, and this monk has armed him and commanded him to march against Mamai." Grand Prince Oleg of Riazan', hearing this, took fright and trembled greatly. He asked, "Why did you not tell me of this before? I would have gone to beseech impure Khan Mamai not to do any harm to anyone. [Now] I will have no way either to bring people to my land or to return the dead to life, or to get back the captives. Whatever happens, it will be according to God's judgment. As God wills, so will it come to pass. Now I have ruined my soul: with whom have I to keep alliance? If I remain with Mamai, I will perish because he is godless and heathen. It will be the same if I join Iagailo Olgerdovich. But let God's will be done. My allegiance will be to him, whomsoever Lord God, the Most Pure Theotokos and all the saints aid!"

As he had promised before, Grand Prince Iagailo of Lithuania assembled a large force of Lithuanians, Varangians and Zhemat', and others, and marched to the aid of Khan Mamai.[15] When he reached Odoev, he halted there to obtain the news; hearing that Oleg, Prince of Riazan', had taken fright and trembled greatly, he, himself, began to grieve and grew sad, saying, "In vain did I become persuaded by my friend, Oleg of Riazan'. Why did I trust him? Lithuania has never been advised by Riazan', and how did I enter into such madness?" He decided to wait to learn what would occur between Mamai and [the Prince of] Moscow.

In the year 6889/1381.[16] In the month of September Grand Prince Dmitrii Ivanovich came to a place called Berezui, twenty

15. In this case, "the Lithuanians" are western Russians, who formed by far the largest part of the population of Lithuania, and whose language till the end of the seventeenth century was the state language of the Grand Duchy of Lithuania. The Varangians were mercenary soldiers in Lithuanian service. The Zhemat', also Zhmud' or Semigalians, are ethnic Lithuanians who, with the original Prussians and Latvians, formed the Letto-Baltic group of Indo-European languages.

16. The year 6889, according to the Byzantine calendar and chronology, began on September 1. Thus, according to the contemporary Russian and Western calendar, it was still the year 1380 until December 31.

1381 and three *poprishche* before the river Don.[17] There, two Lithuanian princes came to do him homage and to serve him: Prince
Andrei Olgerdovich of Polotsk with the men-at-arms of Pskov,
and his brother, Prince Dmitrii Olgerdovich of Briansk with his
troops. These princes greatly aided Grand Prince Dmitrii Ivanovich for the sake of God.[18] Then the Grand Prince sent into the
prairie toward Mamai's Horde his chosen boiar and staunch
voevoda, Semion Melik, and with him the following of his chosen
men: Ignatii Krenia, Foma Tyrnin, Petr Gorskii, Karp Aleksandrov, Petr Chirikov, and many other outstanding and courageous
men and scouts. They were trained for this purpose, and their
task was to locate the Tatar outposts and send tidings rapidly.
From this place the Grand Prince moved quietly toward the Don,
gathering reports, when, suddenly, two of his scouts, Petr Gorski
and Karp Aleksandrov, came to him with a Tatar prisoner who
was well informed about the Khan's court because he was one of
the Khan's courtiers.

This prisoner told the following: "Now the Khan is at Kuz'ma
Barrage. He is not in a hurry but awaits Oleg, Prince of Riazan',
and Prince Iagailo Olgerdovich of Lithuania. He does not know
that prince Dmitrii of Moscow has amassed a host and he does not
expect to encounter him, according to the long written missives[19]
of Oleg of Riazan'. In three days hence he must be on the Don
river." And they inquired of him concerning Mamai's forces—
how large they were—and he responded, "There is a numberless
multitude of them."

Then Grand Prince Dmitrii Ivanovich summoned his cousin,
Prince Vladimir Andreevich, and all the princes, voevodas and
magnates, and held council with them: "What should we do? How
should we plan the battle against those godless Tatars? On this
side of the Don, or should we cross to the other bank of the Don?
For all of us the day and hour are approaching." And they spoke
at length of this, and spent much time on it, and all grieved greatly.

---

17. *Poprishche*: an Old Russian unit of distance, roughly one *versta*,
or about two-thirds of a mile, according to Cherepnin, *Russkaia metro-
logiia*. In the nineteenth century, however, according to Dal', *Tolkovyi
Slovar'*, a *poprishche* is about twenty versts, one day's travel.

18. See the campaign against Lithuania, year 1379.

19. *Knigi* —books.

Then more footmen and people from the neighboring regions **1381**
came, and merchants from various lands and cities. It was awesome to see what a great number of people had gathered for the
march into the prairie against the Tatars. They began to count
their number, and counted more than four hundred thousand,
both horse- and footmen.[20] Then the Lithuanian princes, Prince
Andrei and Prince Dmitrii, the sons of Olgerd, brothers of Iagailo
Olgerdovich of Lithuania, arose and said, "If we remain here, the
Russian host will be weak; but if we cross to the other side of the
Don we will be strong and courageous. For everyone will give up
all thought for his life and will be prepared to die, which may
happen from hour to hour. If we overcome the Tatars, there will
be great glory to you and to us all; but if we are vanquished by
them, we will die together, sharing a common death. And let us
not be frightened at their great forces. God is not with the strong
but with the just, and on whomsoever He bestows His mercy, him
will He help."

The many messengers approached, announcing the Tatars'
advance. Grand Prince Dmitrii Ivanovich strengthened his heart
with the Name of Christ, prayed to Lord God and to the Most
Pure Theotokos, to the great wonderworker Peter and to all the
saints, and he addressed all present courageously. "Brethren! An
honorable death is better than an evil life! It would be better not
to march at all against these godless ones than, having come, to
achieve nothing and then retreat. So let us today cross the river
Don and then sacrifice our heads there for the sake of the holy
Orthodox churches, for the Orthodox faith, for our brethren and
for Christianity!" And so he commanded all his troops to build
bridges over the Don and to don their armour for precaution.
And they crossed the Don; having crossed over it, they destroyed
the bridges [behind them, so as to cut off all retreat].

Through the night the wolves howled frightfully, and ravens
and eagles croaked and screeched day and night in anticipation
of the dreadful day of bloodletting which would arrive by God's
will: as it is said, "Wheresoever should lie a corpse, there would
eagles gather together." The valiant hearts of these courageous
warriors grew stronger and bolder, while some weak and timorous

20. About the size of the Russian army, see the footnotes at the beginning of this tale.

1381 ones became apprehensive and morose, seeing death before their eyes.

Then came the night before the holiday of the Nativity of the Most Pure Theotokos[21]. That year the fall was very long, the days were sunny, bright and warm; and the night, itself, was also warm and still.

Together with both Lithuanian princes, there came an outstanding voevoda, a cunning and bold army commander by the name of Dmitrii Bobrok, who was a native of the Volynian land and was widely known; and [his enemies] feared him for his valour. He approached the Grand Prince and said, "If you want, I will show you the omens when it is deep night and thus you will learn beforehand what will happen later." The Grand Prince ordered him to tell nothing of this to anyone, and when it was dark and the night was well advanced, Dmitrii Bobrok, the Volynian, mounted his horse, took the Grand Prince with him, and they rode out into Kulikovo Prairie ["Prairie of Snipes"], where they halted between the two hosts. Then they turned toward the Tatar army, from whence they heard clamor and great commotion like the noise of carts rolling from market or like the building of a fortress, and trumpets blared. But behind them wolves howled horribly. On the right side where the river Nepriadva was there was a loud noise of birds shrieking and beating their wings, of crows croaking and eagles screaming. It was terrible because it seemed that already among the birds there was battling and fighting, which foretold bloodshed and the death of many men. The Volynian asked the Grand Prince, "What did you hear there?" And the Grand Pprince replied, "I hear [that they are seized by] fear and ominous foreboding." Then Dmitrii Bobrok, the Volynian, said, "Prince, turn toward the Russian host." And he turned: there it was very quiet. Then Dmitrii, the Volynian, asked, "What did you hear there, my lord Prince?" And the Grand Prince replied, "Nothing. It only looks like dawn from the multitude of the campfires."

Then Dmitrii Bobrok, the Volynian, added, "My lord Prince! Thank God and the Most Pure Theotokos, and great wonder-worker Peter and all the saints! These lights are good portents.

---

21. September eighth. According to the contemporary calendar, it was still 1380.

Appeal to Lord God and pray to Him frequently, and do not **1381**
abandon your Faith in Him, in the Most Pure Theotokos and in
your shepherd, the great man of prayer and wonderworker Peter.
All these omens are good; but there is yet another omen."

He dismounted his horse, fell onto his right ear, pressed it
to the ground, listened to the earth and, after remaining thus for
a long while, stood up, his head hanging. The Grand Prince
asked him, "What is it, brother Dmitrii? Tell me." Dmitrii did
not want to tell him and forebare at length from speaking; but the
Grand Prince again insisted, asking him to speak. The other shed
tears. Seeing his tears, the Grand Prince became afraid and importuned him, "Brother Dmitrii, tell me, for my heart pains me
greatly."

Dmitrii [Bobrok] began to console him and replied,

"Grand Prince! I will tell you—but only you. Do not reveal
it to anyone. There are two portents: one foretokens great joy
for you, and the other, great grief. When I put my ear to the earth,
then I discerned that the earth weeps twice. Both sounds are
fearsome and terrifying. From this side it sounds as though a
woman were weeping, wailing and shrieking in the Tatar tongue
about her children—tremulously, lamentingly, as if shedding
torrents of tears. On the other side of the ground it sounds as
though a maiden were weeping and wailing with the voice of a
mournful flute, as if she were greatly grieved and saddened. I
have experienced many battles and discerned many augurings
in many fights, and they are known to me and are clear. Rely upon
divine mercy. You will defeat the Tatars, but many from your
Christian army will fall at sword's edge."

When Grand Prince Dmitrii Ivanovich heard these words
he wept and shed tears at great length, saying, "The will of God
be done. It will happen according to the Lord's will. Who can
resist His will?" Then Dmitri Bobrok, the Volynian, said, "Lord
Prince! It is unmeet that you should mention this to anyone in
your host, so that they do not grieve or become sad at heart. Appeal, however, to Lord God for help, with faith and humility,
to the Most Pure Theotokos, to great Wonderworker Peter and
to all the saints, and arm yourself with the Lifegiving Cross of
Christ because That is His mightiest invincible armour against
visible and invisible enemies."

The wolves howled terrifyingly all night and their multitude

1381 was such as if they had gathered together from the entire universe; the ravens croaked and cawed and the eagles screeched direly throughout the night. The same night a certain man named Foma Katsybei, who once used to be a highwayman but then repented and who was very strong and bold, had a vision. He had been chosen by the Grand Prince to guard the outpost on the river Chiura Mikhailova and to take close heed of the Tatars. To strengthen his faith God had sent him a vision that same night: he saw in the sky, coming from the east, a large host; and then, suddenly, two radiant youths came against this host from the south, both in arms, and they began to flay this host, exclaiming, "Who commanded you to destroy our fathers' land?"[22] And they killed some, and chased the others away.

The same night Vasilii Kapitsa and Semion Antonov also saw a vision. In the field they saw a multitude of Ethiopians[23] advancing in great force, some on chariots, some on horseback, and it was awesome to view them. Then, suddenly, St. Peter, Holy Metropolitan of all Russia, appeared holding a golden staff and he moved against them fiercely, asking, "Why have you come to destroy my flock which the Lord entrusted to me?" Then he flayed them with his staff and they ran away: some escaped, others drowned in the waters, and some fell, wounded.

All of them imparted these visions to Grand Prince Dmitrii Ivanovich, who told them not to reveal these visions to anyone; and he prayed tearfully to Lord God, to the Most Pure Theotokos, to the great Wonderworker Peter, patron of the Russian land, and to the holy martyrs, Boris and Gleb, asking them to protect the Russians from the Tatars' ferocity so that these dogs would not defile holy places or Tatar swords kill Orthodox Christians.

And that night, toward dawn—the eighth day of the month of September, the holiday of the Nativity of the Most Pure Theotokos —when the sun began to rise, thick fog still hung over the entire land and it was dark, and so it remained till the third hour of the day,[24] and then it began to lift. The Grand Prince sent his cousin,

---

22. This was a vision of the holy passion martyrs, saintly Princes Boris and Gleb.

23. "Ethiopians" here denote just darkskinned people.

24. "Third hour of the day"—that is, the third hour after sunrise, sunrise being considered the beginning of the day.

Prince Vladimir Andreevich, upstream on the Don into an oak **1381** forest with troops, to lie there in ambush, and he gave him the chosen and foremost men from his own personal guard. He also sent with him the renowned voevoda, Dmitrii Bobrok, the Volynian, and this voevoda Dmitrii prepared these troops for the battle.

The entire Christian host readied itself for battle; everyone donned his armour and the host took a position on the Kulikovo Prairie at the mouth of the river Nepriadva. The Tatar troops marched from the hill down the slope. The Christian forces also marched downhill and took a position in the open field on firm ground. The Grand Prince changed his horse frequently and rode alongside the troops, speaking to them with tears, saying, "My beloved fathers and brethren! For the sake of the Lord and the Most Pure Theotokos, and for the sake of your own salvation, stand firm for the Christian faith and for our brethren. For all of us, from the small to the great, are brothers, the same grandchildren of Adam; we are of the same tongue and nation. We are of the same baptism, of the same Christian faith; we have but One God, Our Lord, Jesus Christ, Who is glorified in the Trinity. Let us die now for His Holy Name, for the Orthodox faith and the holy churches, for our brethren, for all Orthodox Christendom!" Hearing this, everyone shed tears and took heart, becoming as courageous as the soaring eagles, and roared like lions against the Tatar hosts.

Having thus encouraged them, the Grand prince raised his black banner,[25] dismounted, took off his royal mantle and, summoning Mikhail Andreevich Brenk, his favorite man, whom he loved more than any other, commanded him to mount his horse and don his royal mantle, with all the royal badges. Then he commanded his guard to carry his black banner over Mikhail Andreevich Brenk. He took up the holy cross, on which was represented the Passion of Christ and which contained a particle of [wood from] His Lifegiving Cross[26] and, shedding tears, he proclaimed, "In Thee do I put my trust, Christ-God! By the power of Thy

25. He bore a black banner which apparently was emblazoned with an icon of Jesus Christ.

26. According to Orthodox tradition Empress Helen, mother of Emperor Constantine, recovered in Jerusalem the Cross on which Christ was crucified, and a piece of it was inlaid on Grand Prince Dmitrii's cross.

1381 Cross, give us the victory over our enemies, as Thou gavest it to Emperor Constantine in the days of old."

At that time messengers from Abbot Sergius of Radonezh approached him bearing the latter's blessing and missive, wherein was written, "May Lord God and the Most Pure Theotokos, and holy Wonderworker Peter be your helpers!" He also sent him liturgic bread consecrated [on the occasion of the feast] of the Most Pure Theotokos.

The Grand Prince partook of this holy bread and stretched out his arms, exclaiming loudly, "Great is the Name of the Most Holy Trinity! Most Holy Lady Theotokos, help us! Our Lord, Christ, hearken to the prayers of holy Wonderworker Peter, of great Metropolitan Cyprian and reverend Abbot Sergius, and have mercy upon us and protect us against these Moslems who have taken up arms against us!" And he commanded his troops to advance slowly.

The voevodas of his vanguard regiments were Dmitrii Vsevolodich, and the latter's brother, Vladimir. On the right wing marched Mikula Vasilievich, Semion Ivanovich, Semion Melik with numerous forces. It was already the sixth hour of the day.

As they advanced to meet [the enemy] at the mouth of the Nepriadva river, there suddenly appeared a powerful Tatar force moving toward them rapidly from the hills. They [the Russians] halted because there was no room to align themselves, and they stood with lowered lances, wall upon wall, each man resting his lance on the shoulders of the one before him. Those in the first row extended just a part of their lances, while those behind thrust their lances forward for a greater length. The Grand Prince, also with a large Russian force, moved against the Tatars from another hill. It was terrifying to view the two hosts marching to the onset against each other for bloodshed and rapid death. The Tatar force [with the sun behind it] loomed dark, while the Russians shone in their armour. Their army looked like a great, flowing river or the undulating sea, and the sun shone brightly against the Russians so that from a distance they resembled shining lights.

With five of his foremost lords the impure Khan Mamai rode onto a high place on the hill, where he remained, wishing to watch the human bloodshed and fast death: indeed, many a lifespan was nearing its end.

The Russian vanguard advanced and so did the Tatars. The Grand Prince rode with the vanguard but stayed with them only a short while, then returned to the main host. And so both forces moved toward each other: from one side, the massive Tatar troops, and from the other, Grand Prince Dmitrii Ivanovich, himself, with all the Russian princes. One could see the unspeakably vast Russian troops, more than four hundred thousand horse- and footmen.[27] The Tatar force, however, was also vast.

As the two hosts prepared to clash, there emerged from the Tatar line a very stalwart, broadshouldered and bold Tatar warrior. It was most awesome to gaze upon him and no one dared to go against him or to accept his challenge. Men said to each other that they should step out against him but no one did. Then Peresvet, the illustrious monk, disciple of the reverend Abbot Sergius of Radonezh, addressed the Grand Prince and all the princes: "Do not be discomfitted for Our Lord is Great, and Great is His Power! With the Lord's help and that of His Most Pure Mother and of all His saints, and relying on the prayers of reverend Abbot Sergius, I will engage him in combat!" This Peresvet, when he was still a layman, was a renowned knight *[bogatyr]* and had great strength and vigour, surpassing all in stature and power; he was very skilled in the martial arts. On the advice of the reverend Abbot Sergius he had taken the highest monastic vows of the holy schema. He made the sign of the Holy Cross, sprinkled himself with holy water and asked forgiveness of his spiritual father, of the Grand Prince and of all the princes, and of all the Christian army, and of his spiritual brother, Osliabia.

The Grand Prince wept bitterly and all the princes and the entire army wept with him. With tears in his eyes, he—Dmitrii—said, "Help him, Lord, for the sake of the prayers of Thy Most Pure Theotokos and of all the saints, just as in ancient times Thou didst aid David against Goliath." And so caloyer Peresvet, the disciple monk of reverend Abbot Sergius, rode against the Tatar knight, Temir Murza, and they came together so fiercely that the clash resounded loudly and mightily, the earth shook and both fell dead; and this was the end of them both. Their horses also died at the same time.

27. See footnote 5. above regarding the strength of the Russian army.

1381   But now the seventh hour arrived[28] and the Grand Prince addressed his princes and boiars and all the army: "Brethren! It is time to drink the bitter cup! This place may be our grave in the Name of Christ, for the Christian faith and for all Orthodox Christians!" And so the two mighty hosts clashed in battle and it was a fierce struggle and most evil slaughter, the blood ran like water and a numberless multitude of dead fell on both sides—on the Tatar and on the Russian. Tatar bodies fell upon Christian ones, Christian upon Tatar, and Tatar blood mixed with Christian; everywhere lay such a multitude of dead that the horses could not advance because of the bodies. They killed each other not only with arms but in bodily encounter, and died under the horses' hooves. Men suffocated in the crush because there was not enough room on the Kulikovo field between the rivers Don and the Mecha for such a multitude of mighty warring legions. Felled like trees or mown hay, here lay the great Russian army of footmen, and it was awful to see. Nevertheless, the Christian soldiers fought, unrelenting. Still, to punish us for our sins, God allowed the Tatars to gain the upper hand and, already, many illustrious great princes, boiars and voevodas fell to the ground like trees. Grand Prince Dmitrii Ivanovich, himself, was unsaddled; and then, when he mounted another horse, the Tatars again unhorsed him and wounded him. So, wearied, he was obliged to go from the battlefield into an oak wood, where he crouched under a recently felled tree with many branches and rich foliage, taking refuge there, and he lay upon the ground.

The Tatars, gaining, slashed the Grand Prince's great banner, and his beloved comrade, Mikhail Andreevich Brenk, was killed; and they killed a great many princes, boiars, voevodas and squires. This was about the eighth hour of the day; and the ninth hour commenced, the Tatars gaining the advantage everywhere.

In the meantime, Prince Vladimir Andreevich, grandson of Ivan [Kalita], great grandson of Daniil, gr. gr. grandson of Aleksandr [Nevskii], cousin of Grand Prince Dmitrii Ivanovich— who, together with the wise and valiant voevoda, Dmitrii Bobrok the Volynian, was lying with the secret [reserve] selected western troop in the oak wood. Seeing the Christian warriors slain, he

---

28. The seventh hour after sunrise in September: thus, it was about one or two P.M. at the onset of the battle.

wept and shed tears. Only a few of them still moved on the battle- **1381**
field. Thereupon Prince Vladimir Andreevich asked Dmitrii the
Volynian, "What is the use of our lying in ambush, and what
manner of aid do we provide them? And whom can we help, for
nearly all the Christian troops are already lying dead?" But the
great and wise voevoda and daring fighter, Dmitrii Bobrok the
Volynian, responded, "Woe is me, my Prince, woe is me! For our
sins, the wrath of God has come upon us; but it is not yet time for
us to strike the enemy! Let us bide our time, praying to God in the
humility of our hearts, and He will defeat our adversaries!"
Prince Vladimir Andreevich cried out, lifted his arms up to the
heavens, praying tearfully to Lord God, to the Most Pure Theotokos and to all the saints. When, however, they wanted to move
to the onset, the wind still blew in their faces so strongly that it
hindered the sortie. And Dmitrii Bobrok, the Volynian, said,
"In no case should any now enter the battle: the Lord forbids it
us." His words moved all to tears and weeping, and all shed tears,
and with tears they prayed fervently to Lord God, to the Most
Pure Theotokos and to all the saints. Dmitrii Bobrok, the Volynian, himself, wept bitterly and shed many tears.

Suddenly, toward the end of the ninth hour of the day, the
wind turned and began to blow from behind them, forcing them
forth against the Tatars.[29] And now Dmitrii Bobrok said to Prince
Vladimir Andreevich, "My lord Prince! Our hour has come!
The time is at hand!" Then he addressed all the host: "My lords,
fathers, brethren, children and friends! Charge! Our favorable
moment has arrived! The might of the Holy Ghost helps us!"

So everyone, filled with God-inspired fierceness and fury,
charged the infidel and adverse foes. The fearless Christian host
struck them in the manner of most illustrious warriors. [At that
moment] the faithful saw angels coming to aid the Christians, and
there [in the heavens] appeared the host of holy martyrs—of
St. George, Christ's great warrior, and St. Demetrius, as well as

29. Bobrok was waiting for a favorable turn of the wind, because as
long as the southern wind continued the dust raised on the battlefield
would have blinded the Russians. During the first phase of the battle the
wind blew and the sun shone into the Russians' faces, thus greatly aiding
the Tatars. When the wind turned, however, and the sun moved to the
west later in the day, these natural phenomena worked to the Tatars'
disadvantage.

1381 the Russian princes, St. Boris and St. Gleb; and with them was the great *archistrategos* Michael, commander of the supreme host of heavenly power.[30] And the pagans also saw the radiant supreme host of these two heavenly commanders, who marched against them and showered them with fiery arrows; and thus these godless Tatars fell, slain by divine wrath and Christian arms. This happened because God exalted the arm of Grand Prince Dmitrii Ivanovich in order to defeat these aliens.

Then, thanks to the help of God and the Most Pure Theotokos, the impure Ishmaelites were seized by great fear and fright, struck by invisible divine power, and they cried out, "Woe to us! Woe to us! The Christians have outwitted us! The best and most valiant princes and voevodas, with fresh forces, have remained in ambush; but now our arms have grown weak, our shoulders have tired, our knees have stiffened. Our horses are weary! Woe to you, great Mamai! Your pride rose as high as the clouds but now your madness has led you to hell! And you have destroyed us all in vain!" The Tatar armies fled, pursued, slain and flayed by the Christian troops.

Mamai saw it when the fresh Christian hosts sallied forth against his Tatars, and thanks to God's aid and that of the Most Pure Theotokos which was bestowed on Orthodox Christendom, Mamai and his Tatars imagined that tens and tens of thousands of Christian troops had sallied out of the oak forest.[31] Therefore none of the Tatars could oppose them; and Mamai, his lords and a small personal guard fled. Thanks to the aid of the Theotokos and of great Wonderworker Peter, many Tatars fell, killed by the weapons of Christ's warriors, while many others drowned in the river. They were pursued up to the river Mecha[32] and the Prince's troops [even] followed the Tatars as far as their encampments, and took much spoil and wealth.

[From thence] the Christian warriors returned and saw that everywhere lay the dead. And such was the victory and the help of God, and the wonders and signs wrought by the Holy Theo-

30. *Archistrategos*: supreme commander, Greek work for Archangel Michael.

31. "Tens of thousands"—"*tmochislenye:*" as mentioned earlier, *t'ma* denoted a military unit, an army corps theoretically consisting of ten thousand warriors.

32. River Mecha: presently called the "Krasnaia Mecha."

tokos, great Wonderworker Peter, reverend Abbot Sergius, by the
holy passion martyrs, Boris and Gleb, and by all the saints, as well
as the power of the prayers of the fathers and mothers of the
Orthodox Christians, that even in places not reached by Christian
troops there lay dead Tatars smitten by the Invincible Power of
God and the Most Pure Theotokos and His Saints. Prince Vladimir Andreevich also returned and halted over the bones [of the
dead], viewing the great many slain Christian warriors: numberless princes, boiars, voevodas, squires and footmen lay dead, and
everywhere flowed rivers of blood. Then Prince Vladimir Andreevich started to search for his brother, Grand Prince Dmitrii Ivanovich; but, not finding him, he grieved so greatly that he beat his
brow in torment.

Then he commanded the buglers who had gathered around
him to sound their bugles, and the surviving Christian warriors
assembled. He asked them, "Who has seen my brother, Grand
Prince Dmitrii Ivanovich, and where?" And someone told him,
"We saw him being sorely wounded; perhaps he is among the
corpses of the dead." Another told him, "I saw him fighting fiercely, and then escaping, and later I saw him fighting four Tatars,
and then he escaped from them; but I do not know what happened
to him." Thereupon Prince Stepan Novosil'skii also spoke, saying,
"I saw him grievously wounded, walking with difficulty from the
battlefield, but I could not aid him because I, myself, was being
chased by three Tatars." Then Prince Vladimir Andreevich, who
was the cousin of Grand Prince Dmitrii Ivanovich, summoned
everyone to him and asked them, weeping and with many tears,
"My lords, brethren, sons and friends! Search carefully for Grand
Prince Dmitrii Ivanovich. Whosoever finds him, verily, I say, that
one, if he be glorious, great and honorable, will be still more
glorified, lauded and honored; and if he be one of the common and
poor, even one of the poorest paupers, then he will be first in
wealth, honor and glory!"

The men scattered everywhere and searched. Some of them
found Mikhail Andreevich Brenk, the Grand Prince's closest
friend, who had been killed and was in the mantle, armour and
helmet of the Grand Prince, with all the royal badges. Some others
found Prince Fedor Semionovich Belozerskii, taking him for the
Grand Prince because he resembled him very much. But two
simple warriors rode to the right toward the oak forest; one of

1381 them was Fedor Zov by name;[33] the name of the other was Fedor Kholopov, and both were common people. While riding, they came upon the body of the Grand Prince, badly hurt, hardly breathing, lying as though dead under the branches of a newly felled tree. Leaping from their horses, they did obeisance to him and one quickly returned to Prince Vladimir Andreevich to tell him that the Grand Prince was still alive.

[Prince Vladimir Andreevich] mounted his horse at once and rode rapidly thither with his warriors. Approaching, he addressed him, "Oh, my brother, my dear Grand Prince Dmitrii Ivanovich! You are like Iaroslav of old, you are a new Alexander! But, first of all, we must glorify Our Lord Jesus Christ, His Most Pure Theotokos, great Wonderworker Peter, reverend Abbot and Wonderworker Sergius, the holy passion martyrs in Christ, Boris and Gleb, and all the holy servants of God because, thanks to invisible divine aid, the Ishmaelites have been defeated and divine grace has shone upon us." Grand Prince Dmitrii Ivanovich spoke, barely audibly, "Who is speaking and what is the meaning of these words?" Prince Vladimir Andreevich told him, "It is I, your cousin, Prince Vladimir Andreevich, who speaks to you!"

They raised him with difficulty, and all his armour was badly broken, and he was wounded; but no mortal wounds were found upon his body. Still, he had been foremost in battle, had fought in the first onset, and had done battle for a long time, face to face with the Tatars. Albeit, many of his princes and voevodas had told him, "Our lord Prince! Do not do battle ahead of all, but stay behind or in the wings, or in some other place on the side." He had answered them, however, "How can I tell the others, 'Let us fight staunchly, brethren, against the enemy,' whilst I, myself, remain in the rear, hiding my face? I can not do thus, covering myself; but I want before all, not only in word but also in deed, to sacrifice my head for the sake of Christ and His Most Pure Mother, as well as for the Christian faith and for Orthodox Christendom. Then the others, seeing my fighting, would also stride into action with their whole hearts."[34] He did as he said, and he began before

33. "Zov:" in some *mss.* of *Nik.* this name is also spelled "Zernov" or "Morozov."

34. Here, in the printed text of *Nik.*, appears a paragraph whose content has been given before and which is to be found only in one of the *mss.* of this chronicle.

anyone else to fight with the Tatars. The Tatars encircled him **1381**
from the right and from the left, striking him on his head, on his
shoulders, on his chest, slashing and stabbing. But thanks to the
mercy of Lord God and the prayers of the Most Pure Theotokos,
and of Wonderworker Peter and of all His saints, he was protected
from death. He was so utterly wearied, however, and so much exhausted from the Tatars' assaults that he was close to death. He
was, however, very strong and valiant, had a mighty and stalwart
body, with broad shoulders, and a large belly, and he was very
heavy; his beard and his hair were black, and his mien was handsome.

When he understood that he had been told a great joy, he
recovered himself and said, "This day was the work of the Lord.
Let us rejoice and be glad!" And so they put him on his horse and
the bugles sounded over the bones with great joy [announcing the
victory]. And then he was asked by Prince Vladimir Andreevich,
"Are you aware how great was God's grace and that of His Most
Pure Theotokos? Even in such places which were not reached by
our warriors—even there can be found a great many Tatars,
slain by invisible divine might and by the power of the Most Pure
Theotokos, great Wonderworker Peter, and all the saints."[35]
Then the Grand Prince raised his arms toward the heavens and
said, "Great is the Lord and wonderful are His deeds! There are
no words which suffice to glorify Thy miracle, oh, Most Pure
Theotokos! Who can worthily glorify Thee and Thy unspeakable
miracles? Oh, blessed Peter, our strong intercessor! How can we
render to thee what thou hast rendered to us?"

Then, after resting from his labors and recovering from his
sweat and wounds, he expressed his joy with sweet words to his
cousin, Vladimir Andreevich, to the other princes and to all the
warriors, praising them and lauding them, for they had fought
for the Orthodox faith and for all Christendom. And he went
with his cousin, with the other princes and voevodas—although
only a few remained alive—to look upon the dead, who lay like
haystacks, and where Christian bodies lay together with Tatar
ones, and where Christian blood flowed together with Tatar blood;
and it was a terrible and awesome sight. The Grand Prince wept

35. Here in the printed text appears a sentence found only in one
ms., which repeats a paragraph already printed. It is omitted.

1381   loudly and with tears, and came to the place where, together, lay
eight dead princes of Belozersk. They had been very daring and
mighty, brave and courageous warriors, and they died for each
other, and with them many of their boiars died. Then, nearby,
they came upon the body of his great voevoda, tysiatski Mikula
Vasilievich,[36] together with the bodies of fifteen princes, and with
them lay a great multitude of dead boiars and voevodas. He also
came upon the body of his bosom friend, whom he loved more
than any other—Mikhail Andreevich Brenk, near whom was likewise a multitude of dead princes and boiars. There lay Semion
Melik, alongside Timofei Voluevich, both slain. And they moved
to another place, where they saw the body of Abbot Sergius' monk,
Peresvet; and near him was the body of the outstanding Tatar
warrior *[bogatyr]*. Turning, the Grand Prince said to those with
him, "Look, brethren! Here you see the one who was the first to
begin the battle and who defeated one equal to him, from whom
many of our men might have drunk the bitter cup." The Grand
Prince mourned them all, shedding bitter tears, and said, "Glory
to God, it was His will."

The number of men killed by Mamai's men in this deadly
battle was beyond counting. Among the slain were outstanding,
great and valiant men, whose names are: Prince Fedor Romanovich of Belozero and his son, Prince Ivan; Prince Fedor Semionovich; Prince Ivan Mikhailovich; Prince Fedor of Tarussa; his
brother, Prince Mstislav; Prince Dmitrii Monastyrev; Semion
Mikhailovich; Mikula Vasilievich, the son of the tysiatskii; Mikhailo and Ivan Akinfovich; Ivan Aleksandrovich; Andrei Shuba;
Andrei Serkizov, also sometimes called Volui; Timofei Vasilievich; Okatii's grandson; Mikhailo Brenk; Lev Mozyrev; Taras
Shatnev; Semion Melikov; Dmitrii Minich;[37] Abbot Sergius' monk,
Peresvet, whose lay name was Aleksandr and who used to be the
boiar of [the prince of] Briansk. He was a daring and great fighter,
very illustrious and very experienced in the martial arts and weaponry. All of them, whose names have been aforementioned, were
daring and great warriors. But there were also killed tens of thou-

36. Mikula Vasilievich was not tysiatskii, but the son of the last
tysiatskii, V. V. Veliaminov, who died in 1374.

37. Some names are corrected after *Novg. IV* and *Late Muscovite
15th century chronicles*, which were the sources of *Nik.*

sands of others: princes, boiars, voevodas, princes' sons, junior   **1381**
boiars, squires and footmen, and who would be able to count them
all or write down [all their names], for their number was legion?

Then Grand Prince Dmitrii Ivanovich addressed everyone,
"My lords! My fathers! My brethren! My sons! I thank you for
your valorous feat of arms. It behooves you to be in my service
and it behooves me to reward you according to your deeds. When
Lord God grants me again to be in my patrimony, in the Grand
Principality of Moscow, then I will honor and reward you. Now,
let us labor once more, as much as we can, and bury our Orthodox
Christian brethren who have been killed by the Tatars on this field."

The Grand Prince remained eight days on this field beyond the
Don, separating Christian bodies from those of the impure Tatars,
as far as possible. They did as much as they could, and as far as
the other [dead] are concerned only God knows, because all this
happened by the will of God. Because of our sins Lord God permitted this calamity. Still, thanks to His mercy alone, He responded to the prayers of His Most Pure Mother and great Wonderworker Peter, and, thus, thanks to His invisible divine power, these
Ishmaelites were vanquished.

Now Grand Prince Dmitrii Ivanovich spoke: "Brethren!
Count how many of us remain." They counted and the Moscow
boiar, Mikhailo Aleksandrovich, reported, "Lord Prince! There
remain forty thousand of us; but there were more than four hundred thousand horse- and footmen."[38] And the Grand Prince
responded, "The Lord's will be done! Everything happens as
pleases our God. Who can resist His will and who can contradict
the Lord? All events occur according to His will and His desire."
And the Grand Prince commanded the priests to chant the funeral service for those who had been slain, and they buried them as
far as they could manage to do. The priest sang "Eternal Memory"
to all the Orthodox Christians who had been killed by the Tatars
on Kulikovo Field, between the rivers Don and Mecha. Then the
Grand Prince, himself, together with his cousin and with all the
surviving warriors, weeping and with many tears, exclaimed in a
loud voice, "May their memory live for ever!" Then the Grand
Prince, himself, addressed [the dead]:

38. As to the size of the Russian host, see footnote 5. at the beginning of this story.

1381   "My brethren and friends, Orthodox Christians! May the memory of all of you who suffered for the sake of the Orthodox faith and all Christendom on Kulikovo Field, between the rivers Don and Mecha, live for ever! This place was preordained for you by God. Forgive me and give your me blessing in this and the future age, and pray for us since you have won imperishable crowns from Christ God!"

And now a man from Vladimir Andreevich's host approached the Grand Prince, saying, "My lord Prince! When I was in the oak forest, lying in ambush together with Prince Vladimir Andree-vich's host, we all wept before Lord God and His Most Pure Mother and great Wonderworker Peter because we witnessed our Ortho-dox Christians being slain by the Tatars. We all grieved greatly and dolefully; but then, suddenly, I fell into a state of ecstasy and saw an endless number of crowns descending upon the slain Chris-tians; and these are my true words: that they were crowned with the imperishable crowns of Christ God and they received honor and great glory in Heaven and pray for us [there]."

Lord God also delivered us from Prince Iagailo of Lithuania, who was marching from the Lithuanian land with all his forces to aid pagan Mamai and the Tatars and to do harm to the Christians. He did not succeed in coming on time, although he was merely one day's march from the field of battle. Prince Iagailo Olgerdo-vich and all his forces received tidings of the battle between Grand Prince Dmitrii Ivanovich and Mamai, and that the Grand Prince defeated the latter and that Mamai fled, not waiting even for awhile. So Prince Iagailo retreated forthwith with all his Lithuanian forces, albeit none pursued them. They saw then neither the Grand Prince [Dmitrii], nor his host, nor his arms but they feared and trembled at the mere mention of his [Dmitrii's] name.

Thereupon Grand Prince Dmitrii Ivanovich told his cousin, Prince Vladimir Andreevich, "My brother! Let us return to our land beyond the forests *[Zemlia zaleskaia]*, to the most glorious city of Moscow, and let us resume ruling the domains of our fathers and forefathers. We have won honor and glory for gen-erations and generations to come."

When they recrossed the river Don and the Grand Prince marched into the Riazan' land he was told that Prince Oleg of Riazan' had sent his forces to aid Mamai, that he had destroyed the bridges over the rivers and that he had ordered that those boiars

and squires returning to their homes from the battle on the Don   **1381**
be robbed and stripped naked as they passed through his patrimony—the land of Riazan'. Thereon Grand Prince Dmitrii
Ivanovich determined to send troops against Prince Oleg. When
Prince Oleg of Riazan' received tidings that the Grand Prince,
having defeated his enemies, was advancing, he hid himself and
exclaimed, "Woe is me, sinful apostate of the Christian faith!
What did I attempt to do? What did I envision? I made common
cause with the godless Khan!" And he departed from his city of
Riazan', fleeing to Iagailo, Prince of Lithuania. Arriving at the
Lithuanian confines, he told his boiars, "I purpose to await here
tidings that Grand Prince Dmitrii has crossed my land and gone
to his own domain. Only then will I return home."

The boiars of Riazan', however, gave up [their service to]
Oleg and went over to the Grand Prince, whom they told that
Prince Oleg had abandoned his patrimony—the land of Riazan'
—and had fled with his princess, his children and the boiars. They
petitioned him—Dmitrii—humbly not to send an army against
them, and they asked him for a treaty, promising to accept it.
The Grand Prince accepted their petition, sent no army and assigned his own namestniks in the principality of Riazan'. He also
commanded that whosoever in his army crossed the land of Riazan'
should not touch even a single hair [of the people of Riazan'].

From the Don the Grand Prince came to Kolomna on the
twenty-first day of the month of September, when the memory of
the Holy Apostle Quadratus[39] is remembered, and he was met at
the city gate by Bishop Gerasimus of Kolomna, and the entire
Sacred Council, with lifegiving crosses and holy icons. They
entered the cathedral church and chanted a thanksgiving service
to Lord God and His Most Pure Mother; then the holy liturgy
was celebrated by Bishop Gerasimus, and throughout all the city
the priests celebrated prayers and liturgies on behalf of the health
of the Grand Prince, of all the princes and of the entire Christ-
loving host. Sojourning in Kolomna four days, he—Dmitrii—
rested somewhat from his deeds, for he was sorely wearied and
fatigued. Then he went to the glorious city of Moscow and entered
the city of Moscow, where he was met by his spiritual father,

39. St. Quadratus (in Russian, *Kondratii*) was a disciple from among
the seventy.

1381   Cyprian, Metropolitan of Kiev and all Russia, and by the entire
Sacred Council, with crosses.[40] The Grand Prince addressed the
Metropolitan:

"My father! Thanks to the mercy of God and His Most Pure
Mother, and great Wonderworker Peter, as well as your prayers
and those of venerable Abbot Sergius, we overcame impure
Mamai and defeated those with him. He was obsessed with pride,
while we were humble. You saw, yourself, how much gold and
silver I sent him, and how greatly I entreated him, but he did not
heed me and exalted himself in his pride, and was put to shame.
We have escaped [conquest by him] thanks to divine mercy, we
have defeated them and have taken much booty and their wealth,
and have brought with us large herds: horses, camels, yoke-
buffalo, great sheep—and there is no end to them; and we have
seized their arms, their armaments, their clothing, and an endless
amount of their goods."

Metropolitan Cyprian answered,

"Glory to Thee, Lord, glory to Thee, Our Holy One, glory to
Thee, Our King, that Thou didst manifest to us Thy great
mercy and didst vanquish our enemy! We magnify Thee, Most
Holy Virgin Theotokos, because Thou hast bestowed Thy great
mercy upon us and hast wrought upon us Orthodox Christians
Thy great miracles. Praise be to thee, Christ's Bishop Peter, because you intercedest on behalf of your spiritual flock and defeated
our enemies."

"How can we now exalt you, my lord and beloved son in
Christ, Grand Prince Dmitrii Ivanovich? You are a new Constantine! You are a glorious [new] Vladimir! You are a most marvelous [new] Iaroslav! You are a most wonderful [new] Alexander!
What manner of thanks, honor and laud can we render you, for
you have fought and labored for the sake of all Orthodox Christendom?"

And the Metropolitan blessed him with the honorable cross
and also blessed his cousin, Prince Vladimir Andreevich. Then
they embraced each other and entered the holy church of the
Dormition of the Most Pure Theotokos, and they chanted a
thanksgiving service. The Metropolitan, himself, celebrated the
divine liturgy, assisted by all the Sacred Council, and through-

40. As mentioned before, Cyprian was not in Moscow in 1380.

out the entire city the priests celebrated thanksgiving services
and liturgies, praying for the health of the Grand Prince and of
all the princes and of all the Christloving host. Thereafter the
Grand Prince distributed large gifts to the churches, to the monasteries, to the poor and to the paupers, and he enjoyed the company
of his spiritual father, Cyprian, Metropolitan of Kiev and all
Russia, as well as of his cousin, Prince Vladimir Andreevich,
and all the surviving warriors. Thereafter he disbanded them and
everyone went home.

Later, the Grand Prince journeyed to the monastery of the
Lifegiving Trinity in Radonezh, to venerable Abbot Sergius,
and he prayed there, shedding tears, to Lord God and His Most
Pure Mother and to all the saints, and he received a blessing from
venerable Abbot Sergius, whom he told, "My father! Thanks to
your holy prayers we have defeated the Ishmaelites! If it were
not for your wonderful servant, monk Peresvet [whose lay name
was] Aleksandr, who slew the great Tatar warrior, many of us
would have had to drink our cup of death at the hands of this
Tatar. Withal, my father, by God's will and because of our many
sins, a very great many Christian warriors were slain by the Tatars.
Please, celebrate a memorial service and liturgy for all those who
were killed." And so this was done, and he made bestowals and
provisions for the needs of venerable Abbot Sergius, and his
brethren, and then he returned to the city of Moscow and re-
sumed his rule in the domain of his father and grandfather, of the
Grand Principality, resting after many deeds and hurts which he
received for the sake of the Orthodox faith and all Christendom.

Grand Prince Dmitrii, how great and mighty was your valor!
You did not fear to march beyond the river Don into the open
prairie against the great forces of the Tatars and you were first,
yourself, to do battle against them and to slay the Ishmaelites!
But all this happened, thanks to the aid of God and His mercy,
as well as thanks to the prayers of His Most Pure Mother, of great
Wonderworker Peter, of all the saints and of the warriors' mothers and fathers.

Oh, Lord Christ! Be not wroth at us for our iniquities but
forgive us because of Thy great mercy, and defeat our enemy!

Oh, Most Holy Virgin Mother of God! Entreat Thy Son and
Our Lord Jesus Christ on our behalf and bring peace in place of
quarrels, fighting and rebellions, and still all those who arise

1381   against us! And give us, Thy servants, tranquility, peace and love!
Oh, great and blessed shepherd, [St. Metropolitan] Peter!
Do not abandon us, your orphans, who are [so often] injured and
offended by our enemy; but intercede always for your flock and
keep it safe, as you promised. Drive afar off from us calumny,
envy and pride. Dispatch by your prayers humility, tranquility,
meekness and love into our hearts because the Lord is love
[I John 4:16] and His is the glory unto the ages of ages. Amen.
[End of the tale about the victory on the Don.][41]

[TOKHTAMYSH]

At that time, with his surviving lords and a rather small escort,
Mamai escaped from the deadly battle on the river Don, attained
his own land and, again, became wroth and angered at Grand
Prince Dmitrii Ivanovich. He reassembled his remaining forces
and decided once more to attack Grand Prince Dmitrii Ivanovich and the entire Russian land because the host he amassed was
still a considerable legion.

Hardly had he undertaken his preparations and begun in
great fury to move his forces against Grand Prince Dmitrii Ivano-
ovich than he received tidings that another khan, named Tokhtamysh, was marching against him from the east, from the Blue
Horde.[42] Mamai, who had mustered his host against Grand Prince
Dmitrii Ivanovich, now moved with his entire force against Tokhtamysh, and they met on the river Kalka[?], where a fierce fray
ensued. Tokhtamysh defeated Mamai and chased him away.
Then, secretly, Mamai's lords took counsel, saying, "There is
nothing good in remaining in Mamai's realm because everywhere
we are nought but offended and defeated by our enemies. How
does it profit us to be under his reign? Let us join Khan Tokhtamysh and then we will see what happens." And so Mamai's
lords dismounted from their horses, made great obeisance before
Tokhtamysh according to their faith, promised him fealty, swore
allegiance to him and thus became his vassals.

41. Let us remember that September of the year 6889 was, according to the modern calendar, still in the year 1380 and not 1381.

42. Tokhtamysh was another Turkic army commander and descendant of Genghis Khan who succeeded in building an empire in
Central Asia and subjugated there most of the "White"—or, as the Russians called it, "Blue"—Horde.

Now Mamai was left with but few troops, ashamed and of-   **1381**
fended. Seeing that his lords had betrayed him, Mamai, with his
advisors and supporters, fled at once. Khan Tokhtamysh despatched troops in pursuit; but, though chased, Mamai nonetheless escaped from Tokhtamysh's pursuers and attained the vicinity of the city of Kafa.[43] There he contacted the people of
Kafa, according to his agreement with them and requested refuge until his pursuers should withdraw. They ordered him to
enter the city and Mamai, with his advisors and supporters, entered the city of Kafa with a great amount of wealth—gold, silver,
gems and pearls. When the people of Kafa saw his large treasure
they conspired and cunningly slew him. Thus did Mamai badly
end his accursed life.

Khan Tokhtamysh assumed Mamai's entire Horde, his wives,
his treasure, his markets, his tribes, his wealth, his gold, silver,
pearls and gems, all of which were in very large quantity, and he
divided them among his warriors. The same fall he despatched
his envoys to Grand Prince Dmitrii Ivanovich of Moscow and to
all the Russian princes, announcing to them his conquest of the
Khanate of the Volga and informing them how he had assumed
it, how he had defeated his and their enemy, Mamai, while he,
himself, had marched forward and taken over the reign of the
Volga Khanate.

All the Russian princes honored his envoy fairly and let him
return with honors and gifts to the Horde, to Khan Tokhtamysh.
The same winter and spring, rapidly and without delay, they each
sent their own envoys with many gifts for Khan Tokhtamysh, for
his wives and for his lords. The same fall, on the twenty-ninth day
of the month of October, when the venerable martyr, Anastasia
of Rome, is remembered, Grand Prince Dmitrii Ivanovich despatched his own emissaries, Tolbuga and Moksha, to Tokhtamysh, the new Khan of the Volga Horde, with gifts and presents. The same fall on the first day of November all the Russian
princes assembled and confirmed concord among them.

The same year on the fouteenth day of the month of August
the envoys of Grand Prince Dmitrii Ivanovich, Tolbuga and
Moksha, as well as the envoy of the other princes, returned from
Khan Tokhtamysh in the Horde, bearing the latter's bestowals
and honors. There was great joy in Russia although grief did

43. Italian (Genoese) colony in Crimea.

1381 not abate over the princes, boiars, voevodas, squires and innummerable Christian warriors who had been slain on the Don by Mamai. The entire Russian land at that time was impoverished for want of its voevodas, squires and warriors [who had been killed in the Kulikovo battle], and great fear still filled the whole Russian land.

In the year 6889/1381 Metropolitan Pimen came to Russia from Constantinople. Grand Prince Dmitrii Ivanovich did not accept him, and when he arrived in Kolomna he commanded that the white mitre be removed from Pimen's head and placed him under arrest. About this it was written earlier in the narrative about Mitiai, in the seventh year of this decade [6887/1379].

The same year Dionysius, Bishop of Suzdal', sent from Constantinople with monk Malachias the Philosopher, an icon which was a copy of the icon of the Most Pure Theotokos *Odigitria*, which in the Russian language is called *"Nastavnitsa,"* "One Who Shows the Way," or, in Greek, *"Cathodigitria."*[44] This *Odigitria* icon left Constantinople on Tuesday. Bishop Dionysius had this icon painted according to the actual width and length [of the original]. Then he had the other icon painted of the same Most Pure Theotokos *Odigitria*, likewise of the same size in width and length, and he sent it to Russia. One of these icons was placed in the church of the Holy Saviour in Nizhnii Novgorod and the other one in the cathedral church of Suzdal'.

The same year a son, Ivan, was born to Prince Vladimir Andreevich and he was baptised by His Holiness Cyprian, Metropolitan of all Russia, and by reverend Abbot Sergius of Radonezh.

[TOKHTAMYSH'S ENVOYS]

The same year Khan Tikhtamysh sent Ak Khodzha, son of a khan, with seven hundred Tatars to Grand Prince Dmitrii Ivanovich and to all the Russian princes. They went as far as Nizhnii Novgorod and then returned because they did not dare to go to Moscow. Then he sent some of his Tatars, though but a very small troop of them; but even those did not venture further.

---

44. On this type of icon the Theotokos points at the Infant Christ, thus indicating the way to salvation.

The same winter and spring before early sunrises a certain portent appeared in the eastern skies: there would appear a manner of fiery column and a star which looked like a lance.[45] This portent foretold the wicked invasion of Tokhtamysh and the bitter attack of the pagans. The same year during the week of All Saints there was fearsome thunder and a very strong storm with tornadoes.

45. A comet.